Terrorism

Terrorism

THE ESSENTIAL REFERENCE GUIDE

Colin P. Clarke, Editor

An Imprint of ABC-CLIO, LLC
Santa Barbara, California • Denver, Colorado

Library of Congress Cataloging-in-Publication Data

Names: Clarke, Colin P., editor.
Title: Terrorism : the essential reference guide / Colin P. Clarke, editor.
Description: Santa Barbara, California : ABC-CLIO, 2018. | Includes bibliographical references
    and index.
Identifiers: LCCN 2017052603 (print) | LCCN 2017054827 (ebook) | ISBN 9781440856297
    (ebook) | ISBN 9781440856280 (hardcopy : alk. paper)
Subjects: LCSH: Terrorism—Encyclopedias.
Classification: LCC HV6431 (ebook) | LCC HV6431 .T4977 2018 (print) | DDC
    363.32503—dc23
LC record available at https://lccn.loc.gov/2017052603

ISBN: 978-1-4408-5628-0 (print)
      978-1-4408-5629-7 (ebook)

22   21   20   19   18   1   2   3   4   5

This book is also available as an eBook.

ABC-CLIO
An Imprint of ABC-CLIO, LLC

ABC-CLIO, LLC
130 Cremona Drive, P.O. Box 1911
Santa Barbara, California 93116-1911
www.abc-clio.com

This book is printed on acid-free paper ∞

Manufactured in the United States of America

Contents

List of Entries

List of Documents

Preface

Since the rise of the Islamic State in the summer of 2014, there has been a renewed focus on counterterrorism worldwide. But the truth is, this preoccupation has never really left us. Well before the al-Qaeda attacks of September 11, 2001, countries have been concerned with countering terrorism and insurgency throughout the globe. The scope, characteristics, and nature of terrorism have changed over time, but political violence remains a constant in the realm of international politics. Terrorism has been a favored tactic of insurgents, warlords, militias, and mercenaries, each seeking to achieve different objectives and pursuing wide-ranging strategies along the way.

The United States is at a critical juncture in dealing with the challenges of terrorism and violent nonstate actors. Admittedly, one would be hard-pressed to identify a period in the past three decades when this statement was not true, but the current wave of global instability can truly be described as unprecedented. Given this volatility, projecting the future of terrorism and violence is a precarious undertaking. Terrorism is shifting, evolving, and spreading. Many previous projections, such as the prospects for conflict resolution, have not come to pass, while new fault lines have formed.

What will shape the nature of terrorism and violence in the coming years? We are currently witnessing the decentralization of the threat, from an organized and controlled al-Qaeda to an atomized jihadist militancy writ large. The Islamic State has lost its claim to a caliphate in Iraq and Syria, while some of its franchise and affiliate groups have grown stronger, from the Sinai Peninsula in Egypt to parts of Libya, Yemen, Afghanistan, and the Philippines. This trend is likely to continue, posing challenges to counterterrorism efforts and changing the nature of plots that surface.

States or regions where governments lack the capacity or the will to project power or to maintain security correspond with areas that experience high degrees of violence and where extremism has flourished. Rarely has the Middle East, the locus of much of the terrorism and violence worldwide, been more unstable and unpredictable. *Uncertainties* abound. In particular, how (and when) current conflicts resolve will be a key determinant of how terrorism and violence develop. The Syrian Civil War—more than just the struggle with the Islamic State— likely will be the most important factor in how violence and terrorism develop in the region. Syria has become the centerpiece of conflict between and among Muslims, and the resolution of this conflict will determine whether the region can begin to recover. Will Iraq and Syria be put back together in a way that allows refugees to return and ameliorates the flash point of the religious struggles between Sunni, Shia, and the West? Will Kurds, Shia, and Sunni find reason to cooperate? How will Western military involvements in the Middle East shape Muslim sentiment? Will any civil societal improvements be achievable in the midst of conflict, thus dealing with the problems disenfranchisement brings? Beyond the Middle East, how might the competition between ISIS and al-Qaeda unfold? Will more Indonesians, Chinese Uighurs, Chechens, and others be attracted to the ISIS's clarion call?

At this point, there are more questions than answers. This volume attempts to place these questions in perspective while providing readers with a historical context to make informed judgments about the past, present, and future.

Colin P. Clarke, PhD

Acknowledgments

I would like to thank my thoughtful colleagues at Carnegie Mellon University, the University of Pittsburgh, the International Centre for Counter-Terrorism (ICCT)–The Hague, and the RAND Corporation for countless hours of fascinating conversations on the topic of terrorism. At ABC-CLIO, I owe a debt of gratitude to Steve Catalano, whose guidance and encouragement helped me finish this project. I'd also like to thank Padraic (Pat) Carlin, who picked up where Steve left off. Finally, I would like to thank my family, especially my wife Colleen, for her support, encouragement, and patience as I worked on this book. This book is dedicated to my daughter, Fiona Catherine. May the world be a less dangerous and violent place as you continue to grow. You are my inspiration more than you will ever know.

Colin P. Clarke, PhD
Pittsburgh, PA 2018

Introductory Essays

Introduction

Terrorism has evolved considerably over the course of time. From the earliest known conception of the use of terrorism as a tactic to inflict violence and fear to its place in modern annals, it is a phenomenon that both enthralls and perplexes, all while avoiding an agreed-upon definition. It is employed by both nation-states and nonstate actors, organizations and groups motivated by varying ideologies over time, from anarchy to Marxism, and from radical religious beliefs to the quest for an independent homeland.

The old adage, "one man's terrorist is another man's freedom fighter" is but one of several well-known maxims that have become conventional wisdom. But terrorism has never been easy to define as it is constantly evolving and takes different forms based on geography, culture, and other important factors.

At its most basic level, terrorism is political violence. Of course, there are other important elements to consider, namely, whether or not civilians are targeted; the intended psychological impact of a terrorist attack or action; and the extent to which an individual acts alone (a so-called "lone wolf") or is part of a broader organization with a defined ideology and core set of objectives.

The field of terrorism studies began to emerge, in earnest, in the 1970s, when scholars like Martha Crenshaw and David Rapoport began studying it as a field distinct from political science, even if it has remained a subfield of the international relations discipline of that field. Indeed, David Rapoport's *The Four Waves of Modern Terrorism* is one of the best guides to understanding the evolution of terrorism over time. Rapoport describes the changing tactics and ideologies of terrorist organizations in generational terms, which he breaks down accordingly, "anarchist wave" (1880s–1920s), "anticolonialist wave" (1920s–1960s), "New Left wave" (1960s–1990s), and "religious wave" (present day). In her classic 1981 work, "The Causes of Terrorism," Martha Crenshaw notes that "the study of terrorism can be organized around three questions: why terrorism occurs, how the process of terrorism works, and what its social and political effects are." Jerrold Post has argued that individuals are drawn to the path of terrorism to commit acts of violence and that as such, their logic is grounded in their psychology and reflected in their rhetoric and propaganda, which seek to justify their violent activities.

Walter Laqueur's *A History of Terrorism* remains one of the most comprehensive and authoritative treatments of the subject, providing an in-depth understanding of assassinations, bombings, hijackings, kidnappings, and other terrorist tactics as they have evolved over time. Similarly, Bruce Hoffman's *Inside Terrorism* continues to be one of the most important works of scholarship in the field of terrorism studies, a true tour de force that covers domestic terrorism within the United States as well as international terrorism, including a comprehensive assessment of the various groups, motivations, and methods of global terrorist organizations. Paul Wilkinson's *Terrorism and the Liberal State* examines the relationship between terrorism and other forms of violence, as well as the implications for democracy and the international community, with specific attention to the period immediately following the end of the Cold War. Paul Pillar's *Terrorism and U.S. Foreign Policy* is another must-read, in which Pillar identifies the necessary elements of comprehensive counterterrorism policy, while also analyzing the reasons he believes the United States to be a frequent target of terrorists. Finally, Andrew Silke's work has repeatedly provided a rigorous assessment of the state of terrorism research itself and the methods employed by researchers studying the subject.

In the post-9/11 era, much of the focus has inevitably homed in on Salafi jihadism and groups like al-Qaeda and the Islamic State of Iraq and Syria (ISIS). Lawrence Wright's *The Looming Tower* and Steve Coll's *Ghost Wars* remain two of the most important accounts of al-Qaeda and the growth of this organization in the late 1980s and throughout the 1990s. Other important works, including Ali Soufan's *The Black Banners* and Seth Jones's *Hunting in the Shadows,* provide deep insight into the inner workings of al-Qaeda's transnational network. There have also been some excellent analyses on the new way of war, including Mark Mazzetti's *The Way of the Knife,* Aki Peritz and Eric Rosenbach's *Find, Fix, Finish,* and Eric P. Schmitt and Thom Shanker's *Counterstrike.*

Daniel Byman, Patrick Johnston, and Jenna Jordan have all conducted excellent research on the elimination of leadership in terrorist organizations; R. Kim Cragin, Brian Jackson, Michael Kenney, and Chad C. Serena have explored how terrorist organizations adapt and evolve over time; and Matthew Levitt and Juan Zarate have highlighted the importance of funding and financing to terrorist groups. Robert Pape and Mia Bloom have examined the factors and variables that lead groups to adopt suicide tactics, while many other important scholarly works have been published by John Horgan, Rohan Gunaratna, Fernando Reinares, Peter Neumann, Assaf Moghadam, Mohamed Hafez, Max Abrahms, Marc Sageman, Olivier Roy, Alex Schmid, Thomas Hegghammer, James J. F. Forest, and many others. Since the emergence of ISIS in the summer of 2014, several notable works by William McCants, Brian Fishman, Jessica Stern and J. M. Berger, Hassan Hassan and Michael Weiss, and Graeme Wood have all been published on that group.

Wrestling with Definitions

Although there is usually a clear distinction between terrorism and insurgency—the former is a tactic while the latter is a movement—this distinction is not always recognized in the broader academic literature. With the proliferation of post-9/11 studies, this problem became even more acute. Furthermore, literature on civil wars also bleeds into the insurgency literature, with distinctions between civil war, guerrilla warfare, and insurgency occasionally hinging on a body count threshold (per year or throughout the duration of the conflict), tactics employed (low intensity vs. conventional military), the actors involved (state vs. non-state, indigenous vs. foreign), or other categorical variables that classify conflicts as coups, countercoups, mutinies, insurrections, or other "revolutionary" activities. There is also no clear agreement on what differentiates irregular warfare from asymmetric warfare, or if a difference even exists between the two.

There are many different ways to analyze terrorism and insurgency and to highlight differences and identify similarities. In their study of the role of airpower in counterinsurgency, Alan Vick et al. reviewed the key differences between terrorists and insurgents. Among the differences Vick and his colleagues highlighted are the various targets, operations, and territory between terrorists and insurgents. The most important difference to keep in mind, though, is the role of politics. Insurgency is armed politics; terrorism is not.

To date, the most lucid explanation of the differences between insurgency and terrorism has been conceptualized by Dr. Thomas A. Marks, a scholar of Maoist insurgency and a professor at the National Defense University (NDU). Marks described insurgency as an armed political campaign whereas terrorism is a form of armed political communication. Insurgency uses mass mobilization by substate actors of a counterstate to challenge a national government for political power. Terrorism, on the other hand, is characterized by the use of violence by substate actors to attack innocent civilians to garner attention for their cause. This "propaganda by deed" was first popularized by Russian anarchists in the 19th century who hoped that their attacks would transform them from "a small conspiratorial club into a massive revolutionary movement."

Although the authors focus on territorial size, Daniel Byman et al. believe that the tactics used to gain and control territory are a more appropriate indication of whether the group is a terrorist or an insurgent group. Each of the groups analyzed in this dissertation—Provisional IRA, Hezbollah, Tamil Tigers, African National Congress—were consistent practitioners of terrorism but also used a range of other tactics in their effort to control territory. Terrorism expert Bard O'Neill finds that terrorism is merely a form of warfare in which violence is used primarily on civilians, whereas insurgent terrorism has a purpose. Unlike the former, the latter is used in the pursuance of a range of objectives, from short-term goals to intermediate and long-term. Although some scholars define religious or millenarian terrorists as irrational, even religious terrorists have goals, however unrealistic.

Definitions play a vital role in analysis. However, far too often academics and policy makers get tied up arguing over the definition of a term, rather than what the implications of that term might or might not be. In the end, a circuitous debate transpires, amounting to little more than mere semantics. Meanwhile, the problem continues unabated until a more serious attempt at remedying the issue is addressed, with or without ever agreeing upon a single definition of the subject under consideration.

And inasmuch as the al-Qaeda terrorist attacks of September 11, 2001, opened the eyes of many, especially Americans, to the evils of international terrorism, this tactic has existed for millennia prior.

Early Beginnings

The earliest known practitioners of terrorism were the Zealots in Jerusalem (AD 66–73), the Hindu Thugs in India (7th century), and the Muslim *assassins,* or "hashish eaters"

(1090–1272), although the use of the word *terrorism* was not popularized until the French Revolution and the *Regime de la terreur,* in which Maximilien Robespierre sought to purge French society through violence, terror, and death.

In the late 1800s and early 1900s, anarchist terrorism and "propaganda by the deed" took center stage. Russian anarchists, driven by the belief that society should have no government or laws, successfully assassinated Czar Alexander II in March 1881. Following the assassination of the czar, a worldwide panic spread that anarchism would take root as a popular ideology as subsequent attacks by anarchists in the United States led to an overinflated impression of the threat.

Around this same time, Irish Republican terrorism took aim at the British Empire. Groups such as the Fenian Brotherhood, Irish Republican Brotherhood (IRB), and Clan na Gael led an unsuccessful campaign to drive British occupiers from Ireland. Even though terrorism was an unsuccessful tactic to achieve the revolutionaries' goal, these early terrorist groups laid the groundwork for other violent organizations, including several variations of the Irish Republican Army, to emerge later on.

Violence perpetrated by nonstate actors was overshadowed throughout the first half of the 20th century as World War I and World War II were primarily about nation-states fighting with and among each other. Accordingly, many scholars point to the assassination of Archduke Franz Ferdinand of Austria, as the spark that lit the fuse leading to the beginning of the first world war. Ferdinand was assassinated by members of Mlada Bosna, a revolutionary organization with links to the Serbian Black Hand, or Crna Ruka.

It was not so much that terrorism disappeared altogether over the course of the two world wars, but rather that it was now being practiced by totalitarian and Fascist heads of state, including Adolf Hitler of Germany, Benito Mussolini of Italy, and Joseph Stalin of the Soviet Union (USSR).

During the Cold War, the issue of state-sponsored terrorism was a major theme. Both the United States and the Soviet Union helped finance, equip, and train terrorist and insurgent groups in Africa, Latin America, the Middle East, and Asia. These groups were used as proxy forces in the broader struggle for power between the Americans and the Soviets in the quest for global hegemony. Some of the dominant ideologies that defined terrorism during the Cold War, driven in part by decolonization, included ethnonationalism, left-wing/Marxism, and irredentism and separatism.

The Internationalization of Terrorism

Most scholars pinpoint the beginning of the phase where "terrorism goes global" to the events of July 22, 1968. On this date, three terrorists belonging to the group the Popular Front for the Liberation of Palestine (PFLP), part of the Palestine Liberation Organization (PLO), hijacked an El Al flight en route to Rome, Italy, from Tel Aviv, Israel. Although the passengers and crew from the flight were ultimately released, traded in exchange for imprisoned terrorists, the event garnered widespread media attention and led many terrorists to recognize the propaganda value of such publicity. This event also marked the trend of terrorists crossing international borders to conduct attacks, a trend that continues to the present day.

In short, the Palestinians dominated the headlines related to international terrorism throughout much of the 1970s. In 1972, a Palestinian group by the name of Black September attacked Israeli athletes at the 1972 Olympic Games in Munich, Germany. Eleven Israeli Olympians were taken hostage and eventually killed, while 5 Black September terrorists and a West German police officer were also killed. Director Steven Spielberg made the event into a Hollywood film in 2005, focusing on what became known as Operation Wrath of God, a plan by the Israeli government to retaliate against terrorists involved with the plot.

Other terrorist groups active during the 1970s include the Secret Army for the Liberation of Armenia, 17 November (Greece), Red Brigades (Italy), the Provisional Irish Republican Army (PIRA), and Red Army Faction (RAF) in Germany. One of the earliest known "terrorist entrepreneurs," Ilich Ramirez Sanchez, a Venezuelan national also known as "Carlos the Jackal," led a group of other terrorists in an attack on a meeting of leaders from the Organization of the Petroleum Exporting Countries (OPEC) in December 1975 in Vienna, Austria.

Other notable terrorism-related events during the 1970s include an Israeli raid to free hostages at Entebbe International Airport in Uganda in July 1976; the kidnapping and murder of Italian politician Aldo Moro by the left-wing terrorist group known as the Red Brigades in March 1978; and a wave of political violence that followed the Iranian Revolution in 1979.

Terrorism during the 1980s was dominated by several well-known groups, including the PIRA and Basque Homeland and Liberty (ETA) in Europe; the Revolutionary Armed Forces of Colombia (FARC), Sendero Luminoso, and M-19 in Latin America;

Egyptian Islamic Jihad (EIJ), Abu Nidal Organization, and the government of Libyan strongman Muammar Gadhafi in the Middle East; and the Liberation Tigers of Tamil Eelam (LTTE) in Asia.

In addition to continued airline hijackings, other notable terrorism-related events during this decade include the assassination of Egyptian President Anwar Sadat in October 1981 by members of EIJ; the continuous targeting of U.S. military personnel abroad, especially throughout Europe; the Hezbollah bombings of U.S. Marine Corps barracks in Beirut, Lebanon, in October 1983; the assassination of Indian prime minister Indira Gandhi by her Sikh bodyguards in India in October 1984; the hijacking of the Italian cruise ship the *Achille Lauro* in October 1985 by militants from the PFLP; attacks against the international airports in Rome, Italy, and Vienna, Austria, by the Abu Nidal Organization in December 1985; the bombing of a discotheque frequented by U.S. military members in West Berlin, Germany, by Libyan terrorists; the Remembrance Day bombings in Enniskillen, Northern Ireland by the PIRA; and the 1988 Pan Am Flight 103 bombing of an airplane over Lockerbie, Scotland, sponsored by Gadhafi's Libya.

With the end of the Cold War, many terrorist groups once considered vital to the proxy conflict between the United States and the Soviet Union lost their funding, with most fading away and others engaging in various types of crime to fund their operations. The use of terrorism throughout the 1990s was diverse and deadly, with groups motivated by ideologies from right-wing extremism to millenarian and cult-like objectives.

Moreover, the 1990s brought the slow and steady drumbeat of al-Qaeda terrorism targeting the United States, although this only became apparent in retrospect. Indeed, many opportunities to counter al-Qaeda during the 1990s were missed, as the group was involved (either directly or indirectly) in a bomb attack on the World Trade Center in 1993, and extremely lethal attacks against the American embassies in Nairobi, Kenya, and Dar es Salaam, Tanzania, in 1998. Osama bin Laden, the leader of al-Qaeda, made no effort to disguise his hatred of the United States and the West, declaring a fatwa in 1996, imploring his followers to strike out against "the far enemy," as he labeled the United States.

Some devastating and spectacular terrorist attacks occurred in the 1990s. In 1992 and 1994, respectively, Hezbollah attacked Jewish targets in Argentina, including the Israeli embassy and a Jewish Community Center; the use of sarin gas by Aum Shinrikyo in the March 1995 Tokyo subway attack; Timothy McVeigh's bombing of the Alfred P. Murrah Federal Building in Oklahoma City, Oklahoma, in April 1995; the bombing of Khobar Towers, a housing complex for American servicemen in Saudi Arabia in June 1996; as well as attacks by Palestinian Hamas, the Tupac Amaru Revolutionary Movement (MRTA) in Peru, the Armed Islamic Group of Algeria (GIA) in Paris, the Kurdistan Workers' Party (PKK) in Turkey, and Gamaa Islamiya in Egypt.

The Threat Evolves

In 1975 Brian Michael Jenkins declared, "Terrorists want a lot of people watching, not a lot of people dead." Although this quote mostly rang true for decades, the al-Qaeda attacks of September 11, 2001, were in many ways a total paradigm shift for how the world viewed terrorism. Although the al-Qaeda attacks on New York City and Washington, DC, were in no way the first use of suicide operations by terrorists—indeed Hezbollah, the Tamil Tigers, and many other groups had favored this tactic long before al-Qaeda—the scale and scope of the attacks led many to suggest that the "old terrorism" was dead and that "new terrorism" had arrived and the consequences were unknowable.

As Jenkins has gone on to point out, the new age of terrorism is characterized by several important trends: it is more lethal; terrorists are less financially dependent on state sponsors; terrorists have adopted different forms of organization (more horizontally structured); terrorism is unbound by borders; and terrorists have sought to exploit new technologies.

Throughout the Cold War, the primary adversary of the United States was the Soviet Union, while terrorism was considered a lower-tier threat, something that happened in distant lands of former colonial empires. Compared to the prospect of nuclear warfare against the Soviets, terrorism was a mere nuisance, lumped together with topics such as low-intensity conflict, insurgency, and guerrilla warfare. It was anything but an existential threat.

Of course, terrorism was a fact of life in the United States during this time. From the Weather Underground to Ted Kaczynski ("the Unabomber"), the United States has dealt with terrorism from all points of the political spectrum, left wing to right wing. Terrorists linked to al-Qaeda first attacked the World Trade Center in 1993, although that attack only resulted in the deaths of six individuals. Although many in the United States quickly moved on, al-Qaeda was determined to finish the job.

Post 9/11

To put it simply, the al-Qaeda terrorist attacks of September 11, 2001, were in many ways a complete "game changer." Al-Qaeda, or "the base," headed by a Saudi-Yemeni religious zealot named Osama bin Laden, is a transnational terrorist network motivated by Salafi-jihadist ideology and extremely opposed to Western intervention in Muslim lands. The 9/11 attacks killed over 3,000 American citizens and led the United States military to invade Afghanistan, where al-Qaeda was headquartered after receiving sanctuary from the Afghan Taliban, which had ruled the country since 1996.

The American response to 9/11 was to declare a "global war on terrorism," which essentially translated to a worldwide effort to capture and kill al-Qaeda members throughout the globe. In turn, al-Qaeda responded by dispersing its fighters to failed states and ungoverned spaces in an effort to continue its ability to conduct terrorist attacks while remaining a coherent organization, even if it was scattered throughout dozens of countries.

Al-Qaeda and Salafist Jihadism

The origins of al-Qaeda can be traced back to an organization called Maktab al-Khidamat, or MAK, established by a Palestinian jihadist named Abdullah Azzam. The organization's early efforts focused on recruiting Arab fighters to join the resistance in Afghanistan, where the so-called mujahedin, or holy warriors, were fighting to expel Soviet troops from the country. Early members of MAK, which was founded in 1984, included Azzam, Osama bin Laden, and the Algerian, Abdullah Anas. In the mid-1980s, bin Laden met and joined forces with Ayman al-Zawahiri, the current leader of "core" al-Qaeda. Al-Zawahiri eventually merged key members of his group, Egyptian Islamic Jihad (EIJ), with al-Qaeda, once it emerged as its own entity in

the late 1980s, at which point MAK had become more focused on humanitarian efforts rather than actual fighting. Al-Qaeda has continued to evolve over the years. Now entering its third decade, al-Qaeda is many things—terrorist organization, global jihadist network, brand and franchise group for Salafist jihadists throughout the world.

Individuals like Ayman al-Zawahiri, Abu Musab al-Suri, Anwar al-Awlaki (deceased), and Abu Yahya al-Libi (deceased) serve as al-Qaeda's main insurgent theorists, proffering advice on strategy, operations, and tactics (in addition to a host of other issues including diet, grooming, and marriage). These modern-day insurgency theorists are highly adept at propagating the narrative that the Muslim *ummah* is being oppressed by an American-Israeli (or "Crusader-Zionist") nexus that seeks to subjugate all Muslims worldwide while draining their natural resources, sullying their honor, and besmirching their traditions.

Abu Musab al-Suri, aka Mustafa Setmariam Nasar, is a Syrian jihadist with Spanish citizenship and al-Qaeda's most prolific author on insurgent and terrorist strategies and tactics. Dubbed the "architect of the new al-Qaeda," al-Suri perhaps has done more to shape al-Qaeda's new strategy since 9/11 than any other individual. Al-Suri penned a 1,600-page tome, "*Call to Global Islamic Resistance*," which called for individual terrorism to replace al-Qaeda's hierarchically structured design. His magnum opus argues that a decentralized, looser network will present more problems for the West, and calls for cells to form spontaneously and autonomously. The result will be "thousands, even hundreds of thousands of Muslims participating in *Jihad*." Al-Suri's call to arms has not fallen on deaf ears, as evidenced by the 46 incidents of domestic radicalization and recruitment in the

United States alone since September 11, 2001. Perhaps most troubling of all, these incidents involved 125 people, with about half of the cases involving single individuals. The prospect of "lone wolf" terrorism on U.S. soil becomes more of a reality with each passing year, as recently disrupted plots in Detroit, New York, Portland, and Baltimore suggest. Still, these plots have been relatively amateurish in nature.

Eclipsing al-Suri as the vanguard of al-Qaeda's thinking on insurgency was a former member of the Libyan Islamic Fighting Group (LIFG), Abu Yahya al-Libi. At one point referred to as bin Laden's successor, al-Libi was seen as "young, media-savvy, ideologically extreme, and masterful at justifying savage acts of terrorism with esoteric religious arguments." Unlike Al-Qaeda in Iraq's former leader and cult hero Abu Musab al-Zarqawi, al-Libi blended jihadist credentials with scriptural knowledge. He fought against the Soviets in Afghanistan, trained insurgents in Libya and Mauritania, and was arrested by Pakistani intelligence, only to escape captivity at Bagram prison in Afghanistan while under the watch of American soldiers. In other words, his bona fides were genuine and he had "street cred" with both jihadist fighters and scholars alike. The ability to boast leaders with a mastery of the Quran and the AK-47 makes al-Qaeda not just a terrorist group, but also an "intellectual and religio-ideological insurgency," according to al-Qaeda expert Jarret Brachman. To his followers, al-Libi was as much of a scholar-warrior as General David Petraeus, the former International Security Assistance Force commander in Afghanistan and former director of the Central Intelligence Agency (CIA).

If al-Suri is the strategist, and al-Libi represented the "new guard," then al-Qaeda's current leader is the group's operational planner. In his seminal work, *Knights Under the Prophet's Banner,* al-Zawahiri lays out a two-phase strategy to instigate a global Islamic insurgency. First, al-Zawahiri proposes a focus on the "near enemy," to include the corrupt and apostate regimes of the Middle East, with his native country of Egypt drawing particular ire. Next, he argues, after an Islamic caliphate is restored in Egypt, the caliphate will be used as a staging ground to launch attacks against the West and eventually usurp the United States and its allies and reclaim its rightful place as a global example of strength and wisdom.

Other noted jihadist insurgent theorists build upon al-Zawahiri's vision of an Islamic caliphate and contribute to the idea of a global insurgency against the West. In his principal work, *Management of Savagery,* Abu Bakr Naji urges his followers to study Western works on management, military principles, political theory, and sociology to better understand the strategies that Western governments employ and how to exploit American and European vulnerabilities. He even implores his followers to study the Arabic translation of Paul Kennedy's *The Rise and Fall of Great Powers.* Bakr Naji advocates attacks on the American economic and financial infrastructure, including tourist sites and oil facilities. These attacks should be carefully planned to avoid harming other Muslims, so as not to alienate potential followers and supporters.

In 2002, al-Qaeda successfully conducted terrorist attacks in Djerba, Tunisia; Bali, Indonesia; and Mombasa, Kenya. The Bali attacks killed 202 people and were attributed to Jemaah Islamiyah, an Indonesian terrorist group with direct links to al-Qaeda. Over the course of the next several years, al-Qaeda would go on to launch attacks in

Riyadh, Saudi Arabia; Casablanca, Morocco; Jakarta, Indonesia; Istanbul, Turkey; Madrid, Spain; and London, England, demonstrating a truly global reach in its ability to wreak havoc and sow terror in various parts of the world.

The 2004 Madrid train bombings killed 192 people and occurred just before national elections were to be held in Spain. Most terrorism analysts believe that the attack had a significant impact on the elections, with Jose Maria Aznar's party losing to the opposition, which favored withdrawing Spanish troops from Iraq in line with al-Qaeda's stated demands.

The al-Qaeda terrorist attack in London on July 7, 2005, popularly known as the 7/7 bombings, featured a series of coordinated suicide attacks against the public transport system during rush hour. The perpetrators were British citizens who had received training in Pakistan and were linked to al-Qaeda.

Throughout the remainder of the 2000s, al-Qaeda went on to plan and execute more high-profile, spectacular attacks, even though not all were successful. Perhaps the most devastating attack, were it not prevented, would have been the 2006 Heathrow bomb plot, otherwise known as the Transatlantic aircraft plot.

In 2007, al-Qaeda took responsibility for the murder of Pakistani politician Benazir Bhutto, who died after a suicide bomber detonated his explosives near her motorcade. She was also shot during the attack. Al-Qaeda militants were reportedly part of the assault force of Taliban fighters that engaged U.S. troops during the Battle of Wanat, a bloody battle in Nuristan Province in eastern Afghanistan in which 9 American troops were killed and another 27 wounded.

Several high-level plots and successful attacks by al-Qaeda unfolded over the next three years. In September 2009, Afghan American Najibullah Zazi was stopped before he could execute an attack on the New York City subway system. Zazi received weapons and explosives training at an al-Qaeda training camp in Pakistan prior to his plot. As part of Zazi's network, Abid Naseer and Tariq ur-Rehman were arrested and charged with plotting an attack against the Arndale Center, a shopping mall, in Manchester, England.

Also in 2009, Al-Qaeda in the Arabian Peninsula (AQAP), instructed Umar Farouk Abdulmutallab, to conceal a homemade bomb in his underwear and detonate it aboard a flight from Amsterdam, Netherlands, to Detroit, Michigan, on Christmas Day in 2009. The bomb failed to detonate and Abdulmutallab was detained, arrested, and successfully prosecuted, and now faces four consecutive life sentences. Less than a week later, an al-Qaeda triple agent, Humam Khalil Abu-Mulal al-Balawi, detonated a suicide vest at a meeting with CIA operatives, killing numerous agents and himself at Camp Chapman in Khost Province, Afghanistan.

Given its failures to successfully pull off several plots, al-Qaeda remained proactive in planning more attacks. In May 2010, Faisal Shahzad, a Pakistani American who received training at an al-Qaeda camp in Pakistan, attempted to detonate an SUV full of explosives in New York City's Times Square. The bomb failed to explode, however, and Shahzad was apprehended, prosecuted, and imprisoned. Two months later, three al-Qaeda members were arrested in Oslo, Norway, where authorities claim that the terrorists were planning to attack Chinese targets in Norway. Finally, in October 2010, two packages containing plastic explosives were discovered on cargo planes en route from Yemen to the United States. AQAP claimed responsibility for the plots.

Throughout the 2000s, al-Qaeda evolved from an organizational core based in Pakistan to a network of affiliates and franchise groups stretching from North Africa to Southeast Asia. One of al-Qaeda's most capable spin-off groups, Al-Qaeda in Iraq, eventually morphed into an even more dangerous threat—ISIS.

The Islamic State

The Islamic State of Iraq and Syria (ISIS) grew out of its predecessor organization, Al-Qaeda in the Land of Two Rivers or Al-Qaeda in Iraq (AQI), which itself was an outgrowth of a group named Jamaat al-Tawhid wa'a-Jihad (JTWJ), headed by the Jordanian terrorist Abu Musab al-Zarqawi.

ISIS's ideology is defined by a very narrow interpretation of sharia on social and criminal issues and has been described as "untamed Wahhabism," Salafi jihadism, and *takfirism*. Those deemed to be unbelievers are to be killed to purify the community of the faithful. ISIS relentlessly targets Westerners, Christian and Yazidi religious minorities, Shiite Muslims (perhaps the groups' most frequent target), Kurds, Alawites, and even other Sunni Muslims who are labeled as infidels, *kuffar* (derogatory term for "nonbelievers"), apostates, and so on.

The two primary factors most commonly cited as leading to the rise of ISIS are the Iraqi prime minister Nouri al-Maliki's sectarian agenda against Sunnis in Iraq and the resulting power vacuum from the Syrian Civil War.

Under the al-Maliki regime, sectarianism intensified, pushing Iraqi Sunnis, many of whom were formerly associated with Saddam Hussein's Baath Party, into the arms of ISIS. At the same time, foreign fighters from around the globe flocked to join the group, emboldened by its recent string of successful military victories and a slick marketing media campaign unrivaled in its sophistication, technical prowess, and reach. The estimates vary widely, but some intelligence officials believe that currently approximately 15,000 citizens from 80 countries are fighting with ISIS in Syria and Iraq, making it the most significant transnational jihadist conflict of all time. Fighters have traveled from far afield, including many fighters from the United States, various European countries, Australia, and even other countries not normally associated with global jihad, like Chile and Cambodia.

ISIS did use social media to broadcast the beheading of several Westerners it had kidnapped, but it also used Twitter, Instagram, YouTube, and Facebook to show its humanitarian efforts, including fighters handing out ice cream cones to children in an attempt to appeal to its constituents. It has even developed its own video game modeled after *Grand Theft Auto*. ISIS has produced several popular video series such as *Knights of Martyrdom* and *Risen Alive,* which emphasize the camaraderie of jihad by showing militants fighting together on the battlefield. *Dabiq* is ISIS's magazine, which is an English-language production used to help lure more recruits. The magazine is multifaceted, reporting battlefield statistics, but also laying out a thoroughly detailed religious explanation for its actions, especially its attempt to establish an Islamic caliphate in Syria and Iraq. Some of the hashtags promoted by ISIS include #One BillionMuslimCampaigntoSupportIS.

Domestic Terrorism in the United States

Although the threat from terrorism abroad is apparent, there has also been a growing concern about the threat posed by homegrown extremists and radical jihadists in the United States as well. Since 2013, there have been numerous domestic terrorist attacks in the United States, including several high-profile attacks such as:

- The Boston (Massachusetts) Marathon Bombing (April 2013)
- Curtis Culwell Center Muhammad Art Exhibit Shooting in Garland, Texas (May 2015)
- San Bernardino (California) shooting (December 2015)
- Pulse nightclub shooting in Orlando, Florida (June 2016)
- New York-Chelsea Bombing, Seaside Park, New Jersey Bombing (September 2016)
- Ohio State attack, Columbus, Ohio
- Charlottesville, Virginia, attack

Where Do We Go from Here? The Future of Terrorism

The United States is facing an important moment in dealing with the challenges of terrorism and violent nonstate actors. And although one would be challenged to identify a period in the past three decades when this statement was not true, the current wave of violence in the Middle East could have disastrous consequences for the United States and its allies. Given the situation and the post-Arab Spring instability, projecting the future of terrorism and violence is a fraught endeavor. Terrorism—as it has been from the earliest epoch—is shifting, evolving, and spreading. Many previous projections, such as the prospects for conflict resolution between Israel and the Palestinians, for instance, have not come to pass, while new

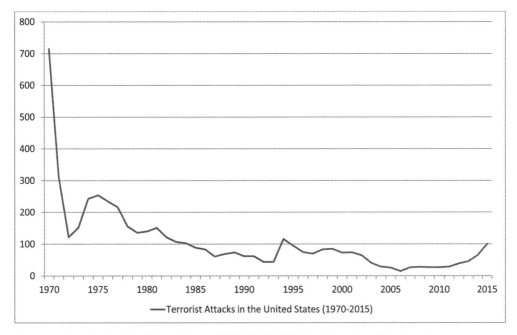

Terrorist Attacks in the United States (1970–2015) (Global Terrorism Database).

xxvi | **Introductory Essays**

fault lines, for example, the global jihad, have formed and spread.

What will shape the nature of terrorism and violence in the coming years? Three broad factors are the most critical in shaping future trends:

- The resolution or continuation of the many intra- and interstate conflicts currently under way—most importantly the Syrian Civil War, but also conflict in Libya and the Sahel, Somalia, Syria, Iraq, Yemen, Afghanistan, and elsewhere—will determine the intensity and geography of future violence. The spread of ungoverned space during the past five years created an environment conducive to extremism and encouraged thousands of volunteers eager to fight. Until some semblance of security is established, militancy will breed.
- The second factor is the unprecedented movement of people out of war zones in Africa and the Middle East into, mostly, the West. This generation of migrants, unless better integrated than their predecessors, could become the recruiting pool for tomorrow's violent nonstate actors.
- The third factor is the multifaceted conflict within Islam—between the vast majority of moderate Sunnis and the small sliver of violent jihadists; between Shia and Sunni as represented by the proxy duel between Iran and Saudi Arabia; and between Islam in general and the West, mostly fed by Western reactions (or overreactions) to the perceived threat from groups like ISIS or al-Qaeda.

What Does the Future of Terrorism Look Like?

With the advent of information technology and unimpeded advance of globalization,

all politics may still be local, but in 2018 *all conflict is global*. What were once considered parochial issues are now magnified far beyond national borders. The increased momentum of human interaction, accelerating speed of change, and ubiquitous media are converging in densely populated (and growing) urban areas. And although many would prefer to "move past" the counterinsurgencies in Afghanistan and Iraq, wars in Libya, Yemen, Somalia, and Syria, and significant extremist influence in much of the Middle East, the fact remains that even if violent conflict declines in most plausible futures, certain regions of the world are likely to experience persistent volatility, especially the belt of territory stretching from the Maghreb through southern Asia. It is important to carefully distinguish between what may be sheer opportunism by terrorists who move to secure ungoverned space and an overall increase in the capabilities of specific groups and the likelihood that they possess the wherewithal to threaten core global security interests.

Globalization will facilitate the movement of nonstate actors and, especially, their interactions. Private entities outside government control are gaining power as information that governments once owned is now more widely available. Encryption, mass dissemination, and instant communication—once the realm of governments—are now available to all. This ease of communication works both ways, enabling nonstate actors but also increasing opportunities to combat violence and terrorism—organizing global efforts on radicalization and Internet hate speech, for example, or arranging more global information sharing.

Disenfranchisement has been a feature of global politics for hundreds of years, but why this disenfranchisement is particularly acute today, and will continue to be in the future is that as they become further empowered, individuals and small groups could gain access to lethal and disruptive technologies, including precision strikes, biological weapons, and cyber instruments. New technologies are likely to continue to create opportunities for hostile state and nonstate actors to pursue specific economic activities to evade, subvert, and steal from established "traditional" state entities and large corporations.

Hacktivists and profit-driven cyber criminals have already found ways to create alternative markets, such as the Silk Road online drug bazaar; disrupt banks and other major companies through cyber theft and data compromises; and create new digital currencies whose encryption enables users to transact quickly and secretively. These challenges are in their early stages, and terrorist organizations such as ISIS are only beginning to exploit new technologies to finance their operations.

The analysis of current trends demonstrates that, over the next five years, and even over the next 20, the most likely scenario seems one with the United States in much the same place it was more than a decade ago in 2005—battling insurgencies in both Iraq and Afghanistan and waging a global war against violent extremist organizations with no end date in sight.

The question of democratization in the post-Arab Spring years and the relationship between religion, disenfranchisement, and growing areas with little or no governance may prove to be vexing problems in the future for Western democracies. We have witnessed many countries that have undergone democratization, or stunted democratization, during the past 50 years, and those lessons may offer clues about which characteristics will spur violence and haunt nation-states in the future. Many of the countries where terrorism is most common have undergone wrenching religious or ethnic conflict, and all have undergone some type of test of leadership. Most have seen major change in the past 10 years alone.

Insecure states make weak partners, and the impact of terrorism and nonstate-actor violence will undermine partner ability to project power, secure borders, and to engage regionally or internationally in trade, diplomacy, and other normal state functions. A broader crisis of governance afflicts the traditional Westphalian nation-state, which in many parts of the world is eroding due to either a lack of will or capacity (and in many cases both) to govern. The resulting power vacuum is often filled by violent nonstate actors (for example, terrorists, insurgents, warlords, sectarian militias). The violence that emerges from a wide range of factors means the United States will face another generation-long debate about whether to support security states that provide some measure of safety to citizens but fail to democratize, and democracies that better reflect U.S. values but are sources of instability in the absence of strong central security apparatuses. The situation in Egypt, where a military dictator overthrew the popularly elected government led by the Muslim Brotherhood, is but one example of a country, faced with a choice between security and democracy, choosing the former. Decades down the road we may face another version of the Arab Spring. Engagement with civil society in these countries, even at the risk of alienating local autocrats, might help ease the transition during the next outbreak of popular revolt.

In the end, it is nearly impossible to predict where terrorist groups may emerge in the future. But by studying what has happened in the past, students of terrorism will know the history and evolution of these organizations, their tactics, their ideologies and objectives, and as such, will have a firmer grasp on how to counter these groups in the future.

A

Abu Nidal Organization

The Abu Nidal Organization (ANO) was the most notorious terrorist group in the Middle East in the period from 1974 until the early 1990s. Sabri al-Banna founded the group on November 22, 1974, and he assumed the name Abu Nidal ("father of the revolution"). His purpose was to protest the involvement of Syrian forces in the Lebanese civil war. For a time, the group had the name Black June to commemorate the uprising of the Palestinians against the Jordanians in June 1974. He modeled the ANO on the strategy and tactics of the Jewish terrorist group, the Stern Gang. His opposition to Syrian intervention in Lebanon moderated, and he turned his attention to Israeli targets.

Abu Nidal had success in recruiting activists, and soon the Abu Nidal group had several hundred hard-core members ready to carry out operations. His hit team consisted of three or four members who were to study and then attack a designated target. From 1974 to 1990, the ANO carried out operations in 20 countries, and it killed or injured nearly 900 people. One such example was the bombing of a Gulf Air aircraft on September 23, 1983, near Abu Dhabi, United Arab Emirates, that killed 111 passengers and crew. During its heyday, the ANO's headquarters was in Baghdad, Iraq, but most of its operations came out of Lebanon. With an operation base in Lebanon, Abu Nidal was able to recruit from the Palestinian refugee camps. Many of the ANO's operations targeted the Palestine Liberation Organization and its head, Yasser Arafat. A blood feud developed between Abu Nidal and Arafat that continued to Abu Nidal's death.

Since 1990, the Abu Nidal Organization has deteriorated and has become almost inactive. In the 1980s, terrorist experts classified the ANO as one of the most active and dangerous terrorist groups operating. Political pressure from Western and Middle Eastern governments, internal dissention, and the health of Abu Nidal have all played roles in weakening the ANO. Political pressure on Iraq (1983), Syria (1987), Libya (1999), and Egypt (1999) caused the ANO to move its operations to Baghdad, Iraq.

Another major factor in the eclipse of the group was a purge of members of the ANO by Abu Nidal in 1989. Abu Nidal became fearful of dissidents in the ANO at his training camps in Libya. He purged 150 of his 800 followers and had them executed. This action caused two leaders of the ANO, Atef Abu Baker and Abdel Rahman Issa, to break with Abu Nidal in November 1989. In addition, news of the executions hurt the ability of ANO to recruit, and membership has lagged since the purge. Much of ANO's financial support has also dried up because of its lack of support from patron states. Barry Rubin reported in *The Jerusalem Post* in 2002 that Abu Nidal and his supporters "are reported to have killed 300 people and wounded more than 650 others in a wide variety of attacks, most of them in Western Europe."

Abu Nidal had periodic health problems, including a heart condition, and he was in virtual retirement in Baghdad, Iraq. He retained control over the Abu

Nidal Organization, but its last major operation was the assassination of a Jordanian diplomat in 1994. Nidal had some form of skin cancer, and he was receiving medical attention in Baghdad until August 2002. On August 16, 2002, Iraqi intelligence agents of the Mukhabarat surrounded the villa where Abu Nidal was living and attacked it. Abu Nidal was either shot or he shot himself to evade arrest. He died in a local hospital later the same day. The Abu Nidal Organization died with him.

Stephen E. Atkins

See also: Al-Fatah; Arafat, Yasser; Palestine Liberation Organization (PLO); Popular Front for the Liberation of Palestine (PFLP)

Citations

Colvin, Marie, and Sonya Murad. "Executed," *Sunday Times,* August 25, 2002.

Coughlin, Con. "He Who Lives by Terrorism," *Sunday Telegraph,* August 25, 2002.

Labich, Kenneth, James O. Goldsborough, and Tony Clifton. "War among the Terrorists," *Newsweek,* August 14, 1978.

Melman, Yossi. *The Master Terrorist: The True Story behind Abu Nidal.* New York: Adama Books, 1986.

Seale, Patrick. *Abu Nidal: A Gun for Hire.* New York: Random House, 1992.

Abu Sayyaf Group

The Abu Sayyaf Group (ASG) was founded on Basilan Island in 1991 under the leadership of *ustadz* (teacher) Abdurajak Janjalani. Originally known as the al Harakat-ul al Islamiya, the group has stated its goals as the eradication of all Christian influence in the southern Philippines and the creation of an Islamic state of Mindanao whose "nature, meaning, emblem and objective are basic to peace" (Surah I-Al Fatiha, undated ASG proclamation).

Although Janjalani originally created his movement as one dedicated to establishing an Islamic state of Mindanao, he quickly tied this objective to the regional and global supremacy of Islam through armed struggle. Toward that end, the ASG paralleled its anti-Christian agenda in Mindanao with an effort to forge and consolidate logistic and operational links with external terrorist groups. Concrete evidence of these transnational ambitions first emerged in 1995 when five ASG cells were directly implicated in Oplan Bojinka (Bojinka Operation), a multipronged plot aimed at assassinating the pope and President Clinton, bombing Washington's embassies in Manila and Bangkok, and sabotaging U.S. commercial airliners flying transpacific routes from American West Coast cities. The plan was hatched by Ramzi Yousef, the convicted mastermind of the 1993 attack against the World Trade Center in New York, and was foiled only when volatile explosive compounds ignited a fire in the apartment he was renting in Manila.

The fervor of the ASG's Islamist agenda, both domestic and international, began to atrophy in the wake of the discovery of Bojinka, a process that rapidly gathered pace three years later when Janjalani was killed in a shoot-out with Philippine police on the island of Basilan. This particular event proved to be a defining moment in the ASG's evolutionary history, triggering a leadership crisis that was followed by the loss of ideological direction and subsequent factionalization that saw the group degenerate into a loosely configured but highly ruthless kidnap-for-extortion syndicate. A number of subsequent operations proved to be highly profitable. The abductions of Western tourists in the first half of 2000, for instance, are believed to have netted the ASG an

Abu Sayyaf Group fighters have waged a guerrilla warfare style insurgency against the government in the Philippines since the early 1990s. The group has links to both al-Qaeda and the Islamic State and funds its organization through crime, especially kidnapping. (AFP/Getty Images)

estimated $20 million in ransom payments (allegedly arranged through the "good offices" of Libya).

The criminal disaggregation of the ASG proved to be short-lived, however. Beginning in 2003, concerted attempts were made to reenergize the group as an integrated and credible Islamist force. The bulk of these efforts were coordinated under the combined auspices of Khaddafi Janjalani (the younger brother of Abdurajak) and Jainal Antel Sali (also known as Abu Solaiman), a self-proclaimed ASG spokesman, both of whom sought to return the group to its militant jihadist origins following the arrest and killing of several leading bandit commanders. Notably, these included Ghalib Andang (also known as Commander Robot) and Aldam Tilao (also known as Abu Sabaya), two domineering personalities who had orchestrated many of the earlier kidnap-for-extortion operations claimed in the group's name.

Although they are now dead, Khaddafi and Solaiman's influence has been significant in reorienting the tactical and strategic direction of the ASG. The group, though disaggregated, now routinely refers to itself by its original nomenclatureal Harakat-ul al Islamiya, and has steadily scaled back its lucrative kidnap-for-extortion activities in favor of a more directed focus on attacking high-profile civilian and Western targets in major metropolitan areas.

Arguably more important, the ASG has sought to consolidate ties with the pro-bombing bloc of Jemaah Islamiyah (JI), acting as the main vehicle for furthering its operational and logistic activities in Mindanao. Intelligence sources in the Philippines confirm that militants associated with the faction continue to pass through areas under ASG control and that at least two of the most wanted men in Southeast Asia—Joko Pitono (also known as Dulmatin) and Zulkifi bin Hir (also known as Marwan)—are now based in Patikul under the group's protection.

Despite this reenergized jihadist focus, the ASG is weaker today than at any other time in the past. Ongoing raids by the Philippine military, carried out with U.S. military assistance, have seen the group's numbers dwindle to around 100 hard-core members supplemented by at most 200 part-timers. Most of these militants are split between 18 separate cells scattered across Sulu, Basilana, and Zamboanga. Compounding matters, the ASG has still to identify a universally accepted emir (leader) to replace Khaddafi and reunite the organization under a single command structure.

So long as this remains the case, the ASG's ability to perpetrate long-range, strategically disruptive attacks will be constrained. That said, the organization still has the capacity to pull off limited, localized strikes when opportunities arise. On August 4, 2010, for example, an individual suspected of being tied to ASG staged an attack on the Zamboanga City Airport, killing 2 and injuring 22. Just over two months later, on October 21 the group was tied to the bombing of a passenger bus in Cotabato that left 9 people dead and 13 wounded, 4 critically. Most recently, in November 2011, ASG was connected to an explosion at a budget hotel in Zamboanga that was hosting a wedding. The blast resulted in 3 fatalities and 27 additional casualties.

Peter Chalk

See also: Global War on Terror; Jemaah Islamiyah (JI); Jihad

Citations

Bowden, Mark. "Jihadists in Paradise," *The Atlantic,* March 2007.

Chalk, Peter, Angel Rabasa, William Rosenau, and Leanne Piggott. *The Evolving Terrorist Threat to Southeast Asia: A Net Assessment.* Santa Monica, CA: RAND, 2009.

Elegant, Simon. "Asia's Own Osama," *Time,* April 1, 2002.

Maydens, Seth. "Libyan Aid Helps to Free Hostages Held in the Philippines," *The New York Times,* October 21, 2001.

O'Brien, McKenzie. "Fluctuations between Crime and Terror: The Case of Abu Sayyaf's Kidnapping Activities," *Terrorism and Political Violence* 24, no. 2 (2012): 320–336.

Adnani, Abu Muhammad al-

Abu Muhammad al-Adnani was born Taha Subhi Falaha in northern Syria in 1977. A committed jihadist, he fought against U.S. forces in Iraq and was captured in 2005. He was detained in Camp Bucca, an American detention facility, where he reportedly first met Abu Bakr al-Baghdadi, the leader of the Islamic State in Syria and Iraq (ISIS) and would go on to become Baghdadi's deputy, responsible for the terrorist group's media campaign and information operations. In June 2014, al-Adnani was the first member of ISIS to officially declare a caliphate in Iraq and Syria. A caliphate is an Islamic state led by a caliph, or a political and religious leader who is a successor (*caliph*) to the Islamic prophet Muhammad and who retains absolute power and religious authority.

He was designated as a terrorist by the U.S. Department of State in August 2014, and a $5 million bounty was subsequently placed on his head. Al-Adnani's legacy continues to live on through audio recordings. In the most notorious of these, a nine-minute audio recording titled "Die in Your Rage" from September 2014, he implores Muslims in Western nations to carry out lone wolf attacks. In addition to serving as ISIS's main spokesman, al-Adnani headed ISIS's *Emni,* or external operations unit, which was responsible for planning attacks outside of ISIS territory. Al-Adnani is thought to have had a hand in planning some of the most spectacular attacks ever conducted by the group, including the Paris November 2015 attack and the Brussels March 2016 attack.

Al-Adnani was also known for his professional level of operations security and tradecraft, skills which helped him evade counterterrorism forces for many years, until he ultimately met his demise in late August 2016 when he was killed by a U.S. precision air strike near al-Bab, Syria. At the time of his death, al-Adnani was considered one of ISIS's longest-serving and most prominent commanders. The U.S. Department of State confirmed his death on September 12, 2016.

Colin P. Clarke

See also: Baghdadi, Abu Bakr al-; Brussels Terrorist Attacks (2016); Islamic State of Iraq and Syria (ISIS); Paris Terrorist Attacks (2015)

Citations

Callimachi, Rukmini. "How ISIS Built the Machinery of Terror Under Europe's Gaze," *New York Times,* March 29, 2016.

McCants, William. *The ISIS Apocalypse: The History, Strategy, and Doomsday Vision of the Islamic State.* New York: St. Martin's Press, 2015.

Warrick, Joby. "ISIS's Second-in-Command Hid in Syria for Months. The Day He Stepped Out, the U.S. Was Waiting," *Washington Post,* November 28, 2016.

Wright, Robin. "Abu Muhammad al-Adnani, the Voice of ISIS, is Dead," *The New Yorker,* August 30, 2016.

Al-Awlaki, Anwar

Anwar al-Awlaki was an American-born cleric of Yemeni descent that went on to become the spiritual leader and chief propagandist of Al-Qaeda in the Arabian Peninsula (AQAP). Al-Awlaki was born in Las Cruces, New Mexico, in April 1971, and moved back and forth between Yemen and the United States. Following the attacks of 9/11, al-Awlaki was actually considered a moderate Muslim and a go-to source for the media with questions about Islam. Interestingly, al-Awlaki was arrested in the mid-1990s several times for soliciting prostitutes.

Al-Awlaki's sermons have lived on through the Internet, and millions of individuals have gone on YouTube to view his lectures, which have served as a radicalizing influence and inspiration for scores of jihadists over the past decade. Al-Awlaki's influence can be seen in the cases of Major Nidal Hasan, the failed 2009 underwear bomb plot with Umar Farouk Abdulmuttalab, and many others. His speeches and writings have also been found among the possessions of several homegrown American terrorists, including the Boston Marathon bombers, the Tsarnaev brothers, and Omar Mateen, and the Pulse nightclub shooter.

In a 2010 recording titled "Call to Jihad," al-Awlaki smoothly and confidently lectures Muslims on why it remains their religious duty to kill Americans. Al-Awlaki was killed by a CIA drone strike eight kilometers from the town of Khashef in the province of Jawf in Yemen in September 2011.

With little doubt, the legacy of AQAP propagandist Anwar al-Awlaki—American-born, English-speaking ideologue who perfected the ability to preach al-Qaeda's rhetoric over the Internet—lives on today. Al-Awlaki successfully established a cult of personality that lives on today and continues to influence and inspire jihadist attacks. Al-Awlaki has remained a popular figure in the global jihad, even long after his death. Moreover, he has been one of the rare few ideologues to remain above the fray in terms of the ongoing dispute between al-Qaeda and the Islamic State. In early 2016, al-Shabaab released a video of Donald Trump announcing a call to ban Muslims from the United States, juxtaposed next to a clip of Anwar al-Awlaki warning Muslims that "the West will eventually turn against its Muslim citizens."

Some scholars, like Yemen and AQAP expert Gregory Johnsen, have argued that the American counterterrorism mission was been distracted by focusing too much on al-Qaeda propagandists like al-Awlaki, who, at least according to Johnsen, was afforded undue influence by the Obama administration far beyond his true position as a "mid-level religious functionary." Johnsen goes on to point out that far more dangerous individuals should have been a higher priority, including the leader of Al-Qaeda in the Arabian Peninsula (AQAP), Nasir al-Wuhayshi; deputy commander, Said Ali-al Shihri; AQAP's top religious scholar, Adil al-Abab; its chief of military operations, Qassim al-Raymi; its bomb maker, Ibrahim Hassan al-Asiri; and its leading ideologue, Ibrahim Suleiman al-Rubaysh.

Colin P. Clarke

See also: Al-Qaeda in the Arabian Peninsula (AQAP); Global War on Terror; Homegrown Terrorism; Jihad

Citations

"Anwar al-Awlaki: An American Citizen, A CIA Target," *NPR Fresh Air,* May 18, 2010.

Ingram, Haroro J., and Craig Whiteside. "The Yemen Raid and the Ghost of Anwar al-Awlaki," *The Atlantic,* February 9, 2017.

Shane, Scott. "The Lessons of Anwar Al-Awlaki," *The New York Times Magazine,* August 27, 2015.

Al-Fatah

Al-Fatah is a Palestinian political and military organization with roots stretching back to the 1950s. Led by Yasser Arafat, "al-Fatah" is Arabic for the reverse acronym of *Harekat at-Tahrir al-Wataniyyeh,* meaning "conquest by means of jihad." The organization originally began as the Palestinian National Liberation Movement and is currently considered one of several organizations under the umbrella of the Palestine Liberation Organization (PLO). Although al-Fatah was initially opposed to the PLO, it is currently the group's most prominent faction. Over time, it has been closely associated with a bevy of other international terrorist organizations, including providing military training to some of them. It was originally formed by members of the Palestinian diaspora living in Cairo and Beirut, along with professionals working in the Persian Gulf. Its founding members included not just Yasser Arafat, but also Salah Khalaf, Khalil al-Wazir, and Khaled Yashruti.

Al-Fatah's ideology has been described as a mixture of nationalism, secularism, and social democracy. It has clashed frequently with Hamas and also suffered from serious

An eight year old boy, known as "Le Monstre," in training with al-Fatah at the Palestine Liberation Organization training camp. (Leif Skoogfors/CORBIS/Corbis via Getty Images)

bouts of internal strife among its members and leadership. Although al-Fatah lost its majority in 2006 parliamentary elections, it regained control of the Palestinian National Authority in the West Bank and exercised an interim self-government body.

When al-Fatah was created in the late 1950s, its original mission was to organize and train Palestinian commandos to launch raids into Israel. Al-Fatah completed its first military operation in December 1964, blowing up an Israeli water-pump installation. It then gained further support after the Arab loss in the Six-Day War of 1967, the same year it officially joined the PLO, which increased its recognition and prominence. In 1968 during the Battle of Karameh, the Palestinian militants fought with the Jordanian military against the Israel Defense Forces. It

lost 150 fighters in that battle. Arafat took over as chairman of the PLO in 1969.

But al-Fatah's relationship with Jordan and other nations ebbed and flowed. Within Jordan, al-Fatah and other Palestinian groups essentially created a state within a state. In 1970, Jordan fought to expel al-Fatah, and in the process, the leadership moved to Beirut, Lebanon. There were over 3,500 Palestinian casualties resulting from those clashes.

In July 1971, Jordanian authorities killed Abu Ali Iyad, a high-ranking al-Fatah official. An extremist group of al-Fatah emerged called Black September in November 1971. Black September is responsible for the murder of 11 Israeli athletes at the Olympic Games in Munich, West Germany in September 1972. Following the Olympic Games attack, Black September continued to do more terrorist attacks, typically against Israel.

In 1978, during the Coastal Road Massacre, al-Fatah commandos attacked and killed 37 Israelis. The Israel Defense Forces (IDF) responded with Operation Litani in southern Lebanon, in what became the early stages of a 20-year occupation.

Israel invaded southern Lebanon, where al-Fatah was headquartered, in 1982. Around this same time, al-Fatah's leadership relocated to Tunis, the capital of Tunisia, although many of the group's foot soldiers remained in Lebanon and fought the "war of the camps" and other bloody battles against a panoply of adversaries and enemies in the ever-changing kaleidoscope of conflict that defined the Lebanese civil war.

The Israeli army defeated the PLO and al-Fatah in areas of Lebanon not controlled by Syria, and subsequently took control over these areas. After the defeat, rival factions began to develop within al-Fatah. Fatah remained a major player throughout Lebanon's 15-year civil war, which finally ended in 1990. Especially during the Cold War, al-Fatah received weapons, explosives, and military training from the Soviet Union and an assortment of Eastern Bloc countries.

The first intifada, the Palestinian uprising, was organized by al-Fatah leader Marwan Barghouti in 1987. It began after an Israeli army truck hit a group of Palestinians, killing four. In 1993, Israel and the PLO, which was dominated by the al-Fatah, signed the Oslo Peace Accords, marking the end of the first intifada. The accords set up the Palestinian Authority (PA), which grated Palestinian control of the Gaza Strip and sections of the West Bank.

The PA held its first elections in 1996, also the last year the national council met. Arafat won the presidency, and al-Fatah won a majority of the seats in the Palestinian Legislative Council (PLC). The second intifada began in 2000 and lasted until 2005, with attacks carried out by supporters of al-Fatah. During the second intifada, Palestinians blew up Israeli nightclubs and buses. Israel's responses to the attacks weakened Arafat, and al-Fatah and left the PA in disarray.

Arafat passed away from a mysterious blood disorder in 2004, and Mahmoud Abbas was named as his successor. Abbas was elected PA president in 2005 as al-Fatah's candidate. However, al-Fatah lost the majority of seats in the PLC to its rival party, Hamas. Late in 2005, a widening internal rift within the party led to the popular Marwan Barghouti breaking ranks and siding with the younger generation of al-Fatah supporters and officials. Meanwhile, Mohammed Dahlan would go on to lead al-Fatah in Gaza.

Al-Fatah's leadership of the PA was viewed as inept and corrupt by Palestinians, especially the older generations often referred to as "the Tunisians" for the time spent in Tunis. Tensions escalated between the two parties, which led Abbas to declare a state of emergency in June 2007 and to dissolve the Hamas-led government, diminishing al-Fatah's reputation.

Al-Fatah held its first congress in two decades in August 2009. Tensions between Hamas and al-Fatah continued, and the two groups reached a reconciliation agreement in 2011. The groups elected Abbas as interim prime minister. In April 2014, al-Fatah and Hamas signed a reconciliation agreement and formed a unity government. However, tensions still remain between the two groups.

Colin P. Clarke

See also: Arafat, Yasser; Palestine Liberation Organization (PLO); Popular Front for the Liberation of Palestine (PFLP)

Citations

"Profile: Fatah Palestinian Movement," *BBC News,* June 16, 2011.

"What Is an Intifada?" *The Economist,* January 24, 2017.

Schanzer, Jonathan. *Hamas vs. Fatah: The Struggle for Palestine.* New York: St. Martin's Press, 2008.

Al-Qaeda

Al-Qaeda is an international, radical Islamic organization, the hallmark of which is the perpetration of terrorist attacks against various Western and Western-allied interests in the name of Islam. In the late 1980s, al-Qaeda (meaning the "base" or "foundation" in Arabic) fought against the Soviet occupation of Afghanistan. The organization is, however, best known for the September 11, 2001, terrorist attacks in the United States, the worst such attacks in the history of that nation.

The founding of al-Qaeda, which is comprised chiefly of Sunni Muslims, is shrouded in controversy. Research from a number of Arabic scholars indicates that al-Qaeda was created sometime between 1987 or 1988 by Sheikh Abdullah Azzam, a mentor to Osama bin Laden. Azzam was a professor at Jeddah University in Saudi Arabia. Bin Laden attended Jeddah University, where he met and was strongly influenced by Azzam. The group al-Qaeda grew out of the Afghan Service Bureau, also known as the Maktab al-Khidmat lil-mujahidin al-Arab (MAK). Azzam was the founder of the MaK, and bin Laden funded the organization and was considered the deputy director. This organization recruited, trained, and transported Muslim soldiers from any Muslim nation into Afghanistan to fight the jihad (holy war) against the Soviet armies in the 1980s.

Sayyid Qutb, a philosopher of the Muslim Brotherhood, developed the credo for al-Qaeda, which is to arm all Muslims in the world and to overthrow any government that does not support traditional Muslim practice and Islamic law. Following the mysterious death of Sheikh Azzam in November 1989, bin Laden took over the leadership of al-Qaeda. He continued to work toward Azzam's goal of creating an international organization comprised of mujahideen (soldiers) who would fight the oppression of Muslims throughout the world. Al-Qaeda actually has several goals: to destroy Israel; to rid the Islamic world of the influence of Western civilization; to reestablish a caliphate form of government throughout the world; to fight against any government viewed as contrary to the ideals of Islamic law and religion; and to aid any Islamic groups trying to establish an Islamic form of government in their countries.

The organization of al-Qaeda follows the *Shur majlis,* or consultative council form of leadership. The emir general's post has been held by Osama bin Laden, who was succeeded by Ayman al-Zawahiri upon bin Laden's death in May 2011. Several other generals are under the emir general, and then there are additional leaders of related groups. There are 24 related groups as part of the consultative council. The council consists of four committees: military, religious-legal, finance, and media. The emir general personally selects the leader of these committees, and each committee head reports directly to the emir general. All levels of al-Qaeda are highly compartmentalized, and secrecy is the key to all operations.

Al-Qaeda's ideology has appealed to both Middle Eastern and non-Middle Eastern groups who adhere to Islam. A number of radical Islamic terrorist groups are also associated with al-Qaeda that have established a history of violence and terrorism in numerous countries in the world today. Most notably, these associated groups include Al-Qaeda in Iraq, which merged with the Islamic State of Iraq and Syria (ISIS), and the al-Nusra Front in Syria. ISIS has been waging a bloody insurgency in both Iraq and Syria since 2011 and has become a key player in the internecine Syrian Civil War. The al-Nusra Front serves as al-Qaeda's Syrian branch, which is also operational in parts of Lebanon. The al-Nusra organization is also involved in the civil war in Syria and, like ISIS, is waging war against President Bashar al-Assad's government. Nigerian-based Boko Haram, another organization of jihadist extremists, also has alleged ties to al-Qaeda.

Bin Laden was able to put most of the radical Islamic terrorist groups under the umbrella of al-Qaeda. Indeed, its leadership spread throughout the world, and its influence penetrates many religious, social, and economical structures in most Muslim communities. The membership of al-Qaeda remains difficult to determine because of its decentralized organizational structure. By early 2005, U.S. officials claimed to have killed or taken prisoner two-thirds of the al-Qaeda leaders behind the September 11 attacks. However, some of these prisoners have been shown to have had no direct connection with the attacks.

Al-Qaeda has continued to periodically release audio recording and videotapes, some featuring bin Laden and Zawahiri, to comment on current issues, exhort followers to keep up the fight, and prove to Western governments that it is still a force with which to be reckoned. Despite the decimation of al-Qaeda's core leadership in Afghanistan and Pakistan after 9/11, it continues to be a major threat. According to experts, the organization

moved from a centralized organization to a series of local-actor organizations forming a broad, loosely organized terrorist network. Al-Qaeda in Iraq was substantially weakened by the end of the Iraq War in 2011, but it subsequently regained control of many of its former staging areas and the ability to launch weekly waves of multiple car bomb attacks. It has also joined forces with ISIS, and in so doing has greatly amplified its ability to sow chaos and terror within Iraq.

On May 2, 2011, bin Laden was killed in an attack mounted by U.S. Special Forces on his compound in Pakistan. President Barack Obama called it the "most significant achievement to date" in the effort to defeat al-Qaeda. In July 2013, however, more than 1,000 people were killed in Iraq, the highest monthly death toll in five years. Most of the attacks were led by al-Qaeda and its affiliates, including ISIS. That same year, in Syria, al-Qaeda's affiliate, the al-Nusra Front, rose to prominence. Al-Nusra reports directly to al-Qaeda's leadership hierarchy. Between 2009 and 2015, in Libya, terror groups affiliated with al-Qaeda have been blamed for scores of attacks, many of them including civilians. Indeed, al-Qaeda has been blamed for the September 11, 2012 attack on the U.S. consulate in Benghazi, Libya, that left the U.S. ambassador and three other Americans dead. In Yemen, al-Qaeda leaders in strongholds in the country's south have not been vanquished by a Yemeni military backed by U.S. and Saudi forces and drone strikes.

Al-Qaeda affiliates in Iraq, Syria, Yemen, and West Africa have expanded their operating areas and capabilities and appear poised to continue their expansion. By January 2014, a resurgent al-Qaeda, along with ISIS, had secured much of Iraq's Anbar Province, including Fallujah, and was making significant headway in Afghanistan, often colluding with a resurgent Taliban. Al-Qaeda has also successfully established itself in parts of Lebanon, Egypt, Algeria, and Mali. By early 2014, the Obama administration had begun shipping Hellfire missiles and other weaponry to the Iraqi government to suppress the growing insurgency there, which is now dominated by ISIS.

In a telling sign of ISIS's recent excesses, al-Qaeda formally disassociated itself from the group in February 2014, citing the organization's brutality and inability to submit to authority. In June 2015, al-Qaeda's second-in-command, Nasir al-Wuhayshi, died in a U.S. air strike in Yemen. The Obama administration trumpeted this as a major blow to the al-Qaeda leadership, but the organization appears not to have suffered unduly because of it. In Afghanistan, meanwhile, President Obama reluctantly agreed to keep a force of more than 10,000 troops there through 2016, in part because of increased activity by al-Qaeda and its affiliates throughout 2015. Saudi Arabia mounted a major military intervention in the Yemeni Civil War in 2015, which was designed in large measure to defeat Al-Qaeda in the Arabian Peninsula. That intervention was limited to air strikes, however. Although al-Qaeda has endured many setbacks since 2001, it remains a potent force for worldwide terrorism. Perhaps its greatest influence in recent years has been its ability to form spin-off organizations like ISIS and to encourage allied groups such as Boko Haram.

Harry Raymond Hueston II

See also: Al-Qaeda in Iraq (AQI); Al-Qaeda in the Arabian Peninsula (AQAP); Al-Qaeda in the Islamic Maghreb (AQIM); Bin Laden, Osama; Jabhat al Fateh al Sham (Jabhat al-Nusra); Zawahiri, Ayman al-

Citations

Bergen, Peter L. *The Holy War, Inc.: Inside the Secret World of Osama bin Laden.* New York: Free Press, 2002.

Gunaratna, Rohan. *Inside Al Qaeda: Global Network of Terror.* New York: Berkley Publishing Group, 2003.

Hueston, Harry R., and B. Vizzin. *Terrorism 101.* 2nd ed. Ann Arbor, MI: XanEdu Press, 2004.

Mendelsohn, Barak. *The Al Qaeda Franchise: The Expansion of Al Qaeda and Its Consequences.* Oxford: Oxford University Press, 2015.

Zuhur, Sherifa. *A Hundred Osamas: Islamist Threats and the Future of Counterinsurgency.* Carlisle Barracks, PA: Strategic Studies Institute, U.S. Army War College, 2006.

Al-Qaeda in Iraq (AQI)

Al-Qaeda in Iraq (al-Qa'ida fi Bilad al-Rafhidayn, AQI) is a militant Sunni jihadist organization that took root in Iraq after the 2003 Anglo-American–led invasion of that nation. The U.S. government once characterized AQI, sometimes referred to as al-Qaeda in Mesopotamia, as the deadliest Sunni jihadist insurgent force in Iraq. Opponents of the continuing U.S. presence in Iraq argued that the 2003 invasion sparked the growth of Salafi jihadism and suicide terrorism in Iraq and its export to other parts of the Islamic world. AQI first formed following the invasion and toppling of the Iraq regime in March 2003, under the name Jama'at al-Tawhid wa-l Jihad (Group of Monotheism and Jihad) under Abu Musab al-Zarqawi. Since 2011 or so, AQI has been gradually subsumed by the Islamic State of Iraq and Syria (ISIS), which has been waging a bloody insurgency in both Iraq and Syria.

Al-Zarqawi had fought in Afghanistan in the 1980s and 1990s, and upon traveling to Jordan, he organized a group called Bayt al-Imam with the noted Islamist ideologue Abu Muhammad al-Maqdisi (Muhammad Tahir al-Barqawi) and other veterans of the war in Afghanistan. Al-Zarqawi was arrested and imprisoned, but was released in 1999. Returning again to Afghanistan and setting up camp in Herat, he reportedly took charge of certain Islamist factions in Kurdistan, from there moving into Iraq and sometimes into Syria. Once Mullah Krekar, the leader of the Kurdish group Islamist Ansar al-Islam, was deported to the Netherlands in 2003, certain sources claim that al-Zarqawi led some 600 Arab fighters in Syria.

Tawhid wa-l Jihad was blamed for, or took credit for, numerous attacks, including bombings of the Jordanian Embassy, the Canal Hotel, that killed 23 at the United Nations (UN) headquarters, and the Imam Ali mosque in Najaf. It is also credited with the killing of Italian paramilitary police and civilians at Nasiriyah and numerous suicide attacks that continued through 2005. The group also seized and beheaded hostages. A video of the savage execution of U.S. businessman Nicholas Berg, murdered in Iraq on May 7, 2004, reportedly by al-Zarqawi himself, was followed by other killings of civilians. AQI targeted Iraqi governmental and military personnel and police because of their cooperation with the American occupying force. AQI's recruitment videos highlighted American attacks and home searches of defenseless Iraqis and promised martyrdom. Estimates of AQI members ranged from 850 to several thousand. Also under dispute were the numbers of foreign fighters in relation to Iraqi fighters.

Foreign fighters' roles were first emphasized, but it became clear that a much higher percentage (probably 90 percent) of fighters were Iraqi: members of the Salafist jihadist, or quasi-nationalist jihadist, groups. In October 2004, al-Zarqawi's group issued a statement acknowledging the leadership of al-Qaeda under Osama bin Laden and adopted the name al-Qa'ida fi Bilad al-Rafhidayn. The Iraqi city of Fallujah, in western Anbar Province, became an AQI stronghold. U.S. forces twice tried to capture the city, first in the prematurely terminated Operation Vigilant Resolve from April 4 to May 1, 2004. The Fallujah Guard then controlled the city. U.S. military and Iraqi forces conquered the city in Operation Phantom Fury (code-named Operation Fajr) during November 7 to December 23, 2004, in extremely bloody fighting. Al-Zarqawi formed relationships with other Salafist jihad organizations, announcing an umbrella group, the Mujahideen Shura Council, in 2006.

After al-Zarqawi was reportedly killed during a U.S. air raid on a safe house in June 2006, the new AQI leader, Abu Ayyub al-Masri, announced a new coalition, the Islamic State of Iraq (the immediate precursor to ISIS), that included the Mujahideen Shura Council. Al-Qaeda, along with other Sunni Salafist and nationalist groups, strongly resisted Iraqi and coalition forces in Baghdad, Ramadi, and Baqubah, and continued staging very damaging attacks into 2007. However, by mid-2008, U.S. commanders claimed dominance over these areas. Nevertheless, AQI was acknowledged to still be operative southeast of Baghdad in Jabour, Mosul, Samarra, Hawijah, and Miqdadiyah. The United States believed that AQI's diminished presence was attributable to the Anbar Awakening, which enlisted numerous tribes, including some former AQI members, to fight al-Qaeda. The Americans further believed that AQI had been diminished because of the troop surge strategy that began in early 2007. From then until his death on May 2, 2011, bin Laden had urged the mujahideen to unify in the face of these setbacks.

AQI strongly influenced other jihadist groups and actors, particularly through its Internet presence. In sparking intersectarian strife in Iraq, the group also badly damaged Iraq's postwar reconstruction efforts and tapped into the intolerance of many Salafi groups as well as other Sunni Iraqis and Sunni Muslims outside of Iraq who were threatened by the emergence of Shia political parties and institutions that had suffered under the Baathist regime of Saddam Hussein. Iraq's al-Qaeda affiliate claimed responsibility for the July 23, 2013, jailbreak from the infamous Abu Ghraib prison that unleashed 500 to 600 militants into an already unstable region and boosted the group's resurgent fortunes in Iraq and Syria. The prisoners were freed in two coordinated assaults in which fighters used suicide bombs and mortars to storm the two top-security prisons on Baghdad's outskirts at Abu Ghraib and Taji. Both were once run by the U.S. military and housed the country's most senior al-Qaeda detainees. At least 26 members of the Iraqi security forces and more than a dozen prisoners were killed.

The scale of the attacks against the heavily guarded facilities reinforced an impression among many Iraqis that their security forces were struggling to cope with a resurgent al-Qaeda since U.S. forces withdrew in December 2011. That withdrawal resulted in the loss of much expertise and technology that had been used to hold extremists at bay. Iraqis' fears about a resurgent al-Qaeda were further vindicated when the group, now closely allied with the Islamic State of Iraq and Syria (ISIS), took control of Fallujah and Ramadi and much of the Anbar Province by January 2014. Meanwhile, car bombings, kidnappings, and other violence perpetrated by al-Qaeda and ISIS accelerated rapidly during 2014 and 2015.

By 2015, AQI was virtually indistinguishable from ISIS, as it had become ISIS's de facto affiliate operating within Iraq. ISIS has also been fighting a bloody insurgency in neighboring Syria, and also has operatives in Lebanon, Egypt, and other Middle Eastern nations. In the late summer of 2014, the Obama administration cobbled together an international coalition designed to take back territory gained by ISIS and AQI and, ultimately, to defeat them. The United States also dispatched a small contingent of Special Forces soldiers to bolster Iraq's ground campaign against the insurgents. These efforts, however, had resulted in only very modest success by the end of 2015. Indeed, Iraq and its allies still face a daunting task in their quest to vanquish AQI and ISIS militarily. Meanwhile, in 2014, al-Qaeda's worldwide leader Ayman al-Zawahiri disavowed al-Qaeda's ties to ISIS, citing its wanton brutality and unwillingness to yield to authority.

Sherifa Zuhur

See also: Al-Qaeda in the Arabian Peninsula (AQAP); Al-Qaeda in the Islamic Maghreb (AQIM); Jabhat al Fateh al-Sham (Jabhat al-Nusra)

Citations

Associated Press. "In Motley Array of Iraqi Foes, Why Does U.S. Spotlight al-Qaida?" *International Herald Tribune,* June 8, 2007.

Brisard, Jean-Charles, and Damien Martinez. *Zarqawi: The New Face of al-Qaeda.* New York: Other Press, 2005.

Burns, John, and Melissa Rubin. "U.S. Arming Sunnis in Iraq to Battle Old Qaeda Allies," *The New York Times,* June 11, 2007.

Congressional Research Service, Report to Congress. *Iraq: Post-Saddam Governance and Security.* September 6, 2007. Washington, DC: U.S. Government Printing Office, 2007.

Al-Qaeda in the Arabian Peninsula (AQAP)

Al-Qaeda in the Arabian Peninsula is an underground Muslim militant group based chiefly in Saudi Arabia and Yemen that is loosely affiliated with Osama bin Laden's and Ayman al-Zawahiri's transnational al-Qaeda network. Al-Qaeda in the Arabian Peninsula (al-Qaida fi Jazirat al-Arabiyya, AQAP) was organized in 2001–2002 and emerged publicly in 2003 when it carried out a series of deadly bombings against the Saudi government and expatriate residences in the kingdom's major cities, including the capital city of Riyadh and the key Red Sea port city of Jeddah.

The group came under attack in 2004 and 2005 during a series of arrests and shoot-outs with Saudi police and soldiers. These shoot-outs resulted in the deaths of several top AQAP leaders and operatives including its founder, Yusuf Salah Fahd al-Uyayri (Ayiri) (d. 2003) and his two successors, Abd al-Aziz bin Issa bin Abd al-Muhsin al-Muqrin (d. 2004) and Salah al-Alawi al-Awfi (d. 2005). AQAP's primary goal was to overthrow the House of Saud, the kingdom's ruling family, that is seen as corrupt and anathema to the "pure" society that the group's members and other unaffiliated and nonmilitant opponents of the monarchy seek to establish.

The monarchy is harshly criticized by both the opposition and many of its own supporters among the ranks of the kingdom's official religious scholars (*ulama*) as being too closely aligned with foreign powers, such as the United States, to the detriment of Saudi interests and social values. AQAP members proved to be adept users of the Internet, creating websites and widely read online publications such as the online magazine *Sawt al-Jihad (Voice of Jihad)*.

Despite a series of small-scale attacks on Europeans and Americans in the kingdom during 2002 and early 2003, Saudi authorities did not acknowledge the existence of AQAP as a fully operational group until May 12, 2003. On that day, the group carried out three simultaneous suicide vehicle bombings at housing compounds used by foreign (mainly Western) expatriates. The attacks killed 35 people, including 9 of the terrorists, and wounded 200 others. According to senior U.S. diplomats and Saudi intellectuals, this attack drove home to Crown Prince Abdullah (later King Abdullah) the need to vigorously combat homegrown Saudi radicalism.

In response to the attacks, hundreds of suspects were arrested by Saudi authorities, many of them with ties to AQAP and to the resistance in Iraq, although many were also probably figures from the nonmilitant religious opposition whom the authorities wished to silence under the guise of combating terrorism. Al-Uyayri (or Ayiri), AQAP's founder and first leader, was killed in June 2003 at the height of this sweep by Saudi authorities. He was succeeded by Abd al-Aziz al-Muqrin. On November 3, 2003, Saudi security forces had a shoot-out with AQAP operatives in the city of Mecca, the location of the Kaaba, Islam's holiest shrine, that resulted in the deaths of two militants and the capture of a large weapons cache. Five days later AQAP launched a successful suicide bombing attack against the Muhayya housing complex in Riyadh, which was home to many non-Saudi Arab expatriate workers; the attack killed 18 people and wounded scores of others.

The group continued to launch attacks on Saudi and foreign targets, including a Riyadh government building on April 21, 2004, and an oil company office in Yanbu on May 1 that resulted in the killing of five Western workers. AQAP suffered another setback on March 15, 2004, when Khalid Ali bin Ali al-Haj, a Yemeni national and senior AQAP leader, was killed in a shoot-out with Saudi police along with his companion, AQAP member Ibrahim al-Muzayni. The group retaliated with a host of deadly attacks on expatriates, killing Herman Dengel (a German, on May 22, 2004), BBC cameraman Simon Cumbers (on June 6), Robert Jacob (an American, on June 8), Kenneth Scroggs (an American, on June 12), Irish engineer Tony Christopher (on August 3), British engineer Edward Muirhead-Smith (on September 15), and Laurent Barbot (French, on September 26). The most widely publicized attack, however, was the June 12, 2004, kidnapping and June 18 beheading of Paul M. Johnson Jr., an American employee of U.S. defense contractor Lockheed Martin. His kidnappers demanded the release of all detainees held by Saudi authorities, which was denied. The beheading was filmed and released on websites associated with and sympathetic to AQAP. That same day, al-Muqrin was killed by Saudi security forces during a raid on an AQAP safe house. Meanwhile, on May 29 the group succeeded again in successfully carrying out attacks on three targets in the city of Khobar, taking hostages in oil business offices and housing complexes associated with foreign companies. Saudi police and soldiers stormed the buildings the next day and rescued many of the hostages but not before the attackers had killed 22 others. Shortly after this attack, the U.S. Department of State issued a statement that urged U.S. citizens to leave the kingdom. The year was capped off with a spectacular attack on December 6 on the U.S. consulate in Jeddah in which five consulate employees, four Saudi national guardsmen, and three AQAP members were killed.

The Saudi government waged a successful campaign against AQAP throughout 2004 and into 2005, killing dozens of the group's members and nearly wiping out its senior leadership. In April 2005, several senior operatives were killed in a shoot-out in Rass, and in August, Saudi security forces killed Muqrin's successor and AQAP leader Salah al-Alawi al-Awfi in the holy city of Medina. Other members were arrested. Many of the group's members remain at large, and Saudi and foreign intelligence agencies continue to warn that AQAP poses a threat. The Saudi government has responded with antiterrorist measures at home, such as conferences and public pronouncements, a highly structured in-prison counseling program designed to deradicalize detainees, and the Sakinah program that analyzes and engages Internet postings. In 2007 and 2008, Saudi security forces detained and imprisoned hundreds of people, some of them suspected militants and others in a variety of incidents, including those planning an attack during the hajj, the annual Islamic pilgrimage to Mecca.

On September 30, 2011, a U.S. drone attack in Yemen resulted in the death of Anwar al-Awlaki, one of the group's leaders, and Samir Khan, the editor of *Inspire,* its English-language magazine. Both men were U.S. citizens. AQAP claimed responsibility for the May 21, 2012, suicide attack at a parade rehearsal for Yemen's Unity Day, killing more than 120 people and injuring 200 others. The attack was the deadliest in Yemeni history. The pace of U.S. drone attacks quickened significantly in 2012, with over 20 strikes in the first five months of the year, compared to 10 strikes during the course of 2011. During 2013, targeted killings by U.S. drones and Special Forces increased in number, thanks in part to the erection of secret U.S. bases in the Horn of Africa and the Arabian Peninsula. Meanwhile, on October 4, 2012, the United Nations 1267/1989 Al-Qaeda Sanctions Committee and the U.S. State Department designated Ansar al-Sharia as an alias for Al-Qaeda in the Arabian Peninsula, although the two groups remain somewhat distinct.

In the summer of 2013, in response to news that AQAP was planning an offensive against U.S. diplomatic posts abroad, the American government temporarily closed more than two dozen embassies and legations as a precaution. This corresponded with an uptick in U.S. drone attacks, which now began to target lower-level AQAP members and other militant jihadists. In 2014, AQAP launched several attacks against Yemeni government targets, and in early December of that year it released a video of kidnapped American journalist Luke Somers and demanded an unspecified ransom for his return. The Obama administration mounted a military rescue effort, but the AQAP terrorists murdered Somers on December 6, before U.S. commandos could reach him. In January 2015, AQAP claimed responsibility for the Charlie Hebdo shootings in Paris that left 11 people dead. Three months later, the group seized the Yemeni port city of Al Mukalla after a protracted battle with Yemeni armed forces. Meanwhile, U.S. drone strikes killed dozens of AQAP militants between April 19 and 20, 2015, part of a much larger American campaign that continues to witness drone and air strikes against extremist fighters within Yemen.

Yemen has been plagued by a costly civil war since 2011, and AQAP has been heavily involved in that struggle. Iran, which supports the Houthi rebels, has essentially been fighting a proxy war with the Yemeni government and its allies, including the United States and Saudi Arabia. Meanwhile, in late March 2015, the Saudis, now leading a nine-nation Arab coalition to aid the Yemeni government, intervened in the conflict by way of air strikes and a blockade of key ports. Although the chief target remained the Houthi fighters, AQAP also fell within the coalition's crosshairs. By the end of April, however, the Saudis had scaled back their air strikes and began to seek a diplomatic end to the fighting. Peace talks were under way by September 2015, but that effort suffered a setback when the exiled Yemeni government pulled out of the negotiations. As of December 2015, the civil war in Yemen continued virtually unabated.

Christopher Anzalone

See also: Al-Awlaki, Anwar; Al-Qaeda; Al-Qaeda in Iraq (AQI); Al-Qaeda in the Islamic Maghreb (AQIM); Jabhat al Fateh al-Sham (Jabhat al-Nusra)

Citations

Al-Rasheed, Madawi. *Contesting the Saudi State: Islamic Voices from a New Generation.* Cambridge: Cambridge University Press, 2006.

Ambah, Faiza Saleh. "In Saudi Arabia, Fresh Recruits for Al Qaeda," *Christian Science Monitor,* April 16, 2004.

Cordesman, Anthony H., and Nawaf Obaid. *Al-Qaeda in Saudi Arabia: Asymmetric Threats and Islamist Extremists.* Washington, DC:

Center for Strategic and International Studies, 2005.

Ghafour, P. K. "Death of Top Terrorists in al-Rass Gunbattle Confirmed," *Arab News,* April 10, 2005.

Murphy, Caryle. "Saudi Arabia Indicts 991 Suspected Al Qaeda Militants," *Christian Science Monitor,* October 22, 2008.

Riedel, Bruce, and Bilal Y. Saab. "Al Qaeda's Third Front: Saudi Arabia," *Washington Quarterly* 21 (2008): 33–46.

Zuhur, Sherifa. "Decreasing Violence in Saudi Arabia and Beyond." In *Home Grown Terrorism: Understanding and Addressing the Root Causes of Radicalisation among Groups with an Immigrant Heritage in Europe,* Vol. 60, edited by Thomas M. Pick, Anne Speckhard, and B. Jacuch, 74–98. NATO Science for Peace and Security Series. Amsterdam: IOS Press, 2010.

Zuhur, Sherifa. *Saudi Arabia: Islamic Threat, Political Reform and the Global War on Terror.* Carlisle Barracks, PA: Strategic Studies Institute, 2005.

Al-Qaeda in the Islamic Maghreb (AQIM)

Al-Qaeda in the Islamic Maghreb is an Algerian-based clandestine jihadi organization founded on January 24, 2007, that employs terrorist tactics in support of Islamist ideology. It seeks to overthrow the Algerian government and establish an Islamic state. Al-Qaeda in the Islamic Maghreb (Tanzim al-Qaida fi Bilad al-Maghrib al-Islamiyya, AQIM) symbolizes Algeria's continuing political instability, North Africa's increasing vulnerability to militant Islam, and al-Qaeda's little-discussed ability to expand not by diffusing or splintering into local cells but rather by skillfully drawing established organizations into its sphere of influence. AQIM draws its members from the Algerian and local Saharan communities, including clans in Mali, as well as Moroccans.

AQIM has been branded a terrorist organization by the United Nations, United States, Russia, and a number of other countries. AQIM's origins lie in Algeria's modern history. The Algerian War (1954–1962) freed Algeria from French colonialism and led to rule under the wartime resistance movement, the National Liberation Front (Front de Liberation Nationale, FLN). In 1989, however, militant Muslim opponents of the FLN regime formed the Islamic Salvation Front (Front Islamique du Salut, FIS). In the early 1990s, the FLN manipulated and canceled elections to prevent the FIS from ascending to power, sparking a bloody civil war. This conflict radicalized and fragmented the opposition, with extremists gathering in the Armed Islamic Group (Groupe Islamique Arme, GIA), a faction bent on utterly destroying the FLN regime and installing a Muslim state under Sharia (Islamic law) through indiscriminate terrorist attacks against moderates and foreigners. The FLN weathered the storm, and as the civil war reached a horrendously violent stalemate, a new Islamist group, the Salafist Group for Preaching and Combat (Groupe Salafiste pour la Predication et le Combat, GSPC), superseded the GIA by denouncing the widely detested violence against civilians.

Founded in 1998, the GSPC would adopt the al-Qaeda moniker nearly a decade later. The transition from GSPC to AQIM was the result of a political dilemma facing Algerian Islamists and deft diplomacy by al-Qaeda operatives. GSPC's first leader, Hassan Hattab (aka Abu Hamza), kept the popular promise to attack only government officials and forces, hoping to regain the far-reaching support for Muslim militancy enjoyed by the FIS. But building a broad backing was slow going, and time suggested that the FLN could withstand a conventional insurgency. Impatient elements within the GSPC forced Hattab's resignation in 2004. His successor, Nabil Sahraoui (aka Abu Ibrahim Mustafa), enjoyed only a brief reign before Algerian soldiers located and eliminated him in June 2004. Abdelmalek Droukdel (aka Abu Musab Abd al-Wadoud) has run the organization since, overseeing its radicalization, renaming, and return to GIA tactics.

Al-Qaeda worked to influence the GSPC from its inception. It helped to fund Muslim militants in Algeria in the early 1990s but refused to fully endorse the GIA despite experiences that so-called Afghan Arabs in the two organizations shared while fighting the Soviets in Afghanistan in the 1980s. In 1998 al-Qaeda leader Osama bin Laden welcomed the advent of the GSPC, a group manned in part by al-Qaeda trainees who tied their renunciation of terrorism to an international jihadi agenda. The new ideology harnessed the GSPC to al-Qaeda, and 12 days after the terror attacks of September 11, 2001, U.S. president George W. Bush labeled the GSPC a terrorist organization and froze its assets. This confrontation with the West, along with defections after 2000 of the halfhearted adherents, further sharpened the GSPC's anti-Western extremist edge.

In 2002, al-Qaeda sent an emissary to Algeria for meetings with sympathetic figures within the GSPC. Two years later Chadian forces captured a key GSPC regional commander moving through the Sahara, and his colleagues decided to pressure Chad's ally, France, for his release. They reached out to al-Qaeda for assistance, and an obliging Abu Musab al-Zarqawi, head of

al-Qaeda in Iraq, agreed to support the GSPC by kidnapping French citizens as bargaining chips. The plan did not materialize, but the congenial link remained, and after 2004 the GSPC's new hard-line leaders ultimately developed the link. Al-Qaeda, for its part, grew increasingly interested in the GSPC after 2005, after the attempt to forge an affiliate terrorist network in Morocco had failed. Al-Qaeda's strategists came to recognize that within North Africa, a critical region supplying long-standing Muslim immigrant communities to nearby western Europe, only Algeria lacked a pervasive security apparatus capable of rooting out terrorist cells.

The two organizations issued cordial statements throughout 2005, and by late 2006, a formal merger between al-Qaeda and the GSPC was announced, with the latter's name change coming the following year. Since this merger, AQIM has grown more powerful and dangerous. Al-Qaeda is probably funneling resources into AQIM, supplementing funds that the Algerian organization can gather on its own through the European financial network it inherited from the GIA. In return, AQIM is internationalizing its purview. Some fear that it could make Europe a central area of operations, and it forwent expansion to send newly trained North African recruits to fight in Iraq. The al-Qaeda–AQIM alliance has been most pronounced in terms of tactics. The GSPC initially acquired conventional weaponry for guerrilla ambushes, false checkpoints, and truck bombs against military and government targets. With al-Qaeda's help and encouragement, AQIM has executed impressive terrorist attacks featuring suicide bombers and civilian casualties. Since December 2006, AQIM has bombed not only the Algerian prime minister's office and an army outpost but also foreign oil-services contractors and United Nations (UN) staff.

AQIM has declared its intention to attack European and American targets. One of the best-armed and well-financed terrorist organizations, AQIM raises most of its funds through kidnapping and holding individuals for ransom. It is believed to have secured more than $60 million in this fashion during the past decade. One of its leaders, Oumar Ould Hamaha (who was killed in northern Mali in 2014) put it this way: "The source of our financing is the Western countries. They are paying for jihad." In December 2012, one of AQIM's commanders, Mokhtar Belmokhtar, split off from AQIM and took his brigade with him, executing the In Amenas hostage crisis a month later, after France had begun Operation Serval, its military intervention against Islamists in Mali. The hostage crisis began on January 16, 2013, when Belmokhtar and his men took more than 800 people hostage at the Tigantourine gas facility near In Amenas in southern Algeria. After four days, Algerian special forces attacked the site, endeavoring to free the hostages. At least 39 foreign hostages were killed along with an Algerian security guard, as were 29 Islamists. A total of 685 Algerian workers and 107 foreigners were freed. Three Islamist militants were captured. In the late winter of 2013, French forces killed a top-level AQIM leader, although this did not appear to weaken the organization. Meanwhile, in July 2014, Operation Serval ended in a victory, with northern Mali largely freed from Islamic militants. On November 20, 2015, AQIM operatives attacked a Bamako, Mali hotel, taking more than 100 guests hostage. Mali security forces eventually ended the standoff, but not before 19 people had died. In December 2015, AQIM reportedly joined forces with Al-Mourabitoun, an Islamic militant organization that operates in Mali, Libya, and Niger.

Benjamin P. Nickels

See also: Al-Qaeda; Al-Qaeda in the Arabian Peninsula (AQAP); Al-Qaeda in Iraq (AQI); Jabhat al Fateh al-Sham (Jabhat al-Nusra)

Citations

Gunaratna, Rohan. *Inside Al Qaeda: Global Network of Terror.* New York: Berkley Publishing Group, 2003.

Hansen, Andrew, and Lauren Vriens. "Al-Qaeda in the Islamic Maghreb (AQIM) or L'Organisation Al-Qaida au Maghreb Islamique (Formerly Salafist Group for Preaching and Combat or Groupe Salafiste pour la Predication et le Combat)," Council on Foreign Relations, *Backgrounder,* Updated July 31, 2008. Available online at www.cfr.org/backgrounder/al-qaeda-islamic-maghreb.

Hunt, Emily. "Islamist Terrorism in Northwestern Africa: A 'Thorn in the Neck' of the United States?" Washington, DC: The Washington Institute for Near East Policy, *Policy Focus* #65, February 2007, www.washingtoninstitute.org/templateC04.php?CID=266.

Ibrahim, Raymond. *The Al Qaeda Reader.* New York: Doubleday, 2007.

Stora, Benjamin. *Algeria: A Short History.* Ithaca, NY: Cornell University Press, 2004.

Al-Shabaab

Originally, al-Shabaab (literally "the youth") was the hard-line youth militia of the Islamic Courts Union (ICU), which briefly took control of Mogadishu, Kismayo, and other areas of southern Somalia in June 2006. When a combination of Ethiopian and Somalian transitional federal government (TFG) troops forced the ICU to withdraw from the capital in December 2006, al-Shabaab reconstituted itself as an independent organization, and in early 2007 initiated an insurgency in an attempt to gain control of the country. Originally led by Aden Hashi Farah Aero, the group has used assassinations, bombings, and more recently suicide attacks to target TFG forces, African Union Mission to Somalia (AMISOM) peacekeepers, the United Nations, and foreign nationals. The group's declared intention is to establish a caliphate in Somalia based on a strict Wahhabi interpretation of Islam. Formally called Harakat al-Shabaab al-Mujahideen, or Movement of Warrior Youth, the organization was led by Sheikh Ahmed Abdi Godane after U.S. air strikes killed Farah and several other commanders on May 1, 2008. Under Godane's leadership, al-Shabaab overran Kismayo in August 2008, and by the summer of 2010 had seized most of southern and central Somalia, including much of the capital, Mogadishu. After Godane was killed by U.S. air strikes on September 1, 2014, he was replaced by Ahmad Umar, about whom little is known. Al-Shabaab appears to be divided into three commands: the Bay and Bokol, South Central and Mogadishu, and Puntland and Somaliland. An affiliate group also exists in the Jubba Valley. The group funds itself mainly through charitable donations raised in areas it controls, although there have been repeated allegations that it has diverted aid in these regions to buttress its war chest. Al-Shabaab's strength is very hard to determine with any amount of accuracy. Some sources claim it directly controls as few as 1,000 fighters, while other sources claim that it has as many as 8,000 to 9,000 active combatants. Some of al-Shabaab's most significant early attacks included a suicide car attack on an AMISOM base in Mogadishu, killing six peacekeepers (February 22, 2009); a suicide car bomb at the

Medina Hotel, Beledweyne, killing 35, including TFG security minister Omar Hashi Aden (June 18, 2009); the truck bombing of an AMISOM base in Mogadishu, killing 21 peacekeepers (September 17, 2009); and a suicide attack at Hotel Shamo in Mogadishu, where a ceremony was being held for medical students, killing three TFG ministers. In addition to these domestic attacks, there is increasing concern that al-Shabaab has forged close links with foreign extremists, many of whom are thought to be based in Somalia and helping with the training of the group's members. Fears were further heightened in February 2010 when al-Shabaab formally declared its organizational and operational allegiance to al-Qaeda. More recently, al-Shabaab is believed to have forged informal alliances with Al-Qaeda in the Islamic Maghreb as well as Boko Haram, the latter of which is a militant Islamist group operating chiefly in northeastern Nigeria, but also in portions of Cameroon, Chad, and Niger. In 2015, the Islamic State of Iraq and Syria (ISIS) released several recruiting videos in an attempt to entice al-Shabaab members to join its ranks. The move was met with open hostility among al-Shabaab's leadership, which cautioned its members not to engage with ISIS. Moreover, it now appears that the group has made a conscious strategic decision to strike international targets. Al-Shabaab has been linked to a 2009 plot to attack the Holsworthy Barracks in Australia, efforts aimed at recruiting Americans to carry out bombings on U.S. soil, and the attempted assassination in January 2010 of Danish cartoonist Kurt Westergaard, who created controversy in the Muslim world by drawing pictures depicting Muhammad wearing a bomb in his turban. More seriously, the group claimed responsibility for the July 11, 2010, suicide bombings in

Kampala, which killed 74 people and wounded another 70, as well as an attack against a bus station in Nairobi on November 31 that left 3 people dead and injured 39. Al-Shabaab justified the strikes as retaliation for Ugandan and Kenyan support of the AMISOM mission in Somalia. During a famine in Somalia in 2011, al-Shabaab was accused of blocking the delivery of aid from Western relief agencies. The organization claimed responsibility for the attack on a UN compound in 2013 that killed 22 people. In September 2013, al-Shabaab militants assaulted an upscale suburban shopping mall in Nairobi, Kenya, resulting in the deaths of 61 civilians and 6 Kenyan security officers. In May 2014, the group launched an attack on a Djibouti restaurant, killing three people and wounding several others. In Garissa, Kenya, al-Shabaab militants staged a massive assault on Garissa University College in April 2015, during which 152 people died and 72 others were wounded. Meanwhile, in February 2015, the extremist group released a video online in which it vowed to attack shopping malls in the United States and Canada; although no such attacks have yet occurred, mall operators increased security for the remainder of 2015 and into 2016. At the same time, al-Shabaab attacks continued in Somalia, with Mogadishu the favored target. By August 2014, al-Shabaab had suffered a series of military reversals, as TFG and AMISOM forces gradually retook more and more territory once held by the rebel group. That same month, the Somali government announced a major military campaign to flush out remaining al-Shabaab strongholds from the countryside. The Somali government also issued a blanket 45-day amnesty for all al-Shabaab members in an effort to eviscerate the organization and convince members to engage in peace talks with the TFG. By 2016, a number of ranking al-Shabaab members had turned themselves in; meanwhile, military operations against the group continued, including U.S. drone and air strikes. On March 5, 2016, U.S. warplanes bombed al-Shabaab's Raso training camp, situated some 120 miles to the north of Somalia's capital at Mogadishu. The Pentagon indicated that an estimated 150 al-Shabaab militants were killed in the attack. U.S. air strikes against al-Shabaab and its leadership have continued well into 2017 as the United States continues to work to dismantle the organization through kill-and-capture operations.

Richard Warnes

See also: Al-Qaeda; Garissa University Attack; Westgate Mall Attack

Citations

Fergusson, James. *The World's Most Dangerous Place: Inside the Outlaw State of Somalia*. Boston: Da Capo Press, 2013.

Hansen, Stig Jarle. *Al-Shabaab in Somalia: The History and Ideology of a Militant Islamist Group*. Oxford, UK: Oxford University Press, 2013.

Jones, Seth, et al. *Counterterrorism and Counterinsurgency in Somalia: Assessing the Campaign Against al-Shabaab*. Santa Monica, CA: RAND Corp., 2016.

Anthrax Attacks

On September 18, 2001, one week after the terrorist attacks of September 11, five letters contaminated with anthrax bacteria were mailed in the United States to five media outlets. Over the next month, two more letters were sent. Altogether, the anthrax letters (which were mailed from a postal box in

New Jersey) resulted in the deaths of 5 people and the infections of 17 more.

The anthrax-laced letters originally sent on September 18 were sent to the offices of ABC News, CBS News, NBC News, the *New York Post,* and the *National Enquirer.* Nearly a month later, two more letters were sent to Democratic senators Tom Daschle and Patrick Leahy at the Senate building in Washington, DC. The postal service misdirected Leahy's letter, but the letter addressed to Daschle was opened by an aide, who became infected. Unlike the earlier letters, the second set of letters contained higher-quality weapons-grade anthrax capable of infecting victims with greater lethality.

In response to the attacks, thousands of people who came in contact with or near the envelopes began taking strong doses of ciprofloxacin ("cipro"), an antibiotic capable of preventing anthrax infections. In addition, the federal government began radiation treatment of all incoming mail to defuse any possible anthrax inside. Post office employees began wearing gloves and masks and warned all Americans to carefully examine their mail and report any suspicious letters or packages.

Five people died from the anthrax infection: one employee at the *National Enquirer,* two post office employees, and two other unconnected people whose mail was likely cross-contaminated by the anthrax letters. Government officials began an investigation immediately after discovering the anthrax letters. Following a variety of leads, the investigators profiled the suspect as a chemical or biological engineer in the United States who had likely worked at government facilities in the past. Some microbiologist experts who examined the anthrax stated that its quality was likely greater than that of the anthrax found in either U.S. or Russian stockpiles and

thus was likely created in recent government anthrax programs.

The Federal Bureau of Investigation eventually concluded that Dr. Bruce Ivins, a microbiologist working at the U.S. Army's Bio-Defense Laboratory in Maryland, was responsible for the attacks. To this day, however, questions remain about his guilt, and there continues to be speculation that the true perpetrator is still on the loose. Ivins committed suicide in 2008.

Peter Chalk

See also: Global War on Terror

Citations

"American Anthrax Outbreak of 2001," University of California at Los Angeles (UCLA) Department of Epidemiology, August 24, 2008. www.ph.ucla.edu/epi /bioter/detect/antdetect_intro.html.

Croddy, Eric A., and James Wirtz, eds. *Weapons of Mass Destruction: An Encyclopedia of Worldwide Policy, Technology, and History.* Santa Barbara, CA: ABC-CLIO, 2005.

Shane, Scott. "Colleague Rebuts Idea That Suspect's Lab Made Anthrax in Attacks," *The New York Times,* April 23, 2010.

"Troubled Scientist's Anthrax Attack May Have Been Misguided Attempt to Test Cure," Associated Press, August 1, 2008.

"2001 Anthrax Attacks," History Commons. www.historycommons.org/project.jsp ?project=2001anthraxattacks (accessed July 9, 2012).

Arab Spring

The term "Arab Spring" refers to a wave of popular protests and demonstrations, beginning in Tunisia in December 2010, that swept rapidly throughout North Africa and the Middle East in 2011 and 2012. Although

Egyptians protest against the Supreme military council management of the post-revolution transformation to democracy in Alexandria, Egypt, on April 20, 2012. These protests were part of the Arab Spring revolutions that swept across the Middle East and North Africa in 2011, and 2012, radically transforming governments from Tunisia to Egypt to Libya. (Mohamed Hanno/Dreamstime.com)

responding in part to economic difficulties, including rising fuel and food costs and high unemployment, protesters generally also rebelled against repressive, authoritarian, and corrupt governments, demanding more open political systems. Most expressed frustration with regimes that were often effectively one-party systems or family dictatorships.

The precise form and course of protests varied across different countries, as did the responses of different governments. Jordan, Algeria, Iraq, Kuwait, and Morocco all experienced significant protests and unrest, which resulted in the implementation of a range of political, economic, and social reforms and constitutional changes. In Tunisia and Egypt, expressions of popular discontent were so widespread and intense that within weeks they forced the president then in power from office and brought the overhaul of the

political system. In Yemen, the process was slower, extending over the better part of a year, and further complicated by long-term sectarian violence from two rival groups of Muslim insurgents, one Shiite, the other the Sunni Al-Qaeda in the Arab Peninsula.

Although many Arab governments eventually made at least some concessions to protesters, others were determined to repress all dissent, using whatever force might be needed for the purpose. In both Libya and Syria, opposition to the entrenched one-party governments of Colonel Muammar Gadhafi and President Bashar al-Assad was met by government military crackdowns. In both cases, a brutal and violent civil war was the result. In Libya, estimates of the numbers killed between February and October 2011 ranged from several thousand to 50,000 or more. United Nations' declaration of a "no-fly zone" and air strikes by Western NATO forces played a significant part in the relatively swift resolution of the war, which ended in Gadhafi's capture and execution. In Syria, civil war began in March 2011.

The Syrian conflict proved a magnet for Islamic militia forces of different complexions, while the international community divided over whether to support the government or the rebels. Militia units from Hezbollah and the Muslim Brotherhood, long-time allies of the Syrian government and its president, Bashar al-Assad, rallied to its support, as did Russia and Iran. Al-Qaeda forces with backing from Saudi Arabia, by contrast, threw their lot in with the rebels. While calling on al-Assad to negotiate, the United States initially declined to intervene militarily. However, with the Islamic State of Iraq and Syria (ISIS) seizing more Syrian territory and terrorizing its citizens, the Obama administration began air strikes against ISIS targets in Syria in September 2014; that campaign, now a coalition effort, continues.

The United States also began arming anti-Assad insurgents. In 2015, the Obama administration began sending small detachments of special operations forces into Syria to work with moderate Syrian rebel groups. By May 1, 2016, about 400 U.S. troops were in Syria. The Syrian Civil War became even more complicated when the Russians intervened in the conflict in September 2015. The intervention was mainly conducted by Russian warplanes, which hammered anti-Assad rebel targets. Moscow insisted that it was targeting ISIS, but the facts on the ground did not support that. Indeed, the Russian intervention seemed calculated chiefly to prop up the Assad government and to give the Kremlin more of a say in Syrian affairs. Russia and the United States brokered a shaky cease-fire in late 2015, but by the spring of 2016, violence flared anew as some rebel groups refused to participate in peace talks. Meanwhile, the Russian intervention had strengthened Assad's grip on power by March 2016, and government forces began undertaking offensive operations against insurgent forces.

After many weeks of difficult negotiations, Russia and the United States brokered a new cease-fire agreement on September 9, 2016. The deal stipulated that the Assad government was to stop bombing targets that were not clearly those belonging to ISIS or the al-Nusra Front; it also required the government to permit humanitarian aid into the country. Moscow and Washington, meanwhile, pledged to work together in a military capacity to target and defeat ISIS and the al-Nusra Front and to foster dialogue that would lead ultimately to a permanent peace arrangement within Syria. Within days, however, the deal showed signs of unraveling, as neither side fully abided by the cease-fire and Moscow and Washington blamed each other for that development.

The Syrian Civil War has proven calamitous for much of the Syrian population. By the fall of 2016, it was estimated that as many as 500,000 people had died since the insurrection began in 2011. In addition, several million Syrians had been displaced from their homes, with many of them fleeing Syria and seeking asylum in western Europe. This development created a massive humanitarian crisis and a major immigration problem for many countries.

Consequences of the Arab Spring

Initially, many outside commentators, especially Westerners, hailed the Arab Spring with delight, believing that it would usher in the swift and near painless spread of democracy throughout the Middle East and Arab world. Many also hoped that any new governments that emerged would be liberal in outlook, committed to supporting human and civil rights, including women's rights and religious freedom, political transparency, democracy, equality, and the cause of peace. Yet it soon became clear that the governments that emerged from the upheavals of 2011 might well be strictly limited in terms of democracy and liberal values, and that the reforms that were implemented, far from representing a wholesale remodeling of the entire political, social, and economic fabric, would often be rather limited in scope.

Not all the political forces unleashed by the Arab Spring were liberal or secular in nature. In Egypt, Jordan, and Algeria, for example, for decades governments had sought to discourage sectarian Islamic political parties, for fear that allowing religious extremists too much influence might prove politically destabilizing, both domestically and externally. In Egypt, in particular, the overthrow of President Hosni Mubarak in February 2011 opened the way for Mohamed Morsi, an official of the Muslim Brotherhood, to gain the presidency in July 2012. Within months, he sought to implement drastic increases in his own powers, which many feared marked the beginning of a new dictatorship. After several months of ever-larger demonstrations in which millions of Egyptians ultimately participated, the Egyptian military finally ousted Morsi in July 2013, installing a caretaker president until a new constitution could be drafted and new elections held. The new Egyptian government ended up being controlled by the Egyptian Army. In Jordan and Algeria, constitutional reforms meant that Islamic political parties also made some gains.

Given that sectarian extremism enjoyed significant political support among the general population on the "Arab street," greater democracy might even inflame such issues as the ongoing Israeli-Palestinian disputes. In some cases, especially in Libya and Syria, and perhaps Yemen, the fighting and violence that characterized the Arab Spring were in themselves destabilizing, unleashing tribal and other antagonisms and rivalries that were liable to continue indefinitely. And, just as in Iraq and Afghanistan in the early 21st century, in those states outside groups and elements that participated in the fighting might well stay on and become political forces to reckon within their host countries.

The initial optimism that the Arab Spring betokened an era in which democracy and liberalism would spread swiftly and benignly spread throughout the Middle East, transforming the region permanently for the better, soon came to seem premature and misplaced. The Arab Spring unleashed new, extremist elements in several Middle Eastern nations. ISIS grew exponentially in strength in Iraq and Syria, taking advantage of power vacuums created by civil war and great political and social instability. As Libya descended into chaos after its government fell in 2011, that nation too became ripe for extremist activities. By 2015, ISIS had spread its tentacles into Libya as well.

Priscilla Roberts

See also: Al-Qaeda; Islamic State of Iraq and Syria (ISIS); Jihad; Muslim Brotherhood

Citations

Achcar, Gilbert. *The People Want: A Radical Exploration of the Arab Uprising.* Translated by G. M. Goshgarian. Berkeley: University of California Press, 2013.

Amar, Paul, and Vijay Prashad, eds. *Dispatches from the Arab Spring: Understanding the New Middle East.* Minneapolis: University of Minnesota Press, 2013.

Bradley, John R. *After the Arab Spring: How Islamists Hijacked the Middle East Revolts.* New York: Palgrave Macmillan, 2012.

Dabashi, Hamid. *The Arab Spring: The End of Postcolonialism.* London: Zed Books, 2012.

Danahar, Paul. *The New Middle East: The World after the Arab Spring.* London: Bloomsbury, 2013.

Dawisha, Aweed. *The Second Arab Awakening: Revolution, Democracy, and the Islamist Challenge from Tunis to Damascus.* New York: Norton, 2013.

Noueihed, Lynn, and Alex Warren. *The Battle for the Arab Spring: Revolution, Counter-Revolution and the Making of a New Era.* New Haven: Yale University Press, 2012.

Ramadan, Tariq. *Islam and the Arab Awakening.* New York: Oxford University Press, 2012.

Wright, Robin. *Rock the Casbah: Rage and Rebellion across the Islamic World.* Updated ed. New York: Simon and Schuster, 2012.

Arafat, Yasser

Palestinian nationalist and leader of the Palestine Liberation Organization (PLO) for 36 years (1969–2004), Yasser Arafat, officially named Mohammed Abdel Raouf Arafat al-Qudwa al-Husseini, was born on August 24, 1929. Arafat always stated that he was born in Jerusalem, but Israeli officials began to claim in the 1970s that he was born in Cairo to discredit him. There is also some dispute about his date of birth, which is occasionally given as August 4, 1929. He went by the name Yasser as a child. Arafat's father was a Palestinian Egyptian textile merchant. Neither Arafat nor his siblings were close to their father. His mother, Zahwa, also a Palestinian, was a member of a family that had lived in Jerusalem for generations. She died when Arafat was five years old, and he then lived with his mother's brother in Jerusalem. Arafat vividly remembered British soldiers invading his uncle's house one night, destroying possessions and beating its residents. When Arafat was nine years old his father brought him back to Cairo, where his older sister raised him.

As a teenager in Cairo, Arafat became involved in smuggling arms to Palestine to aid those struggling against both the British authorities and the Jews living there. He attended the University of Fuad I (later Cairo University) in Cairo but left to fight in Gaza against Israel in the Israeli War of Independence of 1948–1949. When the Arabs lost the war and Israel was firmly established, Arafat was inconsolable. He briefly attended the University of Texas but then returned to Cairo University to study engineering. He spent most of his time with fellow Palestinian students spreading his hopes for a free Palestinian state. Arafat became president of the General Union of Palestinian Students, holding that position from 1952 to 1956. He joined the Muslim Brotherhood in 1952. He finally graduated from college in 1956 and spent a short time working in Egypt. During the 1956 Suez Crisis, he served as a second lieutenant in the Egyptian Army. In 1957 he moved to Kuwait, where he worked as an engineer and formed his own contracting company. In 1958 Arafat founded the Fatah organization, an underground guerrilla group dedicated to the liberation of Palestine. In 1964 he quit his job and moved to Jordan to devote all his energies to the promotion of Palestinian nationhood and to organize raids into Israel. The PLO was founded that same year.

In 1968, the Israel Defense Forces (IDF) attacked Fatah at the small Jordanian village of Al-Karameh. The Palestinians eventually forced the Israelis back, and Arafat's face appeared on the cover of *Time* magazine as the leader of the Palestinian movement. In consequence, Palestinians embraced Fatah, and Arafat became a national hero. He was appointed chairman of the PLO the next year, and within four years controlled both the military (the Palestine Liberation Army, or PLA) and political branches of the organization. By 1970, Palestinians had assembled a well-organized unofficial state within Jordan. However, King Hussein of Jordan deemed them a threat to security and sent his army to evict them. Arafat enlisted the aid of Syria, while Jordan called on the United States for assistance. On September 24, 1970, the PLO agreed to a cease-fire and agreed to leave Jordan. Arafat moved the organization to Lebanon, which had a weak government that was not likely to restrict the PLO's operations. The PLO soon began launching occasional attacks across the Israeli border.

Arafat did not approve of overseas attacks because they gave the PLO a bad image abroad. He publicly dissociated the group from Black September, the organization that killed 11 Israeli athletes at the 1972 Munich Olympics, although there is now evidence of his involvement. In 1974 he limited the PLO's attacks to Israel, the Gaza Strip, and the West Bank. Although Israel claimed that Arafat was responsible for the numerous terrorist attacks that occurred within the country during the 1970s, he denied responsibility. In 1974 he spoke before the United Nations (UN) General Assembly. During the Lebanese Civil War, the PLO initially sided with the Lebanese National Resistance Front against the Lebanese forces, who were supported by Israel

and backed by Defense Minister Ariel Sharon. As such, when Israeli forces invaded southern Lebanon, the PLO ended up fighting against the Israelis and then the Syrian militia group Amal. Thousands of Palestinians, many of them civilians, were killed during the struggle, and the PLO was forced to leave Lebanon in 1982 and relocate to Tunisia, where it remained until 1993. During the 1980s, Iraq and Saudi Arabia donated millions of dollars to Arafat to help him rebuild the PLO. Arafat approved the First Intifada (1987) against Israel. In 1988, Palestinians declared Palestinian statehood at a meeting in Algiers. Arafat then announced that the Palestinians would renounce terrorism and recognize the State of Israel. The Palestinian National Council elected Arafat president of this new, unrecognized state in 1989.

Arafat and the Israelis conducted peace negotiations at the Madrid Conference in 1991. Although negotiations were temporarily set back when the PLO supported Iraq in the 1991 Persian Gulf War, over the next two years the two parties held a number of secret discussions. These negotiations led to the 1993 Oslo Peace Accords in which Israel agreed to Palestinian self-rule in the Gaza Strip and the West Bank. Arafat also officially recognized the existence of the State of Israel. Despite the condemnation of many Palestinian nationalists who viewed Arafat's moves as a sellout, the peace process appeared to be moving in a positive direction in the mid-1990s. Israeli troops withdrew from the Gaza Strip and Jericho in May 1994. Arafat was elected leader of the new Palestinian Authority (PA) in January 1996 with 88 percent of the vote in elections that were by all accounts free and fair (but with severely limited competition because Hamas and other opposition groups refused to participate). Later that same year, Benjamin Netanyahu of the Likud Party became prime minister of Israel, and the peace process began to unravel. Netanyahu, a hard-line conservative, condemned terrorism and blamed Palestinians for numerous suicide bombings against Israeli citizens. He also did not trust Arafat, who he charged was supporting terrorists. Arafat continued negotiations with the Israelis into 2000. That July, with Ehud Barak having replaced Netanyahu as Israeli prime minister, Arafat traveled to the United States to meet with Barak and President Bill Clinton at the Camp David Summit.

Despite generous concessions by Barak, Arafat refused to compromise, and a major chance at peace was lost. On the collapse of the peace process, the Second (al-Aqsa) Intifada began. From the beginning of the Second Intifada in 2000, Arafat was a besieged man who appeared to be losing influence and control within the Palestinian and larger Arab communities. His inability or unwillingness to stop Palestinian terrorist attacks against Israel resulted in his virtual captivity at his Ramallah headquarters from 2002. In declining health by 2004, the PLO leader was beginning to look increasingly like a man past his time.

Flown to France for medical treatment, Arafat died on November 11, 2004, at Percy Military Hospital outside Paris, France. There was much conspiratorial conjecture concerning his mysterious illness and death. Rumors persist that he was assassinated by poisoning. In November 2012, three teams of forensic investigators (from Russia, France, and Switzerland) conducted tests on Arafat's body and the soil from his grave, located at his former headquarters in the city of Ramallah. The Swiss team claimed to have found abnormally high traces of polonium, a radioactive element, in Arafat's body. Other experts, however, claim that the likelihood of contamination was high and that the findings did not definitively prove that Arafat died from polonium poisoning. A Russian expert later concluded that Arafat died from natural causes. Despite these investigations, assassination theories persist.

Amy Hackney Blackwell

See also: Al-Fatah; Palestine Liberation Organization (PLO); Popular Front for the Liberation of Palestine (PFLP)

Citations

Aburish, Said K. *Arafat: From Defender to Dictator.* New York and London: Bloomsbury, 1998.

Hart, Alan. *Arafat: A Political Biography.* Rev. ed. London: Sidgwick & Jackson, 1994.

Peleg, Ilan, ed. *Middle East Peace Process: Interdisciplinary Perspectives.* Albany: State University of New York Press, 1998.

"Yasser Arafat—Biography," Nobelprize.org. http://nobelprize.org/peace/laureates/1994/arafat-bio.html.

Aum Shinrikyo

Aum Shinrikyo, known in the West as Aum Supreme Truth, is a Japanese religious group that mixed Buddhist and Hindu beliefs. The group made headlines around the world in 1995 when several of its followers carried out a deadly sarin nerve gas attack on the Tokyo subway. The group's name is made up of the Hindu syllable "omm," representing the creative and destructive forces of the universe, and three kanji characters: *shin* (truth, reality, Buddhist sect), *ri* (reason, truth), and *kyo* (teaching faith, doctrine). The name translates loosely as the "teaching of supreme truth."

The group was founded by Chizuo Matsumoto, a half-blind yoga instructor who began to gather followers through his yoga classes in Tokyo in 1984. During a trip to India in 1986, Matsumoto claimed to have received enlightenment while on a hike in the Himalayas. Upon his return to Japan the following year, Matsumoto changed his name to the "holy" Shoko Asahara. He altered the title of his group to Aum Shinrikyo, and it started to take on an explicit apocalyptic character based on predictions concerning the impending destruction of the universe.

Aum's application for religious tax-exempt status under Japanese law was denied in 1989, but was granted several months later after the group mounted a legal campaign against the government. In fact, the group would use legal recourse on several occasions, both to defend its views and rights and to gather public attention.

In the same year, the group came under fire through a growing public outcry against brainwashing carried out on young people who joined the group. A group of families hired Tsutsumi Sakamoto, a lawyer from Yokohama with experience in cult brainwashing. At the same time the *Sunday Mainichi,* a prominent Japanese newspaper, began to run an exposé of the group's activities based on reports from former members and families of members. Already under attack from the press, the group could hardly accept Sakamoto's discovery of a series of fake tests concerning Asahara (the group's founder had claimed to have a unique type of blood that made him different from all other people; Sakamoto's investigation found out that the alleged tests done at Kyoto University never took place). Soon after, Sakamoto and his wife and infant son disappeared. The bodies were found six years later in remote mountain locations, but despite suspicions that the group had been responsible, no direct evidence implicating Aum Shinrikyo was ever found.

In 1989 the group established a political party with the hopes of broadcasting their views within the Japanese society at large, but all 25 candidates failed to gain enough votes to be elected. Their complete defeat made the group the subject of numerous jokes, further distancing them from mainstream public opinion. This also enhanced the feeling of persecution among the group's followers and their sense that they needed to prepare for the coming Armageddon.

In 1995, following the Tokyo subway sarin gas attack that left 12 commuters dead and thousands injured, Asahara and several other senior members of the group were arrested and accused of masterminding the attack. Asahara himself was found guilty and sentenced to death. Although it is unclear why Aum committed these atrocities, some believe it was an effort to divert police attention away from the group, which was coming under increased scrutiny from the authorities.

Despite the trials of Asahara and other top members, the group continues to operate and is currently led by Fumihiro Joyo, a charismatic leader and one of Asahara's main executives. The group is now called Aleph, the first of the Hebrew letters, a name that stands for a new beginning. As of January 2010, the group is still under police surveillance. Small branches of the group exist in New York, Sri Lanka, and Russia.

Jose M. Valente

See also: Weapons of Mass Destruction

Citations

Hall, John R., Philip D. Schuyler, and Sylvaine Trinh. *Apocalypse Observed: Religious Movements and Violence in North America, Europe, and Japan.* London: Routledge, 2000.

Stalker, Nancy. "Religious Violence in Contemporary Japan: The Case of Aum Shinrikyo," *Pacific Affairs* 75, 2002.

Wessinger, Catherine. *How the Millennium Comes Violently: From Jonestown to Heaven's Gate.* New York: Seven Bridges, 2000.

Autodefensas Unidas de Colombia (AUC)

The Autodefensas Unidas de Colombia (AUC, or United Self-Defense Forces of Colombia) was a loose umbrella movement of self-defense militias and paramilitary groups that battled left-wing guerrillas in Colombia for over a decade. The organization was formed in April 1997 under the leadership of Carlos Castano Gil. Although many Colombians initially considered the AUC as a necessary evil to contain the violence and insurgency of the Fuerzas Armadas Revolucionárias de Colombia (FARC, or Revolutionary Armed Forces of Colombia) and Ejercito de Liberacion Nacional (ELN, or National Liberation Army), they increasingly came to be viewed as a significant threat in their own right. The United States, European Union, and several other countries all shared this view and proscribed the AUC as a terrorist organization.

At its height the AUC could count on a membership of around 31,000 cadres that effectively controlled large tracts of territory in Colombia's northern Antioquia province and eastern plains. The movement's strategy and tactics closely mirrored those of FARC and the ELN, with the basic aim to extend control at the local level through intimidation and bribery. The movement was responsible for most of the mass killings attributed to organized armed groups in Colombia during the late 1990s and 2000s. It is estimated that in its first two years alone, the AUC (and related paramilitary affiliates) killed over 19,000 people. According to the Colombia National Police, during the first 10 months of 2000, the AUC carried out 804 assassinations, 203 kidnappings, and 507 murders. Most violence was directed against FARC and the ELN, their sympathizers, and villages suspected of providing the two guerrilla groups with sanctuary. The movement also routinely terrorized local populations to instill fear and compel support.

The AUC funded itself almost exclusively on the drug trade, working in collaboration with Mexican cartels to ship cocaine to the United States. In a televised interview in March 2000, Castano himself admitted that narcotics trafficking and taxation of coca production in Antioquia and Cordoba provided up to 70 percent of the financing for his forces (with the rest largely coming from extortion). A 2003 Colombian peace commission report claimed that the AUC derived possibly as much as 80 percent of its revenue from drugs and that self-defense militias in general monopolized up to 40 percent of the country's entire narcotics industry.

There have been repeated allegations that the AUC cooperated both tacitly and openly with the Colombian military. In one paramilitary massacre at the town of El Tigre in January 1999, eyewitnesses said the gunmen arrived in trucks belonging to the army's 24th Brigade. Left-wing guerrillas and human rights activists both claimed this incident was consistent with an established relationship aimed at eliminating the civilian supporters of FARC and the ELN. Press reports have also alleged that a number of senior militia leaders in the province of Putumayo previously served as noncommissioned officers in the army.

On April 16, 2004, there was an attack on AUC supreme leader and cofounder Carlos Castano. He was never seen again. Press reports speculated that his disappearance could hurt the peace process with the Uribe government. In 2006 a Venezuelan newspaper, *Nuevo Diario Occidente,* reported that Vincent Castano had hired an assassin, who had confessed to police that he killed Carlos Castano in 2004. The confession led police to a body in August 2006. DNA tests a month later confirmed it was Carlos.

In 2003 Carlos Castano had affirmed that he was ready to discuss a possible cease-fire with the Colombian government. His announcement generated widespread opposition among certain elements of the AUC that rejected any notion of laying down arms. As noted, Castano later disappeared following an attack on his headquarters in April 2004.

Although there was speculation that Castano's murder could hurt the slowly unfolding peace process, talks proceeded and culminated in 2005, when the AUC declared a cease-fire and agreed to disarm in accordance with a so-called Justice and Peace Law (Law 975) passed that same year. The legislation, which originated from the 2003 Santa Fe de Ralito Accord, limited jail terms for the highest-ranking members of the AUC to eight years if they confessed the entirety of their crimes and returned all stolen property. More junior paramilitaries who demobilized were enrolled in an 18-month program that provided them with a stipend, living accommodations, counseling, and help with reincorporating into mainstream society.

Not surprisingly, the law was the subject of considerable controversy, with critics in both Colombia and the United States charging it effectively shielded paramilitary leaders from prosecution or extradition for serious crimes. Despite these objections, the demobilization, disarmament, and reintegration (DDR) process continued and had largely been completed by 2006, by which time up to 30,000 paramilitaries had surrendered and laid down their arms.

Problematically, the DDR program was quickly overwhelmed (the government estimated that there were no more than 20,000 paramilitaries who needed to be processed), and many of those who entered it never received a job and complained that Bogotá had not lived up to its side of the bargain. Initial dissatisfaction with the peace dividend translated into widespread disillusionment, driving many to join preexisting criminal gangs. These reconfigured entities, euphemistically referred to as *bandas criminales* (criminal groups), are thought to number around 5,000 members, organized into 11 main syndicates. Four of these have since become central players in the Colombian cocaine trade and make no pretense of seeking political or ideological objectives: the Don Mario Gang, the Ejercito Revolucionario Popular Anticomunista (ERPAC), Los Rastrojos, and Los Paisas.

Peter Chalk

See also: Ejercito de Liberacion Nacional (ELN); Fuerzas Armadas Revolucionárias de Colombia (FARC)

Citations

Bergquist, Charles, Ricardo Penaranda, and Gonzalo Sanchez, eds. *Violence in Colombia 1990–2000: Waging War and Negotiating Peace.* Wilmington, DE: SR Books, 2001.

Chalk, Peter. *The Latin American Drug Trade: Scope, Dimensions, Impact and Response.* Santa Monica, CA: RAND, 2011.

Cragin, Kim, and Bruce Hoffman. *Arms Trafficking and Colombia*. Santa Monica, CA: RAND, 2003.

Kirk, Robin. *More Terrible than Death: Violence, Drugs, and America's War in Colombia*. New York: Public Affairs, 2004.

Porch, Douglas, and Maria Rasmussen. "Demobilization of Paramilitaries in Colombia: Transformation or Transition?" *Studies in Conflict and Terrorism* 31, no. 6 (2008).

Romero, Mauricio. "Changing Identities and Contested Settings: Regional Elites and the Paramilitaries in Colombia." *International Journal of Politics, Culture and Society* 14, no. 1 (2000).

Saab, Bilal, and Alexandra Taylor. "Criminality and Armed Groups: A Comparative Study of FARC and Paramilitary Groups in Colombia," *Studies in Conflict and Terrorism* 32, no. 6 (2009).

B

Baader-Meinhof Gang

The Baader-Meinhof Gang, named after two of its key members and later to become known as the Rote Armee Fraktion (RAF, or Red Army Faction), had its roots in the radical student movement of the late 1960s and a resurgence of Marxist-Leninist theories in Europe. This coincided with protests against the Vietnam War and what was perceived as U.S. imperialism. Opposition to the political "grand coalition" between the Christian Democrats and Social Democrats heightened tensions, as did the younger generation's criticism of their parents for the Nazi period and the unwillingness of German society to confront its past.

In 1967, during a visit to West Berlin by the shah of Iran, protests erupted; during increasingly violent scenes with the police, a young student protester, Benno Ohnesorg, was shot dead on June 2. This in turn led to violent student protests across the country. The West German authorities responded by amending the Constitution with a "Basic Law" extending their ability to introduce emergency measures. A small core element of the extreme left took these events to signal that demonstrations and protests were ineffectual and that the only way forward was the use of terrorism.

Consequently, during March 1968, left-wing activist Andreas Baader, his partner Gudrun Ensslin, and their colleagues Horst Sohnlein and Thorwald Proll firebombed two Frankfurt department stores in emulation of a similar attack the previous year in Brussels. Although no one was actually injured, the group was quickly arrested and convicted in October 1968. However, they were granted bail pending an appeal, and when this was rejected in November, they fled abroad.

In early 1970 Baader and Ensslin returned to Germany under false identities, but in April, Baader was recaptured and imprisoned. However, on May 15, with the assistance of left-wing *Konkret* journalist Ulrike Meinhof, other members of the group, including Horst Mahler, Ingrid Schubert, and Irene Goergens, freed Baader during an escorted visit to the German Central Institute for Social Issues. On June 5, 1970, the organization formally established itself as the RAF, appointing Ensslin as the group's leader; however, it was still popularly known as the Baader-Meinhof Gang.

That summer, in the first phase of Baader-Meinhof terrorism, a group of over 20 male and female members traveled to a Palestinian al-Fatah training camp near Amman in Jordan. There they practiced the use of firearms with Kalashnikov rifles, grenades, and "urban guerrilla tactics." Although they met Ali Hassan Salameh, a leading figure in the Black September movement, their liberated attitude upset their Palestinian hosts, and they were asked to leave.

Upon returning to Germany, the Baader-Meinhof Gang launched a series of attacks on property and carried out a number of fund-raising bank robberies, becoming the focus of a massive manhunt by the authorities. Inevitably, confrontations with the police occurred, and during 1971, while the group shot and killed three officers, several of its members were arrested.

In May 1972, an expanded Baader-Meinhof Gang that by this time had established a number of regional cells commenced a systematic terrorist campaign against more high-profile "imperialist" German and U.S. targets. Prominent incidents included an attack on the U.S. Army's V Corps headquarters in Frankfurt on May 11, 1972; the bombing of the U.S. Army European headquarters on May 24, 1972; and an assault on the Axel Springer press building in Hamburg.

Police eventually traced Baader to a bomb-making garage at the end of May 1972, where he was captured along with several of his colleagues. Within weeks Meinhof and Ensslin were also arrested, dealing a crippling blow to the organization. However, a new generation of RAF activists would soon arise and conduct a wave of terrorism throughout the 1980s and 1990s that would pose a far more serious threat to German democracy.

Richard Warnes

See also: Al-Fatah; Japanese Red Army; Munich Olympic Games Massacre

Citations

Alexander, Yonah, and Dennis Pluchinsky. *Europe's Red Terrorists: The Fighting Communist Organizations.* London: Frank Cass, 1992.

Aust, Stefan. *The Baader-Meinhof Complex.* London: Bodley Head, 2008.

Otte, Thomas. "Red Army Faction: The Baader-Meinhof Gang," in *International Encyclopedia of Terrorism,* edited by Martha Crenshaw and John Pimlott. Chicago: Fitzroy Dearborn, 1977.

Peters, Butz. *Todlicher Irrtum: Die Geschichte der RAF.* Frankfurt: Fischer Taschenbuch, 2007.

Baghdadi, Abu Bakr al-

Born Ibrahim Awwad Ibrahim Ali Muhammad al-Badri al-Samarrai in Samarra, Iraq in 1971, Abu Bakr al-Baghdadi has been the leader of the Islamic State since its founding in April 2013. Much of Baghdadi's background remains shrouded in mystery, although it is believed that he has two wives and as many as six children. Baghdadi moved to Baghdad in the early 1990s, where he was influenced by Abu Mohammed al-Mufti al-Aali, one of the leading ideologues providing inspiration to jihadist groups in Iraq. He studies at the Islamic University in Baghdad, where he ultimately received his doctorate in Quranic studies.

Baghdadi became involved with militant groups following the U.S.-led invasion of Iraq in 2003. Over time, he assumed greater responsibility and even presided over his own sharia court, where he earned a reputation for brutality toward anyone he suspected of spying for the U.S. and its coalition allies. His connections to known militants landed him at Camp Bucca in 2004, where he expanded his network and likely grew further entrenched in his radical beliefs.

Baghdadi's education allowed him to burnish religious credentials that other jihadist leaders have never been able to claim, including al-Qaeda leaders Osama bin Laden and Ayman al-Zawahiri. The legitimacy afforded by Baghdadi's religious education was one of several factors—along with familial lineage traced back to the Prophet—that cleared Baghdadi's way to declare himself caliph, or ruler of all Muslims, in a historic speech at the Grand Mosque in Mosul in June 2014.

And although news of the new caliph's declaration was largely met with indifference in Western security and intelligence

As of January 2018, al-Baghdadi was still thought to be alive, but on the run, as the ISIL caliphate collapsed and its fighters scattered throughout the globe. The sermon by al-Baghdadi in the mosque in Mosul was a key point for inspiring tens of thousands of foreign fighters to travel to Iraq and Syria to join ISIL. (Al-Furqan Media/Anadolu Agency/Getty Images)

circles at the time, the net result was to usher in an unprecedented wave of foreign fighters from around the globe. Tens of thousands of Muslims flocked to Iraq and Syria to join the Islamic State as it simultaneously sought to construct a modern-day caliphate while vanquishing all enemies in sight.

There have been several reports of Baghdadi's death, including reports by the Russian military in June 2017 that it killed the ISIS leader, but there has never been any proof of his death.

Colin P. Clarke

See also: Adnani, Abu Muhammad al-; Al-Qaeda in Iraq (AQI); Brussels Terrorist Attacks (2016); Islamic State of Iraq and Syria (ISIS); Jihad; Paris Terrorist Attacks (2015)

Citations

Arango, Tim, and Eric Schmitt. "U.S. Actions in Iraq Fueled Rise of a Rebel," *The New York Times,* August 10, 2014.

Beaumont, Peter. "Abu Bakr al-Baghdadi: The ISIS Chief with the Ambition to Take Over Al-Qaeda," *The Guardian,* June 12, 2014.

Clarke, Colin P. "Is ISIS Leader Baghdadi Still Alive?" *Foreign Affairs,* June 22, 2017.

McCants, William. "The Believer," Brookings Institution, September 1, 2015.

McCoy, Terence. "How the Islamic State Evolved in an American Prison," *Washington Post,* November 4, 2014.

Bali Bombings (2002)

On October 12, 2002, devastating suicide bombings rocked the Indonesian island of Bali. The attacks, carried out by an Indonesian-based Islamist group known as Jemaah Islamiyah (JI), were the deadliest in Southeast Asian history and remain the most serious act of international terrorism since the 9/11 strikes in the United States.

About an hour before midnight on October 12, a suicide terrorist walked into Paddy's Bar in the resort town of Kuta and detonated an explosive device hidden in his backpack. As panicked civilians ran into the street to flee the scene, another 400-pound vehicle-borne improvised explosive device (VBIED) concealed in a Mitsubishi L300 van detonated across the street outside the Sari nightclub. This blast caused the majority of fatalities. A third, significantly smaller bomb also exploded at the U.S. consulate in the nearby city of Denpasar, although it caused only minor injuries and minimal property damage.

The attacks killed 202 individuals, including 88 Australians, 38 Indonesians, 24 Britons, and 7 Americans. Another 240 people were injured, many with severe burns. The local hospital was soon overwhelmed, and many of the wounded had to be flown to the Australian city of Darwin for extensive burn treatment. Two days later, the United Nations Security Council (UNSC) unanimously passed Resolution 1438 condemning the attacks.

Although JI, a Southeast Asian Islamist organization with suspected links to al-Qaeda, was immediately suspected, its leader, Abu Bakar Bashir, quickly denied the group's involvement, instead blaming the United States for the attacks. Several days after the bombings, the Arab news network Al Jazeera released an audio recording from al-Qaeda leader Osama bin Laden, who claimed that the attacks were conducted in retaliation for the U.S. war on terror and Australia's involvement in securing East Timor's independence from Indonesia in 1999.

Because of the limited and at times contradictory information released by the Indonesian government in the immediate days after the attack, there are conflicting reports about the composition of the VBIED. Some sources claim the device was made out of ammonium nitrate, others believe it consisted of 1.2 tons of black powder connected to a cable detonator with PETN, while still others say it was constructed of TNT, chlorate, and RDX detonators. Whatever the exact nature of the compound, it is now known that the explosives were mixed in Denpasar (about 15 minutes from Kuta) and packed in at least a dozen filing cabinets that were then stored in the back of the minivan in place of the vehicle's rear seats. This device and the other two bombs were detonated by cell phone.

Police quickly traced the purchase of the Mitsubishi L300 van to Amrozi bin Haji Nurhasyim, largely because he had used his own name to purchase the vehicle. Other key individuals who were rounded up within months of the attack included Amrozi's two brothers, Mukhlas (also known as Ali Ghufron) and Ali Imron, Imam Samudra, and Wan Min Wan Mat (arrested in Malaysia). The chief architect of the operation, Riduan Isamuddin (also known as Hambali), was captured in Thailand in 2003. Two other main individuals who played a direct supervisory role, Azahari bin Husin and Noordin Mohammad Top (who acted as JI's principal explosives and financial experts, respectively) escaped arrest. However, both were later killed in police raids, the first in 2005, the second in 2009.

Subsequent testimony from the captured terrorists revealed that the funding for the bombings amounted to around $35,000, the bulk of which came from the theft of a gold store in Central Java. The targets were selected just two days prior to the attack and largely chosen on account of their patrons: Western tourists. Following his arrest, Samudra asserted, "I saw lots of whiteys dancing and lots of whiteys drinking there. That place Kuta and especially Paddy's Bar and the Sari nightclub was a meeting place for U.S. terrorists and their allies, who the whole world knows to be the monsters" (cited by the Australian Broadcasting Corporation/ABC).

It also became apparent that the sites had advantages owing to the nature of their construction. Paddy's had an open front, which both allowed easy access for Iqbal and ensured that its occupants would be quickly funneled to the site of the main VBIED. The Sari Club consisted of bars with highly flammable thatched roofs and high walls that would act to force the direction of the minivan blast back toward the street where most people were congregated. The operatives apparently developed four backup plans for detonating the explosives in the event that the initial attempt failed: the first by cell phone; the second by a trigger that would be manually armed; the third by a timer; the fourth by a secondary switch set to go off if one of the drawers of the filing cabinet was opened.

Legal proceedings against those arrested began on April 30, 2003. Three were sentenced to death: Amrozi, Samudra, and Mukhlas. After several appeals and stays, the executions were eventually carried out by firing squad on November 9, 2008. Ali Imron, who reportedly showed remorse for his role in orchestrating the attacks, received a sentence of life imprisonment on September 18,

2003. Wan Min Wan Mat, the financial conduit for the attacks, agreed to testify in the trial against Mukhlas in return for a reduced jail term. He was subsequently released in 2005 after Malaysian authorities concluded that he no longer posed a threat to national security.

On October 15, 2004, Bashir was charged with complicity in the Bali attacks as part of a larger indictment for a 2003 bombing in Jakarta. Although acquitted of the latter, he was convicted of conspiracy in connection with the former. He was not indicted on any specific charge of terrorism and received a sentence of only two and a half years in prison (which was later commuted to time served). Bashir was again arrested in 2011, this time for running a militant training camp in Aceh, northern Sumatra. After a highly charged trial he was incarcerated for 15 years.

One of the more important implications of the Bali bombings was that it forced the Indonesian government to admit it had a serious domestic terrorist threat in its midst; prior to the attack, Jakarta had insisted that if there were any extremists in the country, they were foreign and it was the responsibility of these states to deal with them. A slew of initiatives were quickly passed, including two antiterrorism regulations, an overhaul of the law enforcement and intelligence infrastructures, the formation of a new elite counterterrorist unit (Detasemen Khusus 88/Special Detachment 88), and the establishment of a coordinating body to better streamline and integrate counterterrorism responses within the security forces (the Terrorism Eradication Coordinating Desk).

These various measures have paid dividends, substantially eroding JI's operational and organizational presence in the country. Many of the group's top leaders have been either arrested or killed, and at least 450 additional militants have been detained. Although Bali was hit by another suicide attack in 2005 (which resulted in 26 deaths and 100 injuries), there have been no major incidents since then. Reflecting the improved situation, the United States lifted its travel warning for Indonesia in 2008, with Washington's embassy in Jakarta affirming that the decision stemmed from the objective improvements that have been made in internal security and progress against JI.

On October 12, 2004, the second anniversary of the Bali bombings, a memorial to the victims of the attacks was unveiled in Kuta. Similar monuments have been erected in Melbourne, Sydney, Perth, and London. The atrocity was also immortalized in a 2007 Indonesian film called *The Long Road to Heaven*. Directed by Enison Sinaro, this cinematic production chronicles the planning and execution of the attacks, as well as the sentencing of the suspects.

Spencer C. Tucker

See also: Al-Qaeda; Jemaah Islamiyah (JI)

Citations

"Bali Death Toll Set at 202," *BBC News*, February 19, 2003, http://news.bbc.co.uk/2/hi/asia-pacific/2778923.stm, accessed October 21, 2011.

Chalk, Peter, Angel Rabasa, William Rosenau, and Leanne Piggott. *The Evolving Terrorist Threat to Southeast Asia: A Net Assessment.* Santa Monica, CA: RAND, 2009.

Firdas, Irwan. "Indonesia Executes Bali Bombers," *Jakarta Post* (Indonesia), November 9, 2008.

Onishi, Norimitsu. "Indonesia Sentences a Radical Cleric to 15 Years," *The New York Times,* June 17, 2011.

Parkinson, Tony. "Bin Laden Voices New Threat to Australia," *The Age* (Australia), November 14, 2002, www.theage.com.au/articles/2002/11/13/1037080786315.html.

Ramakrishna, Kumar, and See Seng Tan, eds. *After Bali: The Threat of Terrorism in Southeast Asia.* Singapore: Institute of Defense and Strategic Studies, 2003.

Benghazi Attacks (2012)

On September 11, 2012, as many as 150 people stormed the U.S. compound for the U.S. diplomatic mission at Benghazi, Libya. Armed with rocket-propelled grenades, machine guns, hand grenades, and other weapons, the mob breached the main gates of the compound and later fired mortars at a nearby consular annex, where staff had taken refuge. Four Americans were killed in the incident: U.S. Ambassador to Libya J. Christopher Stevens; security personnel Tyrone S. Woods and Glen Doherty, both former Navy SEALs; and foreign service officer Sean Smith. Although many details of the attacks remain mysterious, it was captured by surveillance cameras and witnessed by the surviving guards.

The causes and motives of the attackers are murky. Initially, the attacks were said to be a spontaneous response to an anti-Muslim film created in the United States. The film had already led to protests in Benghazi and Cairo. However, the attacks were later described as intentional and preplanned. In the investigation that followed, the State Department reported that the attacks were carried out by a North African branch of al-Qaeda as well as an extremist militia called Ansar al-Sharia. In the meantime, as the November 6 presidential election approached, Republicans sharply criticized the Obama administration for its handling of the attacks, the Arab Spring, and instability in Libya.

In late 2010 and well into 2011, popular uprisings throughout the Arab world overthrew governments in Egypt, Libya, Yemen, and Tunisia. In Libya, Muammar Gadhafi lost power in late 2011 to rebel forces aided by the North Atlantic Treaty Organization (NATO). Western forces hoped the new leadership in Libya would bring in a new democratic government. However, after the overthrow, Libya remained unstable despite having an interim government and parliament. After the fall of the Gadhafi government, the Obama administration approved reopening the U.S. embassy in Tripoli. However, in the months prior to the attack, intelligence had reportedly reached the Obama administration that security in Libya was faltering. Extremist groups connected to al-Qaeda were training in the mountains near Tripoli, and there had been attacks on a British motorcade and the Red Cross. In an email, Stevens told Washington officials that he was nervous about a lack of security in Benghazi. In the week before the attacks, in fact, there was a car bombing in Benghazi, and the Libyan government issued security warnings. The State Department responded to these warnings by increasing the fortification of the U.S. compound in Benghazi, but it is not clear that the government received direct warnings of a specific threat. Stevens's email was later cited by Republicans who criticized the Obama administration's handling of the security threats in Libya. Ansar al-Sharia, the militant group that has taken credit for the attacks, was training openly near Benghazi. The group's location was so well known that local citizens stormed it in protest after the attacks. U.S. intelligence and even Libyan intelligence reported that there was a certain loss of control over these areas.

The U.S. compound in Benghazi is a collection of buildings surrounded by walls. Security at the compound included five diplomatic security officers and four members of a local militia provided by the Libyan government. A rapid response team was housed at an annex facility approximately a mile away. The time line of events, according to the State Department, shows that the attacks took place over a very short period of time on September 11 and 12. Sometime around 9:40 p.m. on September 11, 2012, security agents reported hearing loud noises and gunfire at the front gate of the compound, and cameras showed an armed group entering it. Calls were made to officials at the U.S. embassy in Tripoli as well as officials in Washington and Libya, and the quick reaction force at the nearby annex was also contacted. Armed security personnel took Stevens and Smith to a safe room inside the compound's main residence building. Attackers stormed this building. The attackers were unable to break into the room Stevens and Smith were hiding in, so they lit fires around it with diesel fuel. The smoke made breathing nearly impossible. Other members of the U.S. security team returned and pulled out Smith, but he had died from smoke inhalation. They were not able to find Stevens in the smoke-filled building.

With security forces unable to hold the perimeter, the decision was made to evacuate the compound and retreat to the annex facility. Between 4:00 and 5:00 a.m. on September 12, a six-man security team from the embassy in Tripoli arrived at the annex, after being told that a search for Stevens at the compound would be futile. The annex was hit by mortar fire, killing Woods and Doherty around this time. After the mortar attacks, the decision was made to evacuate all remaining personnel to Tripoli, with the last plane leaving around 10:00 a.m. In the hours after the initial attack on the compound, locals found Stevens, who had tried to escape the smoke, and took him to the closest medical center. There he was pronounced dead due to asphyxiation. On September 12, Obama used the word *terror* to describe the attacks in his first public statement but did not specifically label the incident as terrorist attacks.

Republican presidential candidate Mitt Romney argued that the failure to do so immediately showed weakness and that the situation was mishandled. On September 16, U.S. Ambassador to the United Nations Susan Rice stated on several talk shows that the events at the compound were the result of spontaneous protests. However, at the same time new intelligence reports stated this was not the case. In her remarks, Rice was using the Obama administration's talking points based on preliminary intelligence assessments, but because the administration also conveyed what it learned from the newer intelligence reports, it seemed to shift its explanation of the attacks. This led to severe criticisms from congressional Republicans and Romney in what many described as a political attack. Congressional Republicans called for an investigation into the Obama administration's handling of the event. They questioned why the attacks were not immediately labeled terrorism and why the administration allegedly ignored calls for increased security at the consulate in Benghazi.

On September 26, Secretary of State Hillary Rodham Clinton announced that militant groups with al-Qaeda ties planned the attacks. The events in Benghazi showed that Libya was still very unstable and that the government did not have complete control of the country. On October 10, Charlene Lamb of the State Department said she did not approve increased security for Benghazi despite the increased violence because she wanted local Libyan forces to be trained for security purposes. On October 15, Clinton officially took the blame for the security

oversights. At a Senate hearing in mid-December, Sen. John Kerry (D-Mass.) said Congress also must accept blame for the attacks, as it had not approved increased funding for embassy security. In January 2013, Clinton was called to the Senate to testify about the Obama administration's handling of the attacks. The White House and intelligence officials maintained that they were searching for answers and the people behind the attacks. The one person held in connection to the attacks was picked up at an airport in Turkey and was sent to his native Tunisia, where he was later released due to a general lack of evidence.

The Benghazi attacks led to an ongoing internal investigation as well as congressional testimony from top State Department officials. Although some said the investigation and attacks from Republicans were merely political, others say the investigation was necessary not only for understanding what went wrong and how to improve security, but also for understanding the instability caused by the Arab Spring. On November 21, 2014, following nearly two years of hearings and investigation, the Republican-led House Select Committee on Intelligence released its long-awaited report on the Benghazi attack. The report found that the U.S. military and CIA had responded appropriately during the attacks, and that the CIA had ensured sufficient security and bravely assisted the night of the attacks. The panel also found no intelligence failure prior to the attacks. The committee also concluded that there was no evidence that the military had been ordered, as some had charged, to stand down during the attacks. It also determined that appropriate U.S. personnel made reasonable tactical decisions that night, and it dismissed claims that the CIA was involved in arms shipments or other unauthorized activities. Despite the release of the 2014 report, many Republicans continued to insist that the Obama administration had attempted to cover up the events in Benghazi, or to whitewash them for public consumption. Benghazi played a sizable role in the 2016 presidential campaign, with every Republican candidate taking Hillary Clinton to task for her handling of the Benghazi affair.

Daniel Katz

See also: Al-Qaeda; Global War on Terror

Citations

"Briefing by Senior Administration Officials to Update Recent Events in Libya," U.S. State Department, September 12, 2012, www.state.gov.

Kirkpatrick, David. "Election-Year Stakes Overshadow Nuances of Libya Investigation," *The New York Times,* October 16, 2012.

Margasak, Larry. "Timeline of Events, Comments Surrounding Benghazi," BigStory .AP.org, October 19, 2012.

"Times Topics: Libya—the Benghazi Attacks," NYTimes.com, January 8, 2013.

"U.S. Confirms Its Libya Ambassador Killed in Benghazi," *BBC News*, Africa, September 12, 2012.

Beslan School Hostage Crisis

The Beslan school operation was the latest in a series of attacks carried out by Chechen rebels in an effort to gain independence for Chechnya, which first broke away from Russia in November 1991 after the fall of the Soviet Union. In 1994 President Boris Yeltsin sent troops to regain control of the province, triggering a bloody insurgency that has resulted in the fatalities of countless troops and civilians. Less than a month before the Beslan attack, Chechen suicide bombers blew up two civilian airliners;

earlier that year, they assassinated Akhmad Kadyrov, the pro-Russian Chechen president installed by Moscow authorities and, in a separate incident, invaded the Interior Ministry in the neighboring republic of Ingushetia.

The Beslan hostage crisis commenced on the morning of September 1, 2004, when 32 heavily armed Chechen, Ingush, Russian, and Arab terrorists stormed and seized School Number One, where an estimated 1,200 students, teachers, and parents were attending opening ceremonies for the first day of classes. Twelve people were killed within the first few minutes after the attackers opened fire, and a few others managed to escape. The remainder, which numbered more than 1,000, were shepherded into the gymnasium, where they were surrounded by a ring of guns, bombs, and detonators. Temperatures soon rose in the building, and as the days wore on, many hostages fainted and faced dehydration.

Soon after the takeover, Russian and North Ossetian police blockaded the school and managed to make contact with the hostage takers. The terrorists immediately demanded full recognition of Chechnya's independence and the withdrawal of all Russian troops from the province. Although the attackers agreed to release 26 hostages on September 2, they refused to allow any food or water into the school, and negotiations soon broke down. However, talks commenced the next day, and the attackers agreed to allow medical personnel to access the building and retrieve the bodies of those who had been killed when the school was seized two days earlier.

It remains unclear exactly what happened next, but when emergency workers entered the school, a series of explosions went off and the gymnasium roof collapsed. At that point, police stormed the building. Adding to the confusion, hundreds of civilians, mainly hostages' families who had been watching the crisis from the other side of police blockades just over 300 feet away, also ran into the school. In the ensuing gunfight, hundreds were killed, and more than 700 were injured. According to Russian police, all but one of the hostage takers were killed either within the school or after being tracked down nearby. The sole survivor, Nur-Pashi Kulayev, was convicted and sentenced to life in prison in May 2006. Shamil Basayev, commander of the Chechen separatist movement since the mid-1990s, later claimed responsibility for the siege.

Much about the siege, particularly what specifically sparked the September 3 explosions that brought about its violent end, remains unknown, and many victims' families accused then Russian president Vladimir Putin and other top officials of a cover-up. A subsequent report compiled by North Ossetian officials concluded that Russian troops fired rocket-propelled grenades and flamethrowers into the school gym, and this caused the roof's collapse and further explosions. The Kremlin denied the charges, claiming that the hostage takers first detonated the charges and that they were responsible for the high death toll. A Russian legislative commission repeatedly delayed the release of its own findings, saying the final report still had "many holes."

Other investigations have raised the possibility that a bomb hung from the gym's ceiling may have fallen and exploded accidentally. Many have also blamed North Ossetian police for failing to prevent the crisis in the first place, especially given that Moscow officials had previously warned of an imminent attack in the region. Numerous people, including families of the victims, are doubtful that the facts behind the siege will ever be fully known.

Edward F. Mickolus

See also: Jihad; Metrojet Flight 9268; Moscow Theater Attack

Citations

Abdullaev, Nabi. "Beslan Tragedy Reveals Flaws in Russian Security Operations," *Eurasia Daily Monitor* 1, no. 79 (September 7, 2004).

Baker, Peter, and Susan Glasser. "Hostage Takers in Russia Argued before Explosion," *The Washington Post,* September 7, 2004.

Chamberlain, Gethin. "Blood of Beslan's Innocents," *The Scotsman* (Glasgow), September 4, 2004.

Mulvey, Stephen. "The Hostage Takers," *BBC News*, September 9, 2004.

Ostrovsky, Simon. "Over 300 Killed in School Carnage," *Moscow Times,* September 6, 2004.

Walsh, Nick. "When Hell Came Calling at Beslan's School No. 1," *The Observer* (London), September 5, 2004.

Bin Laden, Osama

Osama bin Laden was perhaps the world's most notorious terrorist. He has been blamed for several terrorist attacks against the United States, including the bombing of U.S. embassies in Kenya and Tanzania and the World Trade Center and Pentagon attacks on September 11, 2001. Osama Mohammad bin Laden was born on March 10, 1957, in Riyadh, Saudi Arabia, the 17th son of the owner of Saudi Arabia's largest construction company. He had more than 50 siblings, but his position made him among the least regarded of the clan. Raised as a pious

Perhaps the world's most notorious terrorist, Osama bin Laden was one of the founders of al-Qaeda, and its leader for most of the group's existence. Bin Laden was killed on May 2, 2011, following a United States Special Operations Forces raid on his compound in Abbottabad, Pakistan. His death marked a major turning point in the U.S.-led Global War on Terror, closing a chapter that had begun nearly a decade earlier on September 11, 2001. (Stéphane Ruet /Getty Images)

Muslim, bin Laden turned to religion after the death of his father in 1967.

In the 1970s, bin Laden studied management and economics at King Abdulaziz University, and there he became interested in fundamentalist Islamic groups. He was deeply influenced by a teacher, Sheikh Abdullah Yusuf Azzam, a Palestinian who had become disillusioned with the Palestine Liberation Organization and believed Islam needed to return to its roots. In 1979, bin Laden joined other young Muslims in fighting against the Soviet Union's Afghanistan invasion. The rebels of the Islamic Alliance of Afghanistan Mujahideen were supported by the U.S. government. Although it is not entirely clear, bin Laden probably went to Afghanistan and then returned to Saudi Arabia to raise money for the mujahideen, or "freedom fighters." In Pakistan, he used his expertise in construction to manage logistics for what was becoming a jihad, or holy war. By the mid-1980s, he was working inside Afghanistan, building roads and hideouts. He also established a base and training camp for the mujahideen.

When the Soviet Union pulled out of Afghanistan in 1989, bin Laden returned to Saudi Arabia a hero, full of religious zealotry, enriched by the family fortune, and well trained by U.S. forces. He was not a supporter of the United States, however. That same year, he formed the terrorist organization al-Qaeda with Azzam. Bin Laden's zeal was reserved for Islam, and he bore some of the resentment common to soldiers returning from a bloody and punishing war. Seeing in Saudi Arabia a nation that catered to the United States and that was moving away from Islamic principles, bin Laden became an outspoken critic of the Saudi royal family. He also established a charitable organization to support veterans of the Afghan war, many of whom went on to fight in other wars in Chechnya, Somalia, and Bosnia.

In 1990, Iraqi troops under Saddam Hussein invaded Kuwait and threatened Saudi Arabia. The Saudi royal family accepted the help of U.S. troops to defend the nation. Bin Laden was infuriated by this and was vocal in his opposition of the royal family. In response, his citizenship was revoked. Bin Laden left Saudi Arabia in April 1991 and made his way to Sudan. Working from

Khartoum, bin Laden established terrorist training camps where he passed on the skills and techniques he had learned in Afghanistan to religious zealots who would conduct a jihad against the United States. Although he refrained from publicly calling for attacks on the United States, the U.S. government identified him as a major financier of terrorist organizations. Cut off from his family in 1994, bin Laden nonetheless had a fortune estimated at $400 million.

In February 1993, two terrorists bombed the World Trade Center in New York City. The suspects were connected to the Maktab al-Khidamat, a sort of recruiting office originally established to support the Afghan mujahideen and connected to bin Laden. Also in 1993, 18 American soldiers were killed in Mogadishu, Somalia. Bin Laden claimed responsibility. Two years later, a bomb in Riyadh, Saudi Arabia, killed five U.S. soldiers. Nineteen more were killed when a bomb exploded at a military barracks in Dhahran. In 1996, under pressure from the United States and Saudi Arabia, Sudan forced bin Laden to leave the country. He moved to Afghanistan, where his quiet opposition to the United States became defiant and loud. On August 23, 1996, bin Laden issued a fatwa, a religious decree, calling for jihad against the United States.

Two years later, bin Laden convened a meeting of terrorist leaders and called for attacks on American interests. The response was quick and severe. In August 1998, on the anniversary of U.S. involvement in the Persian Gulf War, two bombs exploded at American embassies in Tanzania and Kenya. Although no conclusive evidence was found to link bin Laden to either bombing, the U.S. government openly pointed the finger at him. In 2001, the U.S. government accused bin Laden of orchestrating the September 11 attacks on the World Trade Center and the Pentagon, the most destructive acts of terrorism in history. Claiming finally to have evidence that implicated bin Laden, the United States, along with the support of the United Kingdom and many other countries, declared a war on terrorism and launched an attack on Afghanistan on October 7. U.S. officials claim that from his base there, bin Laden led a loose confederacy of terrorist groups known as al-Qaeda. The massive bombing campaign by the United States in Afghanistan decimated the Taliban regime and al-Qaeda forces, and enabled the Northern Alliance to regain control of most of the country. The United States believed bin Laden was hiding in caves in the mountains near Kandahar and was using Special Forces and marines on the ground to hunt him down. Bin Laden thereafter remained in hiding for many years, occasionally making public appearances and pronouncements via videotape released by al-Qaeda.

On May 1, 2011 (May 2 Pakistan Standard Time), a group of Navy SEALs stormed bin Laden's compound, and he was subsequently killed in the resulting firefight.

Katherine Gould

See also: Al-Qaeda; Egyptian Islamic Jihad (EIJ); Global War on Terror; Jihad; September 11 Attacks; Zawahiri, Ayman al-

Citations

Bergen, Peter L. *The Osama bin Laden I Know: An Oral History of Al Qaeda's Leader.* New York: Free Press, 2006.

Randal, Jonathan. *Osama: The Making of a Terrorist.* New York: Knopf, 2004.

Black September Organization

Palestinian terrorist group founded in the autumn of 1971, so-named for the conflict between Palestinians and Jordanian armed forces that began in September 1970 (Black September) and saw the forced expulsion of Palestinians from Jordan. The Black September Organization was said to be an offshoot of Fatah, the wing of the Palestine Liberation Organization (PLO) controlled by Yasser Arafat, because some Palestinians connected with Fatah joined Black September. Soon, other Palestinian militants began to join Black September, including certain members of the Popular Front for the Liberation of Palestine (PFLP). The extent to which the Black September Organization was tied to Fatah, or even to Arafat, remains somewhat murky. Nevertheless, it is more than probable that Black September received monetary aid and intelligence information via the PLO. If Arafat did indeed acquiesce to the formation of the Black September Organization and if indeed he did funnel resources to the group, he took considerable pains to disguise such activity. The first significant act Black September took occurred in November 1971, when several members attacked and killed Jordanian prime minister Wasfi al-Tal in Cairo, Egypt. The assassination was said to be retribution for Tal's hard-line policies toward the Palestinians and the PLO's subsequent eviction from Jordan. A month later the group struck again when it unsuccessfully tried to assassinate a Jordanian ambassador. Black September was also likely responsible for two acts of sabotage on foreign soil: one in West Germany and the other in the Netherlands. Three months later, members of Black September hijacked Sabena Airlines Flight 571, a Belgian jetliner that had just left Vienna en route to Tel Aviv. A daring commando raid by Israel's Sayeret Matkal managed to defuse the crisis, and just one passenger died in the event. Two of the Black September hijackers were

killed, and Israelis took two more prisoner. Without a doubt, Black September's most spectacular terrorist scheme unfolded during the 1972 Olympic Games in Munich. There, in front of worldwide media assembled for the Olympics, Black September members murdered 11 Israeli athletes, 9 of whom they had previously kidnapped. The terrorists also shot and killed a West German police officer during an abortive rescue attempt of the hostages. The murders shocked the world, but the Black September Organization undoubtedly achieved its aim of international exposure and notoriety thanks to the venue in which the killings occurred and the concentration of print and broadcast journalists in Munich at the time. The Munich massacre saw the Israelis take immediate and bold steps to crush the Black September Organization and apprehend or kill those responsible for the attacks. Despite Israeli reprisals and an international hunt for Black September members, the organization pulled off another terrorist attack, this time on the Saudi embassy in Khartoum, Sudan, in March 1973. In the course of the assault, two American diplomats and the Belgian chargé d'affaires were killed. In the autumn of that year, around the time of the Yom Kippur War, Arafat allegedly pressured the Black September Organization to disband. The following year, Arafat would only sanction terrorist attacks in Israel proper, in the West Bank and the Gaza Strip. It is likely that the Black September Organization persisted for a time thereafter.

Paul G. Pierpaoli Jr.

See also: Al-Fatah; Arafat, Yasser; Munich Olympic Games Massacre; Palestine Liberation Organization (PLO); Popular Front for the Liberation of Palestine (PFLP)

Citations

Dobson, Christopher. *Black September: Its Short, Violent History.* New York: Macmillan, 1974.

Livingstone, Neil C., and David Haley. *Inside the PLO.* New York: William Morrow, 1990.

Yodfat, Aryeh Y., and Yuval Arnon-OHannah. *PLO Strategy and Tactics.* New York: St. Martin's, 1981.

Boko Haram

Boko Haram is a militant, Islamist terrorist organization based in northeastern Nigeria (as well as portions of Chad, Niger, and Cameroon). The official name of the group is the Congregation of the People of Tradition for Proselytism and Jihad, but it is best known as Boko Haram in the Hausa language. Mohammed Yusuf founded Boko Haram in 2002; since then, it has grown considerably in both membership and influence. The group's agenda is to rid Nigerian society of all traces of Western influence and to create an Islamic state in Nigeria based strictly on sharia law (the traditional moral and religious codes of Islam). In recent years, Boko Haram, which is a largely decentralized organization that lacks a strong chain of command, has been led by Abubakar Shekau and Momodu Bama. Boko Haram is uncompromising in its beliefs and goals and has frequently resorted to violence in order to gain attention. Over the years, it has bombed or attacked government facilities, Christian churches and organizations, schools, and police stations. It has also engaged in the abduction of Westerners and schoolchildren, and has assassinated Islamic leaders believed to have been co-opted by the Nigerian government. The group has also employed child soldiers and suicide bombers. It should be noted that the vast majority of Nigeria's Muslim population does not support Boko Haram and is fiercely critical of its tactics. The organization is strongest in Nigeria's northeastern states, where the government has declared a state of emergency. However, the Nigerian government has had little success in suppressing Boko Haram or its activities, which have become bolder in recent months. Between 2002 and the end of 2013, it is estimated that more than 10,000 people had died from violence perpetrated by Boko Haram; another 90,000 to 100,000 people have been internally displaced.

It has remained somewhat unclear what sort of direct links Boko Haram has to other terrorist organizations. Some observers have alleged that the group has ties to al-Qaeda in the Islamic Maghreb, and may be receiving funding from that outfit, but that claim cannot be completely substantiated. Since early 2015, it is believed that Boko Haram may be coordinating its activities with the Islamic State of Iraq and Syria (ISIS). Although the United States officially declared Boko Haram a terrorist organization in November 2013, thus far the group's attacks outside Nigeria have been few in number. Other observers believe that the group is motivated as much by interethnic tensions as it is by religious dogma. These individuals have claimed that Yusuf's initial goal was ethnic cleansing, which he disguised in religious overtones.

Whatever the group's ties might be, and whatever its sources of funding, Boko Haram remains a dangerous and destabilizing presence in Nigeria. In 2014, the organization was responsible for a series of devastating attacks and abductions. In February 2014, Boko Haram terrorists attacked a small village in Nigeria, resulting in 106 civilian deaths. Only days later, terrorists attacked a government college preparatory school, which resulted in the deaths of 29 male students. On April 14, Boko Haram militants stormed a school and abducted 276 schoolgirls; their whereabouts are still unknown, but Abubakar Shekau claimed that he was going to sell them into slavery. Boko Haram has been targeting schools because they believe the institutions are responsible for corrupting Islam and introducing Western ideas into society. On May 5, near the Nigerian-Cameroon border, Boko Haram launched an attack that left at least 310 innocent people dead.

Despite the Nigerian government's efforts to stem the mounting violence, Boko Haram has seemingly grown in strength. Its highly decentralized structure has made it more difficult for government authorities to pursue and apprehend the militants. The government has also reportedly engaged in human rights abuses against suspected Boko Haram terrorists. In 2013, Amnesty International alleged that the Nigerian government presided over the deaths of some 950 Boko Haram suspects who had been detained in prisons. On October 16, 2014, the Nigerian government announced amid much fanfare that it had reached a cease-fire agreement with Boko Haram. This would have ended the group's multiyear insurgency. At the time, Boko Haram's leadership reportedly assured the Nigerian government that the 276 schoolgirls abducted earlier in the year were alive and well. However, on November 1, Abubakar Shekau flatly denied that his organization had agreed to a cease-fire and claimed that the schoolgirls had been married off. On November 10, press reports from Nigeria attributed a school explosion to Boko Haram that killed at least 46 students.

As further evidence that the October cease-fire agreement was either a sham or had been violated, on January 3, 2015, Boko Haram seized the town of Baga, a town in northeastern Nigeria. The group also captured a key multinational military base located there. The troops stationed there reportedly turned and fled as Boko Haram approached and did not offer much resistance. On January 7, media reports indicated that Baga had been obliterated and that some 2,000 civilians (most of them women, children, and the elderly) had been massacred. On January 10, Boko Haram terrorists reportedly strapped explosives to a young girl (perhaps as young as 10), sent her into a crowded marketplace in Maiduguri, and remotely detonated them. The resulting explosion killed the girl as well at least 21 others. This was the fourth suicide bombing in Maiduguri since July 2014. These developments were viewed as significant setbacks in Nigeria's ongoing fight against Boko Haram.

In early March 2015, Boko Haram leaders pledged their loyalty to the Islamic State of Iraq and Syria (ISIS), a menacing radical Islamic group currently wreaking havoc in the Middle East. That same month, Boko Haram kidnapped some 400 women and children in Nigeria, an event that precipitated widespread condemnation among many Nigerians, who decried their government's inability to protect its citizens from such depredations. On March 28, Boko Haram soldiers murdered 41 Nigerians in Abuja, Nigeria, in an attempt to intimidate voters from casting their ballots during that country's national elections. In June and July 2015, Boko Haram perpetrated several deadly attacks against civilians in Chad. In Nigeria, meanwhile, government forces pressed a new offensive against the terrorist group, pushing it out of several strongholds. By September 2015, Nigerian officials announced that Boko Haram had been driven out of all its strongholds and was incapable of holding any territory. In December, Nigeria's president declared that Boko Haram had been "technically defeated." Nevertheless, the group continued to sponsor terrorist attacks in parts of Nigeria as well as Chad and Cameroon. By early 2016, it was clear that Boko Haram's power within Nigeria had been substantially reduced, but it remained a dangerous and potentially destabilizing force, particularly in Chad, Niger, and Cameroon.

Paul G. Pierpaoli Jr.

See also: Al-Qaeda; Global War on Terror; Jihad

Citations

"310 Killed in Latest Boko Haram Attack; Hundreds of Girls Remain Missing," *CNN,* www.cnn.com/2014/05/08/world/africa/nigeria-abducted-girls.

Pham, J. Peter. "Boko Haram's Evolving Threat," Africa Security Threat, April 2012, http://africacenter.org/wp-content/uploads/2012/04/AfricaBriefFinal_20.pdf.

Breivik, Anders

Anders Behring Breivik is a Norwegian terrorist committed to far-right ideology. He is responsible for the 2011 Norwegian bombing and shooting that killed 77 people. He was convicted of terrorism in 2012 and sentenced to 21 years in prison, but can be held longer if he is found to still be a threat to society. According to his diary, Breivik began preparing for the attack in April 2011. He rented a farm in Aasta with the stated intention of growing sugar beets. However, Breivik instead ordered six tons of fertilizer, which he used to construct his bomb. Breivik rented two vehicles to be used in the attacks.

On July 22, 2011, Breivik parked a vehicle containing the bomb on Grubbegata Street, where several government ministries are located. At around 3:30 p.m., the homemade fertilizer bomb exploded, killing eight people and wounding dozens more. Breivik, dressed as a police officer with a semiautomatic rifle and handgun, then took a ferry over to Utoya, a small island where the Norwegian Labour Party was holding a youth summer camp. He first began shooting at campers on the island, and then began to shoot at those attempting to swim away and escape. Breivik surrendered to police at 6:27 p.m., around an hour after he arrived at the island to begin his rampage. Sixty-nine people were killed in the Utoya attack, many between the ages of 16 and 22.

On the day of the attacks, Breivik distributed a 1,500-page manifesto entitled *2083: A European Declaration of Independence,* which was emailed to officials in the United States and Europe. Breivik claimed that his attack would help bring attention to his manifesto, which in rambling fashion, railed against the evils of "multiculturalism" and provided detailed instructions on how to prepare for the "upcoming civil war," while also complaining of the estranged relationship he had with his father. Breivik's worldview sees Europe as being invaded by Muslims and overtaken by Islam. The main themes of the manifesto were anti-Muslim and antifeminist and he identified himself as a fascist and a national socialist.

Breivik confessed to the attack in November 2011, and was originally declared insane during the attack. Following public outrage, he was reexamined and declared sane. In 2016, Breivik filed a lawsuit stating that being placed in solitary confinement violated his civil rights, although he lost in court.

Colin P. Clarke

See also: Homegrown Terrorism; Improvised Explosive Devices; Lone Wolf Attacks

Citations

Englund, Will. "In Diary, Norwegian 'Crusader' Details Months of Preparation for Attacks," *The Washington Post,* July 24, 2011.

Libell, Henrik Pryser. "Anders Behring Breivik, Killer in 2011 Norway Massacre, Says Prison Conditions Violate His Rights," *The New York Times,* March 15, 2016.

Seierstad, Asne. *One of Us: The Story of a Massacre in Norway—and its Aftermath.* New York: Farrar, Straus, and Giroux, 2015.

Brussels Terrorist Attacks (2016)

On the morning of March 22, 2016, suicide bombers with ties to the Islamic State of Iraq and Syria (ISIS) detonated three bombs—two at the Brussels, Belgium airport, and one at a metro rail station in the center of Brussels, not far from the European Commission headquarters. The bombs, which were laced with nails to magnify their destructive power, resulted in the deaths of 32 people; the three suicide bombers were also killed. An additional 300 people were injured. Among the 32 victims killed were 17 Belgians. The others were from various nations, including the United States.

In the immediate aftermath of the bombings, Belgian officials closed the Brussels airport and launched an extensive manhunt and investigation that resulted in multiple arrests and the discovery of incriminating evidence on several seized computers. The first bomb was detonated in the international terminal of the airport at 7:58 a.m. (local time), a period in which the airport is extremely busy. It went off between check-in kiosks for Iberia Airlines and British Airways. About nine seconds later, a second bomb went off adjacent to a Starbucks coffee concession and a Brussels Airlines check-in desk. The terrorists had planted a third bomb in the airport, but it did not detonate and was later discovered and disarmed by police. A total of 18 people died in the airport bombings. At 9:11 a.m., another bomb was detonated by a suicide bomber at the Maelbeek metro rail stop in central Brussels, about six miles from the airport. Fourteen victims died in that explosion. After first responders arrived on the scene, Belgian officials cordoned off a wide area around the metro station and closed the rail line. The closure lasted for a number of days as investigators combed through the wreckage for clues.

Perpetrators Identified and Profiled

Belgian authorities soon identified the three suicide bombers; at the same time, ISIS formally declared responsibility for the attacks. Two of the attackers were brothers: Ibrahim and Khalid El Bakraoui. They were linked to the same Belgian terror cell that was responsible for the November 2015 terror attacks in Paris, France. Both men were Belgian citizens of Moroccan descent, and both had criminal histories. Ibrahim died in the airport attack, and his brother Khalid died in the metro station attack. The third perpetrator (and the second airport bomber) was Najim Laachraoui (also known as Soufiane Kayal). A Belgian national of Moroccan birth, he too died when the bomb he carried was detonated. Less than two hours after the first bombs were detonated, police raided an apartment the brothers used. There, officials located a laptop computer in the trash that had a suicide note written by Ibrahim El Bakraoui. The note indicated that he had been "stressed out," feared for his safety, and was apprehensive of "ever-lasting eternity." Between March 24 and March 27, officials arrested at least 20 men in conjunction with the bombing investigation; one of the men was arrested in Italy and was suspected of having forged documents for terrorists involved in both the 2015 Paris attacks and the 2016 Brussels attacks. Meanwhile, on March 18, Belgian police had arrested Salah Abdeslam in the heavily Muslim Brussels suburb of Molenbeek. It is strongly suspected that Abdeslam was involved in the Paris attacks and was working with the El Bakraoui brothers. Authorities believe that Abdeslam's arrest may have triggered the March attacks in Brussels.

Brussels a Prime Terrorist Target

In recent years, Brussels has become the epicenter of Muslim extremism and terrorism in Europe. The city and suburbs are home to significant numbers of Muslims, many of whom remain poor, uneducated, and marginalized. Belgium has proportionally contributed more ISIS fighters than any other European nation. The country's security systems have been historically weak, and competition among security organizations has created confusion and vast holes in the country's protective safeguards. Because it is considered the de facto capital of the European Union (EU), Brussels has become an inviting target for terrorists, who reason that a strike against Brussels is akin to a strike against all of Europe.

Many of the EU's governing bodies are headquartered in Brussels, as is the North Atlantic Treaty Organization (NATO). In the aftermath of the Brussels bombings, which stood as the most lethal terrorist attacks in Belgian history, several government officials offered to tender their resignation amid allegations that glaring security lapses had invited the tragedy. The Belgian government subsequently increased security at the country's nuclear power plants; meanwhile, the airport remained closed until April 1. That extended closure wrought havoc on much of western Europe's air travel. ISIS warnings that more terrorist attacks might be in the offing were chillingly confirmed when investigators found detailed floor plans to several Belgian government buildings on suspects' computers. Some officials opined that ISIS-aligned terrorists might have even been planning to assassinate Belgium's prime minister.

Paul G. Pierpaoli Jr.

See also: Baghdadi, Abu Bakr al-; Islamic State of Iraq and Syria (ISIS); Paris Terrorist Attacks (2015)

Citations

"Brussels Attacks: Last Gasp of ISIS Terror in Europe or Sign of Growing Threat?" *The Guardian,* March 26, 2016.

"Brussels Attacks: Two Brothers behind Belgium Bombings," *BBC News*, March 23, 2016.

Chad, Sheldon, Christina Boyle, and Corina Knoll. "Hunt Is on for Brussels Bombing Suspect: Islamic State Warns of More, Worse Attacks," *Los Angeles Times,* March 23, 2016.

C

Charlie Hebdo and Jewish Supermarket Attacks

On January 7 and 9, 2015, three terrorists with links to Islamic extremist groups perpetrated two separate mass shootings that killed 16 civilians in Paris, France. The attacks shocked France and elicited strong condemnations from nations around the world. At approximately 11:30 a.m. on January 7, 2015, two Islamic terrorists—Saïd Kouachi (age 34) and Chérif Kouachi (age 32)—stormed the Paris editorial offices of the satirical newspaper *Charlie Hebdo*. As they entered the building, they shouted "Allahu Akbar" (Arabic for "God is great").

Armed with automatic assault rifles, the two brothers fired more than 50 shots within the newspaper offices, killing 11 people and wounding 11 more. A 12th victim, a French police officer, was gunned down as the assailants fled the building. The terrorists claimed ties to the Islamic terrorist organization Al-Qaeda in Yemen, which promptly claimed responsibility for the attack. The group targeted the newspaper because it asserted that it had insulted Islam by depicting the Prophet Muhammad in an unflattering way. Muslims believe that portraying the Prophet in virtually any form is blasphemous. It should be noted, however, that *Charlie Hebdo* has a long history of critical satire that often targets politics, religion, and social developments and that the newspaper has frequently lampooned Christianity. French law gives such periodicals wide latitude to publish what they wish, and freedom of speech is well protected throughout France.

After the attack, the Kouachis fled Paris, prompting a massive manhunt by French police. The brothers eventually took refuge in a sign company in a Paris suburb on January 9, where they took several hostages. Police surrounded the building, not far from Charles de Gaulle Airport, and a nearly nine-hour standoff ensued. Late in the afternoon of January 9, police assaulted the building, forcing the terrorists to flee; both were shot and killed as they attempted to make their escape. No civilians were killed in the standoff.

Meanwhile, in another part of Paris, also on January 9, another terrorist attack was under way. This one took place in a Jewish supermarket in the 20th Arrondissement. About 1:00 p.m., Amedy Coulibaly, an extremist Muslim who professed ties to the Islamic State of Iraq and Syria (ISIS), burst into the Hypercacher kosher market armed with an assault rifle, a machine gun, and two pistols. He immediately ordered the store's customers—most of them Jewish—to the floor. In all, there were about 20 people now held as hostages. When police arrived on the scene, Coulibaly informed them that he would kill all of the hostages if the Kouachi brothers—who were then in a standoff with police at another location near Paris—were injured or killed.

Coulibaly knew the Kouachis, having met them in jail some years before. Later, Coulibaly was also identified as the killer of a female police officer, whom he had gunned down on January 8 in Montrouge, a Paris suburb. Coulibaly shot and killed four customers almost immediately, recording the murders with a body-mounted camera. As Coulibaly conversed with police who had surrounded the market, he claimed that he had targeted the Jewish market "to defend Muslims, especially Palestinians," from Jewish repression.

The standoff continued until shortly after 5:00 p.m., when police decided to flush out the assailant. As he attempted to exit the store, Coulibaly was shot and killed by police. The remaining 15 hostages in the stores were rescued without further incident. In all, the kosher market attack resulted in five deaths (including the perpetrator); nine others, including at least one police officer, were wounded. During the standoff, one of the hostages managed to describe the situation to police via text messages. This permitted police to storm the store without undue risk to the hostages. One of the heroes of the attack was Lassana Bathily, a young Muslim man from Mali who herded a number of store customers into a walk-in refrigerator, shielding them from potential injury or death.

The two terrorist attacks precipitated much outrage and concern throughout France. French president François Hollande strongly condemned the assaults and decided to mobilize 10,000 French Army troops, who would patrol the streets of France's largest cities. Not since World War II were so many soldiers seen in civilian areas. Much of the world, including many Muslim countries, also denounced the violence. The kosher market attack was especially worrisome for French Jews, who for years had been increasingly concerned with a rising tide of anti-Semitism in France. On January 11, massive demonstrations of grief, sympathy, and support for the victims and their families occurred throughout France. In Paris, some 2 million people joined together in a show of support and unity; among them were 40 leaders from around the world, including Israeli prime minister Benjamin Netanyahu and Palestinian Authority president Mahmoud Abbas, who marched arm in arm through city streets. Nearly 2 million more people demonstrated in cities and towns all over France that same day. The timing of the attacks, coming as they did during ISIS offensives in Iraq and Syria, precipitated concern worldwide that Islamic extremists were on the verge of perpetrating more terrorist attacks worldwide.

Paul G. Pierpaoli Jr.

See also: Al-Qaeda in the Arabian Peninsula (AQAP); Islamic State of Iraq and Syria (ISIS); Jihad; Paris Terrorist Attacks (2015)

Citations

Draper, Lucy. "Gunman 'Neutralized' at Kosher Supermarket Siege," *Newsweek,* last modified January 9, 2015, www.newsweek.com/third-shooting-paris-hostage-taken-kosher-grocery-shop-298082.

"Paris Attacks: Millions Rally for Unity in France," *BBC News,* last modified January 11, 2015, www.bbc.com/news/world-europe-30765824.

Urquhart, Conal. "Paris Police Say Twelve Dead after Shooting at *Charlie Hebdo,*" *Time,* last modified January 7, 2015, http://time.com/3657246/paris-charlie-hebdo-shooting.

Christmas Day Airline Terror Plot (2009)

On December 25, 2009, Nigerian citizen Umar Farouk Abdulmutallab unsuccessfully attempted to bomb Northwest Airlines Flight 253 from Amsterdam to Detroit as it approached its final destination. The device, which consisted of a six-inch packet of powdered PETN (which becomes a plastic explosive when mixed with triacetone triperoxide/TAPN) sewn into his underwear and a syringe of liquid acid, ignited a small fire that was promptly put out by a passenger and flight crewmembers. After the incident, officials discovered that Abdulmutallab had been in regular communication with Anwar al-Awlaki, an American-born Islamist widely believed to be the chief ideologue of Al-Qaeda in the Arabian Peninsula (AQAP) in Yemen.

Public responses included a barrage of criticisms of U.S. national security and intelligence organizations for not preventing the attempted bombing, especially given the millions that had been invested to improve aviation security since 9/11. Of particular concern was the fact that U.S. officials had received a warning from Abdulmutallab's father in November 2009, who was concerned over his son's increasingly extremist views. Although the 23-year-old Nigerian had been put on watch lists and even denied a visa renewal by Britain in May 2009, his name was apparently lost among thousands of others and not flagged. Critics also asked why X-ray checks had failed to detect the explosive materials he carried.

Three days after the attempted attack, President Barack Obama publicly addressed the incident while on vacation in Hawaii, receiving some criticism that he showed a lack of concern for Americans' fear for their safety. He mandated a thorough investigation of the event, which he officially blamed on AQAP a week later. A declassified report subsequently released to the public in January 2010 detailed the intelligence and defense agencies' failures to streamline their information and "connect the dots." The president ordered further reforms to fix these weak links and also instigated heightened security measures at airports, including the installation of whole-body scanners in airports and delaying the release of Yemeni prisoners at Guantanamo Bay. He also announced that he would more than double the $70 million in security aid that Washington had sent to Yemen in 2009 and, along with the United Kingdom, would jointly finance a new counterterrorism unit in in the country.

Abdulmutallab was taken into custody on December 26, 2009, and charged with eight felonies, including the attempted use of a weapon of mass destruction and the attempted murder of 289 civilians.

Peter Chalk

See also: Al-Qaeda; Al-Qaeda in the Arabian Peninsula (AQAP); Awlaki, Anwar-al; Global War on Terror; Jihad

Citations
Baker, Peter. "Obama Says Al Qaeda in Yemen Planned Bombing Plot, and He Vows Retribution," *The New York Times,* January 3, 2010.

Borzou, Daragahi. "Bin Laden Takes Responsibility for Christmas Day Bombing Attempt," *The New York Times,* January 24, 2010.

Margasak, Larry, Lara Jakes, and Jim Irwin. "Man Cites Orders from al-Qaeda in Failed Bid to Blow Up Plane," *Globe and Mail* (Canada), December 26, 2011.

Savage, Charlie. "Nigerian Indicted in Terrorist Plot," *The New York Times,* January 6, 2010.

" 'Underwear Bomber' Abdulmutallab Pleads Guilty," *BBC News*, October 12, 2011, www.bbc.co.uk/news/world-us-canada-15278483, accessed October 27, 2011.

D

Dhaka, Bangladesh Café Attack

A July 1–2, 2016, terrorist attack on a Dhaka, Bangladesh café, which was likely perpetrated by the Islamic State of Iraq and Syria (ISIS), was the worst such attack in Bangladesh's history. Late in the evening of July 1, 2016, six assailants entered a bakery/café in Dhaka's tony Gulshan 2 area, opening fire with automatic weapons and setting off several small bombs. They then precipitated an eight-hour siege during which they took several dozen patrons and workers hostage; the siege was ended early the following morning. In all, 29 people died in the attack—22 civilians/hostages, 2 policemen, and 5 of the 6 assailants. The sixth attacker was captured alive.

The Islamic State of Iraq and Syria (ISIS) immediately took responsibility for the attack, although the Bengali government claimed that the assailants were associated with Jamaat-ul-Mujahideen group, a homegrown jihadist organization. The assailants seemingly targeted foreigners, as the café was in an area that is host to numerous embassies. Indeed, most of the victims were foreigners.

At 11:20 p.m. local time, the six terrorists began their assault on the crowded café. Some patrons and workers managed to escape or hide, but several people died almost immediately from the gunfire. The attackers then barricaded themselves in the café, taking all those remaining in the building hostage, and strapped explosives to a café employee, threatening to detonate them if police tried to enter the café. By 3 a.m., Bengali police and army personnel had set up a perimeter around the building; the assailants, meanwhile, permitted some hostages to leave.

At 7:40 a.m. on July 2, a commando battalion stormed the building, employing nine armored personnel carriers that crashed through a back wall of the café. In less than an hour, the building was secured, and five of the attackers lay dead. At the same time, 13 hostages were rescued. The sixth attacker was taken into police custody. It seemed clear that the terrorists did not wish to hold Muslims hostage, as they released many of them before the early morning raid took place. Because ISIS had claimed responsibility for numerous attacks in Bangladesh between September 2015 and July 2016, many international observers suggested that there was a high probability that ISIS sponsored the assault, even though the Bengali government had stated otherwise. On July 6, ISIS released a video in which three Bengali-speaking narrators warned that "what you witnessed in Bangladesh . . . was just a glimpse. This will repeat, repeat, and repeat until you lose and we win." Others have concluded that as ISIS loses territory in Syria and Iraq, its "home base," it is expanding its terror operations in far-flung locales to demonstrate its continued potency and relevance as a jihadist organization.

Paul G. Pierpaoli Jr.

See also: Adnani, Abu Muhammad al-; Islamic State of Iraq and Syria (ISIS); Jihad

Citations

Hammadi, Saad, Rosie Scammell, and Alan Yuhas. "Dhaka Café Attack Ends with 20 Hostages among the Dead," *The Guardian,* July 3, 2016.

Park, Madison, Saeed Ahmed, and Steve Visser. "Dhaka Café Attack: Bangladeshis Mourn Hostages, Officers Killed," *CNN News*, July 5, 2016.

E

Earth Liberation Front (ELF)

The Earth Liberation Front (ELF) represents an extreme and violent fringe of the American environmental movement that seeks to restore the environment in its entirety and re-create ecosystems that have been despoiled by the immoral and selfish actions of the human race. This is to be achieved by adopting an uncompromising stance on the environment and by emphasizing direct action over lobbying and legal forms of protest.

The ELF has employed a variety of tactics in pursuit of its objectives. Principal attack modalities have included arson, product contamination, tree spiking, destruction of logging infrastructure (monkey wrenching), basic vandalism, and (in conjunction with animal rights extremists) mailing booby-trapped letters.

The bulk of the ELF's violent actions have taken place in the Pacific Northwest, given the volume of logging and wilderness leisure development that characterizes that part of the country. However, the group has also demonstrated a capacity to act on a national basis, carrying out attacks in California, Colorado, New York, Michigan, Minnesota, Pennsylvania, and Indiana. This latter willingness and ability reflects the ELF's highly decentralized, flat structure, which has provided a useful militant "force multiplier" that draws on the resources of individuals across the country; extremely close contacts with animal rights activists, which have led to the development of a common, nationwide antihumanist operational agenda; and affinity with the general imperatives of antiglobalization, which is contributing to the emergence of a radical populist movement prepared to act in any "theater" representative of or derived from the contemporary free-market capitalist system.

An inevitable consequence of the ELF's close identification with the goals and imperatives of antiglobalization and animal rights has been a target menu that covers an extremely broad spectrum of corporate, public, and private-sector interests. Principal targets, chosen both for their symbolic value and for ease of attack, have included (1) logging companies, forestry stations, wilderness recreational firms, and urban developers; (2) facilities and businesses deemed to be detrimental or degrading to animal welfare; and (3) perceived symbols of global capitalism and corporate greed.

ELF attacks have caused substantial economic damage. U.S. law enforcement calculates the group has caused anywhere between US$35 and US$45 million in damage to property since first emerging as a visible militant entity in 1996. Estimates of the costs resulting from monkey-wrenching tactics alone run to roughly US$25 million a year, while in 2003 so-called antisprawl operations—arson directed at urban housing projects—are thought to have generated losses in excess of US$2 million. If one factors in indirect multiplier effects (which are inherently difficult to measure), the true fiscal consequences of ELF actions would be far greater.

Peter Chalk

See also: Homegrown Terrorism; Weathermen

Citations

Chalk, Peter, Bruce Hoffman, Robert Reville, and Anna-Britt Kasupski. *Trends in Terrorism: Threats to the United States and the Future of the Terrorism Risk Insurance Act.* Santa Monica, CA: RAND, 2005.

Davidson-Smith, Tim. "Single Issue Terrorism," *CSIS Commentary* 74 (1998), http://fas.org/irp/threat/com74e.htm.

Eagan, Sean. "From Spikes to Bombs: The Rise of Eco-terrorism," *Studies in Conflict and Terrorism* 19 (1996).

Lee, Martha. "Violence and the Environment: The Case of Earth First!" *Terrorism and Political Violence* 7, no. 3 (1995).

Makarenko, Tamara. "Earth Liberation Front Increases Actions across the United States," *Jane's Intelligence Review,* September 2003.

Nauess, Arne. "Deep Ecology and Ultimate Premises," *Ecologist* 18, nos. 4–5 (1998).

Egyptian Islamic Jihad (EIJ)

Egyptian Islamic Jihad (EIJ) emerged in the late 1970s as a group dedicated to overthrowing the Egyptian government. Founded by Muhammad abd-al-Salam Faraj in 1979 as an offshoot of the Muslim Brotherhood, the group's philosophical roots are best understood through Faraj's pamphlet *The Neglected Duty.* In this text Faraj argued, "We have to establish the Rule of God's Religion in our own country first, and to make the Word of God supreme." EIJ established a Majlis al-Shura (consultative council) by the fall of 1980; Faraj and Karam Zuhdi, the founder of al-Gama'a al-Islamiyya (Islamic Group), were both council members and collaborated to form the Cairo and Saudi branches of the organization.

On October 6, 1981, members of EIJ assassinated President Anwar Sadat, an action that marked it for the first time as one of Egypt's foremost terrorist organizations. At their trial, the perpetrators justified the murder on the grounds that Sadat had not effectively enacted sharia law to ensure the emergence of a true Islamic regime in Egypt. After the assassination, EIJ's northern and southern factions split, with Ayman al-Zawahiri taking over the helm of the former.

Some 1,536 suspects were arrested in connection with Sadat's slaying, a majority of whom were found guilty and given prison sentences. On April 15, 1982, the assassin Khaled Ahmed Shawki Islambouli, Faraj, and 22 others were executed. Although Omar Abdel-Rahman, a radical inspirational cleric to both EIJ and al-Gama'a al-Islamiyya (and more commonly known as the "Blind Sheik"), evaded a death sentence, he leveraged the publicity of his trial to defend Islamist ideologies against his depictions of an insufficiently Islamic, and therefore evil, governing system. From the courtroom Abdel-Rahman addressed Egypt and the Muslim world in its entirety about dutiful obedience to Allah; photographs of him encaged with other "members of the faithful" were transmitted throughout the Middle East. The Blind Sheik further strengthened his position by suing the state for torture during his imprisonment, for which he received $10,000 in damages. In short, Abdel-Rahman had cemented himself as the premier spiritual leader of the new generation of Egyptian jihad.

When the net positions of both the government and the jihadi movements are assessed in the aftermath of Sadat's assassination, however, it becomes clear that despite all the publicity Abdel-Rahman was able to generate, EIJ and al-Gama'a al-Islamiyya had both been dealt substantial blows. Egyptian counterterrorism measures were swift and brutal, resulting in the deaths of, or heavy jail sentences for, many key members, including al-Zawahiri. Others went into hiding or were driven into exile. Combined, these losses made future operations incredibly difficult to plan and carry out.

That said, Sadat's successor, Hosni Mubarak, failed to fully douse the terrorist organizations' raisons d'etre and, by attempting to court certain radical Islamist entities in an effort to boost his own legitimacy, may have actually served to sustain them. This latent ideology would once again come to set the country ablaze in the early 1990s. Moreover, the prison experience cemented the resolve of many. This was especially true of al-Zawahiri, who once released in 1984 was generally recognized as the hardened leader of EIJ. On attaining his freedom, he immediately left Egypt for Saudi Arabia to plan the next stages of the jihad.

While he was in exile, a time that coincided with the Soviet invasion of Afghanistan, al-Zawahiri began interacting with Osama bin Laden. It has been suggested that the intent of these interactions was to gain the latter's backing for EIJ and Faraj's vision of the "near jihad." Over time, a distinctly *takfir* ideology (or "purging" mentality within Islam, globally defined) began to take hold in both men's heads, and after al-Zawahiri won an internal power struggle within EIJ, he increasingly moved to intertwine his group with al-Qaeda. The relationship between the two movements was formalized in 1998 with the signing of the now-infamous Khost fatwa against Zionists and Crusaders. In June 2001, EIJ effectively merged with al-Qaeda, with al-Zawahiri assuming the mantle of second in command.

Although EIJ is arguably most well known for its intimate allegiance with al-Qaeda, it should be noted that although it existed as an independent organization, its capacity for incredibly destructive and murderous terrorist activity, predominantly through armed attacks and bombings, was significant. Despite a brutal counterterrorist effort within Egypt in the years following Sadat's assassination, EIJ managed to remain in existence. Although degraded and arguably sidelined by al-Gama'a al-Islamiyya, the group continued to perpetrate a number of incidents and, indeed, in 1993 nearly succeeded in assassinating Egyptian prime minister Atef Sedky and interior minister Hassan al-Alfi. EIJ also staged a number of high-profile attacks abroad, including the bombing of Cairo's embassy in Islamabad in 1995, an unsuccessful attempt to assassinate President Mubarak in Addis Ababa, Ethiopia, that same year, and a failed strike on the U.S. embassy in Albania in 1998.

On March 25, 1999, al-Gama'a al-Islamiyya, by then long the dominant domestically operating Egyptian terrorist organization, formally announced that it would be suspending all future armed and violent activity. Members of EIJ strongly rebuked this annulment of hostilities and refused to abide by any cease-fire. Accordingly, although the Egyptian government rewarded al-Gama'a al-Islamiyya by freeing some 2,000 of its members from prison, it continued its crackdown on EIJ. As noted, however, by this point, al-Zawahiri and bin Laden had forged a close alliance that largely focused on fighting the "far" enemy, namely, the United States and its Western allies, effectively eliminating the domestic threat posed by the group within Egypt.

Michael E. Orzetti

See also: Al-Qaeda; Bin Laden, Osama; Zawahiri, Ayman al-

Citations

Al-Jihad al-Islami Backgrounder. Monterey, CA: Monterey Institute of International Studies (n.d.).

Boyer Bell, J. *Murders on the Nile: The World Trade Center and Global Terror.* San Francisco: Encounter Books, 2003.

EIJ Backgrounder. Washington, DC: Council on Foreign Relations.

Tal, Nachman. *Radical Islam in Egypt and Jordan.* Brighton: Sussex Academic/Jaffee Center for Strategic Studies, 2005.

Wright, Lawrence. *The Looming Tower: Al-Qaeda and the Road to 9/11.* New York: Knopf, 2006.

Ejercito de Liberacion Nacional (ELN)

The Ejercito de Liberacion Nacional (ELN, or National Liberation Army) is a Colombian left-wing rebel group that was founded in 1964. Unlike the Marxist-oriented, peasant-based leadership of the Fuerzas Armadas Revolucionárias de Colombia (FARC, or Revolutionary Armed Forces of Colombia), the ELN was mostly composed of intellectuals and students from the University of Santander who were adherents of Cuban-style revolutionary thought. At its height, the ELN could count on around 5,000 cadres who operated from five *frentes de guerra* (war fronts) mostly concentrated in an extended region that stretched from the middle Magdalena River Valley to the Venezuelan border.

Aside from its Castroite component, the ELN attracted radicalized Catholics who blended religious teachings on social justice with Marxist ideology. The most notable of these recruits was Father Camilo Torres, a Louvain-educated priest from a prominent Colombian family. He joined the rebel group in October 1965 but was killed four months later in an encounter with the army.

The ELN originally operated in a restricted geographic area, the northern departments of Santander, Antioquia, and Bolivar, which it sought to turn into a Colombian version of the Sierra Maestra, Fidel Castro's mountain stronghold in Cuba. As a military organization, the ELN initially failed to mount any operations of consequence, both due to a lack of popular support in the country (the group was mostly urban based) and on account of internal ideological divisions that the ELN's supreme commander, Fabio Vasquez Castano, failed to reconcile.

The group reemerged as a more credible force in the 1980s, however, under the guidance of another guerrilla priest, Father Manuel Perez (also known as el Cura). The new leader (who died of malaria in 1998) proved successful in bridging the rifts between different factions within the group and, just as important, garnering more grassroots backing beyond the cities. The ELN quickly grew from just 800 fighters in 1986 to 3,000 in 1996 to between 3,000 and 5,000 in 2000. Militant operations focused on acts of urban sabotage, hit-and-run attacks on the security forces, and the abduction or assassination of local political and civil leaders. The group was also linked to a number of civilian bombings, although these were not nearly as frequent as those attributed to FARC.

Virtually all of the ELN's financing has been derived from criminality. Traditionally the bulk of revenue came from kidnap for ransom and the extortion of protection money from energy firms (oil, coal, and gas) and mining companies (gold and emeralds). By the turn of the millennium, the group was

thought to have earned approximately US$150 million from these two endeavors, 30 percent from the former and 70 percent from the latter. Over the last several years the ELN has also sought to fund its operations on the back of the highly lucrative South American drug trade (which under Perez's leadership had been strictly off-limits). The group has been relatively successful in this regard and is now thought to control several coca-growing areas along Colombia's northern Pacific coast, although it remains unclear exactly how much it earns from taxing production (the organization is not thought to have made any decisive inroads into narcotics trafficking per se, which is still dominated by stronger and better-connected FARC and paramilitary rivals).

These resources have allowed the ELN to develop a relatively sophisticated and diverse arms pipeline that delivers everything from pistols, assault rifles, and ammunition to heavy machine guns, mortars (60, 81, and 82 millimeters), and rocket-propelled grenades. Reports of surface-to-air missiles have not been confirmed and, to the extent that they exist, are thought to lie within the inventory of FARC. The majority of weapons are sourced from Central America, with El Salvador and Nicaragua playing a particularly important role. Munitions are smuggled through Panama into Colombia by both land and sea. In the former case, shipments run via the Gulf of Uraba or the Gulf of San Miguel, while in the latter case, routes follow a logistic bridge of between 40 and 50 jungle footpaths through the Darien Gap.

Although the ELN remains a viable force in Colombia, its overall strength has declined as a result of defections and successful army infiltration that has resulted in the capture of several top leaders. The group currently lacks the capacity to execute large-scale

tactical (much less strategic) attacks and is generally confined to carrying out strikes against soft targets when the opportunity arises. Several commentators have also suggested that the ELN's growing interest in the drug trade reflects a militant agenda that has become progressively weaker and is now systematically degenerating into straight criminality.

Edward F. Mickolus

See also: Autodefensas Unidas de Colombia (AUC); Fuerzas Armadas Revolucionárias de Colombia (FARC)

Citations

Chalk, Peter. *The Latin American Drug Trade: Scope, Dimensions, Impact, and Response.* Santa Monica, CA: RAND, 2011.

Maullin, Richard. *Soldiers, Guerrillas and Politics in Colombia.* Santa Monica, CA: RAND, 1971.

Rabasa, Angel, and Peter Chalk. *Colombian Labyrinth.* Santa Monica, CA: RAND, 2001.

Tickner, Arlene. "Colombia: Chronicle of a Crisis Foretold," *Current History* 97, no. 616 (1998).

Ethnike Organosis Kypriakou Agonos (EOKA)

The Ethnike Organosis Kypriakou Agonos (EOKA, or National Organization of Cypriot Fighters) was a Greek Cypriot military group that fought to end British rule in Cyprus and unite the island with Greece. The group was active between 1955 and 1959 and had both a military and political component. George Grivas, a former Greek army officer who served in both World Wars, led the former, while Archbishop Michail Christodolou Makarios (born Michail Christodolou Mouskos) oversaw the latter.

At the height of the military campaign, EOKA had a total membership of around 1,250, which included about 250 guerrillas and 1,000 active underground cadres. Although the group did not enjoy the benefit of an entrenched revolutionary environment (widespread poverty, unemployment, and popular alienation), it did have the support of the Greek government in the form of arms, money, and propaganda. This assistance proved vital in terms of sustaining the struggle against the British, who eventually conceded to a presidential election in 1959 that Makarios easily won.

EOKA commenced its military campaign on April 1, 1955, with simultaneous attacks launched on the British-controlled Cyprus Broadcasting Station in Nicosia, the British Army's Wolseley Barracks, and various targets in Famagusta. Subsequent strikes over the course of the next four years left 156 members of the security forces dead. An unknown number of expatriates, colonial officers, and civilian police officers were also killed, while assassination operations against Greek Cypriots resulted in at least 148 fatalities.

As a counterweight to EOKA, the island's Turkish population formed a rival guerrilla force in 1957. Known as the Turk Mukavemet Teskilati (TMT, or Turkish Resistance Organization), the group quickly moved to target Greek Cypriots in reprisal attacks, setting the scene for rapidly escalating intercommunal violence that peaked in 1958 with over 100 civilian deaths.

EOKA's activity continued until December 1959, when a cease-fire was declared. This paved the way for the Zurich Agreement, which provided for presidential elections that same year. EOKA achieved its primary goal when Cyprus became an independent state on August 16, 1960, with the exception of two British military bases. The settlement ruled out any union with either Greece or Turkey, with Ankara, Athens, and London all committing to equally guarantee the island's sovereignty.

Grivas vehemently rejected the Zurich Agreement because it did not include any road map for Cyprus's eventual unification with Greece. In 1971 he formed EOKA-B, the successor group to EOKA, to overthrow President Makarios (who had been reelected in 1968) and achieve enosis (the union of Greece and Cyprus) through violent means. Although Grivas was in an ideal position to create a new organization (which he oversaw until his death in January 1974) given his role as commander of the Greek Cypriot National Guard, his movement did not have any widespread popular support. Unlike the original EOKA, EOKA-B had no anticolonial anchor to justify its existence and indeed was largely perceived as a renegade outfit that was a threat to both Greeks and Turks on the island.

Despite this, the military junta in Athens saw Grivas's group as a potentially useful proxy for achieving complete Greek control over Cyprus. On July 15, 1974, with the tacit blessing of Dictator Dimitrios Ioannidis and the help of the National Guard, EOKA-B tried to overthrow Makarios. The attempted coup failed and left some 3,000 people dead. Turkey invaded five days later, an intervention that most authorities held to be legal, leading to the partition of Cyprus that holds to this day.

Donna Bassett

See also: Partiya Karkeren Kurdistan (PKK)

Citations

Asprey, Robert B. *War in the Shadows: The Guerrilla in History.* New York: Doubleday, 1975.

Barker, Dudley. *Grivas: Portrait of a Terrorist.* Dallas, TX: Harcourt, Brace, 1960.

Brogan, Patrick. *The Fighting Never Stopped: A Comprehensive Guide to World Conflict since 1945.* New York: Random House, 1989.

Byford-Jones, W. *Grivas and the Story of EOKA.* London: Robert Hale, 1959.

Euskadi Ta Askatasuna (ETA)

Euskadi Ta Askatasuna (ETA, or Basque Homeland and Freedom) is a separatist movement group that seeks the establishment of an independent Basque state in the Western Pyrenees on the border between Spain and France. The group, which is designated as a terrorist organization by the European Union, the United States, and the United Nations, has caused more than 820 deaths over the last 40 years (58 since 2000) despite declaring several cease-fires, the most recent of which, announced in 2011, remains in effect.

A militant youth section of the Basque Nationalist Party (Partido Nacionalista Vasco) formed ETA in 1959 out of frustration with their parent movement's rejection of armed resistance. Over the course of the 1960s, the group developed a distinctly Marxist-Leninist revolutionary ideology and emerged as a fierce opponent of Francisco Franco's regime, which banned the Basque language and suppressed any attempt to promote the region's culture. ETA carried out its

Policemen search through the wreckage of a bombing that killed Spanish prime minister Luis Carrero Blanco on December 20, 1973. The bomb was planted along the route that Blanco regularly took to church. Basque Homeland and Liberty (Euskadi Ta Askatasuna—ETA), the militant wing of the Basque separatist movement, claimed all responsibility for the assassination. (AFP/Getty Images)

first planned assassination in 1968, killing the police chief of San Sebastian, Meliton Manzanas. This was followed up with a car bomb attack on Prime Minister Luis Carrero Blanco in 1973, a murder that some credit with speeding the end of the Franco regime, as the dictator no longer had a clear successor.

During the transition to democracy that began after Francisco Franco's death in 1975, the Basque territories in Spain achieved home rule. Despite this, ETA did not put down its arms, pursuing a policy of full independence that saw almost 100 people killed in 1980 alone. The group's escalating campaign of violence cost it public support, however, with opposition becoming particularly marked after it claimed responsibility for the kidnapping and murder of Miguel Angel Blanco, a young Basque town councillor. The incident led to mass protests across the country and triggered widespread demands for an end to violence. According to a poll conducted by the Spanish Universidad del País Vasco, by 2004 over 71 percent of Basques said they "totally rejected" ETA.

Although ETA has been at the forefront of trying to coerce political change in Spain through violence, arguably the biggest impact on the country's internal governing situation resulted from an attack that it did not carry out. On March 11, 2004, 10 improvised explosive devices (IEDs) were set off in Madrid trains, an event that has since come to be known as 3/11; killing 191 and injuring another 1,800. President Jose Maria Aznar, who himself was targeted by an ETA car bomb in 1995, was quick to blame the group for the bombings. However, it soon became clear that al-Qaeda was behind the incident, which the opposition claimed was directly related to Spain's presence in Iraq. The public agreed, and four days later voted Aznar out of office.

ETA's hierarchy has traditionally been predicated on three pillars: political, military, and logistical. The first is charged with planning and executing attacks, the second with coordinating and harmonizing political directives, and the third with financially underwriting the needs of the group's "commandos," mainly through robbery and the imposition of a "revolutionary tax" on Basque businesses. ETA altered this structure in 2004, creating two new branches under the control of the Zuba, or Zuzendaritza Batzordea ("directory committee"): one to handle foreign relations and one to oversee prisoner activity.

ETA has declared several cease-fires since its creation, including, notably, one in 1998 that lasted 14 months, and one in March 2006 that the organization affirmed would be permanent. In December of that year, however, ETA bombed Madrid's airport. The attack, which left two people dead, was quickly followed up by a formal communiqué that the group was resuming its campaign of violence. In 2010 ETA announced yet another cease-fire, declaring it would not carry out any "armed actions." Former United Nations secretary-general Kofi Annan and Sinn Fein (the political arm of the Provisional Irish Republican Army) leader Gerry Adams, among others, subsequently sponsored a conference in October 2011, the outcome of which was a resolution calling on ETA to renounce violence on Spain and France and to open talks. Quickly thereafter the group issued a statement that it was definitively ceasing all armed activity but would continue to pursue the goal of Basque independence. In April 2017, ETA revealed the locations of its weapons caches and claimed that it had completely disarmed.

Drew Bazil

See also: Madrid Commuter Train Bombings (2004); Provisional Irish Republican Army (PIRA)

Citations

Aviles, Juan. *El Terrorismo en Espana: De ETA a Al Qaeda*. Madrid: Arco/Libros, 2011.

Clark, Robert. *The Basque Insurgents: ETA, 1952–1980*. Madison: University of Wisconsin Press, 1984.

Larranaga, Roberto. Guerrilla y terrorismo en Colombia y Espana: ELN y ETA [Guerrilla terrorism in Columbia and Spain: ELN and ETA.]. Bucaramanga, Colombia: Editorial UNAB, 2003.

F

Fort Hood Attacks

On November 5, 2009, Army major and licensed psychiatrist Nidal Hasan committed a terrorist attack at Fort Hood, an Army base near Killeen, Texas, between Austin and Waco, Texas. The shooting began at the Soldier Readiness Processing Center, where a graduation ceremony was in process. Hasan was apparently upset about his upcoming deployment to Afghanistan, as he did not want to fight fellow Muslims. Hasan carried two laser-sighted pistols and 420 rounds of ammunition. During the course of the attack, Hasan yelled "Allahu Akbar," Arabic for "God is great" before firing shots.

Hasan was shot inside the building, but then left the building and shot at victims trying to escape. Hasan wounded 32 and killed 13. He was first announced to have been killed during the attack, but it was later announced that he was sent to the hospital, unconscious after being shot four times. The base remained on lockdown until around 8:30 p.m. on November 5. The attack was the worst mass shooting at a U.S. military base in history.

Hasan is a practicing Muslim who, according to a family member, grew increasingly more devout following the death of his parents; a review of his computer revealed that he spent time perusing radical Islamist websites and was likely radicalized by his communication with Al-Qaeda in the Arabian Peninsula (AQAP) preacher Anwar al-Awlaki.

Hasan was charged with 13 counts of premeditated murder and 32 counts of attempted premeditated murder. He represented himself during trial, and never denied being the gunman. Hasan was given the death penalty on August 28, 2013. The families of the victims filed a wrongful death lawsuit in 2012, alleging that the officials disregarded the safety of the soldiers, and are seeking that the attack is ruled a terrorist attack. In response to the attack, the army and Pentagon made recommendations for improvements, including how to respond to emergencies.

Fort Hood opened on September 18, 1942, and is named after General John Bell Hood. Fort Hood covers 339 square miles and is home to around 52,000 troops.

Colin P. Clarke

See also: Al-Awlaki, Anwar; Homegrown Terrorism; Jihad; Lone Wolf Attacks

Citations

Fernandez, Manny. "Fort Hood Could Not Have Foreseen 2014 Gun Attack, Army Says," *The New York Times,* January 23, 2015.

Maskaly, Michelle, and the Associated Press. "Army: Fort Hood Gunman in Custody After 12 Killed, 31 Injured in Rampage," *Fox News,* November 6, 2009.

Rubin, Josh, and Matt Smith, " 'I Am The Shooter,' Nidal Hasan Tells Fort Hood Court-Martial," *CNN*, August 6, 2013.

Fuerzas Armadas Revolucionárias de Colombia (FARC)

The Fuerzas Armadas Revolucionárias de Colombia (FARC), or the Revolutionary

Armed Forces of Colombia, is a Marxist guerrilla group that operates with the stated goal of overthrowing the Colombian government and seizing control of the country. Currently, FARC remains on both the U.S. and European lists of terrorist organizations and relies on significant numbers of child combatants to fill its ranks.

FARC was initially formed in 1964 following an attack by the Colombian army on Marquetalia and surrounding areas. Guerrilla fighters from Marquetalia met with other communities and formed the First Guerrilla Conference, which would later evolve into the organization that became FARC. The group named themselves the Southern Bloc, and advocated for land reform and better conditions for those in the countryside, and vowed to defend those in rural areas of the country. The group officially adopted the name Fuerzas Armadas Revolucionárias de Colombia in 1966.

Colombia has been enmeshed in an ongoing cycle of terrorism and insurgency since the late 1940s, when *La Violencia* claimed the lives of over 200,000 of its citizens. The Revolutionary Armed Forces of Colombia (FARC) launched its insurgency in 1964 and is still fighting the Colombian government today. In an effort to counter the influence and power of insurgent groups like FARC and Colombia's second largest guerrilla group, the National Liberation Army (ELN), right-wing paramilitaries formed a nationwide coordination committee under the umbrella of the United Self Defense Forces, or AUC, in the mid-1990s.

In 1984, the group signed a cease-fire agreement and formed the Patriotic Union, which won seats in the 1986 elections. Between 1986 and 1991, right-wing paramilitaries killed more than 2,000 party members, including two presidential candidates and four congressmen.

In 1999, FARC's membership peaked at 18,000. Although the FARC originally taxed large coca plantations and cocaine-processing operations, at the beginning of the 21st century, they began buying coca paste and selling it for a profit to drug traffickers who owned the cocaine-processing labs. President Andres Pastrana held peace talks in 1999 with the FARC but the talks dissolved in 2002. On August 7, 2002, FARC guerrillas launched mortar shells close to the presidential palace during President Alvaro Uribe's inauguration ceremony.

With major sections of the country ostensibly governed by FARC already, and in an effort to demonstrate to insurgents that the government was serious about ending the conflict through negotiations, the FARC was granted near complete autonomy to operate in the demilitarized zone (*zona de despeje*), which consisted of five municipalities in Meta and Caqueta departments. The zone was 16,266 square miles—approximately the size of Switzerland. FARC insurgents were able to use this zone to grow their influence, cultivate illegal narcotics, and establish sophisticated training bases.

Contributing to the dearth of government legitimacy is the massive gap between rural and urban, rich and poor. In Colombia's rural areas, the rate of poverty is around 80 percent, which includes 42 percent of this subpopulation within the category of "extreme poverty." In many of these areas, FARC serves as the only source of opportunity and employment for young people. Over the years, FARC has established a shadow state in the areas it controls. Just a few of the services provided by the insurgents include education, medicine, physical infrastructure, protection, the administration of justice, and even civil ceremonies such as marriage and divorce.

FARC collaborated with other insurgent groups, including ETA and the Provisional IRA. After the Colombian government forced the insurgents to switch from mobile warfare back to guerrilla tactics, FARC sought the expertise of over two dozen training teams comprised of PIRA insurgents. PIRA trainers worked with FARC on building more effective mortars, operating in urban terrain, and constructing improvised explosive devices.

In 2002, President Bush signed National Security Presidential Directive (NSPD) 18. This legislation expanded the authority of the Department of Defense and the State Department to work with the Colombian military in waging a COIN campaign against FARC. One of the main pillars of this campaign would be U.S. efforts to work with Joint Task Force Omega (JTF-O). JTF-O's strategy would be to fight against the FARC as well as offensively attacking drug-trafficking organizations and paramilitaries. Because the insurgents sustained their campaign of violence through funds acquired by the drug trade, going after both the narcotics and the insurgents was within the Colombian military's rules of engagement (ROE).

Colombian police's counternarcotics capabilities were bolstered by the acquisition of 2 UH-60 helicopters, 12 UH-1 Huey II helicopters, and Ayres S2R T-65 and OV-10 armored spray aircraft, paid for with U.S. funds. Additional funding was used to expand the police antinarcotics commandos, known as *Junglas,* from one to four companies. The commandos were trained by United States Special Forces with the mission to destroy cocaine labs throughout the country. U.S. Special Forces training of the mobile brigades attached to JTF-O, which began in 2004 and continued through 2008, had a major impact in the security forces'

fight against FARC. The air mobility program was one of the most successful initiatives, if not *the* most successful initiative of "Plan Colombia" and U.S. effort to build the capacity of the security forces in Colombia. The United States provided helicopters, training, maintenance, and spare parts to JTF-O.

As a result of much-improved air mobility, the Colombian military was able to launch operations against FARC bases in Caqueta and Meta. Plan Colombia has been widely hailed as a success, and some analysts believe that the fight against FARC is nearing a tipping point, when the Colombian security forces will finally gain the upper hand once and for all.

A key element of Plan Colombia was to strengthen Colombia's institutions so that gains made against the FARC and overall progress in security would be sustained through government stability. Once Colombian security forces were able to recapture territory from insurgents and drug traffickers, an immediate move was made to stand up institutions in these areas. This was part of the "build"—in clear, hold, and build—and it allowed the Colombian state to extend its writ further afield from the ministries in Bogota to the rural hinterlands. President Uribe's Democratic Security strategy was able to be implemented so effectively in part due to the progress made with judicial, anticorruption, and security force reforms.

JTF-O was the centerpiece of a sustained offensive against FARC positions surrounding Bogota, as well as in Florencia and La Macarena. Throughout southeastern Colombia, the government regained control of territory and began planning to consolidate the area through a combination of security and development. Once Colombian control was extended to these areas, it facilitated the demobilization of paramilitaries as well. In

2002, there were 1,645 acts of terrorism reported by the Colombian government; in 2010, there was a 71 percent reduction, to 480 reported acts of terrorism.

After the Colombian government began to crack down on the guerrilla's kidnapping and drug trafficking, the group turned to illegal gold mining in the early 2000s. In December 2009, FARC rebels kidnapped and killed the governor of Caqueta, Luis Francisco Cuellar. In April 2012, the rebels released 10 police officers and soldiers they had held captive for over 10 years, and the FARC promised to cease kidnapping for ransom.

To finance itself, the FARC relied extensively on kidnapping for ransom (KFR), primarily targeting politicians and wealthy elites. Later on in its tenure, FARC diversified its funding portfolio through involvement in the cocaine-trafficking business. Beginning in the 1970s and continuing until it disbanded, proceeds garnered from drug trafficking helped accelerate its growth over the course of the next several decades. KFR has consistently been a lucrative crime throughout modern Colombian history. During the 1990s, "common criminals" kidnapped 4,946 people while the FARC kidnapped 3,943, the ELN 3,307, "other groups" kidnapped 2,219, the EPL 1,307, and paramilitary groups an additional 193. During Pastrana's four-year tenure, Colombia averaged nine kidnappings *per day.*

In addition to KFR, FARC funded its insurgent activities through rents from a range of sources, including smuggling and trafficking narcotics, extortion of both local government and other narco-traffickers, as well as investments in front companies and money laundering.

In June 2016, the FARC and the Colombian government signed a cease-fire agreement, ending more than 50 years of conflict.

The government and the FARC signed a peace deal in November 2016. The peace deal came two months after Colombian voters rejected a similar peace deal in a nationwide referendum. The group finished disarming in June 2017, and now cease to be an armed group. However, around 250 FARC fighters refused to disarm. The group is now focused on becoming a legal, political movement.

Although significant progress has been made in Colombia, many challenges still remain. Colombia is still a major source country for illicit narcotics. Moreover, the state continues to share sovereignty with a range of violent nonstate actors, including rebel groups and right-wing paramilitaries allied with narco-traffickers and wealthy landowners. Finally, many observers argue that over the last several years, FARC has undergone a mutation from an ideologically driven insurgent group to an inchoate criminal organization fueled by profits. Stamping out the criminal offshoot of FARC may prove even more difficult for the Colombian government than mollifying the ideologically motivated core group of guerrillas.

Colin P. Clarke

See also: Autodefensas Unidas de Colombia (AUC); Ejercito de Liberacion Nacional (ELN)

Citations

Chernick, Marc. "FARC-EP: Las Fuerzas Armadas Revolucionárias de Colombia-Ejercito del Pueblo," in *Terror, Insurgency, and the State: Ending Protracted Conflicts,* edited by Marianne Heiberg et al. Philadelphia: University of Pennsylvania Press, 2007, p. 58.

Ortiz, Roman D. "Insurgent Strategies in the Post-Cold War: The Case of the Revolutionary Armed Forces of Colombia," *Studies in Conflict & Terrorism* 25, no. 2 (2002): 127–143.

Restrepo, Jorge A., and Michal Spagat, "Colombia's Tipping Point?" *Survival,* 47, no. 2 (2005): 135.

Richani, Nazih. "Fragmentation of Sovereignty and Violent Non-State Actors in Colombia," in *Violent Non-State Actors in World Politics,* edited by Klejda Mulaj. New York: Columbia University Press, 2010, p. 37.

G

Garissa University Attack

On April 2, 2015, four terrorists associated with the radical Sunni Islamist group known as al-Shabaab attacked the campus of Garissa University College, situated in the city of Garissa in east-central Kenya. The resulting siege and assault left 152 dead (including the four attackers) and another 79 wounded. The Garissa incident was Kenya's worst terrorist attack since 1998, when al-Qaeda operatives detonated a massive truck bomb in Nairobi that killed some 220 people, including 12 Americans. In 2012, al-Shabaab formally allied itself with al-Qaeda.

The militants, armed with AK-47 assault rifles and explosives strapped to their bodies, launched their attack at 5:30 a.m. local time, when virtually all of the school's students were still asleep in their dormitories. The militants quickly overwhelmed the lightly armed university security detail and proceeded to hold as many as 700 students hostage. As the attack turned into a tense siege, the gunmen began releasing Muslim students, but retained Christian students, some of whom they began to systematically execute. The Kenyan government quickly dispatched defense and security forces to the school, which was promptly surrounded. After almost 15 hours, government soldiers and security personnel apprehended and shot the terrorists to death, ending the siege. In all, 142 students, three soldiers, and three police officers died in the attack.

In the immediate aftermath of the assault, al-Shabaab issued a public statement in which it took full responsibility for the carnage at the university. The group claimed that the attack was retribution for the Kenyan government's heavy-handed antiterrorist campaign that had witnessed mass arrests and the killings of "thousands of Muslims," some of them in neighboring Somalia. A number of observers had previously warned that Kenya's ham-fisted and repressive approach to counterterrorism was creating an atmosphere of distrust and hate, particularly among that country's Muslim population. After the attack, the Kenyan government was also faulted for not having heeded warnings that universities were becoming prime targets of terroristic activity.

Just days after the Garissa incident, the Kenyan government announced that it had apprehended five terrorists who were suspected of having planned the campus attack. Meanwhile, the city of Garissa and the surrounding area remained under a 12-hour curfew from 6:30 p.m. until 6:30 a.m. until April 16. A bounty has been placed on the head of a suspected sixth mastermind. Classes at Garissa University were suspended indefinitely, and there were no immediate plans to reopen the school to students.

Paul G. Pierpaoli Jr.

See also: Al-Shabaab; Westgate Mall Attack

Citations

Karimi, Faith, and Davis McKenzie. "Kenya Attack Victims: Vigil Mourns 147 Slain by Terrorists in Garissa," *CNN*, April 10, 2015, www.cnn.com/2015/04/07/africa/kenya

-attack-victims-vigil, accessed September 9, 2015.

"Kenya Attack: 147 Dead in Garissa University Assault," *BBC News*, April 3, 2015, www.bbc.com/news/world-africa-32169 080, accessed September 9, 2015.

"Kenya Troops Storm University Campus Held by Al-Shabaab," Al Jazeera, April 2, 2015, www.aljazeera.com/news/2015/04 /gunmen-attack-garissa-university-northern -kenya-150402041939434.html, accessed September 9, 2015.

Global War on Terror

"Global war on terror" is the term used to describe the military, political, diplomatic, and economic measures employed by the United States and other allied governments against organizations, countries, or individuals that are committing terrorist acts; that might be inclined to engage in terrorism; or that support those who do commit such acts. The global war on terror is an amorphous concept and a somewhat indistinct term, yet its use emphasizes the difficulty in classifying the type of nontraditional warfare being waged against U.S. and Western interests by various terrorist groups that do not represent any nation. President George W. Bush coined the term in a September 20, 2001, televised address to a joint session of the U.S. Congress, and the term has been presented in official White House pronouncements, fact sheets, State of the Union messages, and such National Security Council (NSC) position papers as the *National Security Strategy* (March 2006) and the *National Strategy for Combating Terrorism* (February 2003 and September 2006 editions). Since 2001, the global war on terror has been directed primarily at Islamic terrorist groups but has also been expanded to include actions against all types of terrorism. During the Bush administration, Secretary of Defense Robert Gates also called it the "long war."

As with the Cold War, the global war on terror is being waged on numerous fronts, against many individuals and nations, and involves both military and nonmilitary tactics. President George W. Bush's September 20, 2001, announcement of the global war on terror was in response to the September 11, 2001, terror attacks against the United States, which led to the deaths of some 3,000 civilians, mostly Americans but representing civilians of 90 different countries.

Although the war constitutes a global effort, stretching into Asia, Africa, Europe, and the Americas, the Middle East remains a focal point of the effort. The ongoing conflict and the manner in which it has been waged has been the source of much debate. There is no widely agreed-upon estimate regarding the number of casualties during the global war on terror because it includes the invasion of Afghanistan in 2001 and the war in Iraq, as well as many acts of terrorism around the world. Some estimates, which include the U.S.-led coalition invasion of Afghanistan in 2001 and the invasion of Iraq in March 2003, claim that well over 2 million people have died in the struggle.

Following the September 11, 2001, terror attacks, the United States responded quickly and with overwhelming force against the organizations and governments that supported the terrorists. Evidence gathered by the U.S. government pointed to the al-Qaeda terrorist organization. Al-Qaeda at the time was being given aid and shelter by the Taliban regime in Afghanistan. On September 20, 2001, President George W. Bush announced to a joint session of Congress that the global war on terror would not end simply with the defeat of al-Qaeda or the overthrow of the Taliban, but only when every terrorist group and terrorist-affiliated government with a global reach had been defeated. These broad aims implied attacks on countries known to support terrorism, such as Iran and Syria. Bush further assured the American people that every means of intelligence, tool of diplomacy, financial pressure, and weapon of war would be used to defeat terrorism. He told the American people to expect a lengthy campaign. Bush also issued an ultimatum to every other nation, stating that each had to choose whether they were with the United States or against it. There would be no middle ground. Clearly Bush's pronouncements were far-reaching, yet the enemies were difficult to identify and find.

Less than 24 hours after the September 11 attacks, the North Atlantic Treaty Organization (NATO) declared the terrorist attacks of 9/11 to be against all member nations, the first time the organization had made such a pronouncement since its inception in 1949.

On October 7, 2001, U.S. and coalition (chiefly British) forces invaded Afghanistan to capture Osama bin Laden, the head of al-Qaeda, to destroy his organization, and to overthrow the Taliban government that supported him. Eventually Canada, Australia, France, and Germany, among other nations, joined that effort. However, when a U.S.-led coalition invaded Iraq in March 2003, there was considerable international opposition to this campaign being included under the rubric of the global war on terror. One problem for national leaders who supported President Bush's policies was that many of their citizens did not believe that the overthrow of Iraqi dictator Saddam Hussein was really part of the global war on terror and questioned other reasons the Bush administration stated to justify the U.S.-led invasion. International

opinion polls have shown that support for the war on terror has consistently declined since 2003, likely the result of opposition to the Bush administration's preemptive invasion of Iraq in 2003 and later revelations that Iraq possessed neither ties to al-Qaeda nor weapons of mass destruction.

The global war on terror has also been a sporadic and clandestine war since its inception in September 2001. U.S. forces were sent to Yemen and the Horn of Africa to disrupt terrorist activities, while Operation Active Endeavour is a naval operation intended to prevent terror attacks and limit the movement of terrorists in the Mediterranean. Terrorist attacks in Pakistan, Indonesia, and the Philippines led to the insertion of coalition forces into those countries as well and concerns about the situation in other Southeast Asian countries. In the United States, Congress has also passed legislation intended to help increase the effectiveness of law enforcement agencies in their search for terrorist activities. In the process, however, critics claim that Americans' civil liberties have been steadily eroded, and government admissions that the Federal Bureau of Investigation (FBI) and other agencies have engaged in wiretapping of international phone calls without requisite court orders and probable cause have caused a storm of controversy, as have the methods used to question foreign nationals.

The Bush administration also greatly increased the role of the federal government in an attempt to fight terrorism at home and abroad. Among the many new government bureaucracies formed is the Department of Homeland Security, a cabinet-level agency that counts at least 210,000 employees. The increase in the size of the government, combined with huge military expenditures—most of which are going to the Iraq War—has added to the massive U.S. budget deficits.

Proponents of the global war on terror believe that proactive measures must be taken against terrorist organizations to effectively defeat global terrorism. They believe that to meet the diverse security challenges of the 21st century, a larger, global military presence is needed. Without such a force, they argue, terrorist organizations will continue to launch strikes against innocent civilians. Many of the people argue that the United States, Great Britain, Spain, and other countries, which have been the victims of large-scale attacks, must go on the offensive against such rogue groups and that not doing so will only embolden the attackers and invite more attacks. Allowing such organizations to gain more strength may allow them to achieve their goal of imposing militant Islamist rule.

Critics of the global war on terror claim that there is no tangible enemy to defeat, as there is no single group whose defeat will bring about an end to the conflict. Thus, it is virtually impossible to know if progress is being made. They also argue that "terrorism," a tactic whose goal is to instill fear into people through violent actions, can never be truly defeated. There are also those who argue against the justification for preemptive strikes, because such action invites counterresponses and brings about the deaths of many innocent people. Many believe that the Iraqi military posed no imminent threat to the United States when coalition forces entered Iraq in 2003, but the resultant war has been disastrous for both the Iraqi and American peoples. Civil rights activists contend that measures meant to crack down on terrorist activities have infringed on the rights of American citizens as well as the rights of foreign detainees. Furthermore, critics argue that the war and the amount of spending apportioned to military endeavors negatively affects the national and world economies. Others argue that the United States should be spending time and resources on resolving the Arab-Israeli problem and trying to eradicate the desperate conditions that feed terrorism. As support for the global war on terror effort has diminished, the debate over its effectiveness has grown. Terrorist attacks have continued, and the deliberation over the best way to ensure the safety of civilian populations around the world likewise continues.

The Obama administration chose not to use the terms "global war on terror" or "long war," instead using the phrase "overseas contingency operations." White House press secretary Robert Gibbs explained that the name change was made "to denote a reaching out to many moderate parts of the world that we believe can be important in a battle against extremists." However, the term "global war on terror" is still widely used in the media and in public discourse.

On May 1, 2011 (May 2 Pakistani local time), the global war on terror reached a milestone with the death of bin Laden. After intelligence information suggested that bin Laden was in Abbottabad, Pakistan, U.S. Navy SEALs raided a compound at which he was staying, killing bin Laden and four others in the ensuing firefight. President Obama addressed the nation to announce bin Laden's death, declaring that "justice has been done," but admonishing Americans to "remain vigilant at home and abroad." Threats made by al-Qaeda and other extremist groups to seek revenge for bin Laden's killing underscored Obama's assessment that the global war on terror remains far from over.

Stephen E. Atkins

See also: Al-Qaeda; Al-Qaeda in Iraq (AQI); Bali Bombings (2002); Bin Laden, Osama; Islamic State of Iraq and Syria (ISIS)

Citations

Bacevich, Andrew J. *The New American Militarism: How Americans Are Seduced by War.* New York: Oxford University Press, 2005.

Mahajan, Rahul. *The New Crusade: America's War on Terrorism.* New York: Monthly Review, 2002.

Woodward, Bob. *Bush at War.* New York: Simon and Schuster, 2002.

Groupe Salafiste pour la Prédication et le Combat (GSPC)

The Groupe Salafiste pour la Prédication et le Combat (GSPC, or the Salafist Group for Preaching and Combat) emerged in 1996 as an offshoot of the Groupe Islamique Arme (GIA, or Armed Islamic Group) with the aim of establishing a theocratic state in Algeria. The organization split from its parent movement in protest over the latter's systematic targeting and slaughter of Algerian civilians, arguing that these actions were hurting the national Islamist cause. Estimates of the GSPC's size vary from a few hundred to several thousand. The current leader is Abu Musab Abdel Wadoud, who assumed the position of national emir after the former commander, Nabil Sahraoui, was killed in a shoot-out with the Algerian Army in June 2004.

Although the GSPC was initially founded as an organization committed to jihadist struggle in Algeria, it has gradually morphed into a full al-Qaeda affiliate. In October 2003, Sahraoui issued a communiqué asserting the group was operating at the behest of and in full accordance with Osama bin Laden and Taliban leader Mullah Omar. In line with this statement, the GSPC is alleged to have sent significant numbers of combatants to fight alongside Al-Qaeda in Iraq (AQI) as foot soldiers, suicide bombers, and mid-level commanders. Overall, it is thought that about 9 percent of all foreigners participating in the Iraq conflict hailed from Algeria, most of whom were shuttled to the country by Adil Sakir al-Mukni.

In a 2005 interview, Wadoud specifically lauded the actions of Abu Musab al-Zarqawi, then the leader of AQI, following this up with a declaration of solidarity with Islamist extremists in the Palestinian territories, Iraq, Somalia, and Chechnya. These vocal statements were given concrete expression in 2007, when the GSPC officially changed its name to Al-Qaeda in the Islamic Maghreb (AQIM).

AQIM employs conventional terrorist tactics including ambushes, bombings, shootings, and suicide strikes. Although many of the group's attacks have been relatively ineffectual, some have resulted in significant casualties. In April 2007, the group killed 23 people with twin bombings in Algiers (one of which detonated outside the prime minister's office). The following December, AQIM carried out a double suicide bombing, again in the capital, that left 41 people dead, including 17 employees of the United Nations. The organization has also demonstrated an ability to decisively hit military targets. In June 2009, for instance, 24 members of the Algerian army died after two improvised explosive devices detonated as their convoy drove by.

Despite being one of the weakest of al-Qaeda's various affiliates, AQIM retains a significant network of Islamic extremists across Europe, Africa, and Canada. These hubs have been tied to a number of attempted high-profile anti-Western attacks, including a 2002 plot to conduct a chemical bombing against the U.S. embassy in Rome. The group is also largely self-sufficient, deriving most of its income from criminal activities such as credit card theft, passport fraud, and ransoms from kidnappings (in 2003, the group received between US$5 and $10 million for the release of 32 European tourists traveling in the Algerian Sahara). Finally, it may yet benefit from the tumultuous events of the so-called Arab Spring. AQIM quickly moved to endorse the popular Libyan uprising against Colonel Muammar el-Gadhafi, and should the new government fail to deliver, it could become a beacon of support for dissatisfied Muslim radicals in the country.

Donna Bassett

See also: Al-Qaeda; Zarqawi, Abu Musab al-.

Citations

Bennhold, Katrin, and Craig Smith. "Tally in Algiers Attacks Uncertain," *The New York Times,* December 13, 2007.

Crumley, Bruce. "The Algeria Bombings: Target Europe?" *Time,* April 11, 2007, www.time.com/time/world/article/0,85 99,1609181,00.html, accessed January 6, 2012.

Hansen, Andrew, and Lauren Vriens. *Al-Qaeda in the Islamic Maghreb.* Washington, DC: Council on Foreign Relations, July 21, 2009, www.cfr.org/north-africa/al -qaeda-islamic-maghreb-aqim/p12717, accessed January 6, 2012.

Philipps, Mark. "Italy: Cops Thwart Terror Attack," CBS News, February 20, 2002, www.cbsnews.com/stories/2002/02/20 /attack/main329974.shtml, accessed April 3, 2006.

Rabasa, Angel, Peter Chalk, Kim Cragin, Sara A. Daly, Heather S. Gregg, Theodore W. Karasik, Kevin A. O'Brien, and William Rosenau. *Beyond al-Qaeda. Part 1: The Global Jihadist Movement.* Santa Monica, CA: RAND, 2006.

Smith, Craig. "At Least 67 Dead in Algiers Bombings," *The New York Times,* December 12, 2007.

Walsh, Courtney. "Italian Police Explore Al Qaeda Links in Cyanide Plot," *Christian Science Monitor,* March 7, 2002.

H

Hamas

This Islamist Palestinian organization was formally founded in 1987. The stated basis for Hamas (Harakat al-Muqawama al-Islamiyya, or Islamic Resistance Movement) is the creation of an Islamic way of life and the liberation of Palestine through Islamic resistance. Essentially, Hamas combines Islamic fundamentalism with Palestinian nationalism. Hamas gained about 30 to 40 percent support in the Palestinian population within five years because of its mobilization successes and the general popular desperation experienced by the Palestinian population during the First Intifada. In January 2006 Hamas won a majority in the Palestinian Authority's (PA) general legislative elections, which brought condemnation from Israel and a power struggle with PA president Mahmoud Abbas and his Fatah Party.

The word *Hamas* means courage, bravery, or zeal. But it is also an Arabic acronym for the Islamic Resistance Movement. Hamas is an Islamist movement, as are larger and longer-established groups such as the Muslim Brotherhood and the Palestinian Islamic Jihad. The growth of Islamist movements was delayed among Palestinians because of their status as a people without a state and the tight security controls imposed by Israel, which had strengthened the more secular nationalist expression of the Palestine Liberation Organization (PLO).

The Muslim Brotherhood, established in Egypt in 1928, had set up branches in Syria, Sudan, Libya, the Gulf states, Amman in Jordan (which influenced the West Bank),

and Gaza. However, for two decades the Muslim Brotherhood focused on its religious, educational, and social missions and was quiescent politically. That changed with the First Intifada (1987). The Muslim Brotherhood advocated *dawah*, what may be called a re-Islamization of society and thought; *adala* (social justice); and an emphasis on *hakmiyya* (the sovereignty of God, as opposed to temporal rule). The Muslim Brotherhood turned to activism against Israel after Islamic Jihad had accelerated its operations during 1986 and 1987. Eventually Islamic Jihad split into three rival organizations. The new movement coming out of the Jordanian and Egyptian Muslim Brotherhood groups, unlike Islamic Jihad, retained its major programmatic emphasis on the Islamization or re-Islamization of society.

As the new organization of Hamas emerged out of the Muslim Brotherhood, it was able to draw strength from the social work of Sheikh Ahmed Yassin, a physically disabled schoolteacher who had led the Islamic Assembly (al-Mujamma al-Islami), an organization influential in many mosques and at the Islamic University of Gaza. In December 1987, Abd al-Aziz Rantisi, who was a physician at Islamic University, and former student leaders Salah Shehade and Yahya al-Sinuwwar, who had had charge of security for the Muslim Brotherhood, formed the first unit of Hamas. Although Yassin gave his approval, as a cleric he was not directly connected to the new organization. In February 1988, as a result of a key meeting in Amman involving Sheikh Abd al-Rahman al-Khalifa (the spiritual

Supporters of the militant Islamic group Hamas celebrate their victory in Palestinian elections on January 26, 2006, in the West Bank city of Ramallah. Hamas unseated the ruling Fatah party, although it still remains committed to terrorism and revolution, repeatedly threatening Israel and consistently firing rockets into Israeli territory. (Uriel Sinai/Getty Images)

guide of the Jordanian Muslim Brotherhood), Ibrahim Ghawsha (the Hamas spokesperson and Jordanian representative), Mahmoud Zahar (a surgeon), Rantisi (acting as a West Bank representative), Jordanian parliament members, and the hospital director, the Brotherhood granted formal recognition to Hamas.

In 1988, Hamas issued its charter. The charter condemns world Zionism and the efforts to isolate Palestine, defines the mission of the organization, and locates that mission within Palestinian, Arab, and Islamic elements. It does not condemn the West or non-Muslims but does condemn aggression against the Palestinian people, arguing for a defensive jihad. It also calls for fraternal relations with the other Palestinian nationalist groups. Hamas is headed by a political bureau with representatives for military

affairs, foreign affairs, finance, propaganda, and internal security. An advisory council, or Majlis al-Shura, is linked to the political bureau, which is also connected with all Palestinian communities; Hamas's social and charitable groups, elected members, and district committees; and the leadership in Israeli prisons. Major attacks against Israel have been carried out by the Izz al-Din al-Qassam Brigades of Hamas. They also developed the Qassam rocket used to attack Israeli civilian settlements in the Negev Desert. However, much of Hamas's activity during the First Intifada consisted of its participation within more broadly based popular demonstrations and locally coordinated efforts at resistance, countering Israeli raids, enforcing opening of businesses, and the like.

Hamas greatly expanded by 1993 but decried the autonomy agreement between the Israelis and the PLO in Jericho and the Gaza Strip as too limited a gain. By the time of the first elections for the PA's Council in 1996, Hamas was caught in a dilemma. It had gained popularity as a resistance organization, but Oslo 1 and Oslo 2 (the Taba Accord of September 28, 1995) were meant to end the intifada. The elections would further strengthen the PLO, but if Hamas boycotted the elections and most people voted, then it would be even more isolated. Finally, Hamas's leadership rejected participation but without ruling it out in the future, and this gave the organization the ability to continue protesting Oslo. When suicide attacks were launched to protest Israeli violence against Palestinians, Hamas was blamed for inspiring or organizing the suicide bombers, whether or not its operatives or those of the more radical Islamic Jihad were involved.

Hamas funds an extensive array of social services aimed at ameliorating the plight of Palestinians. It provides funding for hospitals, schools, mosques, orphanages, food distribution, and aid to the families of Palestinian prisoners who, numbering more than 10,000 people, constituted an important political force. Given the PA's frequent inability to provide for such needs, Hamas stepped into the breach and in so doing endeared itself to a large number of Palestinians. Until its electoral triumph in January 2006, Hamas received funding from a number of sources. Palestinians living abroad provided money, as did a number of private donors in the wealthy Arab oil states such as Saudi Arabia, Bahrain, and Kuwait, and other states in the West.

Iran has been a significant donor to Hamas. Much aid was directed to renovation of the Palestinian territories and was badly needed, and unfortunately a great deal of that rebuilding was destroyed in the Israeli

campaign in the West Bank in 2002, which in turn was intended to combat the suicide bombings. Over the years, the Israel Defense Forces (IDF) has carried out targeted eliminations of a number of Hamas leaders. These include Shehade (July 23, 2002), Dr. Ibrahim al-Makadmeh (March 3, 2003), Ismail Abu Shanab (August 21, 2003), Yassin (March 22, 2004), and Rantisi (April 17, 2004). Hamas had two sets of leaders, those inside the West Bank and Gaza and those outside. The West Bank leadership is divided along the general structure into political, charitable, student, and military activities. The political leadership is usually targeted for arrests because its members can be located, unlike the secret military units. That leadership has organized very effectively before and since PLO leader Yasser Arafat's death, and has become more popular than the PLO in the West Bank, an unexpected development. Although Arafat was quickly succeeded by Abbas as the PLO leader, a sizable number of Palestinians had already begun to identify with Hamas, mainly because it was able to accomplish what the PA could not, namely, to provide for the everyday needs of the people.

Hamas won the legislative elections in January 2006. Locals had expected a victory in Gaza but not in the West Bank. Nonetheless, both Israel and the United States steadfastly refused to recognize the Palestinian government now under the control of Hamas. The United States cut off $420 million, and the European Union (EU) cut off $600 million in aid to the PA's Hamas-led government, which created difficulties for ordinary Palestinians. The loss of this aid halted the delivery of supplies to hospitals and ended other services in addition to stopping the payment of salaries. To prevent total collapse, the United States and the EU promised relief funds, but these were not allowed to go through the PA. The cutoff in funds was designed to discourage Palestinian support for Hamas. On March 17, 2007, Abbas brokered a Palestinian unity government that included members of both Hamas and Fatah in which Hamas leader Ismail Haniyeh became prime minister. Yet in May, armed clashes between Hamas and Fatah escalated, and on June 14, Hamas seized control of Gaza. Abbas promptly dissolved the Hamas-led unity government and declared a state of emergency. On June 18, having been assured of EU support, he dissolved the National Security Council and swore in an emergency Palestinian government. That same day, the United States ended its 15-month embargo on the PA and resumed aid in an effort to strengthen Abbas's government, now limited to the West Bank. On June 19, Abbas cut off all ties and dialogue with Hamas, pending the return of Gaza. In a move to strengthen the perceived moderate Abbas, on July 1, 2007, Israel restored financial ties to the PA.

In early 2008, rocket attacks on Israel launched from the Gaza Strip began to escalate. Although a six-month cease-fire agreement brought relative calm during the latter half of the year, the agreement's expiration on December 19 saw the immediate renewal of hostilities. Hamas, citing Israel's continued refusal to lift its blockade of the Gaza Strip, began launching rockets the next day. As a result, on December 27, the IDF launched a full-scale assault, code-named Operation Cast Lead, on the area. After the deaths of more than 1,000 Palestinians and intense international pressure, the Israelis halted their campaign on January 18. It was clear, however, that an Israeli-Palestinian peace was still far in the future. In November 2012, violence flared anew between Israel and Hamas, when the Israelis launched Operation Pillar of Defense, designed to punish Hamas for some 100 rocket attacks

against Israeli civilians and other acts of provocation on Israeli territory. Hamas claimed that its attacks were in retaliation for the Israeli blockade of Gaza as well as its continued occupation of East Jerusalem and the West Bank. The operation, comprised chiefly of air strikes against Hamas weapons depots and Hamas military leaders, resulted in the death of Ahmed Jabari, head of Hamas's military establishment.

More than 1,500 strikes occurred within the Gaza Strip, with Hamas claiming 79 militant deaths, 53 civilian deaths, and one police officer killed. Human Rights Watch later claimed that both Hamas and Israel had violated the laws of modern warfare during the seven-day clash. The Fatah-Hamas break was not substantially mended until early June 2014, when Abbas announced the formation of another unity government. However, unlike the 2007 government, this one did not include any Hamas members in the cabinet. Hamas agreed to support the government without direct participation in it. The United States and most of its allies cautiously backed the new set up, but Israel denounced the government because of its ties to Hamas, which it continues to view as a terrorist group. A renewed conflict between Israel and Hamas in July and August 2014, which resulted in substantial bloodshed, unraveled Abbas's unity government, however. On July 17, Israel escalated the conflict as it sent ground forces into the Gaza Strip and Israeli warplanes continued to hammer Hamas targets.

On August 26, Hamas and Israel agreed to an open-ended cease-fire. It is estimated that as many as 2,200 Palestinians in Gaza died during the 50-day conflict. The precise number of civilian deaths is contested, but preliminary estimates range from 700 to 1,675. Israel reported 66 soldiers and 8 civilians killed. Since late 2014, efforts to achieve a full reconciliation between Hamas and Fatah have waxed and waned, and the "unity" government created in 2014 remained unified in name only. Talks between Hamas and Fatah occurred during the winter of 2016, but they yielded no concrete results as Fatah leaders insisted that Hamas turn over control of the Gaza Strip to Fatah. Meanwhile, in May 2015 Amnesty International issued a report asserting that Hamas was guilty of carrying out extrajudicial arrests, kidnappings, and murders against Palestinians suspected of aiding Israel during the 2014 Israeli-Hamas conflict. The same report also accused Hamas of torturing Palestinians; many of the victims were members of the rival Fatah political party.

In 2016, Reporters Without Borders charged Hamas with press censorship and having tortured journalists it considers to be subversive. Recently, Egypt, once a supporter of Hamas, disavowed the Palestinian group. Qatar has since stepped in to fulfill the support role once held by Egypt. Iran, meanwhile, has demonstrated inconsistent support for Hamas. The Turkish government has also sought to aid Hamas, much to the consternation of Israel and the United States. In 2017, Hamas revised its charter and presented a slightly softer tone on Israel, yet it is too early to discern whether this represents a real strategic shift or is more of a rhetorical feint deigned to buy time and support.

Harry Raymond Hueston II, Paul G. Pierpaoli Jr., and Sherifa Zuhur

See also: Al-Fatah; Hezbollah; Jihad; Palestine Liberation Organization (PLO)

Citations

Clarke, Colin. "Hamas's Strategic Rebranding," *Foreign Affairs,* May 17, 2017.

Reeve, Simon. *The New Jackals.* Boston, MA: Northeastern University Press, 1999.

Souryal, Sam. *Islam, Islamic Law, and the Turn to Violence.* Huntsville, TX: Office of International Criminal Justice, Sam Houston State University, 2004.

"Straight from the Mouth of Hamas." Jerusalem Media and Communication Center, March 17, 2005.

Haqqani Network

The Haqqani network is an Islamic extremist organization operating in the Afghan provinces of Paktia, Paktika, and Khost and the North Waziristan (NWA) region of Pakistan. The group is aligned with the Afghan and Pakistani Taliban (TTP) and is known for conducting spectacular terrorist attacks against the Afghan national government and coalition forces. Jalaluddin Haqqani formed the group in the 1980s and his son, Sirajuddin Haqqani, has led the organization since 2005.

Jalaluddin Haqqani was among the first Afghan Islamic extremists to take up arms against the Afghan government after Mohammed Daud's 1973 coup. Haqqani left Afghanistan after the coup to receive training and assistance from the Zulfikar Ali Bhutto government in Pakistan. Haqqani fought the Afghan government and later the invading Soviet forces until the latter's withdrawal in 1989.

During the 1980s, the Haqqani Network received extensive arms and training from the Pakistani Directorate for Inter-services Intelligence (ISI) and the American Central Intelligence Agency. Haqqani and the ISI have maintained a close working relationship ever since. During the anti-Soviet insurgency, Haqqani established a series of training and support bases in North Waziristan, Pakistan, with the help of the ISI.

After initially opposing the Afghan Taliban regime, Haqqani aligned with the group in 1995 under pressure from the ISI and became one of the Taliban's most effective commanders. In recognition of his power and influence, the Taliban appointed him minister of tribal and frontier affairs in 1998, but largely sidelined him from real decision-making power. After the American invasion in October 2001, Haqqani escaped into Pakistan and reconstituted the Haqqani Network, vowing to wage jihad with the Taliban against the United States. The Haqqani Network continues to align with the Taliban while also conducting independent operations.

The Haqqani draws its support from several sources, the most important of which is the Pakistani government. The Haqqanis provide a link to the TTP and brokered a truce between the Pakistani government and the TTP in December 2007. The Haqqanis also help Pakistan to destabilize Indian encroachments into Afghanistan. In return for these services, the Pakistani Army and ISI provide the Haqqani Network a safe haven in NWA to launch attacks into Afghanistan and recruit fighters from local tribes.

The other source of support comes from Jalaluddin Haqqani's connections with foreign jihad groups. The Haqqani Network was the first mujahidin group to incorporate Arab volunteers in 1987. This resulted in a close relationship with Arab sponsors, including al-Qaeda leader Osama bin Laden. In 2001 the Haqqani Network served as key conduit for the escape of al-Qaeda operatives into Pakistan after the U.S.-led invasion. These groups assist the Haqqani Network in financing and training recruits and launching attacks in Afghanistan.

The final source of support is Jalaluddin Haqqani's reputation as an original and authentic mujahidin fighter, his military prowess, and religious devotion. This has allowed the Haqqani Network to co-opt or replace tribal leaders in their areas of operation, and gain access to the highest decision-making counsels of the Taliban. It is uncertain if Jalaluddin's alleged death in 2014 will diminish the group's influence, as his son Sirajuddin is not as respected as his father.

In January 2003, Haqqani Network commenced offensive operations in the group's main area of operations, in the areas of Paktia, Paktika, and Khost provinces dominated by the Zadran tribe. This area known as the "Zadran Arch" provides an access corridor from the group's bases in Pakistan into southeastern Afghanistan. The group specializes in improvised explosive device attacks and was one of the first insurgent groups to adopt the use of suicide bombers in Afghanistan. The group has expanded its operations north toward Kabul and has conducted a series of spectacular attacks against government and coalition targets in the capital, starting with the 2008 Serena Hotel attack. The Haqqani Network has also reportedly been involved in several high-profile kidnappings, including that of *New York Times* reporter David Rohde and U.S. Army Sergeant Bowe Bergdahl.

Alex Stephenson

See also: Al-Qaeda; Taliban; Tehrik-i-Taliban Pakistan (TTP)

Citations

Brown, Vahid, and Don Rassler. *Fountainhead of Jihad: The Haqqani Nexus, 1973–2012.* New York: Oxford University Press, 2013.

Dressler, Jeffrey. "The Haqqani Network: A Strategic Threat," *Institute for the Study of War,* March 29, 2012, www .understandingwar.org/sites/default/files /Haqqani_StrategicThreatweb_29MAR_0 .pdf, accessed January 29, 2016.

Giustozzi, Antonio, ed. *Decoding the New Taliban: Insights from the Afghan Field.* New York: Columbia University Press, 2009.

"Haqqani Network Financing: The Evolution of an Industry—Origins and Financial Evolution, Key Financial Personalities, Sources of Income, Pakistani Support," *Defense Technical Information Center,* July 3, 2012, www .dtic.mil/dtic/tr/fulltext/u2/a562872.pdf, accessed January 29, 2016.

Hezbollah

Founded in Lebanon in 1984, Hezbollah is a Lebanese radical Shia Islamist organization and, along with the Amal Movement, a principal political party representing the Shia community in Lebanon. There have been other smaller parties by the name of Hezbollah in eastern Saudi Arabia and Iraq, and their activities have been mistakenly or deliberately associated with the Lebanese party. The Lebanese Hezbollah also operates a number of social service programs, schools, hospitals, clinics, and housing assistance programs to Lebanese Shiites. (Some Christians also attended Hezbollah's schools and ran on their electoral lists.)

One of the core founding groups of Hezbollah, meaning the "Party of God," actually fled from Iraq when Saddam Hussein cracked down on the Shia Islamic movement in the shrine cities. Lebanese as well as Iranians and Iraqis studied in Najaf and Karbala, and some 100 of these students returned to Beirut and became disciples of Sayyid Muhammad Husayn Fadlallah, a Lebanese cleric who was also educated in Najaf.

Meanwhile, in the midst of the ongoing civil war in Lebanon, a Shia resistance movement developed in response to Israel's invasion in 1982. Israel's first invasion of southern Lebanon had occurred in 1978, but the invasion of 1982 was more devastating to the region, with huge numbers of casualties and prisoners taken and peasants displaced.

The earliest political movement of Lebanese Shia was established under the cleric Musa al-Sadr and was known as the Movement of the Dispossessed. The Shia were the largest but poorest sect in Lebanon and suffered from discrimination, underrepresentation, and a dearth of government programs or services that, despite some efforts by President Fuad Shihab, persist to this day. After al-Sadr's disappearance on a trip to Libya, his nonmilitaristic movement was subsumed by the Amal Party, which had a military wing and fought in the civil war. However, a wing of Amal, Islamic Amal led by Husayn al-Musawi, split off after it accused Amal of not resisting the Israeli invasion.

On the grounds of resistance to Israel (and its Lebanese proxies), Islamic Amal made contact with Iran's ambassador to Damascus, Akbar Mohtashimi, who had once found refuge as an Iranian dissident in the Palestinian camps in Lebanon. Iran sent between 1,000 and 1,200 Revolutionary Guards to the Bekaa Valley to aid an Islamic resistance to Israel. At a Lebanese Army barracks near Baalbek, the Revolutionary Guards began training Shia fighters identifying with the resistance, or Islamic Amal.

Fadlallah's followers now included displaced Beiruti Shia and displaced southerners, and some coordination between his group and the others began to emerge in 1984. The other strand of Hezbollah came from the Islamic Resistance in southern Lebanon led by Sheikh Ragheb Harb, the imam of the village of Jibshit who was killed by the Israelis in 1984. In February 1985, Harb's supporters met and announced the formation of Hezbollah, led by Sheikh Subhi al-Tufayli.

Another militant Shia group was the Organization of the Islamic Jihad, led by Imad Mughniyah. It was responsible for the 1983 bombings of the U.S. and French peacekeeping forces' barracks and the U.S. embassy and its annex in Beirut. This group received some support from the elements in Baalbek. Hezbollah, however, is to this day accused of bombings committed by Mughniyah's group. Although it had not yet officially formed, the degree of coordination or sympathy between the various militant groups operative in 1982 can only be ascertained on the level of individuals. Hezbollah stated officially that it did not commit the bombing of U.S. and French forces, but it also did not condemn those who did. Regardless, Hezbollah's continuing resistance in the south earned it great popularity with the Lebanese, whose army had split and had failed to defend the country against the Israelis.

With the Taif Agreement the Lebanese Civil War should have ended, but in 1990 fighting broke out, and the next year Syria mounted a major campaign in Lebanon. The Taif Agreement did not end sectarianism or solve the problem of Muslim underrepresentation in government. Militias other than Hezbollah disbanded, but because the Lebanese government did not assent to the Israeli occupation of southern Lebanon, Hezbollah's militia remained in being.

The leadership of Hezbollah changed over time and adapted to Lebanon's realities. The multiplicity of sects in Lebanon meant that an Islamic republic there was impractical, and as a result Hezbollah ceased trying to impose the strictest Islamic rules and focused more on gaining the trust of the Lebanese community. The party's Shura Council was made up of seven clerics until 1989; from 1989 to 1991, it included three laypeople and four clerics; and since 2001 it has been entirely composed of clerics. An advisory politburo has from 11 to 14 members. Secretary-General Abbas al-Musawi took over from al-Tufayli in 1991. Soon after the Israelis assassinated Musawi. Hassan Nasrallah, who had studied in Najaf and briefly in Qum, took over as secretary-general.

In 1985, as a consequence of armed resistance in southern Lebanon, Israel withdrew into the so-called security zone. Just as resistance from Hezbollah provided Israel with the ready excuse to attack Lebanon, Israel's continued presence in the south funded Lebanese resentment of Israel and support for Hezbollah's armed actions. In 1996 the Israelis mounted Operation Grapes of Wrath against Hezbollah in south Lebanon, pounding the entire region from the air for a two-week period.

Subhi al-Tufayli, the former Hezbollah secretary-general, opposed the party's decision to participate in the elections of 1992 and 1996. He launched the Revolt of the Hungry, demanding food and jobs for the impoverished people of the upper Bekaa, and was expelled from Hezbollah. He then began armed resistance, and the Lebanese Army was called in to defeat his faction.

In May 2000, after suffering repeated attacks and numerous casualties, Israel withdrew its forces from southern Lebanon, a move that was widely interpreted as a victory for Hezbollah, and boosted its popularity hugely in Lebanon and throughout the Arab world. Hezbollah disarmed in some areas of the country but refused to do so in the border area because it contests the Jewish state's control of the Shebaa Farms region.

Sheikh Fadlallah survived an assassination attempt in 1985 allegedly arranged by the United States. He illustrates Lebanonization of the Shia Islamist movement. He had moved away from Ayatollah Khomeini's doctrine of government by cleric (*wilayat al-faqih*), believing that it is not suitable in the Lebanese context, and called for dialogue with Christians. Fadlallah's stance is similar to that of Ayatollah Sistani in Iraq. He, like some of the Iraqi clerics, called for the restoration of Friday communal prayer for the Shia. He has also issued numerous reforming views, for example, decrying the abuse of women by men. Fadlallah is not, however, closely associated with Hezbollah's day-to-day policies.

Some Israeli and American sources charge that Iran directly conducts the affairs of Hezbollah and provides it with essential funding. Although at one time Iranian support was crucial to Hezbollah, the Revolutionary Guards were withdrawn from Lebanon for some time. The party's social and charitable services claimed independence in the late 1990s. They are supported by a volunteer service, provided by medical personnel and other professionals, and by local and external donations. Iran has certainly provided weapons to Hezbollah. Some, apparently through the Iran-Contra deal, found their way to Lebanon, and Syria has also provided freedom of movement across its common border with Lebanon as well as supply routes for weapons.

Since 2000, Hezbollah has disputed Israeli control over the Shebaa Farms area, which Israel claims belongs to Syria but Syria says belongs to Lebanon. Meanwhile, pressure began to build against Syrian influence in Lebanon with the constitutional amendment to allow Émile Lahoud (a Christian and pro-Syrian) an additional term. Assassinations of anti-Syrian, mainly Christian, figures had also periodically occurred. The turning point was the assassination of Prime Minister Rafik Hariri in February 2005. This led to significant international pressure on Syria to withdraw from Lebanon, although pro-Syrian elements remained throughout the country.

Hezbollah now found itself threatened by a new coalition of Christians and Hariri-supporting Sunnis who sought to deny its aim of greater power for the Shia in government. The two sides in this struggle were known as the March 14 Alliance, for the date of a large anti-Syrian rally, and the March 8 Alliance, for a prior and even larger rally consisting of Hezbollah and anti-Syrian Christian general Michel Aoun. These factions have been sparring since 2005, and in some ways since the civil war.

Demanding a response to the Israeli campaign against Gaza in the early summer of 2006, Hezbollah forces killed three Israeli soldiers and kidnapped two others, planning to hold them for a prisoner exchange as has occurred in the past. The Israel Defense Forces (IDF) responded with a massive campaign of air strikes throughout Lebanon, and not just on Hezbollah positions. Hezbollah responded by launching missiles into Israel, forcing much of that country's northern population into shelters. In this open warfare, the United States backed Israel. At the conflict's end, Sheikh Nasrallah's popularity surged in Lebanon and in the Arab world, and even members of the March 14 Alliance were furious over the destruction of the fragile peace in post–civil war Lebanon. Hezbollah offered cash assistance to the people of southern Lebanon displaced by the fighting and those in the southern districts of Beirut who had been struck there by the Israelis. They disbursed this aid immediately. The government offered assistance to other Lebanese, but this assistance was delayed.

In September 2006, Hezbollah and its ally Aoun began calling for a new national unity government. The existing government, dominated by the March 14 Alliance forces, refused to budge, however. Five Shia members and one Christian member of the Lebanese cabinet also resigned in response to disagreements over the proposed tribunal to investigate Syrian culpability in the Hariri assassination. At the same time, Hezbollah and Aoun argued for the ability of a sizable opposition group in the cabinet to veto government decisions. Hezbollah and Aoun called for public protests, which began as gigantic sit-ins and demonstrations in the downtown district of Beirut in December 2006. There was one violent clash in December and another in January of 2007 between the supporters of the two March alliances. Meanwhile, the United Nations Interim Force in Lebanon (UNIFIL) has taken up position in southern Lebanon. Its mission, however, is not to disarm Hezbollah but only to prevent armed clashes between it and Israel.

In 2008, when a unity government took hold in Lebanon, Hezbollah and its allies captured 11 of 30 cabinet seats, giving the coalition the power to veto. Beginning in 2012, amid the ongoing Syrian Civil War, Hezbollah decided to aid Bashar al-Assad's government in its fight against antigovernment rebels. This resulted in several Israeli air strikes against convoys allegedly bound for Hezbollah fighters; the convoys included antiaircraft missiles. Hezbollah's involvement in the Syrian Civil War has raised concerns that the conflict might further destabilize Lebanon. Meanwhile, Hezbollah and its affiliates have been blamed for several terror attacks, including a 2012 bus bombing in Bulgaria that left six people dead. In 2009, Egypt uncovered and foiled a Hezbollah plot that would have attacked Egyptian and Israeli targets in the Sinai Peninsula. In 2011, Hezbollah brought down the 2008 government; similarly, it also brought down the replacement government in 2013, following a disagreement over the makeup of Lebanese security forces. In the summer of 2014, the group strongly supported Hamas in its conflict with Israel in the Gaza Strip.

In January 2015, Hezbollah militants attacked an Israeli military convoy at Shebaa Farms, along the Syrian-Lebanese border. The attack, which Hezbollah claimed was retaliation for an Israeli assault on a Hezbollah convoy in southern Syria, killed two Israeli soldiers and wounded seven others. Meanwhile, Hezbollah's support of Assad's government has continued unabated; since 2015, the group has also been fighting elements of the Islamic State (IS), which seized large swaths of Syrian territory beginning in 2014. Hezbollah has also been working closely with Iran, which has significantly increased its involvement in the Syrian Civil War. In May 2016, a top-level Hezbollah military commander, Mustafa Badreddine, was killed in an air strike near the Damascus airport. Although the media in Lebanon blamed his death on an Israeli air strike, Hezbollah insisted that anti-Assad rebels had killed Badreddine. As of June 2016, Hezbollah held 12 seats in the Lebanese Parliament and 2 posts in the Lebanese Cabinet.

Harry Raymond Hueston II and Sherifa Zuhur

See also: Hamas; Improvised Explosive Devices; Mahdi Army

Citations

Byman, Daniel. "Should Hezbollah Be Next?" *Foreign Affairs* (November–December 2003): 54–66, www.foreignaffairs.com/articles/lebanon/2003-11-01/should-hezbollah-be-next.

Macleod, Scott. "Hizballah's Herald," *Time,* February 2005.

Ranstorp, Magnus. *Hizballah in Lebanon: The Politics of the Western Hostage Crisis.* New York: St. Martin's, 1997.

Homegrown Terrorism

Homegrown terrorism is a distinct category of terrorism that refers to terrorism perpetrated by individuals who are born in (and usually reside in) the country they are attacking. This differs from transnational terrorism, which involves either the crossing of international borders to conduct attacks, or terrorist groups like al-Qaeda and ISIS that have members from countries throughout the globe.

In the United States, the authorities have referred to numerous acts as homegrown terrorism. The Oklahoma City bombing was perpetrated by an American citizen, Timothy McVeigh. Similarly, the Unabomber, Ted Kaczynski, was a U.S. citizen. Since 2009, there have been several high-profile homegrown terrorist attacks in the United States.

In June 2009, Carlos Bledsoe, a Memphis native who adopted the Muslim name Abdulhakim Mujahid Muhammad after converting to Islam, conducted a drive-by shooting on an Army recruiting center in Little Rock, Arkansas. One soldier was killed and another was wounded in the attack.

In November 2009, Army Major and psychiatrist Nidal Hasan opened fire at Fort Hood, Texas, killing 13 people at the Army base near Kileen. Hasan was heavily

U.S. Army col. John Rossi speaks to the media about U.S. Army major Nidal Malik Hasan who went on a shooting rampage on November 6, 2009, in Killeen, Texas. Hasan, an army psychiatrist, killed 13 people and wounded 30 in a shooting at the military base at Fort Hood. Hasan was inspired by jihadist propaganda and was in direct contact with AQAP terrorist Anwar al-Awlaki prior to committing this attack. (Joe Raedle/Getty Images)

influenced by and likely radicalized under the direction of AQAP chief propagandist Anwar al-Awlaki. Hasan was raised in Virginia by parents of Palestinian descent.

Between April and June of 2014, a Muslim convert named Ali Muhammad Brown, killed four people in three separate locations in Washington State and New Jersey. Brown claimed that he carried out the killings in retaliation for U.S. military action abroad, particularly in Afghanistan, Iraq, and Syria.

In September 2014 in Moore, Oklahoma, Alton Nolen beheaded a female coworker at Vaughan Foods. Although the FBI classified this as a case of workplace violence, Nolen had posted images and statements on his Facebook account that were supportive of Osama bin Laden, al-Qaeda, and Salafi-jihadist ideology.

In July 2015 in Chattanooga, Tennessee, Mohammad Youssef Abdulazeez, born in Kuwait but raised his entire life in Tennessee, shot and killed four marines and one sailor near a Navy reserve center.

In December 2015 in San Bernardino, California, Illinois native Syed Rizwan Farook and his Pakistani-born wife, Tashfeen Malik, conducted a murderous rampage at a holiday office party, gunning down 14 people after later being killed themselves by police responding to the scene. Both Farook and his wife had made supportive statements about ISIS in the past, including on social media.

In June 2016 in Orlando, Florida, Omar Mateen, born on Long Island to parents from Afghanistan, murdered 49 people at Pulse, a gay nightclub, before pledging allegiance to ISIS leader Abu Bakr al-Baghdadi. Mateen was shot dead by police.

In September 2016, Ahmad Khan Rahami who was born in Afghanistan but became a naturalized citizen in 2011, placed explosives in two separate locations in New York and New Jersey, injuring 29 people.

In August 2017, right-wing white supremacists staged a rally in Charlottesville, Virginia, protesting the removal of a statue of Confederate General Robert E. Lee. During the protests, James Alex Fields Jr. rammed his vehicle into a crowd, killing one civilian and injuring over a dozen others.

Although Europe has been attacked by both homegrown terrorists as well as terrorists trained and dispatched by ISIS leaders in the Middle East, over the past decade and a half, all of the terrorist attacks in the United States have been perpetrated by American citizens or legal permanent residents. As such, much of the emphasis on counterterrorism has focused on countering violent extremism, or CVE, because those who have consistently attacked the United States have come from within its own borders, not from outside of the country.

Colin P. Clarke

See also: Global War on Terror; Islamic State of Iraq and Syria (ISIS); Jihad; Lone Wolf Attacks

Citations

Bergen, Peter. "The Real Terror Threat in America is Homegrown," *CNN*, June 13, 2016.

Dorell, Oren. "From Fort Hood to Pulse Night Club: A List of Homegrown Terror in the U.S.," *USA Today*, March 23, 2017.

Jenkins, Brian Michael. *Stray Dogs and Virtual Armies: Radicalization and Recruitment to Jihadist Terrorism in the United States Since 9/11*. Santa Monica, CA: RAND Corp., 2011, OP-343-RC.

King, Colbert I. "The U.S. Has a Homegrown Terrorist Problem—and It's Coming from the Right," *Washington Post*, May 26, 2017.

I

Improvised Explosive Devices

Improvised explosive devices (IEDs) have been employed in warfare almost since the introduction of gunpowder. They remain the weapon of choice for insurgent and resistance groups that lack the numerical strength and firepower to conduct conventional operations against an opponent. IEDs are the contemporary form of booby traps employed in World War II and the Vietnam War. Traditionally, they are used primarily against enemy armor and thin-skinned vehicles. A water cart filled with explosives was employed in a futile effort to assassinate Napoleon Bonaparte in Paris as he traveled to the opera on Christmas Eve 1800. The emperor escaped injury, but the blast killed the little girl the conspirators paid to hold the horse's bridle and killed or maimed a dozen other people.

In more recent times, IEDs have been employed against civilian targets by Basque separatists and the Irish Republican Army. Molotov cocktails, or gasoline bombs, are one form of IED. The largest, most deadly IEDs in history were the U.S. jetliners that al-Qaeda hijacked and used to attack the World Trade Center in New York City and the Pentagon in Virginia on September 11, 2001.

IEDs became one of the chief weapons insurgents and terrorists employed against Israel as well as the chief weapon used by insurgents during the Iraq War (2003–2011) to attack U.S. forces and Iraqi police and to carry out sectarian violence. Extremists and insurgents also used them in the Afghanistan War beginning in 2001. The simplest types of IEDs are hand grenades, rigged artillery shells, or bombs triggered by a trip wire or simple movement. It might be as simple as a grenade with its pin pulled and handle held down by the weight of a corpse. When the corpse is raised, the grenade explodes. Bombs and artillery shells are also used as IEDs. Such weapons may be exploded remotely by wireless detonators in the form of garage door openers, cell phones, two-way radios, or infrared motion sensors. More powerful explosives and even shaped charges can be used to attack armored vehicles. Casualty totals are one way to judge the effectiveness of a military operation, and growing casualties from IEDs in the 1980s and 1990s induced the Israeli Army to withdraw from southern Lebanon. Today, they remain the weapon of choice for terrorists of all stripes, in the Middle East and beyond.

Spencer C. Tucker

See also: Lone Wolf Attacks; Mahdi Army; Provisional Irish Republican Army (PIRA)

Citations

Crippen, James B. *Improvised Explosive Devices (IED)*. New York: CRC Press, 2007.

DeForest, M. J. *Principles of Improvised Explosive Devices*. Boulder, CO: Paladin, 1984.

Tucker, Stephen. *Terrorist Explosive Sourcebook: Countering Terrorist Use of Improvised Explosive Devices*. Boulder, CO: Paladin, 2005.

Islamic Movement of Uzbekistan

The Islamic Movement of Uzbekistan (IMU or Harakatul Islamiyyah of Uzbekistan) was founded in 1998 as a coalition of militants drawn from Uzbekistan and several other Central Asian regions, including Chechnya, Afghanistan, Pakistan, Kyrgyzstan, and Tajikistan. It is a large and well-funded terrorist organization that seeks to overthrow the secular and authoritarian regime of Islam Karimov and replace it with a fundamentalist Muslim state based on the full implementation of sharia law. The group has a close relationship with the Afghan Taliban, and until the overthrow of Mullah Omar's government by the United States in 2001, many of its fighters were based in and trained at camps controlled by the IMU.

Under the leadership of Takhir Yuldashev, the IMU declared a jihad on Uzbekistan in 1999 and commenced a systematic campaign of kidnappings, assassinations, random shootings, and bombings. That same year the group's military commander, Juma Namangani, launched two successful offensives into the heart of Uzbek territory, projecting the group into the spotlight of regional and international publicity.

The IMU has been implicated in a number of terrorist attacks in Uzbekistan, including a 1999 car bomb in Tashkent that killed 16 civilians (and only narrowly missed Karimov); the 1999 abduction of a group of Japanese geologists; the August 2000 kidnapping of four U.S. mountain climbers; and various violent acts against civilian targets that reportedly have little to do with the rebels' ostensible cause. In September 2000, the United States proscribed the group as a designated foreign terrorist organization.

Although much of the group's early activity was orchestrated out of the contested Fergana Valley, where it reportedly controls several Central Asian drug-smuggling routes, it has increasingly reoriented its operational focus to regions located in Pakistan's Federally Administered Tribal Areas. These militants continue to espouse a highly fundamentalist agenda and are known to have participated in Taliban attacks directed against Allied forces in Afghanistan, as well as in al-Qaeda and Tehrik-i-Taliban Pakistan (TTP) suicide bombings in the Northwest Frontier and Sindh Provinces. Although the IMU does retain a presence in Fergana, most of these combatants now act as straight narco-syndicates, merely using religion as a justification for their criminal activities.

In November 2000, Namangani was sentenced to death in absentia for the 1999 Tashkent bombing. By then, he had reportedly fled to Afghanistan, where he was a close associate of Osama bin Laden. In November 2001, press sources reported that Namangani had been killed during fighting between Taliban soldiers and the U.S.-backed Northern Alliance in Mazar-e Sharif, Afghanistan. Yuldashev continued to lead the IMU from a hideout along the Pakistani-Afghan border until his death from a U.S. drone attack in October 2009.

Edward F. Mickolus

See also: Al-Qaeda; Global War on Terror; Taliban; Tehrik-i-Taliban Pakistan (TTP)

Citations

Burgess, Mark. "Terrorism: The Islamic Movement of Uzbekistan," Center for Defense Information, Washington, DC, March 25, 2002.

Child, Greg. *Over the Edge*. New York: Villand, 2002.

Christian, Caryl. "In the Hot Zone," *Newsweek* (Atlantic ed.), October 8, 2001.

Rotar, Igor. "The Islamic Movement of Uzbekistan: A Resurgent IMU?" *Jamestown Terrorism Monitor* 1, no. 8 (2003).

Yakubov, Oleg. *Pack of Wolves*. Moscow: Veche, 2000.

Islamic State of Iraq and Syria (ISIS)

The Islamic State of Iraq and Syria (ISIS), variously known as the Islamic State of Iraq and the Levant, or the Islamic State, is a radical, Sunni jihadist organization currently active in Iraq and Syria. ISIS is a successor organization of Al-Qaeda in Iraq and was formally established in 2006, at which time it became known as the Islamic State of Iraq (ISI). ISIS is currently led by Abu Bakr al-Baghdadi, an Iraqi born in Samara in 1971 who took part in the post-2003 Iraqi insurgency following the Anglo-American–led invasion of Iraq in March 2003; he was also a member of Al-Qaeda in Iraq. Al-Baghdadi has been the acknowledged leader of ISIS since 2010.

Origins of ISIS

As with Al-Qaeda in Iraq, ISIS sought to expel all foreign troops and personnel from Iraq and wage war against the Shia-dominated, secular government of Iraq. These organizations have not only battled coalition and Iraqi armed forces, but they have also engaged in myriad acts of terrorism and war crimes that have frequently involved civilians. ISIS, however, had ambitions beyond these activities. It sought to establish an Islamic regime, based on strict sharia law, within Iraq and Syria. It even hoped eventually to extend its reach into the Levant, which encompasses Lebanon, Palestine, and Jordan. By 2010, al-Baghdadi had emerged as a top leader of Al-Qaeda in Iraq. However, his vision of founding an Islamic emirate clashed with the more modest goals of that group, and so he began to assemble his own rebel group. Thereafter, he co-opted several other jihadist organizations, most notably the Mujahideen Shura Council (MSC), and began recruiting followers who shared his more expansive vision. Observers believed that al-Baghdadi enjoyed success in recruiting fighters (many are foreigners, and some even hailed from western Europe and the United States) because he was a charismatic military strategist and battlefield commander rather than a theologian.

ISIS Control of Iraqi and Syrian Territory

By the spring of 2013, ISIS had become a potent force in both Iraq and Syria. In Syria, ISIS has taken full advantage of the bloody civil war there, which has been raging since early 2011. ISIS rebels have been battling Syrian government forces defending the regime of President Bashar al-Assad, as well as other antigovernment rebel groups. Many Syrians have come to despise ISIS because of its violence toward civilians, attacks on other rebel groups, and its uncompromising positions, which include the subjugation and enslavement of women. In early 2014, Western-backed Syrian rebels and even other Islamist groups launched a major campaign to expel ISIS from Syria. It met with only modest success, however, and since that time ISIS extended its reach within Syria to include areas populated by the Kurds. ISIS had an even greater impact in Iraq, however, and by the summer of 2014, it was threatening the very existence of the Iraqi government of then-president Nouri al-Maliki. Throughout 2013, ISIS made major advances in northern and western

Iraq. By late January 2014, ISIS and affiliated groups had managed to seize control of all of Anbar Province. In early June 2014, the group enjoyed even bigger gains, taking Mosul (Iraq's second-largest city) as well as Tikrit. ISIS forces reached to only some 60 miles north of Baghdad and were attempting to drive farther south. The fall of Mosul stunned the Iraqi government and much of the international community. By mid-June, the United States and other Western nations were involved in urgent negotiations to determine how they should aid al-Maliki's government and prevent all of Iraq from falling into the hands of the ISIS. Unfortunately, the corrupt, ineffectual, and rabidly anti-Sunni al-Maliki regime proved virtually incapable of halting ISIS's advance, and many components of the Iraqi Army simply bolted and fled in the face of ISIS offensives.

Resistance to ISIS

During the summer of 2014, the Obama administration began formulating a comprehensive strategy to reverse ISIS's advances. This would come to include cobbling together a multinational coalition, including a number of Arab states, to participate in air strikes against ISIS targets, arming moderate Syrian rebel groups combating ISIS fighters, sending more military hardware to the Iraqi government, dispatching some 3,000 military "advisers" to Iraq, and commencing air strikes against ISIS. These began on August 8, 2014, and the U.S.-coalition air campaign against ISIS in Syria commenced on September 23. Those operations, code-named Operation Inherent Resolve since October 15, 2014, continued into 2015. At the same time the Obama administration had announced its intent to defeat ISIS, it was lobbying for al-Maliki to be replaced as Iraqi prime minister. Under great internal and international pressure, he finally resigned on

September 8 and was succeeded by Haider al-Abadi, who pledged to pursue conciliatory policies in Iraq and to work cooperatively with the United States and its coalition partners to subdue the ISIS insurgency. By late December 2014, there were signs that the anti-ISIS effort was beginning to show some incipient signs of progress. Although Syrian officials reported that ISIS had killed 1,878 people (the vast majority of them civilians) between June 2014 and January 2015, Kurdish fighters recaptured the Syrian border town of Kobani on January 26, 2015. They also pushed ISIS out of the Iraqi city of Sinjar, a development that was hailed as a turning point in the war against ISIS.

Continued Growth and Violence

The threat from ISIS was considerably larger than its military operations in Iraq and Syria might suggest. Indeed, the group routinely violated basic international law and human rights by kidnapping innocent foreign civilians, beheading them, and then releasing the videos of the executions on the Internet. And in addition to targeting innocent civilians, ISIS also engaged in the severe repression of women in areas under its control, including kidnapping, sexually exploiting, and enslaving women and even young girls. On April 1, 2015, the Iraqi government declared a major victory over ISIS forces after having driven the group from Tikrit. Throughout the spring of 2015, Iraqi forces, aided by air support from the United States and other coalition governments, aggressively pursued ISIS. Meanwhile, since the summer of 2014, Iran has been launching air strikes against ISIS targets within Iraq. Iran has also sent special militia forces, known as the Quds Force, to Iraq to engage ISIS on the ground. The United States and Iran, although fighting on the same side in this instance, have repeatedly declared that the two nations are not coordinating their military operations. Iranian militia units played a major role in the retaking of Tikrit. As of late 2017, ISIS had lost significant swaths of territory, including the vital city of Mosul in Iraq, and was well on its way to losing its capital in Raqqa, Syria.

Paul G. Pierpaoli Jr.

See also: Al-Qaeda in Iraq (AQI); Baghdadi, Abu Bakr al-; Brussels Terrorist Attacks (2016); Jihad; Paris Terrorist Attacks (2015)

Citations

Brisard, Jean-Charles, and Damien Martinez. *Zarqawi: The New Face of al-Qaeda.* New York: Other Press, 2005.

"Profile: Islamic State in Iraq and the Levant," *BBC News,* www.bbc.com/news/world -middle-east-24179084, accessed June 13, 2014.

Istanbul Airport Attacks (2016)

On June 28, 2016, three terrorists armed with an assault rifle, a handgun, and two grenades opened fire on and exploded part of the Ataturk Airport in Istanbul, Turkey. Forty-five people were killed, and over 230 were injured. Although no group claimed responsibility for the attack, Turkish officials believe it was the work of ISIS. The entire incident only took 90 seconds, due to the efficiency of the suicide bombs that were detonated. Although most of the victims were Turkish, 11 nationalities were represented among the dead, including citizens from Saudi Arabia, Jordan, Palestine, Iraq, Chile, China, Iran, Tunisia, Ukraine, and Uzbekistan. The terrorists were discovered to be of Russian, Uzbek, and Kyrgyz nationality, and U.S. intelligence later identified them as Akhmed Chatayev, Rakim Bulgarov, and Vadim Osmanov.

Immediately afterward, airport security was tightened in Turkey, and all around the world. Turkish president Recep Erdogan was quick to denounce the act of terror, explaining that killing even one person is inherently un-Islamic. He received criticism, however, from many Turks who believe he is too focused on fighting the ethnic minority in Turkey, the Kurds, and has not focused enough on fighting ISIS. One research paper published by Columbia University claims that the Turkish government has "covertly supplied, trained, financed, and assisted the recruitment of ISIS' Sunni fighters with their battle with the Kurds." Some academics have criticized Erdogan's lack of assistance to Kurdish fighters against ISIS, and take that as a sign of implicit Turkish government cooperation with ISIS.

Although no direct proof of responsibility has been released to the public, the Turkish government remains convinced that they have "strong evidence" that it was the doing of ISIS. This was the eighth suicide bombing in Turkey in 2016, and by far the most serious. Thus, it is apparent that Turkey is at serious risk for further terror attacks by ISIS, and the government must therefore address whether or not it is worth it to ally with their former enemy, the Kurdistan Workers' Party (PKK) and other Kurds in the fight against Islamic State insurgents.

Colin P. Clarke

See also: Brussels Terrorist Attacks (2016); Islamic State of Iraq and Syria (ISIS); Paris Attacks (2015); Partiya Karkeren Kurdistan (PKK)

Citations

Callimachi, Rukmini. "Turkey, a Conduit for Fighters Joining ISIS, Begins to Feel Its Wrath," *The New York Times,* June 29, 2016.

"Istanbul Airport Attackers 'Russian, Uzbek and Kyrgyz,'" *BBC News*, June 30, 2016.

Karimi, Faith. "ISIS Leadership Helped Plan Istanbul Attack, Source Says," *CNN*, June 30, 2016.

Tisdall, Simon. "Turkey Paying a Price for Erdoğan's Willful Blindness to ISIS Threat," *The Guardian,* June 29, 2016.

Yan, Holly. "Istanbul Terror Attack: 42 Killed; Nation Mourns," *CNN*, July 6, 2016.

Ivory Coast Beach Resort Attack

On March 13, 2016, 6 heavily armed men assaulted a popular beach area packed with tourists in the southern Ivory Coast resort of Grand Bassam. The attack killed 14 civilians and 2 Ivory Coast soldiers. All 6 gunmen were also killed. Almost immediately, Al-Qaeda in the Islamic Maghreb (AQIM) claimed responsibility for the assault. Survivors and witnesses said that the terrorists were clad in black clothing and hoods with face masks and were armed with Kalashnikov heavy assault rifles and hand grenades; they began firing their weapons and throwing hand grenades indiscriminately. When AQIM issued its claim of responsibility on social media, it did so in four languages—English, French, Spanish, and Arabic. Experts claimed that it did so to mimic similar messages sent out by the Islamic State of Iraq and Syria (ISIS).

These same experts have posited that AQIM is modernizing its media campaigns to mirror its recent uptick in terror activities. Indeed, until late 2015, AQIM had appeared nearly extinct, but it subsequently announced an alliance with the jihadist group known as al-Mourabitoun, which was responsible for hotel and resort attacks in Mali (November 2015) and Burkina Faso (January 2016). AQIM also claimed responsibility for those incidents. The Ivory Coast assault seemed to signal an era of increasing AQIM activity in Africa. The beach resort attack occurred at a particularly sensitive time in Ivory Coast's modern history. Once among the most stable nations in West Africa, from 2002 until 2011, Ivory Coast endured political instability and a civil war. The civil strife pitted Ivory Coast's chiefly Muslim northern population against the predominantly Christian population in the south. Ivory Coast's economy suffered for more than a decade before it began a significant recovery over the last several years. Ivory Coast leaders now fear that the attack might derail the economy by driving away tourists and foreign investors. The Ivory Coast attack was the third such attack in West Africa in just five months, a signal that the region had become more vulnerable to terrorist incidents.

Paul G. Pierpaoli Jr.

See also: Al-Qaeda; Al-Qaeda in the Islamic Maghreb (AQIM); Tunisian Beach Resort Attack

Citations

Miller, Michael E. "Horror at the Beach: 22 Dead in Terror Attack on Ivory Coast Resorts," *The Washington Post,* March 14, 2016.

Pearson, Michael, Mariano Castillo, Tiffany Ap, and Tim Hume. "16 Killed in Attack on Ivory Coast Hotels; Al-Qaeda Affiliate Claims Responsibility," *CNN*, March 14, 2016.

J

Jabhat al Fateh al-Sham (Jabhat al-Nusra)

Jabhat al Fateh al-Sham, or JFS, is one of several names for al-Qaeda's Syrian affiliate, a major participant in the Syrian civil war. With approximately 10,000 fighters, JFS is now both the largest al-Qaeda franchise and, by many accounts, the most lethal, eclipsing the capabilities of Al-Qaeda in the Arabian Peninsula (AQAP) and Al-Qaeda in the Islamic Maghreb (AQIM).

As a failed state on the periphery of Europe, Syria remains an ideal staging ground for al-Qaeda to rejuvenate its global campaign of terrorism, with JFS serving as "the tip of the spear." Veteran al-Qaeda leaders like Saif al-Adl are thought to be among the current leadership directing JFS strategy in Syria. A critical centerpiece of this strategy is seeking consent of locals and working to garner political legitimacy in Sunni-dominated parts of northwest Syria, where JFS has established an enclave. This approach stands out in stark juxtaposition to ISIS's ultraviolent scorched-earth campaign. JFS has benefited from the combined Western and Russian campaign against ISIS as it has allowed the al-Qaeda splinter to survive and thrive.

JFS has publicly disassociated itself from al-Qaeda in an attempt to maintain a lower profile with respect to its adversaries, namely the Russian-backed regime of Syrian President Bashar al-Assad and the United States-led coalition. Still, the rebranding has failed to convince the U.S. government, but as prominent terrorism scholars like Daveed Gartenstein-Ross have pointed out, Washington was never the intended audience. A major line of effort within al-Qaeda's broader campaign has been establishing close ties with locals in the areas where it now operates. For the past several years, al-Qaeda has been shifting fighters and resources into Syria and slowly accruing popular support among locals. JFS is focused on political and military targets and has worked to build localized bases of influence and embeds its fighters into established zones of territorial control.

The change in nomenclature from Nusra to JFS serves several specific purposes. One potential outcome is that countries like Saudi Arabia, Turkey, and Qatar may feel more at ease arming or aiding the militants now that they have publicly distanced themselves, even if in name only, from al-Qaeda. Qatar, in particular, has been urging such a move for months.

Another objective of the rebranding is to present JFS as a more inclusive organization, open to working with, instead of against, the myriad Syrian rebel groups aligned against the Assad regime. Compared to ISIS, JFS has been far more selective in recruiting new members, especially among the thousands of foreign fighters that have flocked to Syria since the civil war erupted five years ago. By merging with parts of the local opposition, JFS can present itself as most representative and legitimate alternative among active jihadist groups.

Like its parent organization al-Qaeda, JFS is playing the long game. Its new name allows it to portray itself as a vanguard of the

Syrian people rather than an al-Qaeda puppet. Compared to ISIS—the more technologically adept and media-savvy—al-Qaeda, and by extension JFS, is a more conservative and "old-school" jihadi outfit. There is little doubt that ISIS poses a significant threat to regional stability in the Middle East and has already demonstrated both a willingness and capability to strike the West. But in the grander scheme, ISIS has been compared to an infection that can be treated and contained, whereas al-Qaeda and its affiliates are likened to a cancer that defies treatment and continues to spread.

Another motive of the name change is to integrate JFS within the current patchwork rebel coalition of anti-Assad fighters. If JFS successfully embeds itself within the opposition, there are serious consequences in both the short- and long-term. More immediately, this could prolong the conflict. In the long run, this symbiosis could lead to political legitimacy enabling the militants to emulate the staying power that Hezbollah has demonstrated in neighboring Lebanon.

The West should be doing everything possible to ensure that JFS and its ideological sympathizers are unsuccessful in their attempt to entrench themselves in Syria the way Hezbollah did in Lebanon. This likely means taking aggressive measures to separate or isolate jihadists from the more moderate elements within Syria's rebel opposition. Regardless of whether Assad stays or goes, this should be an overarching goal of Western countries working to resolve the Syrian crisis.

Following recent infighting with other Syrian rebel groups in the northwestern part of the country, Al-Qaeda in Syria appears to have recognized the need to secure legitimacy and present itself as an authentically Syrian entity to the civilian population it seeks to influence. In attempting to do so, al-Qaeda's affiliate in Syria joined with four other jihadist groups in late January to form a new organization—Hay'at Tahrir al Sham, or the "Assembly for Liberation of the Levant," led by Abu Jaber (also known as Hashem al-Sheikh), former commander of the Syrian rebel group Ahrar al-Sham.

The Syrian branch of al-Qaeda has undergone substantial change over the past year. In mid- 2016, the group announced it would no longer be known as Jabhat al-Nusra (Nusra Front) and would instead adopt the moniker Jabhat Fateh al-Sham (JFS), an attempt to distance the "new" group from al-Qaeda. But several prominent terrorism experts were skeptical that the rebranding signaled actual changes to the relationship.

The initial rebranding from Jabhat al-Nusra to JFS was intended to accomplish several different but interrelated objectives. JFS leaders likely said they hoped the rebranding would make it more feasible for the Sunni states in the Gulf to provide the militants with desperately needed resources to continue the fight against Syrian President Bashar al-Assad and his allies.

Another objective of the initial attempt at rebranding was to portray JFS as an inclusive organization capable of working with other Syrian rebel groups fighting against the Syrian regime. By aligning with local elements of the opposition, JFS could claim to be among the most representative and legitimate of literally hundreds of rebel groups on the ground in Syria.

Finally, the exceedingly public disassociation from al-Qaeda was announced so that JFS could attempt to adopt a lower profile and elude the high level of scrutiny the Islamic State receives from the Syrian regime, Russia, and the United States. And although defeating the Islamic State remains the top priority of the United States, the consolidation of territory around Idlib Province in northwestern Syria by extremist groups linked to al-Qaeda has made these militants a target of American air strikes.

A targeted strike in late February 2017 killed veteran al-Qaeda commander Abu al-Khayr al-Masri. Shortly thereafter, the U.S. Treasury Department imposed sanctions on two senior al-Qaeda operatives in Syria. These aggressive moves by the U.S. against al-Qaeda in Syria are designed to cripple the organization while signaling to other jihadist groups that joining the coalition would lead them to be targeted as well.

The more recent move to create Hay'at Tahrir al-Sham (HTS) is less a rebranding than an opportunistic attempt at expansion, as Ahrar al-Sham is divided and weakened and other moderate Syrian rebels are no longer receiving aid from the United States, Turkey, and Saudi Arabia, because these countries fear groups linked to al-Qaeda could co-opt those supplies.

To be sure, HTS is not the first terrorist or insurgent group to attempt to refurbish its image through a name change. In many cases though, the introduction of a new and "separate" entity is an effort to begin developing a legitimate political wing, as the Provisional Irish Republican Army did with Sinn Fein. As was the case in Northern Ireland, the development of Sinn Fein as a legitimate political entity was a major factor in helping bring the conflict to an end after 30 years of fighting, culminating with the Good Friday Agreement of 1998.

One possibility for the name change is that al-Qaeda in Syria believes its rival, the Islamic State, is headed toward defeat and that without ISIS to worry about, the U.S. would elevate HTS to its No. 1 target. Al-Qaeda had eschewed active intervention in many countries during the Arab Spring, and its leadership saw Syria as a chance to reestablish its relevance.

The most likely scenario is that the change in nomenclature is merely an attempt to buy time and live to fight another day. Indeed, the rebranding has done nothing to slow down the group's operations tempo of conducting attacks. In late February 2017, HTS launched a campaign targeting other rebel groups it accused of acting in support of external powers. It also assassinated one of Assad's top commanders, Major General Hassan Daaboul, the regime's military intelligence chief in the city of Homs, Syria. In mid-March 2017, HTS claimed responsibility for a double suicide bombing in Damascus, which killed at least 40 people and was apparently aimed at Shiite pilgrims visiting shrines. A follow-up suicide attack launched less than a week later killed at least 30 inside a historic judicial building close to the site of the shrines.

Despite several attempts at rebranding over the course of the past year, al-Qaeda in Syria (under any name) remains a dangerous and capable terrorist organization with the ability to conduct attacks in the West. Those seeking to grapple with the threat posed by the group should focus less on the game of "What's in a name?" and more on its actions. Six years into the conflict in Syria, al-Qaeda's presence in the country has never been stronger. And although most dismiss the notion of al-Qaeda as a political entity in Syria, the same was said about Hezbollah 30 years ago—the Shia group now holds seats in Lebanon's parliament and still maintains a vast military wing. If the rebranding of jihadist groups linked to al-Qaeda in Syria is effective, this could be yet another step toward positioning itself as a political player if or when negotiations to end the civil war in Syria gain traction.

While the West targets ISIS, JFS is quietly laying the groundwork for al-Qaeda's resurgence by "hunkering down," rebuilding and repositioning itself along several fronts. This should come as no surprise—al-Qaeda and its affiliates are nothing if not resilient.

Colin P. Clarke

See also: Al-Qaeda; Global War on Terror; Islamic State of Iraq and Syria (ISIS); Jihad

Citations

Callimachi, Rukmini. "Protest of U.S. Terror Listing Offers a Glimpse at Qaeda Strategy," *The New York Times,* November 17, 2016.

Clarke, Colin P. "Al Nusra is Stronger Than Ever," *The Cipher Brief,* November 2, 2016.

Lister, Charles. *The Syrian Jihad.* Oxford: Oxford University Press, 2016.

Jammu and Kashmir National Liberation Front

The Jammu and Kashmir National Liberation Front (JKNLF) served as the main insurgent organization in the disputed territory of Jammu and Kashmir (J&K) during the 1990s. The group's principal demand was that India and Pakistan give up control of J&K, half of which makes up Delhi's only Muslim-majority state, and let the area establish its own geopolitical identity. Failing this, the JKNLF would accept Kashmir's incorporation into Pakistan, India's Muslim neighbor.

The roots of the present J&K struggle date back to 1947. In this year the princely state's last Hindu maharaja, Hari Singh, formally elected to join India in return for military assistance to help suppress a Muslim tribal invasion that had allegedly been orchestrated by Pakistan at the time of the subcontinent's partition. Islamabad vigorously rejected the validity of this Instrument of Accession, arguing that Singh had been coerced into signing an agreement of union on terms dictated by Delhi and supported by Britain, the ex-colonial power. Pakistan quickly moved to consolidate control over that part of the state that had fallen to Muslim hands, which it has since referred to as Azad Jammu o-Kashmir (AJK, or Free Jammu and Kashmir). A year of subsequent fighting led to intervention by the United Nations (UN), which determined that the state's future should be decided on the basis of a plebiscite held under international supervision (UN Resolutions of August 13, 1948, and January 5, 1949). This popular referendum never materialized, generating two more Indo-Pakistani wars in 1965 and 1971. In 1972 a 460-mile (740-km) Line of Control (LoC) was delineated from Sangar to map reference NJ9842, which effectively set the division between J&K (administered by India) and AJK (administered by Pakistan) that exists today.

J&K's Muslim majority has always been at odds with the predominantly Hindu orientation of the Indian polity. However, Delhi's lamentable rule in the region has also been a major factor in triggering and entrenching local perceptions of alien and unresponsive rule. The central government has consistently denied outside arbitration and adjudication in determining the state's future and repeatedly refused to allow Kashmiri leaders passports to travel and confer with their counterparts in AJK. Widely documented human rights abuses (especially during the 1980s), corruption, a lack of development, and insufficient employment opportunities have merely confounded the situation, playing a key role in radicalizing the sentiments of a population that by the late 1980s had become bitter, sullen, and disillusioned.

The specific catalyst for militant violence in J&K was state elections of 1987, which were contested by antigovernment groups under the banner of the Muslim United Front (MUF). Following an impressive showing at the polls, Delhi annulled the results of several constituencies that the MUF had won to ensure the return of a pro-Indian administration under the auspices of Farooq Abdullah's National Conference, which has retained the state's seat of government ever since. From the ranks of these cheated victors, the JKNLF was born. The group specifically eschewed the middle ground of political compromise in favor of more direct, militant actions, commencing armed operations in 1989 to achieve full and complete independence for the Kashmiri people.

The JKNLF initially served as the main vehicle for the anti-Indian insurgency in J&K, and at its height had roughly 5,000 cadres in place throughout the Kashmir Valley region. By the mid-1990s, however, the JKNLF had largely ceased to exist as a viable militant force, its demise stemming from the interaction of several factors, including the loss of Pakistani patronage, the capture of its top leadership, and a growing acceptance that Indian rule could not be defeated through the force of arms. From 1995 on, the broad character of the Kashmiri conflict underwent a dramatic change, evolving from one that was primarily indigenously and nationally based to one that was defined in far more explicit religious and transnational terms. Although this transformation certainly began with the void created by the fall of the JKNLF, it is owed, more intrinsically, to decisions taken within Islamabad's Inter-Services Intelligence (ISI) Directorate, which has deliberately fostered the infusion of foreign jihadist elements in an attempt to replicate the success of the anti-Soviet mujahideen campaign it oversaw in Afghanistan during the 1980s.

Peter Chalk

See also: Lashkar-e-Taiba (LeT); Tehrik-i-Taliban Pakistan (TTP)

Citations

Ashraf, Fahmida. "State Terrorism in Indian-Held Jammu and Kashmir," *Strategic Studies* 1 (Spring 2001).

Choudry, Shabir. "Why I Said Goodbye to JKLF?" Counter Currents, July 25, 2008, www.countercurrents.org/choudhry250708.htm.

"Jammu and Kashmir Liberation Front," Global Security, www.globalsecurity.org/military/world/para/jklf.htm.

"Jammu and Kashmir Liberation Front," South Asia Terrorism Portal (SATP), www.satp.org/satporgtp/countries/india/states/jandk/terrorist_outfits/jammu_&_kashmir_liberation_front.htm.

Japanese Red Army

During the late 1960s and early 1970s, mirroring developments in western Europe, several extremist left-wing groups emerged in Japan. Preeminent among these was the Nippon Sekigun, or Japanese Red Army (JRA). The group strongly opposed defense treaties between Tokyo and Washington, the stationing of American military forces on Japanese soil, and Israeli Zionism. It championed itself as a revolutionary vanguard working on behalf of the urban masses and claimed close solidarity with other fighting communist organizations such as the Rote Armee Fraktion, Brigate Rosse, and Action Directe.

In 1970, following the hijacking of a Japan Airlines aircraft that was forced to fly to North Korea, the JRA divided into two main factions. The first was the Rengo Sekigun, or United Red Army (URA), which was led by Mori Tsuneo and merged with the Keihin Joint Struggle Committee. The URA believed it should concentrate its activities within Japan and vigorously enforced a strict internal code of conduct. Indeed, in 1972 the leadership executed 14 of its members for "deviationism." However, this action merely brought the URA to the attention of the local police, forcing its main constituent component to flee. These members seized a holiday chalet and took its female owner hostage. After a weeklong siege in which two police officers were killed and the woman released, the majority of the remaining members were arrested, effectively putting an end to the URA and its actions.

The other faction, comprising around 50 activists, continued to call itself the JRA. Fusako Shigenobu led the group and sought to align its actions with those of other international social revolutionary and Palestinian terrorist organizations. She forged particularly close ties with the Popular Front for the Liberation of Palestine (PFLP) and relocated with her followers to its camps in Lebanon.

In May 1972 the PFLP called a summit meeting with the intention of furthering international cooperation between extreme left and Palestinian groups. Representatives at the summit included Abu Iyad and Fuad Shemali of the Black September Organization (BSO), Andreas Baader of the Rote Armee Fraktion (RAF, or Red Army Faction), and Shigenobu of the JRA. Several other terrorist entities also allegedly attended the meeting, including the Provisional Irish Republican Army (PIRA), South American groups, and the Turkish People's Liberation Army, a forerunner to the current Devrimci Halk Kurtulus Partisi/Cephesi. Three weeks later, in a demonstration of this international solidarity, the JRA carried out its most infamous attack: the attack on Israeli's Lod Airport, undertaken on behalf of the PFLP.

The strike team for the Lod operation consisted of three members: Kozo Okamoto (the leader), Takeshi Okudaira, and Yasuiki Yashuda. All three had undergone training in the use of automatic weapons and grenades at a PFLP camp near Baalbek. The trio flew from Beirut to Paris on May 23, 1972, traveling on to Frankfurt and then Rome, where they met Shigenobu on May 30. She briefed them on their forthcoming mission and provided the three terrorists with false passports, Czech VZ58 assault rifles, and fragmentation grenades. That same evening, Okamoto, Okudaira, and Yashuda caught an Air France flight to Lod Airport, Tel Aviv, checking bags that contained their weaponry.

Upon arrival, the three JRA operatives waited in the arrivals area and calmly collected their suitcases. They then opened their luggage and indiscriminately opened fire and threw fragmentation grenades at the 300 or so passengers around them. During the course of their attack, Okamoto and his JRA colleagues managed to kill 25 people, wounding another 72. Okudaira and Yashuda died in the attack, and Israeli security forces captured Okamoto. He was subsequently sentenced to life imprisonment but released on medical grounds in 1985, having become mentally ill.

In 1982 Shigenobu announced that the JRA had rejected terrorism and the use of violence, justifying the decision on the grounds that the group had failed to win any international support. Over the next five years the group suffered from the arrest of several of its members and by 1987 had become essentially moribund. Despite a brief comeback in 1988, when the JRA took responsibility for the bombing of U.S. Officers Club in Naples, little more was heard from the organization, and in 2001 Shigenobu formally announced that the JRA had disbanded.

Richard Warnes

See also: Popular Front for the Liberation of Palestine (PFLP)

Citations

Farrell, William. *Blood and Rage: The Story of the Japanese Red Army*. Lexington, MA: Lexington Books, 1990.

Harclerode, Peter. *Secret Soldiers: Special Forces in the War against Terrorism*. London: Cassell, 2002.

Jemaah Islamiyah (JI)

Jemaah Islamiyah (JI) is an al-Qaeda–linked terrorist group operating in Southeast Asia, primarily in Indonesia but also with links to Singapore, Malaysia, the Philippines and possibly Thailand and Cambodia. The group's overarching objective is to establish a pan-Islamic state across the region. It has conducted major terrorist attacks in Bali in both 2002 and 2005. The first attack featured three potent bombs planted in a popular tourist destination and vacation spot for Westerners, especially Australians. The 2002 attack killed 202 civilians. The group was also responsible for an attack against a Marriott hotel in Jakarta in August 2003 and against the Australian embassy in September 2004. In October 2005, JI orchestrated a series of suicide bombings that killed 20 and wounded an additional 129 civilians. There was also a foiled plot to attack the American, British, and Israeli embassies in December 2001.

The Islamist terrorist group has links to Darul Islam stretching back to the 1950s and 1960s, when the issue was more about being opposed to policies in place during the decolonization era with the Dutch. Leaders include Abu Bakar Bashir, Achari Husin, Abdullah Sungkar, Riduan Isamuddin (aka "Hambali"), and Noordin Mohammad Top. Jemaah Islamiyah grew in prominence by helping recruit fighters for the anti-Soviet jihad in the 1980s, where the group's fighters trained and fought with the Afghan and Arab mujahideen.

Indonesian authorities have made significant progress in rolling back Jemaah Islamiyah throughout the country, especially through the specialized unit "Detachment 88." Hambali was arrested in Thailand, approximately 60 miles north of Bangkok in 2003, and Abu Dujana apprehended in 2007. Hambali was formerly linked to the 1995 "Bojinka" plot masterminded by al-Qaeda henchman Khalid Sheikh Mohammed.

Before he was arrested, Hambali had assumed an important role within JI as its operational chief, which allowed him free reign to plan and plot terrorist attacks. Hambali also headed JI's regional shura council and was one of the group's main liaisons to al-Qaeda core. In 2014, JI's leader Abu Bakar Bashir allegedly pledged *bayat,* or allegiance, to the Islamic State.

JI relies on a multiphased strategy of violent jihad that first targets local government, next targets regional governments, and finally expands its targets on a global basis. JI is divided into various sections, each of which have varying bureaucratic responsibilities and received funding through a diversified portfolio that spans donations and illicit activities. Its organizational structure is largely decentralized, and cells remain small, likely to avoid infiltration and arrest. It is well known that JI relies on a network of Islamic schools to indoctrinate and recruit new members for its organization in the classic madrassa style.

JI has experienced somewhat of a resurgence since the rise of the Islamic State. Current membership is estimated to be somewhere in the low thousands, so the future of the organization is very much uncertain, although as the world's most populous Muslim country, Indonesia would seem like a fertile recruiting ground for JI as it continues to spread its virulent ideology throughout the region.

Colin P. Clarke

See also: Al-Qaeda; Bali Bombings (2002); Global War on Terror; Jihad

Citations

Abuza, Zachary. *Militant Islam in Southeast Asia.* Boulder: Lynne Rienner, 2003.

Chalk, Peter et al. *The Evolving Terrorist Threat to Southeast Asia: A Net Assessment.* Santa Monica, CA: RAND Corp., 2009.

"Jemaah Islamiyah," Council on Foreign Relations Backgrounder, June 19, 2009.

Jihad

The term *jihad* (*jehad*) is often translated as "holy war." It means "striving" or "to exert the utmost effort," and refers both to a religious duty to spread and defend Islam by waging war (lesser jihad) and an inward spiritual struggle to attain perfect faith (greater jihad). The distinction between lesser and greater is not accepted by all Muslims in all circumstances. Many distinguish between jihad as an individual versus a collective duty, as when Muslims face invasion or cannot practice their faith, or in its defensive or offensive forms. In general, the broad spectrum of modern Islam emphasizes the inner spiritual jihad. Within the spectrum of Islamic belief, definitions of jihad have also rested on historical circumstances. Indian reformer Sayyid Ahmad Khan argued for a more limited interpretation of jihad whereby believers could perform charitable acts in place of armed struggle, which was only incumbent if Muslims could not practice their faith.

The reform movement of Muhammad ibn abd al-Wahhab in 18th-century Arabia, in contrast, reasserted the incumbency of jihad as armed struggle for all believers. As the Quran contains verses that promote mercy and urge peacemaking but also verses (referred to as the Sword Verses) that more ardently require jihad of believers, there is a scriptural basis for both sides of this argument. Quranic thought on the nature of jihad began to evolve when Muhammad moved from Mecca to Medina in 622 and created an Islamic state. The initial Quranic jihadic sanction (22:39) was for fighting in self-defense only, "those who stay at home," that could be taken as condemnation of those who abstained from an early key battle of the Muslims against the Meccan forces. Many Muslim scholars held that the admonition to pursue an aggressive jihad "with their wealth and their persons" (Quran 4:95) overrode verses revealed earlier on. Fighting and warfare (*qital*) are, however, differentiated from jihad, which is always accompanied by the phrase *ala sabil Allah* ("on the path of God") in the same way that just war is differentiated from other forms of conflict. Some scholars differentiate the fulfilling of jihad by the heart, the tongue, or the sword as a means of discouraging Muslims from seeing armed struggle as a commandment, but such teachings have by and large been contradicted by the revival of activist jihad, first in response to colonialism and then again in the 20th century.

The broad spectrum of Islam considers foreign military intervention, foreign occupation, economic oppression, non-Islamic cultural realignment, colonialism, and the oppression of a domestic government, either secular or Islamic, of an Islamic people or country to be a sufficient reason, if not a Quranic mandate, to participate in a defensive jihad. The more militant and fundamental end of the Islamic spectrum asserts that a social, economic, and military defensive jihad is justifiable and necessary. However, a widespread discussion of jihad is ongoing in the Muslim world today in response to the rise of militancy, and there is a concerted effort to separate the concepts of jihad and martyrdom from each other when they are the rallying call of irresponsible extremists such as Osama bin Laden and his ilk. Notable defensive jihads in the more recent history of Islam include the resistance of the Afghan (1979) and Chechnya mujahideen against their respective Soviet and Russian occupations and the Algerian War of Independence against France. Some Islamic religious scholars, such as Dr. Abdullah Yusuf Azzam, a former teacher of bin Laden, argued for jihad against the West. Numerous clerics and scholars have held, along with the views of their communities, that the Palestinian struggle against Israel is a defensive jihad because of the infringements on life and liberty, the use of collective punishment, and the seizure by Israel of *waqf* ("endowment") lands.

Offensive jihad was essentially adopted by the early Muslim community, as no defensive action would have sufficed to protect them against the allied tribal forces determined to exterminate them. In such a jihad, the People of the Book (*dhimma*), meaning other monotheistic traditions including Judaism and Christianity, must be treated differently than enemies who are unbelievers (*kuffar*). However, the People of the Book must submit to Islamic rule, including the paying of poll and land taxes. Rules of engagement, truces, and treatment of prisoners and non-Muslims were all specified in medieval texts concerned with *siyar,* or "Islamic international law." Classical Islamic law and tradition asserts that a jihad that is a collective duty (simplified in Western texts as an offensive jihad) can only be declared by the caliph, the successor to the Prophet Muhammad and the lawful temporal and spiritual authority for the entire Islamic community.

On the other hand, no authority other than conscience or the awareness of an oppression targeting Islam or Islamic peoples is necessary to participate in an individually incumbent jihad. When the Mongols attacked Baghdad in 1258, the caliphate, long since a divided patchwork of sultanates and emirates, ceased to exist. It was the only legal, governmental, and clerical structure recognized by the classical interpretation of Islamic doctrine as being capable of declaring jihad. That did not prevent the Ottoman sultans from declaring themselves caliphs and calling for jihad, but the Muslim world did not recognize them as such. Other jihads were declared in the early modern period, for instance by the Mahdiyya of the Sudan, the Wahhabi movement in Arabia, and the Sanusiyya in today's Libya. Leaders of such movements, like contemporary jihadists, have sometimes proclaimed jihads by issuing a fatwa or statement. Although a fatwa is supposed to be a legal response issued by a qualified jurist, self-proclaimed leaders and clerics sometimes say that the traditional ulama ("a body of mullahs"), crushed by modern state governments, have failed in their duty and therefore claim the right to speak in their stead. Although many Muslims recognize their respective governments and political leaders as worthy of defining and declaring defensive jihads, many others perceive their governments as illegitimate Islamic states or illegitimate Islamic political leaders.

Turkey, Egypt, and Pakistan, for example, are quasi-democratic states that grant secular political parties and politicians the same rights as Islamic political parties and politicians. Islamic militant groups in all three countries see these governments and their leaders as heretical and illegitimate under

Islamic law (sharia). In a similar vein, some Muslims, most notably the takfirists, declare jihad against Muslim governments perceived as oppressive, anti-Islamic, or corrupt (being non-Muslim in their eyes). Additionally, many of the Islamic theocratic monarchies (Saudi Arabia, for example) are deemed illegitimate by fundamentalist Muslims. This perception is due in part to the willingness of some of these monarchies and democracies to cooperate and form alliances with non-Islamic nations or with nations that wage economic, cultural, or military war against Islam and Muslims.

Additionally, some of these monarchies and democracies limit the power of the clerics within their countries. Various Islamic extremist movements, most notably al-Qaeda, Boko Haram, al-Shabaab, the al-Nusra Front, and the Islamic State (IS), have stepped into the void created by the disappearance of the caliphate and the resultant fractured Islamic political and religious world. These groups have interpreted Islam as they wish and declare jihad as they desire, although often with the assistance and support of some clerics and of leaders with a degree of religious knowledge. Because early Muslims killed in jihad were considered martyrs, there is an extensive tradition that exalts martyrdom. This adds to the modern jihadists' appeal, particularly to younger or more desperate followers. Defensive jihad, inclusive of martyrdom, is deemed appropriate to end Israel's occupation of the perceived Islamic territories of the West Bank, East Jerusalem, and Gaza, if not all of Palestine.

A martyr secures a place in paradise and may intercede for other Muslims. Antiterrorist campaigns in the Muslim world have argued, against the weight of literature and popular belief, that modern jihadists are not martyrs if they set out to martyr themselves because suicide is not allowed in Islam. Noncombatant Muslims who perish in a jihad are also considered martyrs. Jihadists thus excuse the deaths of innocents caught in their cross fire with targets or authorities. They explain the deaths of non-Muslim civilians as being deserved for their failure to submit to Islam or for their open oppression of Islam or Islamic peoples. In the case of Israeli civilians, the fact that all provide military service to their country means that they are not really considered civilians by the jihadists. The term *jihad* is incorporated into the organizational names of numerous militant groups, including the Egyptian Islamic Jihad, the Egyptian Tawhid wa-l-Jihad, and the Palestinian Islamic Jihad. The struggle in contemporary Islam to redefine jihad and detach its meaning from adventurism, martyrdom, and attacks on Muslim governments as well as Westerners is one of the most significant challenges at this time in history.

Richard M. Edwards and Sherifa Zuhur

See also: Al-Qaeda; Global War on Terror; Homegrown Terrorism; Islamic State of Iraq and Syria; Lone Wolf Attacks

Citations

Benjamin, Daniel, and Steven Simon. *The Age of Sacred Terror.* New York: Random House, 2002.

Bostom, Andrew G. *The Legacy of Jihad: Islamic Holy War and the Fate of Non-Muslims.* Amherst, NY: Prometheus, 2005.

Delong-Bas, Natana. *Wahhabi Islam: From Revival and Reform to Global Jihad.* Oxford: Oxford University Press, 2004.

Esposito, John L. *Unholy War: Terror in the Name of Islam.* New York: Oxford University Press, 2002.

Fregosi, Paul. *Jihad in the West: Muslim Conquests from the 7th to the 21st Centuries.* Amherst, NY: Prometheus, 1998.

Kepel, Gilles. *Jihad: The Trail of Political Islam.* Cambridge, MA: Belknap, 2003.

K

Kaczynski, Ted

Theodore John "Ted" Kaczynski is an American mathematician who engaged in a mail-bombing campaign over 17 years that killed 3 people and injured 23 others. Many of his victims were university professors and airline employees, which earned him the moniker "Unabomber"; a combination of "university and airline bomber." Kaczynski was the subject of one of the Federal Bureau of Investigation's (FBI) most costly investigations and was eventually captured after his brother tipped off federal authorities in 1995.

Kaczynski was motivated by an idiosyncratic mixture of neo-Luddite and anarchist convictions that modern technology requiring large-scale organization was working to fundamentally erode human freedom. He claimed that his bombings were necessary to draw attention to this malaise and to curtail and ultimately roll back industrial technology. Basing himself out of a remote cabin without electricity or running water in Lincoln, Montana, he mailed or hand-delivered 16 letter bombs between 1978 and 1995. Most of his devices were handcrafted and made with both metal and wooden parts. The initial bomb, sent to an engineering professor at Northwestern University in 1978, adopted a highly primitive triggering mechanism involving a nail tensioned by rubber bands. Over time, however, the sophistication of the detonation techniques improved and would eventually take the form of a combination of batteries and filament wire.

Although most of Kaczynski's attacks targeted individuals, on at least one occasion he attempted to blow up a passenger plane, American Airlines Flight 444 flying from Chicago to Washington, DC, in 1979. Only a faulty timing mechanism prevented the bomb, which had been placed in the cargo hold, from detonating. According to the authorities, had the device been properly wired, it would have obliterated the aircraft.

As aviation sabotage is a federal crime, the FBI assumed responsibility for the postincident inquiry. The agency code-named the ensuing investigation UNABOM and formed a joint task force with the Bureau of Alcohol, Tobacco, and Firearms and the U.S. Postal Inspection Service. Overall, 150 full-time employees were assigned to the case, and a $1 million reward was also posted for anyone who could provide information leading to the Unabomber's arrest.

Despite these measures Kaczynski avoided capture and indeed over the next 15 years carried out attacks that left three people dead: Hugh Scrutton, the owner of a computer store in California; Thomas Mosser, a senior executive with the national advertising firm Burson-Marsteller; and Gilbert Murray, the president of the timber industry lobbying group California Forestry Association. There is speculation that the latter two murders were undertaken in support of the wider radical environmental movement. Following Murray's death, Kaczynski reportedly wrote a letter to Earth First! acknowledging responsibility under the rubric of the "Freedom Club." Following his arrest he also admitted to killing Thomas Mosser after reading an article by the same group charging that Burson-Marsteller

Ted Kaczynski, American domestic terrorist, luddite, and mathematics teacher, gestures as he speaks during an interview in a visiting room at the Federal ADX supermax prison in Florence, Colorado, August 30, 1999. Motivated in part by beliefs hostile to modern technology, the Unabomber mailed parcels and packages containing explosives through the postal system, leading to the death of 3 people, with 23 others injured. (Stephen J. Dubner/Getty Images)

was guilty by association for the Valdez 1989 oil spill in Alaska, as it had advised the company that owned the vessel at the heart of the accident, Exxon-Mobil.

In 1995 Kaczynski sent a letter to the *New York Times* and promised to desist from further acts of violence if that paper or the *Washington Post* agreed to publish a 35,000-word statement of his beliefs and objectives, *Industrial Society and Its Future*. The FBI pressed the *Times* and *Post* to jointly run the so-called manifesto piece in the hope that readers would identify the author. The move paid off as David Kaczynski recognized the style of writing and beliefs as those of his brother. His wife, Linda, pushed him to alert the authorities that Ted was in fact the Unabomber, and after a search, he was eventually traced to the cabin in Lincoln on April 3, 1996. Combing the premises, agents discovered a wealth of bomb-making components, 40,000 handwritten journal pages, one live bomb, and what appeared to be the original manuscript of the manifesto.

In a bargain to avoid the death penalty Kaczynski pleaded guilty to all the government's charges on January 22, 1998. He is currently serving a life sentence without the possibility of parole at the federal Administrative Maximum Facility supermax near

Florence, Colorado. David Kaczynski donated the reward money, less expenses, to the families of his brother's victims.

Edward F. Mickolus

See also: Earth Liberation Front (ELF); Homegrown Terrorism; Improvised Explosive Devices; Lone Wolf Attacks

Citations

"Excerpts of the Unabomber Manifesto," *USA Today,* November 13, 1996, www.usatoday .com/news/index/una6.htm, accessed January 10, 2012.

Ottley, Ted. "Ted Kaczynski: The Unabomber," Crime Library, 2005, accessed June 12, 2005.

"Post, Times Publish Unabomber Manifesto," *CNN News*, September 19, 1995, http:// edition.cnn.com/US/9509/unabomber /index.html, accessed June 12, 2005.

Taylor, Bron. "Religion, Violence and Radical Environmentalism: From Earth First! to the Unabomber to the Earth Liberation Front," *Terrorism and Political Violence* 10, no. 4 (Winter 1998).

Khalid Sheikh Mohammed

Khalid Sheikh Mohammed was the operational chief for the planning for the September 11, 2001, operation. He had been active in extremist Islamist activities with his nephew Ramzi Yousef before and after the 1993 World Trade Center bombing, but it was his role as instigator of the September 11 plot that made him notorious. Until his capture in Pakistan, he rivaled Osama bin Laden as public enemy number one in the United States.

Mohammed came from a family with strong religious and political views. He was born on April 24, 1965, in the Fahaheel neighborhood of Budu Camp, Kuwait. His father was a Muslim cleric from the Pakistani province of Baluchistan. Because of the citizenship rules of Kuwait, the family remained as guest workers instead of Kuwaiti citizens. The young Mohammed grew up in Kuwait resenting his inferior status. Mohammed was a good student and excelled in science. His father died before he graduated high school, and his elder brothers assumed responsibility for his care. Because both brothers had strong political views, they guided his political orientation, which eventually led him to join the Muslim Brotherhood at age 16. He graduated from Fahaheel Secondary School in 1983, and his brothers decided to send Mohammed to the United States to further his education. Mohammed traveled to the United States in 1983 to study mechanical engineering at Chowan University, a Baptist school in Murfreesboro, North Carolina. After a short stay there, Mohammed transferred to North Carolina Agricultural and Technical State University in Greensboro (now University of North Carolina at Greensboro). At both schools, Mohammed remained aloof from American students and American society. Most of his contacts were with other students from Arab countries.

After graduating in 1986 with a degree in mechanical engineering, Mohammed traveled to Pakistan to join the mujahideen in fighting Soviets in Afghanistan. His older brother Zahid Sheikh Mohammed was head of a Kuwaiti charity, the Committee for Islamic Appeal (Lajnat al Dawa al Islamia [LDI]), in Peshawar, Pakistan. His brother Abed worked for Abdul Rasool Sayyaf's newspaper in Peshawar. For a time Mohammed taught engineering at a local university. The three brothers worked together with Abdullah Azzam, Sayyaf, and Gulbaddin

Hekmatyar to determine the strategy of the Afghan resistance. Mohammed's war experiences in Afghanistan changed his life, especially after he lost his brother Abed in the fighting late during the war, at the Battle of Jalalabad. Mohammed became secretary to the Afghan warlord Sayyaf and, through him, made the acquaintance of Osama bin Laden and other Islamist leaders.

After the end of the Afghan-Soviet War in 1989, Mohammed stayed in Pakistan, where he devoted his activities to operations run against the West. When the political situation in Afghanistan deteriorated for Islamist militants, Mohammed looked elsewhere for employment. The conflict in Bosnia attracted him, and he fought with the mujahideen there in 1992. During these years, Mohammed held a number of jobs before ultimately working for the Qatari government as an engineer in its electricity headquarters.

Mohammed's first involvement in a major terrorist operation was with his nephew, Ramzi Yousef. His role in the planning of the February 26, 1993, bombing of the World Trade Center in New York City is still mostly conjecture, but it is known that he sent Yousef $660 to help build the bomb. This bombing, however, proved a disappointment: Although it caused many casualties, it failed to cause the collapse of the Twin Towers or kill the hoped-for thousands. After Yousef returned to Karachi, Pakistan, he met with Mohammed. It was at one of these meetings in 1993 that Yousef and his friend, Abdul Hakim Murad, suggested a way to attack the United States. Murad, who had earned a commercial pilot license at an American commercial pilot school, proposed packing a small airplane full of explosives and dive-bombing into the Pentagon or the headquarters of the Central Intelligence Agency. Mohammed quizzed Murad about details of

pilot training and the ways that such an operation might be carried out. Nothing was done at that time, but Mohammed later used this information in the September 11 plot.

Later in 1993 Mohammed contacted Hambali, the operation chief of the Indonesian Islamist terrorist group Jemaah Islamiyah. Mohammed and Yousef traveled to the Philippines to work on a plan, Operation Bojinka, that envisaged the bombing of a dozen U.S. commercial aircraft over the Pacific during a two-day period. He also worked with Yousef to plan the assassination of Pope John Paul II during his visit to the Philippines, but a chemical mishap caused by Yousef ended this attempt. Mohammed returned to Pakistan, where he kept in touch with Yousef. Only after Yousef was captured in 1995 did Mohammed begin to make separate plans for terrorist operations, one of which was the use of commercial aircraft as terrorist weapons. However, he needed allies before undertaking such a massive operation.

American intelligence was slow to realize the importance of Mohammed in the terrorist world even as he traveled throughout the Muslim world making contacts. Evidence obtained in Yousef's apartment in Manila indicated Mohammed's association with Yousef, but nothing else was known. Beginning in 1993, Mohammed lived in Doha, Qatar, working at the Ministry of Electricity and Water. In his spare time, Mohammed raised money for terrorist groups. Enough evidence about his participation in Yousef's activities existed that a New York grand jury issued a secret indictment against him in January 1996. Although American authorities tried to persuade Qatari officials to extradite Mohammed, the Qatari government was reluctant to do so. Efforts to mount a seizure operation were hindered by a lack of commitment on the part of the American military, the Central Intelligence Agency (CIA), and the Federal Bureau of Investigation (FBI). Eventually the FBI made a halfhearted effort, but Mohammed was long gone, warned by his friend Abdullah ibn Khalid, the minister of religious affairs in Qatar, that the Americans were looking for him.

Mohammed began cooperating with al-Qaeda in 1996. Bin Laden invited him to join al-Qaeda's military committee under Mohammad Atef. Mohammed was to swear loyalty (*bayat*) to bin Laden and to al-Qaeda, bringing with him connections to the Middle East and South Asia, as well as plans to attack the United States. He met with bin Laden and Atef, al-Qaeda's military commander, at bin Laden's Tora Bora mountain refuge in 1996, where Mohammed presented to them a variety of terrorist schemes, the most promising of which was the use of commercial airliners as flying bombs to use against targets in the United States. Yet, though bin Laden asked Mohammed to join al-Qaeda, Mohammed turned him down, wishing to retain his autonomy. Despite this, Mohammed developed a close working relationship with al-Qaeda. Mohammed needed al-Qaeda to supply money and martyrs for his operations even as he supplied the planning, but bin Laden was noncommittal about the plan until 1998, when he proposed that the four leaders of the plane hijackings should be two Saudis (Khalid al-Mihdhar and Nawaf al-Hazmi) and two Yemenis (Walid Mohammed bin Attash and Abu Bara al-Yemeni). This plan, however, fell apart when the two Yemenis were unable to obtain American visas. At this time no need existed for pilots, something that soon changed. This change of plans led to the later recruitment of Mohamed Atta, Ziad Jarrah, and Marwan al-Shehhi from the Hamburg cell. American intelligence had no idea of the extent of Mohammed's growing contacts with al-Qaeda, but the FBI was offering a $2 million reward for his capture because of his role in the Manila plot.

Shortly after his 1996 meeting with bin Laden, Mohammed began recruiting operatives for a future suicide mission. His liaison with al-Qaeda's leadership was Ramzi bin al-Shibh. He briefed bin Laden and the leadership of al-Qaeda orally on his final plan for a suicide mission using commercial aircraft sometime in 1998 or 1999. By this time, Mohammed, who had sworn a loyalty oath to bin Laden, had been integrated into al-Qaeda's leadership hierarchy. Recruits for the mission were trained at the Afghan al-Matar training complex, where Abu Turab al-Urduni, a Jordanian trainer, taught them how to hijack planes, disarm air marshals, and use explosives. Mohammed confessed in a June 2002 interview with the Muslim journalist Yosri Fouda that the operation in the United States had been planned two and a half years before it took place.

Mohammed's original plan included hijacking 10 aircraft and destroying 10 targets but was ultimately reduced to 4 targets. Once the operatives were selected and Mohamed Atta had been picked and briefed as mission leader, Mohammed watched from behind the scenes.

After September 11, Mohammed knew that he was a marked man. He eluded capture for nearly two and a half years. Considerable investigation was required by American authorities before they realized just how important Mohammed was to planning September 11, but once his importance was realized, his capture was only a matter of time. On March 1, 2003, a joint team of Pakistani and American agents arrested Mohammed in

Rawalpindi, Pakistan, seizing his computer, cell phones, and documents.

Khalid Sheik Mohammed Confesses to His Role in the 9/11 Attacks

"About two and a half years prior to the holy raids on Washington and New York, the military committee held [a] meeting during which we decided to start planning for a martyrdom operation inside America. As we were discussing targets, we first thought of striking a couple of nuclear facilities but decided against it for fear it would go out of control. The attacks were designed to cause as many deaths as possible and havoc and to be a big slap for America on American soil." After being detained at a remote prison site in Pakistan, where he was interrogated about his role in al-Qaeda and in the September 11 attacks, Mohammed was transferred to the Guantanamo Bay detention camp in September 2006. In early March 2007, the Bush administration announced that he and others would appear before military courts that would determine whether or not they were enemy combatants; enemy combatants would appear before a military tribunal. Before the proceedings, it was reported that Mohammed had been increasingly forthcoming about his role in the September 11 plot. His confessions included myriad plots, most of which were never carried out or were failures. At his hearing at the Combatant Status Review Tribunal Hearing on March 10, 2007, Mohammed stated that he had been the organizer of the September 11 plot, justifying it as part of a war between the Islamist world and the United States. Mohammed also confessed to complicity in many other plots, among which were the 1993 World Trade Center bombing and the killing of the Jewish journalist Daniel Pearl in Pakistan, in which he claimed personal involvement only, stating that it was not related to his al-Qaeda activities. Although his open confession of participation in these terrorist acts equated to a guilty plea, Mohammed simultaneously claimed that he had been tortured.

In February 2008, military prosecutors charged Mohammed and five other Guantánamo prisoners with war crimes and murder for their roles in the September 11 attacks and said they would seek the death penalty for the six men. During his arraignment hearing before a military tribunal in Guantanamo Bay in June 2008, Mohammed declared he wanted to be put to death and viewed as a martyr. In November 2009, the Obama administration announced that Mohammed and four coconspirators would face a civilian trial in New York City. However, after that news set off a firestorm of controversy, those plans were dropped. In May 2012, Mohammed was arrained and charged with terrorism, hijacking aircraft, conspiracy, murder in violation of the law of war, attacking civilians, attacking civilian objects, intentionally causing serious bodily injury and destruction of property in violation of the law of war.

Stephen E. Atkins

See also: Bin Laden, Osama; September 11 Attacks; World Trade Center (New York) Bombing (1993)

Citations

Eggen, Dan. "9/11 Report Says Plotter Saw Self as Superterrorist," *The Washington Post,* July 27, 2004.

Fouda, Yosri, and Nick Fielding. *Masterminds of Terror: The Truth behind the Most Devastating Terrorist Attack the World Has Ever Seen.* New York: Arcade Publishing, 2003.

Lance, Peter. *1000 Years for Revenge: International Terrorism and the FBI; The Untold Story.* New York: ReganBooks, 2003.

McDermott, Terry. *Perfect Soldiers: The 9/11 Hijackers; Who They Were, Why They Did It.* New York: HarperCollins, 2005.

Richey, Warren. "The Self-Portrait of an Al Qaeda Leader," *Christian Science Monitor,* March 16, 2007.

Soltis, Andy. "I Did 9/11 from A to Z," *New York Post,* March 15, 2007.

Khorasan Group

The Khorasan group is a small group of approximately two dozen veteran al-Qaeda jihadists from the Middle East, South Asia, and North Africa that are forward-deployed to Syria as assets that could be used to strike against the West. This cell is responsible for running a network of training camps and also has access to a communication building and other command and control facilities. These elite al-Qaeda terrorists were dispatched to Syria by the group's current leader Ayman al-Zawahiri to develop plans for external attacks, build and test improvised explosive devices, and recruit Westerners to conduct operations abroad. The Khorasan group is believed to work closely with al-Qaeda's Syrian affiliate, Jabhat al-Nusra, or al-Nusra Front, and has been described by the former U.S. Director of National Intelligence James Clapper as just as much of a threat to the U.S. homeland as ISIS.

The group's leader at the time, a Kuwaiti al-Qaeda veteran named Muhsin al-Fadhli, was killed by a U.S. drone strike in July 2015. The U.S. had previously struck Khorasan group targets west of Aleppo in 2014, with cruise missiles fired from warships stationed in the Persian Gulf and Red Sea. One major concern is potential collaboration between Khorasan group assets and Al-Qaeda in the Arabian Peninsula (AQAP), widely believed to be the most operationally dangerous of all al-Qaeda–affiliated groups, to take down U.S. airliners using explosives smuggled on board.

The term *Khorasan* itself is not an organizational name, but rather an Islamic word used in ancient religious texts to describe the Afghanistan-Pakistan-Iran region. Its existence was not publicly recognized until September 2014. The U.S. government has provided little information about the group, leading to dissent among experts as to whether the group is truly separate from al-Nusra. Although the United States government revealed that the group was a threat, it was never stated how large or what the threat was. U.S. officials have stated that they discovered plots created by the Khorasan group against the United States.

Colin P. Clarke

See also: Al-Qaeda; Global War on Terror; Jabhat al Fateh al-Sham (Jabhat al-Nusra); Jihad

Citations

Schmitt, Eric, "Leader of Qaeda Cell in Syria, Mushin al-Fadhli, Is Killed in Airstrike, U.S. Says," *The New York Times,* July 21, 2015.

"What is the Khorasan Group?" *BBC News,* September 24, 2014.

Wong, Kristina, "The Khorasan Group: 5 Things to Know," *The Hill,* September 24, 2014.

Kosovo Liberation Army

The Kosovo Liberation Army (KLA—Ushtria Clirimtare e Kosoves) was a guerrilla force that fought for Kosovo's independence from Yugoslavia, and later from Serbia. Most of the group's members were ethnic Albanians, who make up approximately

90 percent of Kosovo's 2 million people. Although the KLA officially disbanded in July 1999, many of its commanders and fighters joined forces with the National Liberation Army in Macedonia and other satellite organizations to continue their fight for an independent Kosovo.

The KLA formed around 1990 as a small band of peasants committed to the liberation of Kosovo. The province had been an autonomous region from 1974 to 1989, and its degree of home rule was virtually equivalent to that of any republic of the former Yugoslav federation. However, Kosovo's autonomy was rescinded in 1989 by Yugoslav president Slobodan Milosevic, who cited a need to suppress separatism and protect non-Albanian ethnic minorities living in Kosovo. For several years, most Kosovar Albanians followed a policy of nonviolence in their efforts to restore their autonomy. As severe repression against ethnic Albanians by Serbian police and Yugoslav Army forces continued unabated through the mid-1990s, the KLA began to carry out well-planned attacks against carefully chosen Serbian targets. Beginning in 1997, open clashes erupted between KLA rebels and government forces.

In 1998, Milosevic launched a crackdown on the KLA and also on ethnic Albanian villages throughout the province. In an effort to ferret out the rebels, Serbian police began terrorizing citizens suspected of providing shelter or support for the KLA. The crackdown drove many Kosovars into the arms of the KLA, and the group's membership swelled to an estimated 35,000 fighters. In early 1999, the Serbs began a heightened military campaign to destroy the KLA, burning entire villages, driving tens of thousands of civilians from their homes, and causing many civilian casualties. The North Atlantic Treaty Organization (NATO) responded to this aggression by launching air strikes against Yugoslavia to help prevent further attacks on Kosovar Albanians.

By the onset of the NATO air strikes, the KLA's force had dwindled to roughly 3,000 fighters. However, by June 1999, a groundswell of volunteer fighters from Albania and from among fleeing refugees brought the KLA force within Kosovo to an estimated 17,000—with another 5,000 volunteers in training in Albania. Although the KLA remained far outnumbered by the heavily armed Yugoslav military, the NATO air war hindered the mobility of the Yugoslav troops, further equalizing the battlefield. On June 9, NATO and Yugoslav officials signed the Military-Technical Agreement, paving the way for the complete withdrawal of Serbian troops and the demilitarization of the KLA.

Despite the agreement, factions within the KLA remained divided over the prospect of disarmament under any peace plan negotiated between NATO and the Yugoslav government. The group's most radical members formed a rival armed faction, the Armed Forces of the Republic of Kosovo, led by Bujar Bukoshi. The splinter group comprised former KLA members who refused to accept anything less than full independence.

Although little was known about the KLA's command structure, Hashim Thaci, leader of the Democratic Party of Kosovo, emerged as its nominal head. Former KLA commander Ramush Haradinaj became prime minister of Kosovo in December 2004 but resigned in March 2005 after being indicted for war crimes charges tied to his time as a KLA commander. Haradinaj surrendered to the United Nations International Criminal Tribunal for the Former Yugoslavia in The Hague.

Lisa McCallum

Citations

Clark, Wesley. *Waging Modern War: Bosnia, Kosovo, and the Future of Combat.* New York: PublicAffairs, 2001.

Malcolm, Noel. *Kosovo: A Short History.* London: Pan Macmillan, 2002.

Wrage, Stephen D., ed. *Immaculate Warfare: Participants Reflect on the Air Campaigns Over Kosovo, Afghanistan, and Iraq.* Westport, CT: Praeger, 2003.

L

Lashkar-e-Taiba (LeT)

Lashkar-e-Taiba (LeT, literally, the Army of the Pure) dates back to the mid-1980s when it was created as the military wing of the Markaz-ad-Da'awa Wal Irshad (MDI) madrassa. It is affiliated with the Ahl-e-Hadith sect of Wahhabism (which emphasizes statements attributed to the Prophet Muhammad) and was a creation of Pakistan's InterServices Intelligence (ISI) Directorate to act as a proxy force for prosecuting Islamabad's policy objectives in Jammu and Kashmir (J&K). The group is led by Hafiz Saeed (its spiritual emir) and Zaki ur-Rehman Lakhvi (its operational commander), and has a broader membership of around 150,000 cadres (including 750 insurgents on the ground in J&K). Under international pressure following the 9/11 attacks in the United States, then president Pervez Musharraf banned the group in 2002. However, it has since operated more or less openly under the name Jama'at-ud-Da'awa (which Saeed leads purportedly as an Islamic charity), although this group was also banned in 2009.

LeT possesses a robust network in India and has made strenuous efforts to cultivate ties with various extremist groups in the country, including the Students Islamic Movement of India and the Indian Mujahideen. LeT also enjoys an established international network outside South Asia, with particular strength in the Middle East and a growing presence in the United Kingdom. Financially, most of the group's funds come from diaspora contributions, earnings from legitimate businesses (such as real estate and commodity trading), the Pakistani military, and the provincial government of the Punjab (in the form of donations). Its espousal of Ahl-e-Hadith, which is considered theologically similar to the Salafi Islam practiced in Saudi Arabia, has additionally helped it procure financial support from that country.

LeT has between 100,000 and 150,000 supporters and members and enjoys an extensive infrastructure in Pakistan that includes its sprawling compound in the town of Muridke outside Lahore, training camps in Pakistani Occupied Kashmir (POK, or Azad Jammu o-Kashmir) offices, madrassas, schools, medical clinics, and mosques. The group publishes several periodicals in Urdu and English, has operated websites and promulgated news bulletins via outlets such as Yahoo Groups, recruits openly on Pakistani university campuses, and operates the MDI madrassa (which was heavily involved in relief efforts following the devastating 2005 earthquake in POK).

Although the group was established to fight Indian rule in J&K, most of LeT's personnel are Punjabi and Pashtun, with relatively few Kashmiris in its ranks. In addition, the group has always defined its objectives in local and regional terms, articulating a twofold ideological and operational agenda that aims to (1) exploit ethnoreligious tension in Kashmir in order to (2) trigger a wider religious revolution across the Indian state. To this end, the group has spearheaded terrorist attacks across J&K and has been directly tied to numerous assaults in India, including the attack on India's Red Fort in December 2000, the strike against the Indian

Parliament in December 2001, the Kaluchak massacre in May 2002, serial explosions in Delhi in October 2005, the Varanasi attack in March 2006, the Mumbai assaults in November 2008, and the bombing of a German bakery restaurant in Pune in February 2010. Of these, arguably the most serious and audacious were the November 2008 assaults, which were allegedly undertaken in collaboration with Ibrahim Dawood, the head of D Company (also known as the Bombay Mafia) and one of India's most wanted men.

Besides its J&K and Indian operations, there is evidence to link LeT to attacks and plots outside South Asia. Shezad Tanweer, one of the perpetrators behind the 2005 Underground bombings in London, was thought to have visited the LeT headquarters in Muridke; Willie Brigitte, who was arrested in 2003 on suspicion of planning attacks on the Lucas Heights nuclear reactor and the Pine Gap intelligence-gathering station in Australia, admitted to French authorities that he was trained by the LeT; U.S. officials have periodically claimed that LeT has been instrumental in recruiting Islamists to fight against Allied troops in Iraq; and in November 2009 four suspected operatives of LeT were arrested in Bangladesh for plotting to lead a fedayeen assault against the Indian and U.S. diplomatic missions in Dhaka to coincide with the anniversary of the 2008 attacks in Mumbai.

LeT is known for its sophisticated intelligence and operational planning capabilities. The 2008 Mumbai attacks represent a case in point. David Headley, a Pakistani American, traveled to India on several occasions to reconnoiter targets for the assault, using a fake visa-processing business to establish his cover identity. The attacks were then executed by LeT cadres trained in marine operations and equipped with automatic weapons, grenades, and delayed explosive charges.

Members of the strike team used Google Earth to familiarize themselves with Mumbai, hijacked a fishing trawler to make the trip to India, employed modern GPS receivers to navigate, and communicated with their Pakistani handlers via satellite phones routed through the Internet. The attackers operated in small, heavily armed units, exploiting news broadcasts to ascertain the position, size, and maneuvers of the security forces. These tactics allowed 10 men to not only strike multiple locations across the city but also to decisively overwhelm Mumbai's massive but poorly trained and equipped police force.

LeT is set apart from other Pakistani terrorist groups by its relative obedience to the military and ISI as well as by its espousal of the Ahl-e-Hadith sect of Islam. These traits have frequently caused friction with the major Deobandi militant entities, although it has often cooperated on an operational and logistic level with groups in India and Bangladesh. Unlike many other Kashmiri tanzeems, LeT is additionally characterized by a relatively strong sense of internal cohesion, and at the time of writing, there was little evidence to suggest that it was suffering from the type of internal hemorrhaging that has befallen groups such as Jaish-e-Mohammed and Harakat-ul-Mujahideen.

That said, speculation has arisen that certain globalized elements within LeT have moved to establish concrete ties with al-Qaeda. Fueling this concern is residual evidence linking the two organizations: Abu Zubaydah, a senior al-Qaeda field commander arrested in 2002, was detained in a LeT safe house in Faisalabad. LeT has been suspected of involvement in the 2005 London Underground bombings; although these attacks are not believed to have been directly ordered by al-Qaeda, they were definitely inspired and endorsed by the movement. A sizable proportion of killed or captured LeT militants have been linked to radicals known to have received training in former Afghan camps run by al-Qaeda and/or the Taliban, including militant centers at Tayyba and Aqsa. Indian sources have consistently claimed that al-Qaeda has supplied LeT with money, both directly and through intermediaries in Pakistan (although these assertions need to be assessed in the politically interested context in which they have been made). Indian sources have additionally claimed that contacts exist between Osama bin Laden's international jihadist network and D Company, the crime syndicate that allegedly collaborated with LeT in carrying out the 2008 Mumbai attacks. Pakistani commentators have periodically alleged that al-Qaeda has funneled financial support to aid Kashmiri tanzeems fighting in J&K, including LeT. LeT has shown increased willingness to target Western interests in South Asia, such as the Café Leopold and Jewish Chabad Lubavitch Center, which were attacked during the 2008 Mumbai assault, and a disrupted plot to attack the U.S. and UK embassies in Dhaka in 2009.

Currently, there is no definitive evidence of an established logistic or operational link between LeT elements and al-Qaeda. However, the existence of at least residual ties cannot be discounted. LeT's ideological focus has certainly taken on a much more explicit anti-Western tenor in recent years, reflecting concerns and aspirations that, at least rhetorically, closely accord with the open-ended aims of the broader al-Qaeda jihadist network. Although the group has always promoted an international agenda (promising, for instance, to plant the Islamic flag in the capitals of the United States, Russia, and Israel), it has mostly focused its activities on the local and regional theaters. Today, as much emphasis is given to fighting Washington and allied governments supportive of (what was formerly called) the global war on terror as to staging attacks in India and J&K. This shift in focus is arguably supported by LeT's alleged involvement in the aforementioned attacks and plots in the United Kingdom, Australia, and Bangladesh.

Despite LeT's growing connections to anti-Western violence, the Pakistani government has refused to act against the group, and both the military and the ISI are considered to enjoy somewhat cordial relations with it. Indeed, reports from the Indian media indicated that Saeed was the guest of honor at an *iftar* dinner (the evening meal that breaks the daily fast during the holy month of Ramadan) hosted by the Pakistani Army's 10th Corps in 2009, shortly before he was charged with preaching jihad and raising money for terrorist activities (all of these charges have since been dropped). The general reluctance to act against LeT is considered to be a product of the army's belief that the group continues to be a strategic asset vis-à-vis Pakistan's competition with India. A number of military and intelligence officers also share LeT's religious convictions, further strengthening bonds. A number of sources in Pakistan have additionally suggested that Islamabad is fearful of the consequences of attempting a wholesale crackdown on LeT, given its size and formidable capabilities.

Ben Brandt

See also: Jihad; Mumbai Attacks (2008); Taliban; Tehrik-i-Taliban Pakistan (TTP)

Citations

Rana, Muhammad Amir. *A to Z of Jehadi Organizations in Pakistan.* Lahore, Pakistan: Mashal Books, 2004.

Tankel, Stephen. "Lashkar-e-Taiba: From 9/11 to Mumbai," International Center for the

Study of Radicalisation and Political Violence, London, April/May 2009, www.ps .au.dk/fileadmin/site_files/filer_statskund skab/subsites/cir/pdf-filer/Tankel_01.pdf, accessed December 21, 2017.

Liberation Tigers of Tamil Eelam (LTTE)

The island of Sri Lanka (Ceylon until 1972) is 75 percent Buddhist Sinhalese, with Hindu Tamil people forming the largest minority of some 20 percent. The Tamils live in northern and eastern Sri Lanka and are related to the Tamils of India. Following the independence of Ceylon in 1948, the Sinhalese majority trumpeted Sinhalese nationalism. Thus, Sinhalese replaced English as the official language of Ceylon in 1956, and Ceylon was renamed Sri Lanka in 1972.

As a result of this ethnic pressure, violence increased, as did Tamil demands for autonomy. Velupillai Prabhakaran founded the Tamil New Tigers youth group in 1972, and in 1976 it became the Liberation Tigers of Tamil Eelam (LTTE), now an insurgent organization. The LTTE demanded independence for the Tamil regions and was aided by supporters in the southern Indian state of Tamil Nadu. LTTE guerrillas were effectively organized and well armed.

The LTTE gained infamy for its innovative techniques now widely employed by insurgent groups worldwide, the most notable of which was suicide bombing. The LTTE fought for decades for the creation of an autonomous Tamil homeland. Toward that end, it allied itself in 1985 with the Eelam Revolutionary Organization of Students, the Eelam People's Revolutionary Liberation Front, and the Tamil Eelam Liberation Organization. However, by 1986, the LTTE had turned against its new

antigovernment partners and had assumed control of most of Sri Lanka's northern area, especially the strategically located Jaffna Peninsula, where the LTTE ruled the region as a de facto government.

The withdrawal of Indian troops from Sri Lanka in March 1990 solidified the LTTE's power, but in 1993 the Colombo government mounted a successful campaign to oust the rebels from their Jaffna stronghold. The start of the campaign was spurred by an ambush of government troops in which hundreds of soldiers were killed.

The LTTE was long regarded as the primary obstacle to peace between the Tamils and the Sinhalese Buddhist government because of its terrorist activities, hard-line position, and intolerance of dissent. The LTTE was blamed for the 1991 assassination by suicide bombing of former Indian prime minister Rajiv Gandhi, the May 1993 assassination of Sri Lankan president Ranasinghe Premadasa, and the December 1999 attack on Chandrika Bandaranaike Kumaratunga, elected president of Sri Lanka just days later. The LTTE killed scores of politicians, journalists, and others who opposed it.

The LTTE also established its own navy and air force, and for a time appeared to pose a real military threat to Sri Lanka's government. However, after the World Trade Center and Pentagon attacks of September 11, 2001, the United States classified the LTTE as an international terrorist group, and funding for its cause began to dry up when foreign governments cracked down on its overseas support.

In 2005 new Sinhalese president Mahinda Rajapakse unleashed the military to destroy the LTTE. In early 2008, Sri Lanka's army intensified its offensive against the LTTE in the northeast, despite the plight of Tamil civilians caught up in the fighting. In May 2009, Sri Lankan troops cornered the remnants of the LTTE on a tiny sliver of land in the northeast, killing or capturing the LTTE combatants and ending both the insurgency and the LTTE, with the military displaying what it claimed was the body of LTTE leader Prabhakaran.

Spencer C. Tucker

See also: Improvised Explosive Devices

Citations

Bose, Sumantra. *States, Nations, Sovereignty: Sri Lanka, India and the Tamil Eelam Movement.* Thousand Oaks, CA: Sage Publications, in association with the Book Review Literary Trust, New Delhi, 1994.

Hashim, Ahmed S. *When Counterinsurgency Wins: Sri Lanka's Defeat of the Tamil Tigers.* Philadelphia: University of Pennsylvania Press, 2012.

Lone Wolf Attacks

So-called "lone wolf" attacks, also known as lone actor attacks, are attacks perpetrated by people not specifically aligned with a terrorist or insurgent group, but instead acting individually. Several plays on the phrase have evolved, including "loon wolves," to suggest the attacker suffered from mental illness, and "known wolves," to indicate that attackers were known to authorities before the attack.

Between 2014 and the present, ISIS has continually relied on its extensive use of propaganda to attempt to radicalize people living in Europe in hopes of convincing them to launch terrorist attacks, an example of the classic "lone wolf" or inspired terrorist. ISIS sometimes attempts to make direct contact with individuals through the Internet in what many have called the "virtual planning model" of terrorist attacks, where ISIS members direct individuals through encrypted apps and help them plan each step of the

attack. There is also the possibility that ISIS members are already prepositioned in Europe, either with or without direct instructions, and these members or cells could conduct attacks similar in style to the Paris November 2015 attacks.

The situation is different with the United States, insulated by two oceans and safer as a matter of pure geography. The United States also benefits from more robust defenses, including superior security and intelligence services and far fewer overall targets. Furthermore, it appears to be the case that U.S. policing, intelligence, and border officials have been able to prevent ISIS members from arriving in the United States, although there is no way to be certain of this. ISIS will likely focus its attempts on the first two options listed (lone wolf and virtual planning model) but might also attempt something similar to the July 2017 plot in Australia, where explosives were sent through the mail to terrorists already living in the country. There is a lower probability (albeit not a negligible one) that ISIS will attempt to send fighters directly to the United States via air travel from Europe or the Middle East, or first to Canada and Mexico or points south and then over the border into the United States.

ISIS does not follow one simple model in planning terrorist attacks, but instead hedges their bets to achieve the highest rate of success in conducting an attack. There have indeed been true lone wolves that have merely been inspired by Salafi jihadist ideology—the ISIS and al-Qaeda ideology that seeks to emulate the presumed practices of the earliest generation of Muslims and that believes in violent struggle against non-Muslims and apostates as an important religious duty. But ISIS would prefer to play a more direct role in these attacks, because virtual planner-style attacks or ISIS-directed attacks involving trained militants dispatched to attack a target typically result in higher lethality rates.

Colin P. Clarke

See also: Homegrown Terrorism; Improvised Explosive Devices; Jihad

Citations

Bhojani, Fatima, "America's Lone-Wolf Terrorists Are Unpredictable in Almost Every Regard—Except One," *Quartz,* October 19, 2016.

Byman, Daniel L. "Can Lone Wolves Be Stopped?" *Brookings Institution,* March 15, 2017.

Callimachi, Rukmini. "Not 'Lone Wolves' After All: How ISIS Guides World's Terror Plots From Afar," *The New York Times,* February 4, 2017.

Lord's Resistance Army

Long a country suffering from ethnic and cultural divisions, Uganda has been plagued by the ebb and flow of violence and conflict for decades. To properly understand the context in which the Lord's Resistance Army (LRA) emerged, one must explore the history of Uganda as a nation. Following independence from Britain, Uganda held its first democratic election, which resulted in a win by the Uganda People's Congress, a southern, Bantu-dominated political party led by Milton Obote, who's government held power between 1962 and1971, at which point it was overthrown by the military dictatorship of Idi Amin.

Amin's regime was brutal, primarily characterized by economic failure and violence. Amin was later overthrown by Obote, who subsequently served as the president of Uganda for a second time. Indeed, Obote's second term was marred by the Ugandan

Bush War, a conflict between his government and the National Resistance Army, led by Yoweri Museveni. The National Resistance Army primarily consisted of southern Bantu nationalists and was successful at consolidating power in Uganda. After a brief period of rule by Acholi president Tito Okello, Museveni helped stage a successful coup and soon after assumed the role of president.

Museveni claimed that he was committed to democracy, an expression of faith that helped him secure the support of many Western countries, including the United States. Still, his army and supporters were far from democrats and indeed sought power through political violence. They launched attacks and perpetrated numerous acts of violence against the Acholi northerners. In response, the Acholi people formed a nationalist group called the Holy Spirit Movement, led by Alice Auma. This group was the predecessor to the Lord's Resistance Army.

Alice Auma was a firm believer in Acholi nationalism and spiritual resistance. It was believed that Auma was in possession of a spirit named Lakwena and she used this perception to present herself to her followers as Alice Lakwena. Her goal was to resist the Bantu government of Museveni and retake the captured city of Kampala. This was a popular message to spread, as the northern Acholi people were wary of southern occupation of their territory.

Although initially successful with several victories in battle, the Holy Spirit Movement ended when Alice Auma fled, following a military defeat. Auma's nephew, Joseph Kony, went on to become the founder and leader of the Lord's Resistance Army, which was first known as the Holy Salvation Army and then the Uganda Christian Army, before adopting its modern name in 1992. Kony took over for Alice Auma after her defeat, preaching similar messages in a similar

Joseph Kony, head of the Lord's Resistance Army (LRA), shakes hands with a Ugandan government official during cease-fire talks in southern Sudan on July 31, 2006. Uganda has been wracked by a bloody civil war between LRA and government forces since 1987. Kony, the LRA leader and warlord known to forcibly recruit child soldiers, is still on the run, with his whereabouts unknown. (Adam Pletts/Getty Images)

style. He told his followers that he was a spokesperson of God possessed by certain spirits, and believed strongly in numerous superstitions and unorthodox practices, such as polygamy. Kony's spirited leadership took a sharp turn for the worse in the subsequent decades after the founding of the LRA, as his cult of personality became more demanding. In fact, a warrant for his arrest was issued in 2005 by the International Criminal Court, for crimes against humanity including violence, rape, and the abduction of thousands of children for the purpose of making them soldiers in the LRA.

The LRA is peculiar in that no widely accepted consensus has been reached in identifying its ideology. Its roots lie in the Acholi nationalism of Alice Auma, but also involve

the theocratic Christian tendencies of Joseph Kony. The political goals of the LRA have been to "topple the government of President Yoweri Museveni and to install a regime dedicated to enforcing the Ten Commandments." However, the claims of Christianity and protection of its own people are juxtaposed by the kidnapping, rape, murder, and mutilation of various political enemies and many young Acholis who the LRA wish to indoctrinate into their philosophy. Overall, the ideology of the LRA is a mix of Acholi nationalism, Christian fundamentalism, and support for political stability and peace in Uganda.

Since its peak in the 1990s, the LRA has decreased from a force of more than 10,000 adult and child soldiers to just over 100 soldiers today. Some Ugandans no longer consider Kony a threat, and the search for Joseph Kony was recently called off by the Trump administration, which is withdrawing the 250 special operations forces troops attempting to track Kony down. The last LRA attacks in Uganda took place in 2006, but there have been cross-border attacks launched in the Democratic Republic of the Congo (DRC) and the Central African Republic (CAR). The LRA is also thought to be active in South Sudan, and some rumors suggest that Kony is hiding out in the southern Darfur region.

During the height of its terror, attacks in which over 100 people were killed were not uncommon for the LRA, including several attacks on churches. By 2006, 1.7 million people lived in more than 200 internally displaced person (IDP) camps in northern Uganda, largely as a result of the brutality of the LRA. Over 20,000 northern Ugandan children were reportedly abducted by the LRA between 1987 and 2006 for use as child soldiers, servants, or sexual slaves. Four leaders of the LRA were issued arrest warrants by the International Criminal Court. Interpol wanted person red notices have been issued on five.

Colin P. Clarke

See also: Al-Qaeda in the Islamic Maghreb (AQIM); Al-Shabaab; Boko Haram

Citations

Arieff, Alexis, Lauren Ploch Blanchard, and Tomas F. Husted. "The Lord's Resistance Army: The U.S. Response," *The Congressional Research Service,* September 28, 2015.

Chivers, C. J. "'All People Are the Same to God': An Insider's Portrait of Joseph Kony," *The New York Times,* December 31, 2010.

Cooper, Helene. "A Mission to Capture or Kill Joseph Kony Ends, without Capturing or Killing," *The New York Times,* May 15, 2017.

Pike, John. "Military," *Lord's Resistance Army (LRA),* May 23, 2017.

Shannon, Lisa, and Francisca Thelin. "Out of Kony's Shadow," *The New York Times,* March 16, 2015.

Loyalist Volunteer Force (LVF)

The Loyalist Volunteer Force (LVF) is a Protestant paramilitary group in Northern Ireland. The formation of the LVF came about in the context of the June/July 1996 Drumcree Crisis, in which Protestant Orangemen were prevented from marching along the Garvaghy Road, a predominantly Roman Catholic area. The LVF emerged during this standoff, made up of disaffected members of the Ulster Volunteer Force (UVF), notably Billy Wright (also known as "King Rat"), a self-professed born-again Christian and the UVF's Mid-Ulster "brigade commander." Wright, thought to have been responsible for the deaths of at least 30 people, was expelled from the UVF for the unsanctioned killing of a Roman Catholic taxi driver, which breached the cease-fire that the UVF and the majority of the loyalist paramilitaries had announced in response to the first Provisional Irish Republican Army (PIRA) cease-fire in 1994.

Although the overwhelming majority of UVF members in Belfast remained loyal to their existing leadership, former members of a UVF unit based in Portadown formed the core of the LVF. From the outset, the LVF's objective was to thwart the possibility of reconciliation between the Nationalist and Unionist communities in Northern Ireland. To this end the group carried out a series of notably brutal murders of Roman Catholic civilians during July 1997, including the use of torture and mutilation that was reminiscent of the methods employed by the UVF's Shankill Butchers in the mid-1970s. In August 1997, the LVF also planted four small explosive devices in Dundalk in the Irish Republic, but the devices were rendered safe by security forces.

In parallel, the LVF and their former comrades in the UVF engaged in an increasingly violent feud, with several UVF attempts to kill senior LVF members. Wright himself may have been saved from assassination in 1998 at the hands of the UVF by being sentenced to eight years in prison for witness intimidation. However, any reprieve was short-lived, and on December 27, 1997, Wright was murdered within the high-security Maze prison by three prisoners from the Irish National Liberation Army (INLA) while awaiting transport inside a prison van. The INLA prisoners claimed he had been killed for waging a war on the Nationalist population from inside the high-security Maze prison.

The leadership of the LVF then passed to one of Wright's lieutenants, Mark Fulton, and in retaliation for Wright's murder the LVF stepped up their attacks against Roman Catholic targets, killing 10 civilians and a former PIRA member between December 1997 and April 1998. The LVF also sought to strengthen its position though cooperation with elements of the Ulster Defence Association (UDA)/ Ulster Freedom Fighters (UFF), particularly the unit commanded by Johnny Adair. A number of the killings for which the LVF claimed responsibility in early 1998 were in fact the work of UDA gunmen. These deaths incited a response from the INLA, which retaliated with the murder of a UDA member in Belfast. The PIRA also breached its cease-fire in retaliation for the UDA/ LVF campaign, killing a leading UDA man and bringing about a political crisis in the

ongoing peace process. This led then secretary of state for Northern Ireland, Mo Mowlam, to visit loyalist paramilitaries in prison to ask for a cessation of the violence. Partly as a result of her intervention and political pressure being placed on the UDA's political representatives, the group's leadership reined in its members. However, the LVF continued its killing spree. On April 29 a gunman from the group murdered a Roman Catholic council worker in Portadown, shooting him at point-blank range. The next month LVF members fatally shot a 22-year-old student near Crumlin in Antrim.

However, within a month of this last killing, the LVF announced to general surprise that it was calling its own cease-fire. The statement was formally recognized by the British government in November 1998, which entitled LVF members to the paramilitary prisoner early-release scheme installed under the Good Friday Agreement. In December 1998 the LVF became the first Irish paramilitary group to hand over weapons to the Independent International Commission on Decommissioning.

Despite this official recognition, the LVF was widely believed to have been behind the March 1999 murder of human rights lawyer Rosemary Nelson. The murder was claimed by the Red Hand Defenders (RHD), suspected to be a flag of convenience for loyalist paramilitaries wishing to carry out attacks without breaching their parent organizations' cease-fires. Another incident in September 2001 that involved the killing of Martin O'Hagan, an investigative journalist, caused the British government to withdraw its recognition of the LVF (and the UDA/ UFF) cease-fires. Although the RHD claimed responsibility for the murder, police forensic investigators discovered that the pistol O'Hagan had been shot with was the same one used in a previous LVF murder.

By the end of 1999 the LVF had become openly involved in another round of feuding with the UVF. Tension had built up between the two groups in Portadown, resulting in the UVF raiding an LVF bar and assaulting a number of LVF members, several of whom were badly beaten. In retaliation, the LVF murdered the UVF's regional commander, Richard Jameson. Jameson was a respected figure within his movement and the Protestant community, and thousands of supporters attended his funeral. The UVF subsequently drew up a hit list of those thought to have been responsible for Jameson's killing. In January 2000 two young men, one linked to the LVF, were abducted, beaten, and stabbed to death by a UVF gang in Tandragee. The UVF also tried but failed to kill the gunman who had assassinated Jameson. Members of Adair's UDA unit escorted the intended victim, who had survived the attack, out of Belfast, inflaming tensions between that group and the UVF. Hostility between the two groups turned into open conflict in August 2000, when a UDA parade turned into a violent confrontation with UVF supporters, and the two main loyalist paramilitary groupings embarked on an intensive bout of internecine violence and killing.

In June 2002, the LVF lost its second leader when Fulton was found hanging in Maghaberry prison; he was believed to have committed suicide. Fulton was replaced by his brother Gary, who was himself soon arrested. Robin King then assumed leadership and committed to repairing and restoring the damaged relationship between the LVF and Adair's Belfast UDA. At one point it appeared that the former might fully merge with the latter, but this was prevented by Adair's arrest and reimprisonment.

In 2004 and 2005, the LVF and UVF returned to fighting each other. The violence was so serious that the Independent Monitoring Commission resolved to issue a report dealing solely with the feud. Between May 2004 and August 2005, the UVF killed five individuals it judged to be associated with the LVF, with a further 38 attacks (including 17 attempted murders) on LVF members or associates. The UVF leadership sought to eliminate the LVF altogether, which caused the latter to issue a statement in October 2005 that it was "standing down" its military units. Although the LVF does not appear to have actually disbanded, the International Monitoring Commission described it in 2010 as a "small organization without any political purpose; people historically linked to it were heavily involved in crime, and the proceeds of these crimes were for personal and not organizational use."

Greg Hannah

See also: Provisional Irish Republican Army (PIRA); Ulster Volunteer Force (UVF)

Citations

"Call on LVF to Disband," *BBC News*, January 16, 2000, http://news.bbc.co.uk/2/hi/uk_news/northern_ireland/605553.stm.

Cusack, Jim, and Henry McDonald. *UVF: The Endgame*. Dublin: Poolberg, 2008.

"Politicians Assess Ceasefire End," *BBC News*, October 13, 2001, http://news.bbc.co.uk/2/hi/uk_news/northern_ireland/1596068.stm.

Sixth Report of the Independent Monitoring Commission. London: HMSO Stationery Office, September 2005.

Streeter, Michael. "UVF Disbands Unit Linked to Taxi Murder," *The Independent* (UK), August 3, 1996.

Taylor, Peter. *Loyalists*. London: Bloomsbury, 1999.

Twenty-Third Report of the Independent Monitoring Commission. London: HMSO Stationery Office, May 2010.

M

Madrid Commuter Train Bombings (2004)

The terrorist bombing attacks in Madrid, Spain, on March 11, 2004, also referred to as 3/11, were launched in the morning against the city's commuter train system, killing an announced 191 people and wounding 1,755 others. Later estimates, after reexamination of victim remains, reduced the death toll to 190. The victims included citizens of 17 countries. The attacks took place during the morning rush hour on four commuter trains traveling between Alcala des Henares and the Atocha Station in Madrid in an obvious effort to inflict the greatest amount of casualties possible.

Thirteen bombs, hidden in backpacks, were placed on the trains, and 10 of these exploded within a two-minute period beginning at 7:37 a.m. Two of the 3 additional bombs were detonated by a police bomb squad, as was a suspicious package found near the Atocha Station. An additional unexploded bomb was brought intact to a police facility and later dismantled. This unexploded bomb provided evidence for the investigation and subsequent trial of the terrorists. In the immediate aftermath of the attacks, the Spanish government blamed the attacks on Euskadi Ta Askatasuna (Basque Homeland and Freedom, or ETA), the Basque separatist movement that had launched terrorist attacks in the past. Investigators quickly absolved ETA of the attacks, however, and the blame shifted to the terrorist group al-Qaeda, which had perpetrated the September 11, 2001, terrorist attacks

against the United States. Spanish authorities have claimed that the attackers were a loosely knit group of radical Muslims primarily from Morocco, Syria, and Algeria.

A number of Spanish nationals were also involved, mainly by selling the explosives to the terrorists. The Partido Popular (Popular Party, PP), which then formed the government of Spain, was defeated in national elections held three days later, replaced in power by the left-leaning Partido Socialista Obrero Español (Spanish Socialist Workers' Party, PSOE). Although al-Qaeda later claimed that the attacks had led to the electoral defeat, most experts agree that the PP government's clumsy handling of the aftermath of the attacks was the primary factor in the PSOE victory in the election. The PP had held only a narrow and shrinking lead in the polls prior to the attacks. Many had seen the government's early declaration that the attacks were the work of the ETA as influenced by electoral considerations, and when the claim was quickly shown to be untrue, the government's credibility was badly damaged.

The PSOE had strongly opposed Spain's participation in the U.S.-led invasion of Iraq, which the PP had supported. Shortly after the elections the new government under Prime Minister José Luis Rodríguez Zapatero withdrew Spanish troops from the coalition in Iraq, adding some weight to the al-Qaeda assertion that its attacks had directly affected Spanish foreign policy. The precipitous Spanish troop withdrawal also led to considerable tension in U.S.-Spanish relations. As late as the 2008 U.S.

presidential elections, Republican candidate John McCain said that he would not meet with Spanish prime minister Zapatero. A few weeks after the attacks, on April 2, 2004, an additional explosive device was found on the tracks of a high-speed rail line. The explosives had been prepared for detonation but were not connected to any detonating device. Following this further discovery, new investigations were launched, and Spanish police tracked down suspects in an area south of Madrid. During the raid to apprehend them, an explosion—apparently caused by a suicide bomb—killed seven suspects. Security officials believe that between five and eight suspects managed to escape the police that day. They have not yet been apprehended.

In all, 29 suspects (20 Moroccans and 9 Spaniards) were apprehended and charged for involvement in the attacks. Their trial began on February 15, 2007, and lasted four and a half months. The verdict, handed down on October 31, 2007, found 21 guilty of various crimes, ranging from forgery to murder. Two of the convicted terrorists were sentenced to prison terms that added up to 42,924 years, but Spanish law limits actual imprisonment to 40 years. The court sentences did not mention any direct links between the convicted terrorists and al-Qaeda, however. Although al-Qaeda may have inspired the Madrid terrorists and a connection cannot be ruled out, no irrefutable evidence has been found to connect it with the planning, financing, or executing the Madrid attacks. Nevertheless, the Madrid attacks may well have been the first major success for an al-Qaeda–type terrorist organization in Europe. The attacks did lead to greater cooperation between west European security services in an attempt to prevent further attacks. Yet on July 7, 2005, London suffered multiple terrorist bombings that also appear to have been independent from but inspired by al-Qaeda.

Elliot P. Chodoff

See also: Al-Qaeda; Euskadi Ta Askatasuna (ETA); Global War on Terror; Improvised Explosive Devices

Citations

Jane's Intelligence Review 16, no 8 (August 2004). Coulsdon, Surrey, UK: Janes, 2004.

Puniyani, Ram. *Terrorism: Facts versus Myths*. New Delhi: Pharos Media, 2007.

Von Hippel, Karin. *Europe Confronts Terrorism*. New York: Palgrave Macmillan, 2005.

Mahdi Army

Founded by the Iraqi Shiite cleric Muqtada al-Sadr, the Mahdi Army, also known as Jaish al-Mahdi (JAM), is a powerful Shiite militia organization active in Iraq. As the military wing of al-Sadr's political movement, JAM plays a pivotal role in Iraqi politics. The group rose to prominence for its frequent clashes with U.S. and coalition forces following the U.S. invasion of Iraq and later went on to engage in much of the sectarian violence that plagued the country through early 2007. However, as part of al-Sadr's broader social and religious organization, the group also assumes an active role in the delivery of social services to many of its supporters. The group's posture and its predisposition toward violence have gradually evolved over the years. In August 2007, al-Sadr announced a freeze on all JAM activities. In 2008 the military arm of the movement was reduced in size and largely shelved as al-Sadr reoriented the majority of JAM forces toward social support activities designed to aid its disenfranchised Shiite

Armed members of Iraqi Shiite radical leader Muqtada al-Sadr's militia, the Mahdi Army, shout anti-U.S. slogans under a poster of their leader in Baghdad's Shiite neighborhood of Sadr on April 6, 2004. U.S. troops surrounded the cleric's offices during the demonstration. Al-Sadr has remained a force in Iraqi politics and commands a significant following of Iraqi Shiites, providing him with a large base and serious clout. (AFP/Getty Images)

base. Nonetheless, JAM still maintains a robust military capacity and as such represents a formidable Shiite voice in Iraqi politics.

Following the U.S.-led invasion of Iraq in March 2003, al-Sadr was quick to voice his protest of a U.S. presence in his country. A firebrand critic of the invasion, al-Sadr became the bellicose mouthpiece of much of the country's antioccupation sentiment. He was also quick to match his rhetoric with concrete action; on July 18, 2003, he announced the formation of the JAM and called on his marginalized Shiite supporters

to resist the U.S. occupation. JAM forces quickly heeded the call, clashing with U.S. forces first in Baghdad and later in Karbala in October 2003.

The following year was marked by violent uprisings of JAM forces and the rise to prominence of the overall Sadrist movement. Increasingly threatened by al-Sadr's rhetoric and his confrontational stance, U.S. forces shut down al-Sadr's newspaper, *Al Hawza,* on March 28, 2004. Shortly thereafter, they arrested one of al-Sadr's key deputies, Mustafa al-Yacoubi. JAM retaliated with waves of attacks in major Iraqi cities, including Baghdad, Kufa, Karbala, and Najaf. These violent uprisings led to some territorial gains for the group, further undermining U.S. and coalition forces. Although a cease-fire was reached at the end of May 2004, fighting would soon break out again.

In August 2004, motivated by the belief that U.S. forces were preparing to arrest their leader, JAM militants attacked U.S. military forces. The incident set off a much wider conflict that saw serious clashes between the United States and JAM. Heavy fighting quickly overtook Najaf, where a standoff developed between JAM militants and U.S. forces. As JAM forces occupied some of Najaf's holy sites, including the Imam Ali shrine, U.S. troops strafed the city, hesitant to risk damaging the mosque and further inflaming antioccupation sentiments. It took the intervention of the Grand Ayatollah Ali al-Sistani, a revered Shiite cleric, to convince the two sides to agree to a cease-fire later that same month. In total, the fighting in Najaf killed hundreds. Yet, however bloody the incident was, it will be best remembered as the moment JAM thrust itself onto the Iraqi political stage as a powerful stakeholder.

JAM forces would continue to play an active, albeit slightly different, role in the violent struggle over Iraq's future following the August 2004 Najaf clashes. Instead of solely confronting U.S. forces, the Mahdi Army was forced to confront the maelstrom of sectarian violence that swept over Iraq in 2005. In this context, JAM forces entered the country's internecine conflict, partially assuming the role of protector of the country's Shia. As groups like Tanzom Qa'idat al-Jihadi Bilad al-Rafidyan (QJBR), more commonly known as Al-Qaeda in Iraq (AQI), targeted Shiites across Iraq with mass-casualty bombings and other brutal tactics, JAM forces were quick to retaliate with mass abductions and targeted killings. Alongside rival Shiite militia movements like the Badr Organization, JAM forces dealt retaliatory blows to Iraqi Sunnis, accelerating Iraq's bloody Sunni-Shia conflict and pushing the country to the precipice of civil war.

Sectarian violence in Iraq began to wind down after its peak in late 2006. Nonetheless, JAM remained a potent, lethal force, so much so that in 2006 the United States identified the organization as the single greatest threat to the Iraqi state's security, eclipsing QJBR. This assessment was driven in part by the widespread belief that Iran had begun funding and training JAM forces, whose tactical repertoire already included guerrilla tactics such as ambushes, mortar attacks, and placement of improvised explosive devices (IEDs). Now, with Iranian backing, the Mahdi Army began to deploy explosively formed penetrators, a special type of IED capable of piercing the most advanced U.S. armor. In addition to challenging the United States, the group also challenged the Iraqi state, operating on a Hezbollah-like model of building a state within a state, complete with its own army and its own social services infrastructure.

In effect, the group's capabilities and antagonistic posture naturally pitted it against both the United States and the Iraqi

government. As a result, the United States made a special point of targeting JAM elements during the troop surge of 2007. That summer, JAM elements were confronted directly, and pitched battles erupted between U.S. forces and the Mahdi Army. As these clashes took their toll, al-Sadr eventually pulled back, announcing a freeze on all JAM operations in August 2007.

This freeze on JAM activities proved to be ineffective, however, given al-Sadr's limited ability to exercise total control over his movement. Known for its undisciplined and poorly trained fighters, the group never possessed a strong organizational structure. Fractures and splinters were rife within the movement, most prominently the split of Qais al-Khaz'ali, who would go on to found a rival Shiite movement. Compounding JAM's internal troubles was the fact that many elements of the Mahdi Army at times engaged in predatory criminal behavior, extorting from some of those whom it protected or intimidating rival suppliers of services. Many of these rogue elements would ignore al-Sadr's freeze and continue to fight in Basra, as they jockeyed with rival Shiite militias for control of different funding streams, including the city's lucrative oil industry. The intra-Shiite conflict ultimately worsened to such an extent that the Iraqi government felt compelled to take action, and it descended on Basra in March 2008.

The March 2008 Basra offensive was beset by a number of problems. As Iraqi forces confronted JAM militants in Basra, the offensive quickly stalled, but with the assistance of U.S. military support, the tide of the battle slowly turned. JAM forces agreed to a cease-fire on March 30, 2008, and the Iraqi government emerged bruised but victorious. Although the cease-fire held in Basra, fighting continued in Baghdad's Sadr City as JAM elements unleashed a torrent of rocket and mortar attacks on the Green Zone, the site of the Iraqi government and coalition forces' headquarters. Only when Sadr City was literally cordoned off with blast walls did the attacks cease. The Sadr City clashes would serve as the last major instance of serious military confrontation between U.S. and JAM forces.

On June 18, 2008, al-Sadr further solidified his shift away from violent tactics toward political participation by announcing a major reorganization of his militia movement. JAM forces would now operate in one of two categories: First, the majority of the movement would move away from its role as a militant group and instead rededicate itself to its religious and social role, delivering services to its marginalized Shiite base. Second, a smaller cadre of full-time fighters would remain as JAM forces. However, these forces would in essence end up shelved for the next two years. In effect, al-Sadr essentially disbanded JAM, as he calculated that there was more to gain through conventional political channels than in the role of a combatant.

The next two years saw a continual evolution toward a less confrontational Sadrist movement and a wholly inactive JAM. In the March 2010 national parliamentary elections, al-Sadr fared quite well, gaining 40 seats, up from the 29 his movement won in 2005. The group's peaceful orientation would be tested that year, though. In April 2010 elements of QJBR tried to pull JAM back into the cycle of sectarian violence with a series of bombings targeting Iraq's Shia, including mosques and political offices in Sadr City. Al-Sadr responded calmly, and the Mahdi Army refrained from retaliatory attacks.

Nonetheless, one must be cautious about overstating the reorientation of the Sadrist movement as a peaceful, solely political organization. The permanence of the shift

away from violence remains unclear. Although JAM forces did not retaliate in the wake of the April 2010 bombings, conflicting statements emerged among Sadrists surrounding a possible lifting of the freeze on the movement's militia activities. Moreover, Iraq's political future remains uncertain, and the wounds of the country's painful sectarian conflict are still raw. The Mahdi Army still benefits from a large and fiercely antioccupation base. Iran continues to loom in the background, funding, arming, and training JAM elements for possible use as its proxy. In effect, JAM forces still represent a potential serious threat to the stability of Iraq and peace in the country.

Nate Shestak

See also: Al-Qaeda in Iraq (AQI); Hezbollah; Improvised Explosive Devices

Citations

Cochrane, Marisa. "The Fragmentation of the Sadrist Movement," *Iraq Report* 12, Institute for the Study of War, Washington, DC, January 2009.

Cordesman, Anthony H., and Jose Ramos. "Sadr and the Mahdi Army: Evolution, Capabilities, and a New Direction," Center for Strategic and International Studies, Washington, DC, August 4, 2008.

International Crisis Group. "Iraq's Civil War, The Sadrists, and the Surge," *Middle East Report* no. 72, February 7, 2008.

Management of Savagery

The al-Qaeda strategic guide, *Management of Savagery: The Most Critical Stage Through Which the Islamic Nation Will Pass,* was published online under the nom de guerre Abu Bakr Naji, in 2004. In it, he describes themes of nationalism and religious superiority with an emphasis on violence.

The purpose of this book is to instruct al-Qaeda and other extremists on the most effective way to establish and sustain the administration of an Islamic caliphate. Though the true identity of Naji is still a serious matter of debate, the Al-Arabiya Institute for Studies claims that Naji is actually Muhammad Khalil al-Hakaymah, also known as Abu Jihad Al-Masri, originally from Egypt. Al-Hakaymah was recognized by the United States as the head of media and propaganda for al-Qaeda, until his death by air strike in the North Waziristan area of Pakistan on October 31, 2008.

Al-Hakaymah was known as an extremist Islamic strategist, as he wrote several books and pamphlets on jihad. *Management of Savagery* lays out several variations of strategies used extensively by al-Qaeda and, more recently, by ISIS. The author writes on the assumption that the reason the USSR left Afghanistan was the bravery and violence by the rebelling mujahideen, who slowly attenuated and depleted the will of the Soviets to continue fighting. Soon afterward, the USSR collapsed, politically and economically, and withdrew from Afghanistan altogether. The author contends that this same strategy of attrition will work with regard to the United States and other Western enemies.

In his work, Naji calls for a centralized al-Qaeda organizational structure. He urges jihadists, once they are able to seize and hold territory, to erect a governing apparatus and enforce sharia, while governing a true Islamic society. Interestingly, even though Naji was an al-Qaeda ideologue, his model was essentially adopted by the Islamic State.

What Naji describes in his book is a more "hands-on" organizational structure that would avoid redundancy and be better positioned to plan and orchestrate attacks. His hopes were that his work would be influential enough to mitigate the ongoing "near enemy versus far enemy" debate that had bogged down senior al-Qaeda leaders dating back to the group's founding in the late 1980s. Opposed to Abu Musab al-Suri's viewpoints, Naji's work better with safe haven and sanctuary. Even though al-Qaeda is typically described in networked terms, in reality it has been much more hierarchical than many have recognized, suggested, and portrayed.

Another Naji-ism from the book is that to exhaust the forces of the enemy, it is critical that jihadists work to carry out attacks in their adversaries' home countries. His book has sometimes been referred to as "al-Qaeda's playbook."

The themes Naji continuously returns to throughout this book are that violence should be maximized for propaganda value; the need to provoke Western militaries from overreacting and getting bogged down in civil wars; and the jihadists' need to commit to a strategy of attrition. Once again, although Naji was an al-Qaeda theorist, it seems quite apparent that the Islamic State has adhered very closely to many of these tenets.

Naji was reportedly influenced by the thoughts and writings of Ibn Taymiyyah, and he emphasizes the use of extreme violence and cites the regimes in Jordan, Saudi Arabia, Yemen, Nigeria, Pakistan, and several in North Africa as objects of his ire.

The basis of the book is the term "management or administration of savagery," which refers to the period between the waning of one power (foreign enemies) and the consolidation of power of another (in this case, an Islamic caliphate). Thus, to successfully enter into this transition, Bakr Naji proposes a strategy to "enrage the United States so that it oversteps local security forces and engages directly with local jihadis, which in turn incites other Muslims to join the fight against the 'occupying' power, thereby increasing al-Qaeda's strength and prestige." The author's ultimate goal was a harassment of Muslim nations that exhausted their will to exist, completely eroded the state and its powers, resisted foreign occupation through violence, and, ultimately, established an Islamic caliphate.

In another phase of Naji's tome, he focuses on establishing a "fighting society." In this instance, the caliphate should focus on internal improvements such as security, border control, feeding its people, eliminating spies, and establishing sharia law. This is followed by the plundering of financial resources, wherein the caliphate must evolve to become economically independent, which it might seek to accomplish through the usurpation of oil fields, seizing arms, and selling surplus assets.

The phase titled "No Room for Mercy" leads the author to stress that violence is the key to strength. The logic that follows is that, had the Afghan mujahideen demonstrated mercy toward the Soviets, they could not have succeeded in ending the occupation. Thus, the author encourages brutal techniques such as public beheadings as a strategic move to strike fear into the hearts of sovereign citizens and foreign enemies alike. "A Policy of Polarization" leads the author to contend that there must be two sides in this argument, right and wrong, and that every citizen must take a side. Through the strategy of maximum violence, people will realize the conflict is serious and will strongly ally and believe in the ideology of the side that is stronger, especially if they are to potentially risk their lives for that side of the conflict.

In the words of Bakr Naji, "We must make this battle very violent, such that death is a heartbeat away, so that the two groups will realize that entering this battle will frequently lead to death. That will be a powerful motive for the individual to choose to fight in the ranks of the people of truth in order to die well, which is better than dying for falsehood and losing both this world and the next."

This online book has become a set of guidelines for extremist Islamic terrorists across the world, including al-Qaeda, ISIS, and al-Shabaab. Most significantly, the Islamic State of Iraq and Syria (ISIS) has used these strategies in the last few years. They have invaded and occupied territory and drained resources from the area for the purpose of providing for a new Islamic State. They have also provoked Western intervention with acts of violence, in the hope that these nations will continue to attack until they are economically and militarily depleted. ISIS views itself as currently being in the process of the "management of savagery," as it is working on establishing a fighting society, plundering financial resources, committing acts of violence, and polarizing the population.

Colin P. Clarke

See also: Al-Qaeda; Al-Qaeda in Iraq (AQI); Islamic State of Iraq and Syria (ISIS); Jihad; Suri, Abu Musab al-

Citations

Hassan, Hassan. "Isis Has Reached New Depths of Depravity. But There Is a Brutal Logic behind It," *The Guardian* (Islamic State/The Observer), February 7, 2015.

Jackson, Brian A., and Bryce Loidolt, "Considering Al-Qa'ida's Innovation Doctrine: From Strategic Texts to 'Innovation in Practice,'" *Terrorism and Political Violence* 25, no. 2 (2013): 284–310.

Ryan, Michael W. S. "Al-Qaeda's Purpose in Yemen Described in Works of Jihad

Strategists," The Jamestown Foundation, January 28, 2010.

Wright, Lawrence. "ISIS's Savage Strategy in Iraq," *The New Yorker,* May 24, 2017.

Marine Corps Barracks Bombing (Beirut)

On October 23, 1983, a five-ton suicide vehicle-borne improvised explosive device (VBIED) killed 241 U.S. servicemen and wounded 80 others at the U.S. Marine Barracks at Beirut Airport. Minutes later, another VBIED killed 58 French paratroopers and injured 15 others two miles north of the airport. The twin attacks raised serious questions about sending foreign troops to the Middle East to participate in so-called peacekeeping missions and the wisdom of an American president flexing his military muscle around the world. They were also widely credited for the subsequent decision to withdraw the United Nations' Multi-National Force (MNF) from Lebanon, underscoring the asymmetric power of terrorism and its potential to "level the playing field" for substate actors confronting even the strongest, most advanced militaries.

The first terrorist drove a Mercedes truck loaded with the equivalent of 12,000 pounds of TNT enhanced with explosive gas cylinders. He slid through a gate that had been left open, rammed through both barbed wire and a sandbagged sentry post, and detonated the vehicle in the lobby of a building housing the 1st Battalion, 8th Marines of the 2nd Marine Division. The bomb had been placed on top of marble covering a bottom layer of concrete in the back of the truck. This configuration was designed to direct the blast upward and collapse the four-story building. Even so, the explosive force drove the truck bed 8 feet down into the earth and severed the supporting concrete columns, each of which was 15 feet in circumference and reinforced by steel rods. The entire structure then lifted and collapsed on itself. The death toll—220 Marines, 18 Navy personnel, and 3 Army soldiers—was the highest for the Marines since the World War II battle of Iwo Jima and the most serious for any American military unit since the first day of the 1968 Tet Offensive during the Vietnam War.

The ensuing blast left a crater 30 feet deep and 120 feet across. Marine sentries could not fire at the truck because they were required to keep their weapons unloaded while in the barrack building under the terms of their deployment.

The second suicide bomber drove a car loaded with the equivalent of about 1,200 pounds of TNT into the eight-story apartment building housing the French 1st Parachute Chasseur Regiment in the central Beirut district of Ramlet el-Baida. The resultant fatality count was the single worst French military loss since the Algerian War.

Islamic Jihad Organization (IJO, now thought to be the direct predecessor of Hezbollah) took responsibility for both bombings. In phone messages to Agence France-Presse offices in Beirut and Paris, a caller claiming to be a spokesman for the group said, "We are the soldiers of God and we crave death. Violence will remain our only path if they (U.S. and French troops) do not leave. We are ready to turn Lebanon into another Vietnam." Ten days later, IJO carried out a similar bombing against Israel's intelligence headquarters in the Lebanese town of Tyre. This attack killed 61 Palestinians as well as an unspecified number of Israelis.

The three bombings came on the heels of an earlier assault on the U.S. embassy in Beirut. That attack, which took place on April 18, 1983, and involved a VBIED composed of approximately 1,230 pounds of TNT, killed 64 people and wounded between 88 and 100. Among the fatalities was Robert Ames, the Central Intelligence Agency's (CIA) national intelligence officer for the Near East and Washington's key liaison to the Palestine Liberation Organization's (PLO) leadership. He had just walked into the building when the blast occurred.

A massive rescue operation commenced immediately after the Beirut explosions. Helicopters dispatched from the U.S. Sixth Fleet quickly brought many of the wounded to the USS *Iwo Jima*, which had surgical operating facilities onboard. Others were medevaced to various American and European hospitals in Egypt, Italy, Cyprus, and West Germany.

In Washington, a three-hour National Security Council meeting was held, after which President Reagan announced that Commandant General Paul X. Kelley would be dispatched to Beirut to investigate ways of better protecting Marines deployed as peacekeepers in active conflict zones. In Israel, Prime Minister Yitzhak Shamir said those responsible for the bombing were motivated by a desire to halt the peace process in Lebanon. In Moscow, the Russian newspaper *Pravda* proclaimed, "It appears the Viet Nam story begins to repeat itself. The U.S. is getting drawn deeper into the fighting."

Naturally, the United States, France, and Israel wanted to strike back at the terrorists. However, because Western governments had very little information on IJO—up until that time almost all focus had been on the PLO— exactly how to do this was not immediately apparent. Moreover, there was the question of how to infiltrate a fiercely religious movement that obviously had good intelligence of its own and was well organized. Eventually, Paris carried out a retaliatory air strike

against supposed Islamic Revolutionary Guards in Syria's Bekaa Valley. However, there was no serious response from Washington other than to relocate the Marine peacekeepers offshore where they could not be targeted. That decision set in motion the subsequent withdrawal of the entire MNF, which was completed by April 1984, five months after the bombings.

The U.S. government eventually concluded that Hezbollah had carried out the attacks, operating under the banner of IJO with Iranian and Syrian backing. Washington also asserted that this same sponsor-proxy combination was behind the bombing of the U.S. embassy in Beirut on April 18, 1983. In 1985 an American grand jury secretly indicted Imad Mughniyah as the chief architect behind the operations. Although he was never caught, he was killed by a car bomb in Syria on February 12, 2008.

On October 3 and December 28, 2001, the families of those who died in the Marine barracks bombing, together with some survivors, filed civil lawsuits against the Iranian government and its Ministry of Intelligence and Security (MIS). They sought a ruling that Tehran was responsible for the attack and was therefore obligated to pay both punitive and compensatory damages. Iran denied any link to the incident but, notably, did not file court papers to counter the claims.

Important new evidence surfaced during the trial. This included a National Security Agency electronic intercept that had originated with Iran's intelligence headquarters and that instructed Tehran's ambassador in Syria to organize a "spectacular" act against the Marines. On December 18, 2002, the presiding judge in the case, Royce C. Lamberth, determined that the defendants were in default. Four months later he ruled that Iran had provided both financial and logistical support for the bombing, that Hezbollah had actually executed the operation, and that the group had operated with the direct aid of agents from the MIS. On September 7, 2007, Lamberth awarded $2,656,944,877 to the plaintiffs.

Following the bombing, the U.S. Department of Defense issued a report recommending that Washington look at other ways of reaching its goals in Lebanon. It suggested a broader range of "appropriate military, political, and diplomatic responses to terrorism," and said that the army was in urgent need of improving its doctrine, planning, organization, force structure, education, and training to better combat violent extremism.

The Investigations Subcommittee of the House Armed Services Committee was more explicit. It accused the Marines of inadequate intelligence gathering and lax security, and asserted that the entire military chain of command was guilty of "very serious errors in judgment." The subcommittee went on to declare that the ground commander in Beirut was responsible for egregious security lapses and directly faulted the top military officials overseeing the peacekeeping operation for not thoroughly examining the "guts" of protective measures adopted at the barracks. The committee chairman's statement concluded, "If you want to speak of negligence, then it goes all the way up to the combined Joint Chiefs of Staff."

The findings of another commission appointed by President Reagan and led by Admiral Robert L. J. Long similarly lambasted officials for not exercising better judgment in force protection. It proclaimed that even basic measures could have reduced the casualty count, such as constructing concrete barriers around the barracks and allowing sentries to have loaded weapons. The report was held from release while the White House debated the thorny question of how the military could be blamed without conducting court-martials for negligent generals and, more pointedly, without holding the administration accountable for putting the Marines in harm's way in the first place.

The 1983 bombings in Beirut vastly increased the dimensions of contemporary terrorism, heralding the dawn of a new type of militant extremism, which up until that time had been confined mostly to small-scale strikes designed to attract mass publicity rather than cause widespread physical damage per se. The startling success of the operations, pointedly demonstrated by the withdrawal of the MNF from Lebanon, also heralded the initiation of a new, deadly tactic—large-scale suicide bombings—that was to become a characteristic modus operandi in numerous conflict environments around the world. Indeed, the events of 1983 have since been portrayed as one of the most clear-cut cases demonstrating the coercive success of suicide terrorism inflicting unacceptable punishment. As President Reagan later extolled in his memoirs, "The price we had to pay in Beirut was so great, the tragedy at the barracks so enormous. . . . We had to pull out. . . . We couldn't stay there and run the risk of another suicide attack on the Marines."

Donna Bassett

See also: Hezbollah; Improvised Explosive Devices; Jihad

Citations

Chalk, Peter, and Bruce Hoffman. *The Dynamics of Suicide Terrorism: Four Case Studies of Terrorist Movements.* Santa Monica, CA: RAND, 2005.

Davis, Mike. *Buda's Wagon: A Brief History of the Car Bomb.* New York: Verso Books, 2007.

Fisk, Robert. *Pity the Nation: The Abduction of Lebanon*. New York: Touchstone, Simon & Schuster, 1990.

Tyler, Patrick. *A World of Trouble: The White House and the Middle East—from the Cold War to the War on Terror*. New York: Farrar Straus Giroux, 2009.

Wright, Robin. *Sacred Rage: The Wrath of Militant Islam*. New York: Touchstone Books, Simon & Schuster, 2001.

Zisser, Eyal. "Hezbollah in Iran: At the Cross-Roads," *Terrorism and Political Violence* 8, no. 2 (Summer 1996).

Mateen, Omar

Omar Mateen is the domestic American terrorist responsible for the Pulse nightclub terrorist attacks in Orlando, Florida, that killed 49 people and wounded 58 on June 12, 2016, and was considered the deadliest act of violence targeting LGBT people in American history. Mateen pledged allegiance or loyalty to ISIS caliph Abu Bakr al-Baghdadi during a 911 call, identified himself as a "mujahideen," "Islamic soldier," and "soldier of God" at various points during the call, and claimed that the attack was a reaction to the killing of Abu Wahib, an ISIS commander.

Mateen was born on November 16, 1986, in New Hyde Park, New York. His parents were Afghan immigrants to New York in the 1980s, before moving to Port St. Lucie, Florida, in 1991. In middle and elementary school, Mateen was known to have serious behavioral problems that prevented him from getting good grades. Fights, foul language, and general aggression were commonplace in his childhood, and he was placed in several different high schools as a result. In one particular instance, he was recorded as having been suspended for five days for cheering in support of Osama bin Laden just days after the 9/11 attacks. By the time

he graduated high school in 2003, he had a long history of fighting and other forms of violence.

Mateen attended Indian River State College, receiving a degree in criminal justice technology. He then went on to work as a recruit for the Florida Department of Corrections, but never became a certified corrections officers, as he was dismissed in 2007 following disturbing pro-gun comments he made shortly after the Virginia Tech shooting. He then took a job for G4S Secure Solutions as a guard. While employed there, the FBI investigated him twice for telling coworkers he supported militant groups and briefly placed him on the terrorist watch list, but he retained his job. His coworkers described him as "unhinged and unstable," referencing his abundant use of homophobic, racist, and sexist rhetoric. Mateen had two different wives in his lifetime, both of whom contributed accounts detailing his tendency for violence, domestic abuse, and suspicious behavior.

On June 12, 2016, Omar Mateen entered the Pulse gay nightclub in Orlando and opened fire using a legally purchased semi-automatic rifle and a handgun. He was eventually subdued and killed in a shoot-out with police.

Numerous witnesses, including his father, blame Mateen's actions on his extremist Islamic beliefs, which include intense homophobia. Other accounts, however, claim that he may have been gay himself. A former classmate claims that Mateen asked him out at a gay nightclub, several witnesses claim that they had seen him at Pulse at least a dozen times, and others claim to have seen him use online gay dating apps. Numerous journalists explored one popular theory that Mateen was secretly gay and ashamed of it, believing it was against his religious principles. Thus, he committed the crime out of jealousy and anger at himself and his situation. However, the FBI has not found solid proof to back up this narrative, so as such this is not currently considered as the motive to the crime. Further investigations are ongoing to discover Mateen's true motives.

Colin P. Clarke

See also: Homegrown Terrorism; Islamic State of Iraq and Syria (ISIS); Jihad; Lone Wolf Attacks

Citations

Berman, Russell. "Could Congress Have Stopped Omar Mateen from Getting His Guns?" *The Atlantic,* June 14, 2016.

Fagenson, Zachary. "Gunman in U.S. Massacre Described as 'Quiet' but Grew Hateful," *Reuters,* June 14, 2016.

Robles, Frances, and Julie Turkewitz. "Was the Orlando Gunman Gay? The Answer Continues to Elude the F.B.I.," *The New York Times,* June 25, 2016.

Sandoval, Edgar, Chelsia Rose Marcius, and Ginger Adams Otis. "Ex-Classmate Says Orlando Shooter Omar Mateen Was Gay," *NY Daily News,* June 13, 2016.

Metrojet Flight 9268

Metrojet Flight 9268 was an internationally chartered passenger flight operated by Russian airline Kogalymavia. Shortly after takeoff on October 31, 2015, the plane, originating from Sharm el Sheikh international airport in Egypt's Sinai Peninsula, was blown out of the sky, killing 217 passengers and 7 crewmembers aboard. Most were Russian citizens headed back to St. Petersburg airport in Russia. The suspected perpetrator of the attack was the Islamic State's branch in the Sinai, previously known as Ansar Bait al-Maqdis.

Shortly after the attack, ISIS published photos of what it said were the bomb-making components, including a detonator and a switch fastened around a soft drink can. This was a simply constructed bomb, yet one that was powerful enough to take down the entire airliner and kill everyone on the plane. Egyptian authorities have never revealed details of the investigation, including whether it was an insider threat that allowed the bomb and bomb materials to make it through security.

The reason for the attack that was offered was revenge and retaliation for Russia's role in the Syria conflict, as the attack occurred approximately one month after Russia became involved in backing the Syrian regime and Bashar al-Assad.

Wide-scale flight cancellations and delays occurred immediately following the crash. British, American, and Russian authorities quickly placed heavy restrictions and regulations on flights to and from the Sinai Peninsula. Fifty-nine percent of future bookings at the Sharm el Sheikh tourist resort were canceled, causing an estimated loss of US$87 million.

A bevy of theories were raised in the immediate aftermath of the crash. Most prominent among them were the ideas that the plane fell due to fuel explosion, metal fatigue, aircraft pressure bulkhead failure, and lithium batteries overheating. The head of the investigation in Egypt, Ayman al-Muqaddam, worked tirelessly over the course of the next few weeks, and made some startling conclusions. Due to the discovery that the plane came apart in midair and was largely destroyed before even hitting the ground, in combination with evidence of a heat flash at the time of disappearance and audio from the flight data recorder and cockpit voice recorder, Egyptian authorities concluded that the tragedy was almost certainly caused by a bomb detonated in the luggage hold. Within a week of the crash, the consensus shifted from accident to terrorist attack. By November 6, the leadership of the United States, Australia, Israel, United Kingdom, as well as other Western nations considered the crash an act of purposeful political violence. Slow to react, however, was Russia, which did not acknowledge the cause to be a bomb until November 17.

Russian president Vladimir Putin's response to the attack was uncharacteristically subdued. Known for having a short temper and a nationalistic fervor that leads him to value Russian lives over any other, he surprisingly chose to stay reserved, simply offering condolences and dismissing most terrorism narratives, saying that the possibility of a bomb is just "one of the versions." Putin's spokesman Dmitry Peskov was even more blunt, stating on November 3 that "there was not the slightest evidence indicating there was an act of terror." Peskov and other Kremlin officials were quick to deny any correlation between the crash and Russia's military operations in Syria. Dmitry Kiselev, the Kremlin's top propagandist, blamed the attack on a secret pact between America and the Islamic State. According to political analyst Maria Lipman, "The Sinai victims were touchingly mourned, but society has quickly moved on, giving the government space to calibrate its response. Mr Putin is due to deliver his yearly address at the beginning of December. With the aid of television, the crash can be used to fuel further 'patriotic mobilisation.'" Thus, it is most reasonable to conclude that Russia was slow to react or give credence to the bomb theory because it was not in the government's best interest to do so.

Egyptian authorities consider Abu Osama al-Masri a prime suspect. Al-Masri, the leader of the Islamic State branch in Sinai, known as Wilayat Sinai, claimed responsibility shortly after the crash, stating "We are the ones who downed it by the grace of Allah, and we are not compelled to announce the method that brought it down." Wilayat Sinai, previously known as Ansar Bait al-Maqdis, is known to be affiliated with ISIS and to act in accordance with its goals, hoping to establish an Islamic State in Egypt. Two weeks after the crash, an ISIL video celebrated the act of terrorism, claiming that it was done in retaliation for Russian air strikes in Syria.

Colin P. Clarke

See also: Improvised Explosive Devices; Islamic State of Iraq and Syria (ISIS)

Citations

Hassan, Ahmed Mohamed, and Michael Georgy. "Exclusive: Investigators '90 Percent Sure' Bomb Downed Russian Plane," *Reuters*, November 8, 2015.

"Kremlin Warns against Linking A321 Crash in Egypt with Russia's Operation in Syria," *TASS*, accessed June 14, 2017.

Simon Calder Travel Correspondent. "Russian Plane Crash Q&A: Why Has Russia Now Confirmed Metrojet Flight 9268 Was Bombed?" *The Independent,* November 17, 2015.

Wroe, David. "Russian Plane Likely Felled by Smuggled Bomb in Hold: Intelligence," *The Sydney Morning Herald,* November 5, 2015.

Millennium Plots

Leaders of al-Qaeda planned for a series of terrorist operations to take place on or around January 1, 2000. At least three plots surfaced during investigations in the months and weeks before the millennium. Khalid Sheikh Mohammad has claimed credit for planning and financing these plots, whose targets were in three different places: Amman, Jordan; Los Angeles, California; and Aden, Yemen. Fortunately, none of the plots were carried out, but the news clearly indicated that al-Qaeda's leadership was busy concocting plots to the detriment of the United States. Al-Qaeda operatives had planned to bomb the Radisson Hotel in Amman, along with Christian tourist sites in and around the city, on January 1, 2000, hoping to kill as many Americans as possible. Jordanian authorities, however, learned of the plot and raided the terrorists' bomb factory, which was hidden in an upper-middle-class residence. The terrorists had planned to use poisons and other improvised devices to increase the casualties of their attacks, planning to disperse hydrogen cyanide in a downtown Amman movie theater. News of this plot reached American officials in the middle of 1999.

The terrorists also plotted to plant a large bomb at Los Angeles International Airport, a plan that originated in Canada among Muslim militants there. Ahmed Ressam tried to smuggle the explosives from Canada to the United States through the British Columbia–Washington Ferry entry point. An alert U.S. customs officer, Diana Dean, suspicious of Ressam's nervousness, pulled him over and had begun to check the vehicle when Ressam suddenly drove off. Dean and fellow customs officers soon captured him, and an examination of his vehicle revealed a large quantity of explosives and a map of the Los Angeles International Airport. American authorities believed that Ressam would have received assistance from al-Qaeda members in the Los Angeles area, but no proof of this has surfaced.

Finally, the terrorists planned a marine bombing intended to sink the destroyer USS *The Sullivans* at its berth in the port of Aden, Yemen. Al-Qaeda operatives overloaded a small boat with explosives, to the point of sinking, and nothing remained but to cancel the operation. Both because of the covert nature of this operation and because of its failure, American authorities did not learn about this plot until much later, after the attack on USS *Cole*.

Stephen E. Atkins

See also: Al-Qaeda; Bin Laden, Osama

Citations

Loeb, Vernon. "Planned Jan. 2000 Attacks Failed or Were Thwarted; Plot Targeted U.S., Jordan, American Warship, Official Says," *The Washington Post,* December 24, 2000.

Moscow Theater Attack

Scores of masked Chechen men and women armed with automatic weapon stormed the House of Culture for the State Ball-Bearing Factory (the "Dubrovka") Theater in Moscow on October 23, 2002. They took nearly 900 people hostage, beginning a 58-hour siege that ended with the deaths of at least 115 of the captives and possibly as many as 124. Forty-two rebels were also killed, including their leader (Movsar Barayev) and 18 female suicide bombers. Approximately 600 hostages were hospitalized.

The attack began around 9:00 p.m. After an initial period of confusion during which approximately 100 people managed to escape, the terrorists took control of the theater. One of the rebels issued a statement to Radio Echo Moskvy, calling for the immediate withdrawal of Russian troops from Chechnya. He threatened to kill all the hostages if their demands were not met.

To show good faith, the militants released approximately 150 people (mostly Muslim children). However, they said no more would be freed, that land mines had been planted around the theater, and that 10 hostages would be killed for every rebel injured. Tatyana Solnishkina, an orchestra member, called on her cell phone to confirm that the terrorists had lots of explosives and were serious in their intentions. She also asked that the authorities not try to storm the place or start firing.

The rebels separated their captives into three groups: men, women, and foreigners. The latter included citizens of the United States, the United Kingdom, Germany, Austria, Switzerland, Australia, France, Belarus, Azerbaijan, Georgia, Bulgaria, Ukraine, Israel, and the Netherlands. There were at least three Americans and a Russian with a U.S. green card.

A Chechen website later reported that the leader of the attackers was Movsar Barayev (Yasser), the nephew of Arbi Barayev, a Chechen rebel commander who had died in 2001. Barayev had referred to his organization as the Islamic Special Purpose Regiment of the Chechen State Defense Committee (Majlis al-Shura). He called the specific team that had undertaken the siege the Sabotage and Military Surveillance Group of the Riyadh al-Salikhin Martyrs.

Singer-politician Yosif Kobzon, the Duma member from Chechnya, contacted the rebels with a Red Cross representative and managed to negotiate the release of another five hostages. However, he failed to secure the freedom of any further captives during a second visit. Other officials who opened lines of communications with the terrorists included U.S. ambassador Alexander Vershbow and former prime minister Yevgeny Primakov. Between October 25 and 26, another 34 hostages were released. Whether this was the result of the efforts of the two intermediaries is not known.

The time line for the ensuing events remains unclear. At some point a male hostage apparently threw a bottle at a Chechen woman and tried to charge her. She shot him dead, along with a nearby woman. According to some reports, the terrorists then refused to make any further concessions to improve the condition of their captives and killed another two hostages when a group tried to escape.

Fearing that the situation was spiraling out of control, a decision was made to initiate a rescue operation. A combined team of elite Spetsnaz (literally Special Purposes) Federal Security Service and Ministry of the Interior forces was assembled. After pumping a chemical agent (never identified but thought to be either fentanyl or 3-methylfentanyl) into the building's ventilation system, they stormed the theater. Several rebels were captured or killed, and although the government claimed that all the hostages had been successfully released, many had to be immediately treated for bullet wounds and the side effects of breathing in the incapacitating gas. Many of these people subsequently died. Initially, it appeared that all of the foreign captives had survived. However, it later transpired that an American had died.

The attack prompted President Vladimir Putin to tighten Russia's grip on Chechnya. Two days after the crisis, his government announced that unspecified "measures adequate to the threat" would be taken in response to terrorist activity. Reports subsequently emerged that at least 30 rebel fighters had been killed in Grozny. The Ministry of Defence also canceled plans to reduce the 8,000 troops deployed in the breakaway republic. The theater reopened on January 25, 2003, after undergoing $2.5 million in renovations, including the installation of a completely revamped security system.

Donna Bassett

See also: Beslan School Hostage Crisis

Citations

Mickolus, Edward F., with Susan L. Simmons. *Terrorism, 2002–2004: A Chronology.* Vol. 2. Westport CT: Praeger Security International, 2006.

Murphy, Paul. *The Wolves of Islam: Russia and the Faces of Chechen Terrorism.* Dulles, VA: Brassey's, 2004.

Rabasa, Angel, Peter Chalk, Kim Cragin, Sara A. Daly, Heather S. Gregg, Theodore W. Karasik, Kevin A. O'Brien, and William Rosenau. *Beyond al-Qaeda. Part 1: The Global Jihadist Movement.* Santa Monica, CA: RAND, 2006.

Smith, Sebastian. *Allah's Mountains: The Battle for Chechnya.* London: I. B. Tauris, 2001.

Walsh, Nick, and Jonathan Steele. "Chechen Gunmen Storm Moscow Theatre," *The Guardian,* October 24, 2002, www.guardian.co.uk/world/2002/oct/24/russia.chechnya, accessed September 12, 2011.

Mumbai Attacks (2008)

The Mumbai terrorist attacks of November 2008 struck several locations in India's main commercial center, resulting in a 60-hour standoff and the deaths of 179 people. The highly coordinated assault, which simultaneously hit locations throughout the city on the night of November 26, brought into focus India's increased vulnerability to global terrorism. It also strained relations between the country and its neighbor, Pakistan, where Islamic militants—including those belonging to the group believed responsible for the attacks, Lashkar-e-Taiba (LeT)—are known to train and operate.

Although only 10 well-armed gunmen carried out the Mumbai assault, they quickly killed dozens and took hundreds hostage, focusing in particular on places frequented by tourists, especially Americans and British, as well as a local Jewish center. The attacks began just after 9:00 p.m. on November 26, when the gunmen opened fire almost simultaneously on the Chhatrapati Shivaji railway station, the Cama and Albless Hospital, Café Leopold, the Metro Cinema, the Oberoi-Trident Hotel, the Taj Mahal Palace Hotel, and the Jewish Chabad Lubavitch Center. In addition, at least two taxis exploded, one near Chhatrapati Shivaji Airport and another near a dockyard. Gunshots were also fired that night at a state bank, a municipal building, and a second hospital.

The 2008 assault was the latest in a series of high-profile terrorist acts targeting Mumbai (formerly known as Bombay), including bombings on the city's railway network in July 2006, which killed 187 people; twin explosions in the heart of the financial district in August 2003 that left 53 dead; and a wave of near-simultaneous attacks in 1993 that inflicted a toll of 250 fatalities. Besides these instances, India endured an attack on its national parliament in December 2001, and another at an amusement park in the city of Hyderabad in August 2007. Many of these incidents have also been blamed on LeT, which was first established by Pakistan's Inter-Services Intelligence (ISI) Directorate in 1989 to fight Indian occupation of Jammu and Kashmir—Delhi's only Muslim-majority state. After the November 2008 attack on Mumbai, the United Nations declared LeT a terrorist organization.

Despite the frequency with which India has experienced high-profile terrorist attacks, and although Delhi received specific warnings from the United States about a possible strike on "touristy areas frequented by Westerners" in Mumbai, the government was not prepared for the November 2008 assault in Mumbai. The country's shoreline was inadequately patrolled and protected (the 10 terrorists who carried out the attack arrived by sea); the police who initially responded to the attacks were undertrained and outgunned and lacked basic protective and communication equipment; and India's elite antiterrorist squad, the National Security Guards, could not be rapidly dispatched to secure the situation, as their main base is located hundreds of miles from Mumbai (in Delhi), and they do not have any aviation transport of their own.

In addition to shooting dozens of people throughout the city, the attackers abducted hundreds from two luxury hotels and the Nariman House, which houses the Chabad Lubavitch Center. The National Security Guards first regained control of the Oberoi-Trident Hotel at 11 a.m. on November 28, a day and a half after two of the gunmen had stormed the building and taken close to 400 people hostage. Twenty-four people in the hotel, as well as the two terrorists, were killed. Police next secured the Nariman House at 6 p.m. on November 28, killing two gunmen, who had already executed their six captives.

The longest standoff occurred at the Taj Mahal Palace Hotel, where about 450 people were staying. The siege lasted until 8:30 a.m. on November 29 and left 50 guests dead, in addition to three attackers. Overall, 9 of the 10 militants were killed. The sole surviving member of the assault team, Mohammad Ajmal Kasab, was captured and in May 2010 received the death penalty; he is currently appealing his sentence.

In the aftermath of the assault, tens of thousands of Indian citizens—in both Mumbai and other major cities—launched angry protests over the nation's lack of security. In particular, they vented their anger against a governing and police administration that they charged had not only ignored warnings about a possible terrorist attack in the first place but, when it occurred, also singularly

failed to end it sooner. Outside the United Nations office in Pakistan-administered Kashmir, hundreds of Muslims gathered to chant slogans against Delhi, Washington, and the West in general. The Islamic minority within India, however, universally denounced the terrorist attacks and refused to allow the gunmen to be buried in any of the country's Muslim cemeteries.

Meanwhile, tensions and angry rhetoric grew between India and Pakistan, which have a history of difficult relations over Jammu and Kashmir and other issues, and have fought several wars in the past. Delhi has long accused Islamabad of turning a blind eye to, or even supporting, militant Islamists operating within its borders, and specifically charged that the Mumbai attacks were carried out by LeT with the explicit knowledge and backing of the ISI. India also angrily dismissed Pakistan's defense that LeT had been banned by then president Pervez Musharraf in 2001, pointing out that the group continues to operate openly in many parts of the country through its charitable arm, Jama'at-ud-Da'awa.

For its part, Islamabad has consistently maintained that there is no evidence to support the claim that LeT was behind the attacks and that those involved had any connection to the country's intelligence services. Although a renewed crackdown was launched on LeT in the weeks following the attacks, this basic stance has not changed. Indeed, in 2009 the government cleared the group's leader and founder, Hafiz Muhammad Saeed, of all charges related to the incident and has categorically refused to extradite him to stand trial in India.

Despite Pakistan's denials, many in the West believe that LeT was responsible for the Mumbai attacks, and that even if the ISI did not support the operation directly, it must have had some knowledge of the assault. The episode has also galvanized fears in Europe and the United States that LeT may be emerging as a new and dangerous transnational terrorist threat independent of al-Qaeda, particularly given its purported ties to so-called homegrown militants in Britain, America, and Australia.

Terri Nichols

See also: Lashkar-e-Taiba (LeT)

Citations

Hodge, Amanda. "Death Penalty Looming for Mumbai Gunman," *The Australian*, May 4, 2010.

Kronstadt, Alan. *Terrorist Attacks in Mumbai, India, and Implications for U.S. Interests.* Washington, DC: Congressional Research Service Report for Congress, December 19, 2008, https://fas.org/sgp/crs/terror/R40087 .pdf, accessed December 21, 2017.

McElroy, Damien. "Mumbai Attacks: Foreign Government's Criticize India's Response," *Daily Telegraph* (UK), November 28, 2008.

New York Police Department Intelligence Division. *Mumbai Attack Analysis.* New York: New York Police Department, December 4, 2008.

Page, Jeremy. "Outgunned Mumbai Police Hampered by First World War Weapons," TimesOnline, December 3, 2008, www .thetimes.co.uk/article/outgunned-mumbai -police-hampered-by-first-world-war-weap ons-2q87mkbsqz3.

Rabasa, Angel, Robert Blackwill, Peter Chalk, Kim Cragin, Christine C. Fair, Brian Jackson, Brian Jenkins, Seth Jones, Nate Shestak, and Ashley Tellis. *The Lessons of Mumbai.* Santa Monica, CA: RAND, 2009.

Munich Olympic Games Massacre

The games of the 20th Olympiad, held in Munich from August 26 to September 11, 1972, were the largest ever. The games set records in all categories, with 195 events and 7,123 athletes from 121 nations. But the games themselves were overshadowed and forever marred by a heinous act. These Olympic Games were the first to be held in Germany since 1936, and the Germans hoped they would help erase the racism that marked the 1936 Olympic Games in Berlin during the Nazi era. Yet the most memorable photograph to come out of the 1972 games was not American Mark Spitz receiving his seventh gold medal in swimming but rather the image of a masked Palestinian terrorist standing on a balcony and brandishing an automatic weapon.

Early on the morning of September 5, 1972, with 10 days of the games having gone by without incident and 6 days remaining, eight members of the Black September Organization (BSO) associated with Yasser Arafat's al-Fatah faction of the Palestine Liberation Organization (PLO), dressed as athletes, gained entrance to the Olympic Village, five of them by scaling a fence. Carrying their weapons in gym bags, they sought out the apartment building housing the Israeli athletes.

At about 5:00 a.m. there was a knock on the door of one of the Israeli rooms. Wrestling coach Moshe Weinberg opened it, saw the armed terrorists, and tried to close the door, shouting to other people in the room to flee. Weinberg died in a hail of bullets. An Israeli weight lifter in another room was also shot dead. The terrorists then took nine Israelis hostage.

As 300 German security police cordoned off the area, International Olympic Committee president Avery Brundage met with his staff and decided that the games would continue. At about 9:30 a.m. the terrorists opened negotiations with German authorities, headed by Munich police chief Manfred

MOSHE WEINBERG   KEHAT SHORR   YAAKOV SPRINGER

YOSEF GOTTFREUND   ELIEZER HALFIN   AMITZUR SHAPIRA

Pictures of six Israeli Olympic team members killed in the Palestinian terrorist attack at the 1972 Summer Games in Munich, Germany. They are (L-R from top) trainer Moshe Weinberg, official Kehat Shorr, official Yakov Springer, official Yossef Gutfreund, wrestler Eliezer Halfin, and official Amitzur Shapira. Eleven Israelis were killed in the attack. (Getty Images)

Schreiber. The hostage takers demanded that Israel free 234 Arab prisoners and that West Germany release two German terrorist leaders imprisoned in Frankfurt. The terrorists set a noon deadline and threatened to kill two of the hostages if their demands were not met.

Negotiations continued, and the deadline was repeatedly postponed. The terrorists rejected both a ransom payment and the proposal that Schreiber and two other high-ranking officials take the hostages' place. With Schreiber believing that the building could not be successfully stormed, that evening the two sides reached a deal providing for a plane that would take both the terrorists and their hostages to Cairo. Meanwhile, German sharpshooters took up position.

Security personnel set up a helicopter pad near the apartment complex, and at 8:40 p.m.

the first of three helicopters landed. Fifteen miles away at the Fürstenfeldbruck military air base, a Lufthansa 737 jet stood ready, with German sharpshooters also positioned there.

Shortly after 10:00 p.m. the bound-together and blindfolded hostages and their captors emerged from the apartment building and were herded onto a bus. The terrorists conducted this movement in such fashion that the police were unable to make any attempt to shoot them. Schreiber and two officials joined the bus ride to the helicopters, which then ferried everyone to the airport.

Certain that the incident would end in the deaths of the hostages, German officials were determined to prevent the departure. At 3:00 a.m. on September 6, German sharpshooters opened fire on two terrorists who had just inspected the plane. In the bloody shoot-out that followed, a terrorist threw a grenade into one of the helicopters, killing all within. Other terrorists killed the remaining blindfolded hostages in another helicopter. In all, the incident claimed the lives of 11 Israelis, 5 terrorists, and 1 German policeman. Three of the terrorists were captured alive and imprisoned.

Less than two months later, in response to the hijacking of a Lufthansa jet, the German government released the three imprisoned terrorists and allowed them to fly to Libya. Israeli prime minister Golda Meir and her cabinet, meanwhile, approved a top-secret operation by the Mossad (Israeli intelligence service) to track down and kill those responsible for the Munich atrocity. The Mossad's success in this operation and its moral implications are the subject of the 2005 film *Munich,* directed by Steven Spielberg.

Spencer C. Tucker

See also: Al-Fatah; Arafat, Yasser; Black September Organization; Palestine Liberation Organization (PLO)

Citations

Jonas, George. *Vengeance: The True Story of an Israeli Counter-Terrorist Team.* New York: Atria, 2016.

Klein, Aaron J. *Striking Back: The 1972 Olympics Massacre and Israel's Deadly Response.* New York: Random House, 2005.

Muslim Brotherhood

The Muslim Brotherhood, or Al Ikhwan Al Moslemoon, is an Islamist organization that since 1928 has promoted the Islamic way of life. With branches in over 70 countries, the Muslim Brotherhood provides education, social services, and fellowship for Muslims who want to observe a strict form of the religion. Members have been involved in terrorism and assassination attempts throughout the 20th and 21st centuries. The group has opposed the formation of Israel and has participated in Palestinian attempts to rid themselves of Israeli control. Supporters of the Muslim Brotherhood claim that it is extremely popular with the people of Arab nations, is more moderate than groups such as al-Qaeda, and has not in fact been involved in nearly as much violence as has been claimed. Opponents claim that the Brotherhood is a terrorist organization and is destructive to efforts to create peace in the Middle East.

The Muslim Brotherhood was founded in March 1928 in Egypt. Its founder, Hasan al-Banna, was a 22-year-old elementary school teacher. Al-Banna believed that Islam should be a way of life, not just a religion to be observed on ceremonial occasions, and that Wahhabism, or Islamism, was the proper form of Islam. He opposed Sufism. He particularly wanted to create an organization that would revive Islamic rules of living and family values in the face of secularization and encroaching Westernization. He was motivated by the collapse of the Ottoman Empire and the establishment of a secular Turkish state, which he saw as a threat to the Islamic world. He believed that Islamists should be involved in the government and encourage it to spread and defend Islam. The organization's motto was "Allah is our objective. The Prophet is our leader. Qur'an is our law. Jihad is our way. Dying in the way of Allah is our highest hope."

In its first years, the Muslim Brotherhood sponsored social and educational programs for young people, preaching its strict interpretation of the Quran. The organization quickly became extremely popular, partly because it emphasized fun activities, such as sports and group trips. The group followed a set of eight tenets. These included rejecting anything that contradicted the Quran or Sunna, working to spread the Sunna into every part of life, loving fellow Muslims, working to Islamize the government, engaging in regular physical exercise, and preserving physical health, studying, economically supporting and sponsoring Islamist projects, and fostering social ties with other members of the Muslim Brotherhood. The group emphasized living as a conscientious Muslim, building a good Muslim family and educating children in Islam, and creating a Muslim society and state.

The Muslim Brotherhood became involved in politics in the late 1930s. Al-Banna formed branches of the organization in Syria (1935), Transjordan (1942), and Palestine (1942). By the end of World War II there were branches of the organization throughout the Middle East. The group was adamantly opposed to the creation of Israel, and many of its members fought in the Arab-Israeli War (1948–1949). It disapproved of what it considered the Egyptian government's failure to take action against Zionists and began performing acts of terrorism within Egypt. Egypt banned the group briefly, but it was legal again in 1948, though it was supposed to act only as a religious organization. On December 28, 1948, a member of the Muslim Brotherhood assassinated Egyptian prime minister Mahmud Fahmi Nokrashi. The Egyptian government retaliated by killing al-Banna in February 1949.

When Gamal Abdel Nasser came to power in 1954, the Muslim Brotherhood initially supported him but members were disappointed when he did not put Egypt under sharia law. A member of the organization attempted to assassinate Nasser on October 26, 1954, and Nasser responded by banning the Muslim Brotherhood and imprisoning over 4,000 of its members. Other members moved to Syria, Saudi Arabia, Lebanon, and Jordan. In Jordan, the group supported King Hussein when Nasser attempted to overthrow him. In 1957, King Hussein made the Muslim Brotherhood the only legal political party in Jordan. Syria joined Egypt in the United Arab Republic in 1958, and the Syrian Muslim Brotherhood went underground until Syria left the organization in 1961. The Brotherhood won 10 seats in the next elections, but had to go underground again after the Baath coup in 1963.

Nasser granted amnesty to the imprisoned members of the Brotherhood in 1964. Members of the group responded by trying to kill Nasser three more times in the next year. In 1966 Nasser executed several Muslim Brotherhood leaders and imprisoned many more. Anwar Sadat (president of Egypt, 1970–1981) initially pleased the Muslim Brotherhood by promising to impose sharia law on Egypt. Syria's new president, Hafez al-Assad (president, 1971–2000), however, upset the Brotherhood tremendously because he was an Alawite, so the group did not consider him a Muslim at all. The Muslim Brotherhood declared jihad against al-Assad and began a series of terrorist attacks and assassination attempts. The group tried to assassinate al-Assad in 1980, and in response al-Assad made membership in the Brotherhood a capital offense and had the army wipe out the entire organization. Many members were killed; those who survived fled to other Arab nations. The Egyptian Muslim Brotherhood was deeply angered by Sadat's 1979 peace treaty with Israel. Sadat was assassinated in 1981, by a member of another Islamist group called the Islamic Jihad.

In Israel, Muslim Brotherhood member Ahmed Yassin spent the 1970s running welfare organizations for Palestinian Muslims with the permission of the Israeli government. He became tremendously popular, and in 1987 was one of the founding members of Hamas. The Muslim Brotherhood was once again permitted to operate in Egypt in 1984, though the government kept it under tight control and did not allow it to participate in elections. In 1993 the Muslim Brotherhood became the group with the largest number of seats in Jordan's parliament. The organization is said to be involved in the Afghan resistance and the revolts in Chechnya. It generally supports democracy and free elections.

The Arab Spring, which began in 2010, initially looked promising for the Muslim Brotherhood. In 2011, the organization was legalized in Egypt, and it subsequently participated in parliamentary elections. In the 2012 Egyptian presidential election, the Muslim Brotherhood backed Mohamed Morsi, who was committed to aligning Egyptian laws with sharia law. He won the contest, but soon overreached and was ousted by the Egyptian military in July 2013. This was a significant reversal in the Brotherhood's fortunes. Within weeks, Egypt's military-run government initiated a crackdown against the Muslim Brotherhood; in December 2013, the interim government declared the Brotherhood a terrorist organization. The group has reportedly been involved to some extent in the Syrian Civil War (2011–present). In March 2014 the Saudi government labeled the Brotherhood as a terrorist group.

Amy Hackney Blackwell

See also: Egyptian Islamic Jihad (EIJ); Hamas; Qutb, Sayyid

Citations

Hourani, Albert. *A History of the Arab Peoples.* New York: Warner, 1992.

Kepel, Gilles. *Muslim Extremism in Egypt.* Berkeley: University of California Press, 2003.

Mitchell, Richard P. *The Society of Muslim Brothers.* Oxford: Oxford University Press, 1993.

Smith, Charles D. *Palestine and the Arab-Israeli Conflict: A History with Documents.* 6th ed. New York: Bedford/St. Martin's, 2006.

N

Nice (France) Attacks (2016)

On July 14, 2016, a rental truck driven by Mohamed Lahouaiej-Bouhlel drove onto a promenade sidewalk crowded with people for Bastille Day celebrations in Nice, France. Eighty-seven people died, including the driver, and 450 were wounded. The time and place were chosen because it would cause the most casualties. The truck was driven for about a mile before French police stopped it; the attacker was subsequently killed, and two automatic weapons were recovered.

Mohamed Lahouaiej-Bouhlel was known to have a history of threats, violence, and theft, but was not under any suspicion for terrorism. He was born in Tunisia but had been a resident of Nice since 2005, working as a truck driver. Neighbors and others who knew him described him as a secluded and not very religious man, known for gambling and drinking, who they believe was radicalized shortly before carrying out the attack. Local Muslims say he was not active in any mosque in Nice until April 2016, and it is believed that he turned to radical Islamic terrorism just weeks before the attack, after being convinced by an Algerian member of ISIS living in Nice. ISIS claimed responsibility for his actions, calling him a "soldier of the Islamic State." The nature of this event has been described as a "lone wolf attack," because Lahouaiej-Bouhlel was not known to have been directly involved with ISIS membership; rather, he was influenced by them to take violent action in support of the Islamic State.

Dozens of foreign governments were quick to condemn the attack. U.S. President Barack Obama addressed Americans and their allies by saying that they cannot do the terrorists' work for them by targeting people for their race or religion, noting that nearly a third of the victims were Muslim. French President François Hollande was reportedly booed by crowds while holding a moment of silence for the victims, due to the recent influx of terror attacks in France and the lack of government support to stop it. Popular French politicians such as François Fillon and Marine Le Pen were given warmer receptions in their calls to end Islamic terrorism. The ongoing state of emergency in France was continued in response to the attack. Financial markets were affected, as the Euro fell lower in price and tourism to France suffered. Thousands of homes were raided in the search for suspects, but in the end only one terrorism-related suspect was prosecuted for assisting the perpetrator.

Colin P. Clarke

See also: Homegrown Terrorism; Islamic State of Iraq and Syria (ISIS); Jihad; Lone Wolf Attacks

Citations

Beaumont, Peter. "Mohamed Lahouaiej-Bouhlel: Who Was the Bastille Day Truck Attacker?" *The Guardian,* July 15, 2016.

"Nice Attack: What We Know about the Bastille Day Killings," *BBC News,* August 19, 2016.

Rawlinson, Kevin, Bonnie Malkin, Alan Yuhas, Matthew Weaver, Jason Burke, Rachel Obordo, et al. "Nice Attack: Truck Driver Named as France Mourns 84 Killed in Bastille Day Atrocity—as It Happened," *The Guardian,* July 15, 2016.

Rubin, Alissa J., and Aurelien Breeden. "France Remembers the Nice Attack: 'We Will Never Find the Words,'" *The New York Times,* July 14, 2017.

"Three More Charged over Truck Attack in Nice," *Sky News,* December 17, 2016.

O

Oklahoma City Bombing

On April 19, 1995, a massive explosion caused by the detonation of homemade explosives left in a parked truck tore apart the Alfred P. Murrah Federal Building in Oklahoma City, Oklahoma. The final death toll amounted to 168 people killed in the blast, including 10 children who were being cared for at a day care center. This single act of domestic terrorism brought home to the American people the violent discontent of the so-called militia movement against the federal government in general and against the Federal Bureau of Investigation (FBI) and the Bureau of Alcohol, Tobacco, Firearms and Explosives (BATFE) in particular. Until the World Trade Center and Pentagon attacks of September 11, 2001, the Oklahoma City bombing was the worst act of terrorism in U.S. history, and it underscored the nation's vulnerability to terrorist acts. The investigation into the attack, "OKBOMB," remains one of the largest ever undertaken in the United States, involving 28,000 interviews and the eventual collection of over 3.5 tons of evidence.

The Oklahoma City bombing was supposedly carried out in revenge for the 1993 government siege of the Branch Davidian compound near Waco, Texas. Militia members contended that the deaths of the 82 Branch Davidians in the FBI- and BATFE-led assault were a taste of what lay ahead for similar antigovernment dissidents. Timothy McVeigh, a resident of Kingman, Arizona, initially intended only to destroy a federal building but later decided that his message would be better received if the attack also involved casualties. His eventual criterion for potential venues was that the target should house at least two of three federal law-enforcement agencies: the BATFE, FBI, or Drug Enforcement Agency (DEA). He regarded the presence of additional law-enforcement agencies, such as the Secret Service or the U.S. Marshals Service, as a bonus.

McVeigh apparently considered targets in Missouri, Arizona, Texas, and Arkansas. McVeigh stated in his authorized biography that he wanted to minimize nongovernmental casualties, so he ruled out a 40-story government building in Little Rock, Arkansas, because of the presence of a florist's shop on the ground floor. In December 1994, McVeigh visited Oklahoma City and inspected the Alfred P. Murrah Federal Building. The office complex, built in 1977, housed 14 federal agencies including the DEA, BATFE, Social Security Administration, and recruiting offices for the Army and Marine Corps. McVeigh decided that the building was perfect for his needs, given the number of government bureaucracies represented there, its glass front (expected to shatter under the impact of the blast), and its adjacent large parking lot across the street. In addition, McVeigh believed that the open space around the building would provide better photo opportunities for propaganda purposes.

The bomb that was used to destroy the Murrah Building weighed a massive 4,800 pounds and consisted of 108 bags of ammonium nitrate fertilizer, three 55-gallon tanks

Search and Rescue crews work to save those trapped beneath the debris, following the Oklahoma City bombing, April 26, 1995. The bombing was orchestrated by Timothy McVeigh, who espoused a range of antigovernment beliefs and whose motive was in part, to retaliate for U.S. government raids in Waco and Ruby Ridge. McVeigh was executed in June 2001. (Federal Emergency Management Agency [FEMA])

of liquid nitromethane, several crates of Tovex, and 17 sacks of ANFO. The device was packed into a rented Ryder truck and driven to the site. The detonation occurred at 9:02 a.m. on April 19, 1995, and was timed to coincide with the anniversary of the Waco siege and the 220th anniversary of the Battles of Lexington and Concord. The explosion destroyed 324 buildings in a 16-block radius, killed 168 people, and injured another 680. Total damage exceeded US$650 million.

Following the bombing a nationwide manhunt was launched to search for the person or people responsible for the attack. Two men, Timothy J. McVeigh, a veteran of the Persian Gulf War, and his army friend Terry Lynn Nichols, were ultimately charged with the crime. At a trial held in Denver, Colorado, McVeigh was found guilty by a federal jury and formally sentenced to death on August 14, 1997. Nichols was found guilty of conspiracy and manslaughter and was sentenced to life imprisonment on June 4, 1998. The government prosecution maintained that McVeigh, a militia member who held radical antigovernment views, was primarily responsible for the Oklahoma City bombing and had executed his plan with Nichols's assistance. On April 19, 2000, the former site of the Murrah Building, which had to be completely demolished, was dedicated as the Oklahoma City National Memorial, a unit of the national park system. After several appeals, McVeigh was executed by lethal injection on June 11, 2001. Nichols remains in federal prison.

Peter Chalk

See also: Homegrown Terrorism; Improvised Explosive Devices; Kaczynski, Ted

Citations

Collins, James, Patrick Cole, and Elaine Shannon. "Oklahoma City: The Weight of Evidence," *Time,* April 28, 1997.

"Lessons Learned and Not Learned 11 Years Later," Associated Press, April 16, 2006.

Linder, Douglas. "The Oklahoma City Bombing and the Trial of Timothy McVeigh," Social Science Research Network, November 17, 2007, http://law2.umkc.edu/faculty /PROJECTS/FTRIALS/mcveigh/mcve ighaccount.html, accessed November 10, 2017.

Lou, Michael, and Dan Herbeck. *Alfred Murrah Building Bombing: After Action Report.* Oklahoma City, OK: Oklahoma Police Department, 1995, www.ok.gov/OEM/doc uments/Bombing%20After%20Action%20 Report.pdf.

Lou, Michael, and Dan Herbeck. *American Terrorist: Timothy McVeigh and the Oklahoma City Bombing.* New York: Harper-Collins, 2001.

P

Palestine Liberation Organization (PLO)

A political and military organization founded in 1964 and dedicated to protecting the human and legal rights of Palestinians and creating an independent state for Palestinian Arabs in Palestine. Since the 1960s, the Munazzamat al-Tahrir Filastiniyyah (Palestine Liberation Organization, PLO) has functioned as the official mouthpiece for the Palestinian people. Numerous factions and organizations loosely fall under the PLO's umbrella. In addition to al-Fatah, which is the largest of these groups, the PLO has also encompassed the Popular Front for the Liberation of Palestine (PFLP), the Democratic Front for the Liberation of Palestine (DFLP), the Palestinian People's Party, the Palestine Liberation Front (PLF), the Arab Liberation Front, al-Saiqa (Syrian Baathists), the Palestine Democratic Union, the Palestinian Popular Front Struggle, and the Palestinian Arab Front. Two groups no longer associated with the PLO include the Popular Front for the Liberation of Palestine–General Command (PFLP-GC) and the Fatah Uprising.

The PLO is comprised of centrist-nationalist groups (such as al-Fatah), rightist groups, leftist groups (including communists), militant groups, and nonmilitant groups. It has purposely eschewed embracing any one political philosophy so as to be as inclusive as possible in its membership. The PLO has been enormously successful in attracting funding over the years. Indeed, a 1993 survey estimated the PLO's total assets at between US$8 billion and $10 billion and its average yearly income at $1.5 billion to $2 billion. The PLO was founded in 1964 by the Arab League and Egypt. Its first president was Ahmad Shukeiri. The stated purpose of the PLO was the liberation of Palestine, condemnation of Zionist imperialism, and the dissolution of Israel through the use of armed force. Throughout its existence, the PLO has often used violence to express its viewpoints and gain international attention. This has earned it the reputation of being a terrorist organization, although Palestinians and many international observers dispute that characterization.

In 1988, PLO chairman Yasser Arafat— who led the organization from 1969 to 2004—renounced violence as a means to achieve Palestinian goals, but a number of PLO groups did not follow this decree and have continued to mount terrorist attacks in Israel and elsewhere. Although the PLO has been reorganized many times since its inception, its leading governing bodies have been the Palestinian National Council (PNC), the Central Council, and the Executive Committee. The PNC has 300 members and functions as a nominal legislature. The Executive Committee has 15 members elected by the PNC and holds the PLO's real political and executive power. The Palestinian Revolution Forces are the PLO's military arm. (The Palestine Liberation Army, or PLA, a military group in Syria during the 1970s, was never part of the PLO.)

The PLO has always had a variety of viewpoints represented, some more radical and prone to violence than others, and

Khalil al-Wazir, also known as Abu Jihad, Arafat's right-hand man in the Palestine Liberation Organization, at a preparatory meeting for the Palestinian National Council, February 13, 1983. The PLO was the main force in the Palestinian revolutionary movement, founded on an ideology defined by Palestinian nationalism. It is currently led by Mahmoud Abbas. (Alain Nogues/Corbis Sygma)

Egyptians dominated the organization in its first years. As the 1960s wore on, fedayeen organizations—groups that existed expressly to take up the armed struggle against the Israelis—became more powerful. These groups used guerrilla and paramilitary tactics to resist the encroachment of Israelis on what they considered Palestinian territory. In 1968 al-Fatah took control of the PLO's activities after Arafat appeared on the cover of *Time* magazine as the chairman of the Palestinian movement. On February 3, 1969, the PNC in Cairo officially appointed

Arafat chairman of the PLO. Over the next four years, Arafat had become the commander in chief of the PLO's military branch, the Palestinian Revolution Forces, and the political leader of the organization. He based the PLO in Jordan. In 1968 and 1969, the PLO functioned as a well-organized unofficial state within Jordan, with its uniformed soldiers acting as a police force and collecting their own taxes. In 1968 King Hussein of Jordan and the PLO signed an agreement by which the PLO agreed that its members would stop patrolling in uniform with guns, stop searching civilian vehicles, and act as Jordanian civilian citizens.

The PLO did not comply with this agreement, however, and both attacks on civilians and clashes between Palestinians and Jordanian soldiers increased. By 1970 Hussein decided that the Palestinians threatened national security and ordered his army to evict them. This led to several months of violence, during which Syria aided the Palestinians and the United States aided Jordan. The events of Black September (including an attempt on Hussein's life), several airliner hijackings by the PFLP, and a declaration of martial law in Jordan culminated with the PLO agreeing to a cease-fire on September 24 and promising to leave the country. Arafat now relocated the PLO to Beirut, Lebanon. There, Palestinians moved into existing refugee settlements. The Lebanese government tried to restrict the PLO's movements, which led to tensions, but the Palestinians used their position to launch periodic attacks across the Israeli border. Lebanese Muslims and members of Kamal Jumblatt's progressive coalition supported the Palestinian cause, seeing the Palestinians as allies in their struggle against certain Christian factions who dominated the government and the Lebanese Forces (Maronite militias). The latter disliked the PLO presence and wanted to drive the Palestinians out by force.

During the early 1970s, Arafat and the various groups that comprised the PLO often came into conflict over the proper means of achieving the organization's goals. Although Arafat agreed that a certain amount of violence against Israel was necessary to accomplish the PLO's purposes, he believed that diplomacy and compromise were also key to gaining international support. After 1968, the more politically radical groups, such as the PFLP, the DFLP, and other smaller factions, strongly disagreed because it seemed apparent that the Arab countries could not defeat Israel militarily. Such groups gained notoriety for their airplane hijackings in the late 1960s and early 1970s, carried out in Europe and the Middle East. These attacks were intended to further efforts to destroy Israel and create a socialist secular Arab society in its stead. Arafat himself condemned overseas attacks because he believed that they hurt the PLO's international image. When the radical Black September Organization killed several Israeli athletes at the Olympic Games in Munich in 1972, Arafat promptly stated that the PLO was not responsible for the attacks. Arafat closed down the Black September Organization in 1973, and in 1974 he ordered the PLO to restrict its violent attacks to Israel, the Gaza Strip, and the West Bank.

In 1974 the Arab Summit recognized the PLO as the sole representative of the Palestinian people. Arafat then appeared before the United Nations (UN) that same year as the official representative of the Palestinians. Speaking before the UN General Assembly, he condemned Zionism and said that the PLO would continue to operate as freedom fighters but also said that he wanted peace. This was the first time the international community had heard directly from the PLO, and many international observers praised Arafat and came to support the Palestinian cause. The UN granted the PLO observer status on November 22, 1974. Also in 1974, the leaders of al-Fatah, in the guise of the PNC, created a Ten-Point Program that set forth the PLO's goals. This program called for a secular state in Israel and Palestine that would welcome both Jews and Arabs and provide all citizens equal rights regardless of religion, race, or gender. It also called for the creation of a Palestinian Authority (PA) on free Palestinian territory. Israel rejected the Ten-Point Program. Meanwhile, the radical guerrilla groups of the PFLP and PFLP-GC (which had earlier split from the PFLP) departed from the PLO in protest of its attempt to negotiate with Israel.

In 1975 the Lebanese Civil War broke out. Israel pursued a strategy of support of the Lebanese Forces, the Maronite militias who opposed the Palestinians. The PLO and al-Fatah joined forces with the National Front, a more left-wing coalition of Muslims, Druze, and Christians. Syria intervened at first on behalf of Muslim forces but later came to the aid of the Marionites, and in the 1980s also supported the Shia militias. On January 12, 1976, the UN Security Council voted to grant the PLO the right to participate in Security Council debates. The PLO became a full member of the Arab League that same year. During the late 1970s, PLO members continued to enter Lebanon and maintain positions in Beirut, from which they exchanged attacks with Israel. On July 24, 1981, the PLO and Israel agreed to a cease-fire within Lebanon and on the border between Lebanon and Israel. Arafat interpreted the cease-fire agreement literally and continued to allow the PLO to attack Israel from Jordan and the West Bank. The

Israelis violated the cease-fire numerous times, bombing PLO targets in Beirut. That autumn, Israeli prime minister Menachem Begin and Defense Minister Ariel Sharon planned an invasion into Lebanon to occupy southern Lebanon and territory all the way up to Beirut, where they planned to destroy the PLO. Israeli troops invaded, occupied much of southern Lebanon, and rounded up much of the male population of the area. The UN passed one resolution demanding that Israel withdraw its troops, but the United States vetoed another resolution repeating this demand. The United States demanded that the PLO withdraw from Lebanon. Sharon ordered the bombing of West Beirut beginning on June 15. The UN once again demanded that Israel withdraw, but the United States again vetoed the resolution. On August 12, 1982, the two sides agreed to another cease-fire in which both the PLO and Israel would leave Lebanon. As a result, about 15,000 Palestinian militants left Lebanon by September 1.

The Israelis, however, claimed that PLO members were still hiding in Beirut and returned to the city on September 16, killing several hundred Palestinians, none of whom were known to be PLO members. Sharon resigned as defense minister after the Sabra and Shatila massacres, which were carried out by Lebanese Christian militias with Israeli foreknowledge and approval. Arafat and many surviving PLO members spent most of the 1980s in Tunisia rebuilding the organization, which had been severely damaged by the fighting in Beirut. During this time, Iraq and Saudi Arabia donated substantial sums of money to the organization. But relations between the PLO and Israel remained intractably bad. The Israel Defense Forces (IDF) bombed the PLO headquarters in Tunis in 1985, an attack that killed 73 people.

In December 1987 the First Intifada broke out spontaneously in the West Bank and Gaza, surprising Israelis with its intensity. On November 15, 1988, the PLO officially declared the formation of the State of Palestine. The PLO claimed all of Palestine as defined by the former British Mandate. However, the PLO had decided to seek a two-state solution. That December Arafat spoke before the UN, promising to end terrorism and to recognize Israel in exchange for the Israeli withdrawal from the occupied territories, according to UN Security Council Resolution 242. This was a distinct change from the PLO's previous position of insisting on the destruction of Israel. The PNC symbolically elected Arafat president of the new Palestinian state on April 2, 1989.

Arafat and the Israelis began conducting peace negotiations at the Madrid Conference in 1991. Although the talks were temporarily set back when Arafat and the PLO supported Iraq in the 1991 Persian Gulf War, over the next two years the two parties held a number of secret discussions. These negotiations led to the 1993 Oslo Accords in which Israel agreed to Palestinian self-rule in the Gaza Strip and the West Bank and Arafat officially recognized the existence of the State of Israel. Despite the condemnation of many Palestinian nationalists, the peace process appeared to be progressing apace. Israeli troops withdrew from the Gaza Strip and Jericho in May 1994. In 1994 the PLO established a Negotiations Affairs Department (NAD) in Gaza to implement the Interim Agreement. Mahmoud Abbas, then secretary-general of the PLO Executive Committee, headed the NAD until April 2003, when the Palestinian Legislative Council chose him as the first prime minister of the PA. He was replaced by Saeb Erekat. The Gaza office of NAD handled Israeli affairs, agreements between Israel and Palestine, colonization, and refugees. It also kept careful track of Israeli expansion into Palestinian territory. The NAD also opened an office in Ramallah to handle the implementation of the Interim Agreement and prepare the Palestinian position for negotiations toward permanent status. The government of the United Kingdom began assisting the NAD with its preparation for permanent status talks in 1998.

In 1996 the PNC agreed to remove from the PLO charter all language calling for armed violence aimed at destroying Israel, and Arafat sent U.S. president Bill Clinton a letter listing language to be removed, although the PLO has dragged its feet on this. The organization claimed that it was waiting for the establishment of the Palestinian state, when it would replace the charter with a constitution. Arafat was elected leader of the new PA in January 1996. The peace process began unraveling later that year, however, after rightist hard-liner Benjamin Netanyahu was elected prime minister of Israel. Netanyahu distrusted Arafat and condemned the PLO as a terrorist organization responsible for numerous suicide bombings on Israeli citizens. The accord collapsed completely in 2000 after Arafat and Israeli prime minister Ehud Barak failed to come to an agreement at a Camp David meeting that Clinton facilitated. After that, the Second (al-Aqsa) Intifada began when Palestinians, already experiencing the intractability of the Israeli government, saw Ariel Sharon lead security forces onto the Haram al-Sharif. During that period, suicide bombings increased. These attacks were in some instances claimed by Islamic Jihad of Palestine (PIJ), Hamas sympathizers, and other groups. Arafat and the PLO disavowed any support for such attacks. But whether right or wrong, the Israeli media continued to state or suggest that Arafat clandestinely supported the work of the terrorists. Arafat died on November 11, 2004. There was much dissension over the succession, but Abbas eventually came to represent the PLO's largest faction, al-Fatah. In December 2004 he called for an end to the violence associated with the Second Intifada that began in September 2000. In January 2005 he was elected president of the PA but has struggled to keep the PLO together and al-Fatah from losing its political and financial clout.

In the January 2006 PA parliamentary elections, Abbas and al-Fatah were dealt a serious blow when Hamas captured a significant majority of seats. An even greater blow came in June 2007, when Hamas seized control of Gaza. Since Hamas seized the Gaza Strip, it has been involved in numerous military confrontations with Israel, most notably in 2008–2009, 2012, and 2014. The Fatah-Hamas break was not substantially mended until early June 2014, when Abbas announced the formation of a unity government. However, unlike the short-lived 2007 unity government, this one did not include any Hamas members in the cabinet. Hamas agreed to support the government without direct participation in it. The United States and most of its allies cautiously backed the new setup, but Israel denounced the government because of its ties to Hamas, which it continues to view as a terrorist group. Prior to the beginning of the latest Hamas-Israeli clash in July 2014, the leaders of Hamas and al-Fatah had agreed in principle to hold elections for all Palestinians, including those in Gaza and the West Bank, at the end of 2014. However, the renewed fighting involving Hamas has greatly complicated those plans.

Amy Hackney Blackwell

See also: Abu Nidal Organization; Al-Fatah; Arafat, Yasser; Black September Organization; Popular Front for the Liberation of Palestine (PFLP)

Citations

Abbas, Mahmoud. *Through Secret Channels: The Road to Oslo.* Reading, UK: Garnet, 1997.

Aburish, Said K. *Arafat: From Defender to Dictator.* New York and London: Bloomsbury, 1998.

Palestinian Islamic Jihad

The militant nationalist Palestinian group Harakat al-Jihad al-Islami fi Filastin, known as the Palestinian Islamic Jihad (PIJ), was established by Fathi Shiqaqi, Sheikh Abd al-Aziz Awda, and others in the Gaza Strip during the 1970s. Several different factions identified with the name Islamic Jihad, including the Usrat al-Jihad (founded in 1948); the detachment of Islamic Jihad, identified with the Abu Jihad contingent of al-Fatah; the Islamic Jihad Organization al-Aqsa Battalions, founded by Sheikh Asad Bayyud al-Tamimi in Jordan in 1982; Tanzim al-Jihad al-Islami, led by Ahmad Muhanna; and several non-Palestinian groups. This has caused much confusion over the years. Also, the PIJ movement portrayed itself as being a part of a jihadi continuum rather than a distinct entity. While in Egypt in the 1970s, Shiqaqi, Awda, and the current director-general of the PIJ Ramadan Abdullah Shallah embraced an Islamist vision similar to the Egyptian Muslim Brotherhood. But they rejected the moderation forced on that organization by the Egyptian government's aim of political participation in tandem with *dawa* (proselytizing and education).

The Palestinian group distinguished itself from secular nationalists and antinationalist Islamists in calling for grassroots organization and armed struggle to liberate Palestine as part of the Islamic solution. Shiqaqi returned to Palestinian territory, and the PIJ began to express its intent to wage jihad (holy war) against Israel. Israeli sources claim that the PIJ developed the military apparatus known as the Jerusalem Brigades (Saraya al-Quds) by 1985, and this organization carried out attacks against the Israeli military, including an attack known as Operation Gate of Moors at an induction ceremony in 1986. The PIJ also claimed responsibility for the suicide bombing in Beit Lid, near Netanya, Israel, on January 22, 1994. In the attack, 19 Israelis were killed and another 60 injured. Shiqaqi spent a year in jail in the early 1980s and then in 1986 was jailed for two more years. He was deported to Lebanon along with Awda in April 1988.

The PIJ established an office in Damascus, Syria, and began support and services in Palestinian refugee camps in Lebanon. Shallah had meanwhile completed a doctorate at the University of Durham, served as the editor of a journal of the World and Islam Studies Enterprise, and taught briefly at the University of South Florida. When Shiqaqi was assassinated by unidentified agents (allegedly Mossad) in Malta in 1995, Shallah returned to lead the PIJ. His Florida associations led to the trials of Dr. Sami Al-Arian and Imam Fawaz Damra and others who allegedly supported the PIJ in the United States. The PIJ emerged prior to Hamas. The two organizations were rivals despite the commonality of their nationalist perspectives, but Hamas gained a much larger popular following than the PIJ, whose estimated support is only 4 to 5 percent of the Palestinian population in the territories.

The PIJ has a following among university students at the Islamic University in Gaza and other colleges, and became very active in the Second (al-Aqsa) Intifada, which began in September 2000.

In Lebanon, the organization competes with al-Fatah, the primary and largest political faction in the Palestine Liberation Organization (PLO). Like Hamas and secular nationalist groups known as the Palestinian National Alliance, the PIJ rejected the 1993 Oslo Accords and demanded a full Israeli withdrawal from Palestinian lands. The group has a following among Palestinian refugees and at Ain al-Hilweh, but also suffers from the political fragmentation of Palestinian and Islamist organizations there. The Palestinian Authority (PA) closed down a publication sympathetic to the PIJ but eventually allowed it to reopen. In June 2003, under significant international pressure, Syria closed PIJ and Hamas offices in Damascus, and Shallah left for Lebanon. Khalid Mishaal went to Qatar, but both later returned to Syria.

In the Palestinian territories, the PIJ continues to differ with Hamas. Hamas ceased attacks against Israel beginning in 2004 and successfully captured a majority in the Palestinian elections of January 2006. Hamas moderates have also considered the recognition of Israel and a two-state solution. The PIJ, in contrast, had called for Palestinians to boycott the 2006 elections and refused any accommodation with Israel. It continued to sponsor suicide attacks after 2004 in retaliation for Israel's military offensives and targeted killings of PIJ leaders, including Louay Saadi in October 2005. The PIJ claimed responsibility for two suicide attacks in that year. Israeli authorities continue to highlight Iranian-PIJ links. They cite Shiqaqi's early publication of a pamphlet that praised Ayatollah Ruhollah Khomeini for the 1979 Islamic revolution based on sharia (Islamic law) and for recognizing the Palestinian cause. And an intercepted PA security briefing has led the Israelis to assert that the PIJ continues to rely on Syrian support and Iranian funding.

The PIJ has continued to launch periodic attacks against Israeli citizens and interests. Because the group controls a number of religious and humanitarian groups aimed at helping Palestinians, its following has increased in recent years, even with the PA's efforts to close these organizations down. In 2014, as tensions between Hamas and Israel resulted in a virtual war centered in the Gaza Strip, the PIJ took advantage of this by enlarging its base and clout among Palestinians and by appealing to Iran for more funding.

Sherifa Zuhur

See also: Hamas; Jihad; Palestine Liberation Organization (PLO); Palestinian Stabbing Attacks (2015–2016)

Citations

Abu-Amr, Ziad. *Islamic Fundamentalism in the West Bank and Gaza: Muslim Brotherhood and Islamic Jihad*. Bloomington: Indiana University Press, 1994.

Knudsen, Are. "Islamism in the Diaspora: Palestinian Refugees in Lebanon," *Journal of Refugee Studies* 18(2) (2005): 216–234.

Shallah, Ramadan 'Abdallah, and Khalid al-' Ayid. "The Movement of Islamic Jihad and the Oslo Process: An Interview with Ramadan Abdullah Shallah," *Journal of Palestine Studies* 28 (1999): 61–73.

Palestinian Stabbing Attacks (2015–2016)

Starting in roughly September of 2015 and lasting until halfway through 2016, an influx of terrorist attacks by Palestinians on

Israelis occurred. Some of the perpetrators were affiliated with Hamas, a fundamentalist Islamic group associated with terrorism, but many were "lone wolves" acting by themselves. Between October 1, 2015 and October 1, 2016, there was a total of 166 stabbing attacks and 89 attempted stabbings, 108 shootings, 47 vehicular attacks, and one bus bombing.

A major point of contention in the reignition of the Palestinian-Israeli conflict was the agreement that Jews could not pray at Mount Temple in Jerusalem. This was the arrangement since 1967 when Israel took over all of Jerusalem. However, in 2015, the Jewish holiday of Rosh Hashanah and the Muslim holiday of Eid-al-adha fell on the same day, leading both groups to wish to use the Temple. Violence erupted on September 13, as Israeli police used tear gas and stun grenades to disperse Palestinian youths who had barricaded themselves in the Temple with rocks they had been throwing at Israelis. Palestinian president Mahmoud Abbas expressed approval for the injured and dead occupiers, which was not taken kindly by Israeli president Benjamin Netanyahu. On September 24, Israel passed a series of laws regarding violent rioters, including one that allowed Israeli soldiers to shoot to kill if they believed anyone's life was at risk.

The most well-known crime that led to the influx of stabbing attacks was the murder of Eitam and Na'ama Heiken, an Israeli couple that lived in the claimed Palestinian territory of West Bank. On October 1, 2015, Hamas militants opened fire on their car, leaving them both dead, but their four children alive. The lack of strong condemnation by Palestinian authorities led to further Israeli resentment, both locally and throughout Israel. By the end of the month, 817 violent demonstrations, including numerous stabbing and rock throwing incidents, had occurred.

These attacks continued in rapid succession, with an act of violence being recorded nearly every day from October 2015 to March 2016. Notably, an American student studying abroad was killed on March 8, 2016 in a mass stabbing, the only international victim of the series of attacks. A common series of events that often occurred was a Palestinian stabbing followed by a violent Israeli retaliation that would leave more dead than the initial attack itself. The rate of these events slowed down by March, but tensions would flare again on June 8, 2016, when two Palestinian gunmen opened fire on patrons at a café in Tel Aviv. Unlike most of the events in the preceding attacks, these perpetrators were linked to ISIS, showing that there is more at play here than just Palestine versus Israel.

Intifada is an Arabic word that means "tremor," and is used in Palestine to describe an uprising or resistance against Israeli occupation. The First Intifada lasted from 1987 to 1991, and included civil disobedience, strikes, boycotts, stone throwing, and vandalism. It caused 277 Israeli deaths and 1,962 Palestinian deaths. The Second Intifada was a period of prolonged violence from 2000 to 2005, causing 1,010 Israeli deaths and 3,354 Palestinian deaths. It was characterized by sophisticated weapons such as bombs, tanks, and guns.

The aftermath of this Intifada was the destruction of terrorist infrastructure and an increase in high-tech, high-cost security. The series of Palestinian stabbing attacks is sometimes referred to as the Third Intifada, because it was a period of violent insurgency characterized by attacks with simple weapons such as rocks and knives, which were used as a response to the increased security. It may be harder for a Palestinian to get a bomb or a gun now, but it is always easy to get a knife or a rock. The greatest impact of this strategy has been that it has struck fear into Israeli citizens. Gun sales for self-protection have gone up exponentially, and Israeli politicians often discuss security. Palestinian insurgents hope that this fear will cause Israel to fully consider and respond to Palestine's recurring grievances against the state, which in their opinions Israel has not fairly addressed.

Colin P. Clarke

See also: Hamas; Jihad; Palestinian Islamic Jihad

Citations

Dean, Laura. "Latest Violence in Israel and Palestine Marked by 'Lone Wolf' Attacks," *Global Post,* October 19, 2015.

Leibovitz, Liel. "The Murder of Eitam and Na'ama Henkin," *Tablet Magazine,* June 25, 2017.

Murphy, Kim. "Israel and PLO, in Historic Bid for Peace, Agree to Mutual Recognition: Mideast: After Decades of Conflict, Accord Underscores Both Sides' Readiness to Coexist. Arafat Reaffirms the Renunciation of Violence in Strong Terms," *Los Angeles Times,* September 10, 1993.

Seddon, David (ed.). "Intifada," in *A Political and Economic Dictionary of the Middle East,* p. 284. Oxfordshire, UK: Europa Publications, 2004.

Wedeman, Ben. "Israel-Palestinian Violence: What You Need to Know," *CNN,* October 15, 2015.

Paris Terrorist Attacks (2015)

On November 13, 2015, militants attacked numerous sites in Paris, France, killing 130 people and injuring hundreds more. The attacks, carried out by three teams of gunmen and suicide bombers thought to be associated with Islamic State (ISIS), were coordinated and near simultaneous. The Stade de France was the first location attacked; three suicide bombers detonated bombs just outside the stadium, where a soccer game between France and Germany was in progress. French president François Hollande was at the game and was rushed to safety. Only one bystander was killed, in addition to the three attackers, because the bombers were unable to pass through security checks at the stadium entrances. Meanwhile, a team of gunmen attacked customers in an area popular for its nightlife, closer to the center of Paris. The gunmen traveled to a number of bars and restaurants by car, opening fire on diners. Thirty-nine were killed.

One of the shooters detonated a suicide bomb following the attacks, killing himself. The Bataclan concert hall was the site of the deadliest attack when gunmen opened fire on the crowd of concertgoers. Eighty-nine people died. One of the attackers was shot by police and the other two detonated suicide belts, killing themselves. In response, President Hollande declared a state of emergency that included heightened security measures, and promised to intensify France's efforts to defeat ISIS in Syria.

In fact, on November 15, French bombers attacked ISIS targets in Raqqa, Syria. Hollande also announced he would meet with U.S. president Barack Obama and Russian president Vladimir Putin to discuss coordinating efforts to fight ISIS. In addition, raids to find and arrest suspected terrorists continued for days across France and in neighboring Belgium. Following the attacks, there was an international outpouring of support for France from individuals on social media expressing sympathy and solidarity, as well as from leaders around the world, who promised greater cooperation in fighting ISIS. Media and social media outlets also were criticized because of what some viewed as the lack of attention paid to the ISIS bombing in Beirut, Lebanon, which happened the day before the Paris attacks and killed 43 and wounded more than 200. Less than a month earlier, a Russian passenger jet exploded over Egypt, killing all 224 people on board. Russian officials reported that a two-pound, homemade bomb likely brought down the plane, and many considered ISIS to most likely be behind the bombing. The Russian government offered a $50 million reward for information about those who planted the bomb.

In the United States, a group of mostly Republican governors announced on November 16, that they objected to any Syrian refugees resettling in their states. This announcement came after the discovery that one of the Paris perpetrators was believed to have entered France with a wave of Syrian refugees in October 2015. President Barack Obama criticized the response as based on "hysteria"; his administration countered that all refugees undergo a rigorous screening process. Many international observers speculated that the Paris attacks, the Beirut bombings, and the probable downing of the Russian aircraft signaled an expansion of ISIS's reach from beyond territory it had seized in the Middle East. In addition, many feared the attacks by a handful of suicide gunmen and bombers indicated a change in the group's tactics, and one that would be harder to combat. Nevertheless, many world leaders vowed to intensify the fight against the violent jihadist organization.

Julie Dunbar

See also: Adnani, Abu Muhammad al-; Brussels Terrorist Attacks (2016); Islamic State of Iraq and Syria (ISIS)

Citations

Callimachi, Rukmini. "ISIS Video Appears to Show Paris Assailants Earlier in Syria and Iraq," *The New York Times,* January 25, 2016.

Cragin, R. Kim. "The November 2015 Paris Attacks: The Impact of Foreign Fighter Returnees," *Orbis* (Spring 2017): 212–226.

Partiya Karkeren Kurdistan (PKK)

The Kurdistan Workers' Party (PKK) is an ethno-nationalist terrorist organization based in predominantly Kurdish areas in southeastern Turkey, northern Iraq, and parts of both Iran and Syria. In a further nod to the differences countries have in defining terrorism, the group is considered a terrorist group by NATO, the United States, and the European Union, but not the United Nations, China, Russia, India, and Switzerland. The group was started in 1978 by Abdullah Ocalan, a radical Marxist-Leninist Kurdish student.

The group originally advocated for a communist revolution, but has shifted to support "democratic confederalism." Ocalan describes this as a "strong insurrection movement against cruelty and the exploitation of people and society, and for a people who were deprived of all their rights, denied any kind of fair defense, their language banned and their land occupied and exploited." The group is primarily concerned with justice for the Kurdish people, emphasizing the need for an autonomous republic, free from Turkish rule. The main tenets of the PKK's current political platform include support for heterogeneity, ecology, education, empowerment of women and youth, and the fight against the Islamic State. To date, more than 40,000 people have died in the conflict between the PKK and the Turkish state.

Although the PKK's goals are peaceful in name, its methods of attempting to achieve these goals have included a consistent reliance on terrorism, political violence, and insurgency. From its founding until roughly 2013, the organization has participated in ambushes, sabotage, riots, protests, demonstrations, and armed rebellion. More forcefully, PKK tactics have also included guerrilla warfare, the kidnapping of foreign tourists in Turkey, suicide bombings, and attacks on Turkish diplomatic offices throughout Europe. A cease-fire took place starting in 1999 when Ocalan was arrested and jailed, until 2004, and then again from 2013 to 2015. The PKK attacks Turkish security forces and police, but also civilians, especially civilians who do not cooperate with the group.

The PKK and a significant number of Kurdish nationalists have been on the forefront of the fight against ISIS. This has led to a debate on whether or not the PKK should be removed from international lists of officially designated terrorist organizations. The Kurds' expertise in geopolitically important areas throughout Turkey, Syria, and Iraq allow it to be an effective bulwark against the Islamic State.

Due to the group's designation as a terrorist organization, it is legally prevented from acquiring weapons and supplies abroad and as such, has been consistently under-resourced in its fight against ISIS. This conflict has also reignited long-standing issues of sovereignty between the Turks and the Kurds. The PKK, and the Kurdish population in general, believe the Turkish government has not done enough to help them defend against cross-border incursions from a range of militants in Syria and parts of Iraq. In turn, this has contributed to feelings of resentment toward President Erdogan, and inflamed tensions between Turkey and its Kurdish citizens, at their worst point since the PKK waged a full-blown insurgency in Turkey throughout the 1990s.

The most recent cease-fire collapsed in 2015. The past several years have been met with an upsurge of violence, just as Turkey has been targeted by other terrorist groups, including the Islamic State. In August 2016, the PKK detonated a vehicle-borne improvised explosive device in Cizre, killing 11 policemen and injuring another 78. Just in the past few years, hundreds of people have died as a result of the conflict, particularly in Turkey's Kurdish-majority region in the southeast of the country. Turkey is particularly concerned about the PKK's relationship to other Kurdish militant groups, including the Popular Protection Units, or YPG, operating in Syria.

Colin P. Clarke

See also: Euskadi Ta Askatasuna (ETA); Improvised Explosive Devices; Liberation Tigers of Tamil Eelam (LTTE); Provisional Irish Republican Army (PIRA)

Citations

Bruno, Greg. "Inside the Kurdistan Workers Party (PKK)," Council on Foreign Relations (Backgrounder), October 19, 2007.

Marcus, Aliza. *Blood and Belief: The PKK and Kurdish Fight for Independence.* New York: NYU Press, 2007.

"Who Are Kurdistan Workers Party (PKK) Rebels?" *BBC News*, November 4, 2016.

Popular Front for the Liberation of Palestine (PFLP)

The Popular Front for the Liberation of Palestine (PFLP) is a Marxist-Leninist organization founded in 1967 that seeks to create a socialist state for Palestinians. It has

Hostages from three hijacked aircraft attend a press conference by the Popular Front for the Liberation of Palestine in the desert, in front of a Swissair passenger plane, September 1970. A week later, the women and children were released in Jordan, and the aircraft were blown up. (Keystone/Getty Images)

always been opposed to the existence of Israel and has committed numerous terrorist attacks since 1968, focusing on Israeli and moderate Arab targets. Founded by George Habash on December 11, 1967, just after the Six-Day War, the PFLP arose from the merger of the Arab Nationalist Movement, which Habash had founded in 1953, with the Palestine Liberation Front and Youth for Revenge. Habash created the PFLP to represent the Palestinian working class and stated that its goal was the creation of a democratic socialist Palestinian state and the elimination of Israel. Habash saw the elimination of Israel as a necessary step in purging the Middle East from Western capitalist influences. He also claimed after the 1967 Arab defeat that it would

be necessary to combat the Arab regimes before that could be accomplished. Although Habash was himself a Palestinian Christian, he wanted the PFLP to be an entirely secular organization based on Marxist principles and socialism and positioned on the vanguard of a world socialist revolution.

The PFLP quickly spread into other Arab countries and acquired financial backing from Syria and Jordan. The group joined the Palestine Liberation Organization (PLO) in 1968 and immediately generated two splinter factions, the terrorist organization Popular Front for the Liberation of Palestine-General Command (PFLP-GC) and the orthodox Marxist Democratic Front for the Liberation of Palestine. Most members of the PFLP were trained as guerrillas. The group soon became known for its terrorist activities, especially its airliner hijackings, many of which targeted the Israeli airline El Al. Most of the early attacks were coordinated by Wadi Haddad, known as "The Master." On July 23, 1968, the PFLP commandeered an El Al airplane on its way from Rome to Tel Aviv and landed it in Algeria, mistakenly believing that Major General Ariel Sharon, later to become an Israeli prime minister, was on board. The group held the passengers and crew captive until August 31. Other hijackings and attacks followed. On December 26, 1968, PFLP guerrillas shot at an El Al jet about to leave Athens for Paris, killing a passenger.

On February 18, 1969, its members attacked another El Al jet in Zurich, killing the copilot. Two days later they bombed a supermarket in Jerusalem. That August, the PFLP hijacked a TWA flight flying from Rome to Tel Aviv and forced it to land in Damascus. One of the leaders of this attack was Leila Khaled, who had joined the Arab Nationalist Movement in 1958 at the age of 14. She was arrested in Damascus but was quickly released. On September 9, 1969, 6 Palestinians threw grenades at Iraqi embassies in Bonn and The Hague and at the El Al office in Brussels. The PFLP also attacked a bus at the Munich airport on February 10, 1970. On February 21, 1970, the group detonated a barometric pressure device on Swissair Flight 330, flying from Zurich to Tel Aviv. The bomb damaged the plane sufficiently that the pilots were unable to return to the Zurich airport. The jet crashed and killed all on board, including 38 passengers and 9 crewmembers. On September 6, 1970, the PFLP launched its most ambitious hijacking scheme yet. Group members simultaneously hijacked jets in Brussels, Frankfurt, and Zurich and forced them to fly to Cairo or Zarqa, Jordan. The group hijacked a fourth

plane three days later. They blew up the three aircraft in Zarqa on September 12.

The PFLP announced that the hijackings were intended to teach the Americans a lesson and to punish them for supporting Israel. On September 16, 1970, King Hussein of Jordan formed a military government and began attacking Palestinian guerrillas in Jordan. He ultimately expelled the PLO from the country. This crisis, which became known as Black September, reinforced Habash's claim that Arab regimes were inhibiting the Palestinian guerrilla movement. Khaled, who had undergone six months of cosmetic surgery to disguise her appearance, and her colleague Patrick Arguello attempted to hijack a fourth aircraft departing from Amsterdam on September 6. They failed in this task. Arguello was shot, and Khaled was overpowered and then imprisoned in London. This arrest provoked the PLFP to seize five more civilian airplanes in an effort to persuade British authorities to release Khaled. She was released after 28 days in exchange for 56 Western hostages. In 1973 Habash agreed that the PFLP would cease terrorist activities abroad, on the advice of the Palestinian National Council. Thereafter, he restricted his terrorist activity to Israel, Jordan, and Lebanon.

On May 30, 1972, the PFLP attacked Lod Airport in Israel, killing 24 people. Two months later on July 9, 1972, Israelis killed PFLP member and creative writer Ghassan Kanafani. Throughout the 1970s, the group attacked numerous Israeli targets. The PFLP withdrew from the PLO in 1974, complaining that the PLO was no longer interested in destroying Israel completely and seemed instead to be willing to compromise. When the First Intifada began on December 8, 1987, elements of the PFLP organized terrorist attacks in the Gaza Strip and the West

Bank. In 1990 the Jordanian branch of the PFLP was converted into an actual political party, the Jordanian Democratic Popular Unity Party. Habash stepped down as leader on April 27, 2000, and was replaced by Abu Ali Mustafa, who was killed by Israeli commandos on August 27, 2001.

The PFLP retaliated on October 17, 2001, by killing Rehavam Zeevi, the Israeli minister of tourism. Ahmed Sadat became general secretary of the organization on October 3, 2001, a post he continued to hold as of 2017. The armed militia of this group continued its terrorist activity in the early 2000s, using car bombs and other small-scale bombing techniques and sometimes simply shooting targets. Sadat was subsequently arrested by the Palestinian Authority (PA) and held in Jericho. He has been imprisoned ever since. The PFLP opposed the 1993 Oslo Accords, partially because of its resentment of al-Fatah control over the PLO and subsequently the PA. The group has maintained its Marxist-Leninist beliefs, and this has always contributed to its smaller size and led to its decline as Islamism became much more influential.

The PFLP continues to press for a one-state solution to the Palestinian-Israeli conflict and has gone on record as opposing the Fatah-Hamas split, which began in 2006. That feud was seemingly ended in June 2014, when the two groups agreed to a unity government, but a renewed Hamas-Israeli conflict in Gaza in July 2014 threatened to unravel it. In 2013, however, the PFLP seemed to be siding with Hamas, when it termed the group as "vital" to the Palestinian national movement. After 2004, bombings and suicide attacks attributed to the PFLP fell significantly, perhaps a reflection of the organization's loss of Sadat as its day-to-day leader.

Amy Hackney Blackwell

See also: Al-Fatah; Arafat, Yasser; Palestine Liberation Organization (PLO)

Citations

Hourani, Albert. *A History of the Arab Peoples.* New York: Warner, 1992.

PFLP. *A Radical Voice from Palestine: Recent Documents from the Popular Front for the Liberation of Palestine.* Oakland, CA: Abraham Guillen Press, 2002.

Smith, Charles D. *Palestine and the Arab-Israeli Conflict: A History with Documents.* 6th ed. New York: Bedford/St. Martin's, 2006.

Provisional Irish Republican Army (PIRA)

The Provisional Irish Republican Army (PIRA, or the Provos) was the largest and best-organized Catholic paramilitary organization fighting to end British rule in Northern Ireland. During its operational life, the group spearheaded attacks across the United Kingdom and mainland Europe and was responsible for approximately 1,800 deaths, including at least 630 civilians. In 1997 PIRA agreed to a cease-fire as part of a regional peace process, announcing a full end to its armed campaign on July 28, 2005. Since then several renegade splinter factions have continued to carry out sporadic acts of violence, but nothing approaching the scale or sophistication of their parent movement.

The origins of PIRA can be traced back to the partition of Ireland in 1922 when the six counties of the north, being predominantly Protestant, decided to remain part of the United Kingdom, and the 26 counties of the south, which were overwhelmingly Catholic, chose independence, becoming first the Free State and then the Republic of Ireland. However, the militant Irish Republican

Army (IRA), which had already engaged in a lengthy war against British rule, rejected partition and carried on armed struggle on behalf of the Catholics in the north.

Despite engaging in various clandestine actions, by 1962 the IRA had become essentially moribund due to its total failure to drive the British from Northern Ireland. However, the group reemerged from its enforced period of quiescence amid the sectarian violence that accompanied the civil rights movement of the 1960s, ostensibly defending Catholics against attacks by Protestant extremists.

In 1969 the IRA split into two wings: the Official IRA (OIRA), which favored a political, nonsectarian approach to the status of Northern Ireland, and PIRA, which was firmly dedicated to the use of physical force to wrest Northern Ireland from the United Kingdom and integrate it into the republic to the south to ultimately create an all-Ireland socialist state of Gaelic hue. The following year, OIRA's political wing, Sinn Fein (literally "we ourselves"), which Arthur Griffith had formed in 1905, also divided, making the separation between the two organizations complete.

As noted, the main objective of PIRA was to break the British government's will to remain in Northern Ireland through the force of arms. The military strategy it employed to achieve this goal during the 1970s, 1980s, and much of the 1990s can be split into three main components. First was the "economic war," aimed at undermining business confidence and commercial security in Northern Ireland by disabling commercial and social life in the province, primarily through the use of car bombs and incendiary devices.

Second was the "guerrilla war," the purpose of which was to keep British troops constantly harassed (and demoralized) by subjecting them to constant attacks and

ambushes. During the 1980s, this tact increasingly came to involve the targeting of off-duty Irish security personnel, especially those of the Royal Ulster Constabulary (RUC), RUC reservists, and members of the Ulster Defence Regiment.

Finally, there was the "English war," which sought to make London's involvement in Northern Ireland unacceptable to British public opinion by striking at symbolic representatives of the UK establishment on the country's mainland as well as in continental Europe. In practicing and endorsing this line of action, PIRA calculated that one well-placed bomb in England would have a far greater psychological and political impact than numerous similar attacks in Northern Ireland.

To give meaning to its militant strategy, which one alleged Provo leader blithely summarized as "battering on until the Brits leave," PIRA developed a highly disciplined, hierarchical organizational structure. At the helm was the General Army Convention, which consisted of high-ranking delegates drawn from other structures within the group. The convention elected the 12-member Army Executive, which in turn decided on the makeup of the seven-member Army Council. This latter body was in charge of defining and overseeing the Provos' strategic and tactical direction and was headed by a chief of staff, the primary authority within PIRA.

The General Headquarters implemented the decisions of the Army Council. Based in Dublin, this section of the organization was divided into 10 specific departments: Quartermaster, Operations, Finance, Engineering, Education, Security, Foreign Operations (also known as the English Department), Training, Intelligence, and Publicity. Regionally, PIRA worked through two commands: northern, which was responsible for the nine Ulster counties in addition to County Leitrim and County Louth; and southern, which covered the rest of Ireland.

At the operational level, PIRA was initially built along quasi-military lines, consisting of companies, brigades, and battalions. However, due to concerns over the security vulnerability of these structures, particularly in areas where the Provos could not guarantee full control of the local population, the group moved away from this configuration toward one that was more compartmentalized and cellular in nature. Two parallel teams were subsequently established in the late 1970s. First were support squads that were given the task of policing nationalist areas, gathering intelligence, and hiding weapons. Second were active service units (ASUs), which for the next two decades formed PIRA's main strike force. Typically consisting of between five and eight volunteers (*oglaigh*), ASUs were deployed across Northern Ireland, the United Kingdom, and mainland Europe. They were assigned specific missions and equipped with materiel that was controlled by a quartermaster who came under the direct control of the PIRA leadership. By the early 1990s, the Provos were thought to have around 300 members organized into ASUs in addition to another 450 serving in support roles.

Initially, PIRA was poorly armed, relying mostly on World War II weaponry such as Thompson machine guns and M1 Garands. However, starting in the 1970s, the organization began to build up a far more advanced armory, benefiting from the financial largesse of American sympathizers (much of it channeled through Irish Northern Aid [NORAID]), a growing network of links with international weapons dealers, and, most important, external state support. One of PIRA's main backers in this latter regard

was Libya. The discovery of a secret arms pipeline between Tripoli and Ireland in 1987 underscored the extent of the assistance rendered by the Gadhafi regime. In the course of a single year, PIRA took delivery of nearly 120 tons of munitions, including AK-47 rifles, Webley pistols, rocket-propelled grenades, surface-to-air missiles, hand grenades, ammunition, detonators, fuses, and Semtex-H explosives. Had the weapons link not been discovered, PIRA would have received an additional inventory of assault rifles, more than one million rounds of ammunition, 430 grenades, 1,000 mortar bombs, 120 rocket-propelled grenades, 12 Russian antitank missile launchers, 2,000 electronic detonators, 4,700 fuses, 20 surface-to-air missiles, and two tons of Semtex-H.

Although PIRA's campaign was squarely focused on Northern Ireland, the group did establish cooperative ties with other terrorist movements. Perhaps the closest relationship was with the Spanish Basque group, Euskadi Ta Askatasuna (ETA or Basque Fatherland and Liberty). Representatives from the two movements exchanged visits on several occasions to express solidarity with each other's cause. They also traded weapons and explosives and engaged in joint training programs held in both Ireland and Spain. Apart from ETA, PIRA is known to have worked with various Palestinian organizations, which opened their Middle East camps for militant training, and reportedly had at least some contact with Hezbollah. The Provos were also briefly linked to the Fuerzas Armadas Revolucionárias de Colombia (FARC, or the Revolutionary Armed Forces of Colombia) in 2001, when three members, Niall Connolly, Martin McCauley, and James Monaghan, were arrested at Bogotá International Airport for traveling on false passports. Subsequent investigations revealed that the trio had been training FARC operatives in techniques of urban warfare on a fee-for-service basis. According to British intelligence, the group could have received as much as $2 million for its efforts.

PIRA proved to be one of the deadliest and most active terrorist groups operating in western Europe between 1969 and 1997. During the course of these three decades, the group assassinated Lord Mountbatten (the cousin of Queen Elizabeth II), nearly succeeded in eliminating the entire British cabinet during the ruling Conservative Party's annual conference in 1984, fired mortars that damaged 10 Downing Street in 1991, decimated the financial heart of the city of London in 1996, almost leveled Canary Wharf (one of the largest office and apartment complexes in the UK capital) the same year, and generally disrupted daily life in Britain and Ireland by targeting everything from airports to department stores, train stations, and underground metro systems.

Although PIRA was primarily a violent organization, it also engaged in political activity through a so-called bullet-and-ballot-box strategy. Much of this tactic traces its origins to the 1981 Irish hunger strike when seven Provos (and three Irish National Liberation Army [INLA] members) starved themselves to death while protesting conditions on the H-Block wing of the Maze Prison complex in Northern Ireland. The incident triggered work stoppages and major demonstrations as people from all walks of life came out in sympathy for the strikers. Over 100,000 people attended the funeral of the leader of the group, Bobby Sands, who was posthumously elected to the British Parliament. The success of the hunger strike in

mobilizing popular support encouraged PIRA to increasingly devote time and resources to electoral politics, which was to be carried out through Sinn Fein under the tutelage of Gerry Adams.

During the 1980s several rounds of open and secret meetings were held with moderate nationalist Irish officials and British civil servants, culminating in a 1994 PIRA cease-fire that was called on the understanding that Sinn Fein would be included in any talks for a political settlement to the conflict. When this did not occur, the Provos responded with several major bombings in London (Canary Wharf and Baltic Exchange) and Manchester, which caused in excess of $500 million in combined damage. In 1997 PIRA reinstated its cease-fire, and Sinn Fein was once again admitted into the peace process. The following year, the Good Friday Agreement (also known as the Belfast Agreement) was signed. The accord laid out the basic guidelines for a power-sharing arrangement between London and Belfast (in the guise of a unity government at Stormont) and also required that PIRA lay down its arms and commit to pursuing the aim of a united Ireland through peaceful means alone.

Despite some setbacks in the subsequent peace process, including the brief collapse of the Stormont government, triggered by allegations that republican spies were operating within Parliament buildings and the Civil Service, PIRA moved to dispose of its weapons to the full satisfaction of the Independent International Commission on Decommissioning (IICD). On July 28, 2005, the Army Council announced an end to its armed campaign and indicated that all members of PIRA had been instructed to dump their arms and refrain from all activities other than assisting in "the development of purely political and democratic programmes through exclusively peaceful means." In a news conference on September 26, 2005, the office of IICD chairman John de Chastelain, a retired Canadian general, confirmed that PIRA's arms had been put beyond use and that these weapons represented the totality of the group's arsenal.

PIRA has continued to abide by the terms of the Good Friday Agreement and is no longer considered to be an active operational terrorist entity. However, sporadic attacks, murders, and bombings do persist, almost all of which are the work of splinter factions and renegade groups such as the Real IRA (RIRA) and Continuity IRA (CIRA). In 2009 these dissidents were tied to the shooting deaths of two soldiers and a police officer and were also thought to be behind the deployment of a massive 600-pound (272-kilogram) improvised explosive device that was found and defused near Forkhill in Armagh. Activity spiked again in 2011 when Ronan Kerr, a constable with the Police Service of Northern Ireland, was killed in car bombing near the County Tyrone town of Omagh (the scene of a deadly Real IRA attack in 1998). This was followed by the interception of an improvised explosive device hidden in a tote bag in the luggage compartment of a bus headed toward Dublin just hours before the arrival of Queen Elizabeth II, the first visit to the Republic of Ireland by a reigning British monarch.

Lauren Twenhafel

See also: Improvised Explosive Devices; Loyalist Volunteer Force (LVF); Ulster Volunteer Force (UVF)

Citations

Bell, J. Bowyer. *The Secret Army: The IRA.* Piscataway, NJ: Transaction Publishers, 1997.

Boyne, Sean. "Fresh Troubles: Dissidents Rise Again in Northern Ireland," *Jane's Intelligence Review,* May 2009.

Coogan, Tim Pat. *The IRA: A History.* Greenwood Village, CO: Roberts, 1994.

De Breadun, Deaglan. "Northern Ireland: An End to the Troubles?" *Current History,* October 1999.

Martin, Dillon. *25 Years of Terror: The IRA's War against the British.* New York: Bantam Books, 1996.

Moloney, Ed. *A Secret History of the IRA.* New York: W. W. Norton, 2002.

Northern Ireland Office. Good Friday Agreement. London: Her Majesty's Stationery Office, April 10, 1998. https://peacemaker.un.org/uk-ireland-good-friday98, accessed January 22, 2007.

O'Brien, Brendan. *The Long War: The IRA and Sinn Fein.* Syracuse, NY: Syracuse University Press, 1999.

Q

Qutb, Sayyid

Sayyid Qutb (alternative spellings: Said Qutub, Seyyid Kutb) was an Egyptian author, Islamic theoretician, and leader in the Muslim Brotherhood in the 1950s and 1960s. His writings have given rise to Qutbism, a strain of Islamic ideology that advocates the use of militant jihad to overcome Western power and culture. Due to the widespread popularity and influence of his works, he is commonly referred to as the father of modern fundamentalism. His two seminal pieces, *Milestones* and *Social Justice,* went on to form the ideological foundation of many radical Islamist groups, including al-Qaeda. Qutb mainly focused on the social and political implications of Islam, but he also wrote extensively on his disapproval of the American way of life, which he believed to be fraught with moral pitfalls.

Qutb was born in 1906 in the Egyptian village of Musha. He was introduced to Islam largely through his father, who was well known for his political activism and devotion to the Quran. Qutb moved to Cairo in his 20s to start a career as a teacher in the Ministry of Public Instruction. During this early stage of his career he devoted himself to literary critique and creative writing.

Qutb spent two years living in the United States as a student at the University of Northern Colorado, where he studied teaching. Many believe it was during this trip that Qutb solidified his belief in the moral bankruptcy of America. He wrote an influential piece titled "The America That I Have Seen" that summarized his disdain

of the culture, drawing on aspects such as sexual promiscuity, materialism, racism, individual freedoms, and violence.

Upon his return from the United States, Qutb joined the Egyptian Muslim Brotherhood, where he started working as the editor of their newspaper and was later promoted to head of propaganda. The Muslim Brotherhood, founded in 1928 by Hasan al-Banna, shared many beliefs with Qutb, including a rejection of Western culture and influence in the Middle East.

The Muslim Brotherhood opposed the Egyptian secular monarchy and, as a result, was banned for many of its early years. When Gamal Abdel Nasser and the Free Officers Movement overthrew the pro-Western monarchy, Qutb and the Brotherhood hoped it would pave the way for a partnership toward an Islamic government. In fact, Qutb and Nasser had frequent secret meetings to discuss the future of Egypt. Not until Qutb discovered that Nasser was exploiting their relationship and had created an organization to oppose the Muslim Brotherhood (the Tahreer) did he realize that the secular nationalist ideology of Nasserism would forever be incompatible with his own beliefs.

In 1954, Qutb was arrested for plotting against Nasser and was incarcerated for 10 years. He experienced many horrors during his time in jail, including being physically tortured and witnessing the deaths of fellow members of the Muslim Brotherhood. During this time he also completed one of the most influential commentaries on the Quran ever written, *In the Shade of the*

Quran. Components of this 30-volume piece, along with letters he sent from prison, subsequently came to form the basis of his famous book, *Milestones.* As the popularity of his works spread, the Nasser regime realized that his theories posed an existential threat to its ideology. Qutb was rearrested in 1965, sentenced to death, and killed a year later. Many considered him a martyr because he died at the hands of a government that he vehemently opposed.

The central tenets of Qutb's writings focus on the necessity of sharia law, arguing that following this code in its entirety is the only way to attain personal and societal peace. He believed that true implementation of sharia would not require a form of government but rather would eventuate from and be organized in an anarcho-Islamic structure. Qutb believed that any system where men are subservient to other men, instead of God, could never truly be in accordance with the Quran. To combat this injustice, he advocated both proselytization and the abolishment of such institutions by physical power and jihad.

Despite his hard-line beliefs in sharia, Qutb's early writings focused on a call to secularism, and many scholars contend that an event in his life motivated this radical shift in ideology. Theories range from his time spent in the United States, where he witnessed the societal "harms" that could flow from a Western-style government based on personal freedom, to the horrors he experienced in prison.

Qutb influenced many in his time as well as several modern-day Islamic extremist leaders. Most notably his writings have been credited with forming Osama bin Laden's ideological and theological justifications for terrorism. In addition, they appear to have had a marked impact on Ayman al-Zawahiri, a member of the Muslim Brotherhood, the former head of Egyptian Islamic Jihad, and the current leader of al-Qaeda. In his personal writings, al-Zawahiri credits Qutb repeatedly, particularly his beliefs about the need for a violent overthrow of Western control and cultural norms. The former emir of Al-Qaeda in the Arabian Peninsula, Anwar al-Awlaki, also cited Qutb's works as significant influences on his radicalization, as have senior jihadists in the Taliban.

Stephanie Caravias

See also: Al-Qaeda; Bin Laden, Osama; Muslim Brotherhood; Zawahiri, Ayman al-

Citations

Bergesen, Albert. *The Sayyid Qutb Reader: Selected Writings on Politics, Religion, and Society.* New York: Routledge, 2007.

Calvert, John. *Sayyid Qutb and the Origins of Radical Islamism.* Chichester, NY: Columbia University Press, 2010.

Ibrahim, Raymond. *The Al Qaeda Reader: The Essential Texts of Osama bin Laden's Terrorist Organization.* New York: Broadway Books, 2007.

Musallam, Adnan. *From Secularism to Jihad: Sayyid Qutb and the Foundations of Radical Islam.* Westport, CT: Praeger, 2005.

Qutb, Sayyid. *In the Shade of the Quran.* Falls Church, VA: WAMY International, 1995.

Qutb, Sayyid. *Milestones.* Chicago: Kazi, 1964.

R

Roof, Dylann

Dylann Storm Roof is a right-wing terrorist convicted of killing nine African American churchgoers at Emanuel African Episcopal Church in Charleston, South Carolina. Roof was an uneducated, poor, and apathetic individual who was easily swayed by racist conspiracy theories and seemed to take pride associating with symbols of the Confederate South and American Civil War. He was a self-described sociopath and white supremacist who initially sought out information from racist websites in response to the death of Trayvon Martin, a black teenager.

After the attack, Roof was completely unrepentant and demonstrated no remorse for his monstrous actions. He even went so far as to attempt to justify his actions in a rambling, incoherent jailhouse manifesto. "I have no choice," it reads. "I am not in the position to, alone, go into the ghetto and fight. I chose Charleston because it is most historic city in my state, and at one time had the highest ratio of blacks to Whites in the country. We have no skinheads, no real KKK, no one doing anything but talking on the Internet. Well someone has to have the bravery to take it to the real world, and I guess that has to be me."

In his younger years, Roof had a troubled childhood and cycled in and out of several different schools, all while battling substance abuse problems and social anxiety. He eventually dropped out school after the 9th grade and was never able to develop a career. It seems that he spent some time bouncing around from the homes of friends and family and had a strained relationship with his parents.

Prior to committing his heinous terrorist attack, Roof possessed a police record of two arrests, cited for drug possession and trespassing. Lawyers involved in his case note that due to the nature of his criminal record, he should not have been able to lawfully purchase a gun, as he did to carry out the attack. On June 17, 2005, Roof entered the church and killed nine people with a legally purchased semiautomatic pistol, including pastor and South Carolina state senator Clementa C. Pinckney.

Although Roof initially escaped in his car, he was caught the next morning, easily identifiable with his "bowl-style" haircut, in Shelby, North Carolina, and extradited to South Carolina to be imprisoned and await trial. In an amazing act of forgiveness, in the immediate aftermath of the attack, five of the victims' families came forward to say that they forgave Roof for his heinous crimes and believed that even he could find salvation. A week after the massacre, President Barack Obama visited the site of the slayings and delivered a speech for the victims that included a passionate discussion of race relations in one of the Civil War's most notorious sites.

The location of the attack was deliberately selected for its symbolism—it was the oldest African Methodist Episcopal in the south, and had long maintained a reputation for resistance to slavery as well as ardent civil rights advocacy. Dylann Roof claims that he committed the crime because no one he considered to be part of his twisted ideology would take a stand against what he perceived as an epidemic of black-on-white crime and the usurpation by blacks of white Americans on the ladder of social status and mobility.

At his core, Roof is a white supremacist who strongly believed that black Americans were responsible for an abundance of crime that was destroying the country. He consumed vast quantities of racist and antiblack propaganda online and ultimately informed prosecutors that his intention was to galvanize a war between the races by his actions. He wanted to bring attention to what he saw as rampant discrimination against whites in this United States, an idea first developed and later reinforced by online propaganda distributed by racists and neo-Nazis. A disturbing online manifesto Roof authored contained numerous examples of white nationalist rhetoric and symbolism, including extensive use of the Confederate flag.

Roof's case was somewhat unique as he was the first person in American history to be tried in *both* state and federal court with death penalty charges. Loretta Lynch, the Attorney General of the United States, chose to seek federal charges against him in addition to the state charges because at the time, South Carolina did not have a hate crimes statute on the books, which Lynch believed was necessary for the case at hand. Part of Lynch's statement following his indictment is as follows: "The federal indictment returned today charges Roof with nine murders and three attempted murders under the Matthew Shepard and James Byrd Jr. Hate Crimes Prevention Act. This federal hate crimes law prohibits using a dangerous weapon to cause bodily injury, or attempting to do so, on the basis of race or color. The Shepard/Byrd Act was enacted specifically to vindicate the unique harms caused by racially motivated violence."

Roof entered a plea deal in state court and received a total of nine life sentences, although he was unable to avoid the death penalty in federal court. He was formally sentenced to death on January 10, 2017, and is now located at the United States Penitentiary in Terre Haute, Indiana, awaiting execution.

Colin P. Clarke

See also: Homegrown Terrorism; Lone Wolf Attacks

Citations

"Attorney General Lynch Statement Following the Federal Grand Jury Indictment against Dylann Storm Roof," The United States Department of Justice, Office of Public Affairs, July 22, 2015.

Bever, Lindsey. "'I'm Just a Sociopath,' Dylann Roof Declared after Deadly Church Shooting Rampage, Court Records Say," *The Washington Post,* May 17, 2017.

Blinder, Alan, and Kevin Sack. "Dylann Roof Is Sentenced to Death in Charleston Church Massacre," *The New York Times,* January 10, 2017.

Croft, Jay, and Tristan Smith. "Dylann Roof Pleads Guilty to State Charges in Church Massacre," *CNN,* April 10, 2017.

S

San Bernardino Attacks

In the early afternoon of December 2, 2015, two heavily armed individuals wearing black tactical gear and face masks entered a social services building in San Bernardino, California, and opened fire on a gathering taking place in a conference room. When the shooting stopped, 14 people were dead and 21 others were wounded. The assailants were armed with two AR-15 assault rifles and two semiautomatic handguns. They also left at the scene a knapsack containing pipe bombs with remote-controlled detonators, which fortunately did not explode. Investigators surmised that the bombs were designed to injure or kill first responders arriving on the scene. Police soon identified the attackers—Syed Rizwan Farook and Tashfeen Malik—a married couple who had been previously radicalized by extremist Islamic ideologies. It is believed that the shootings were part of a scheme to unleash a jihad (holy war) against non-Muslims in the area. Virtually all of the victims were colleagues of Farook, who had worked as a San Bernardino County health inspector.

The attack began at approximately 11:00 a.m. local time. Not long before the shootings, Farook had been in attendance at the gathering, which was billed as a holiday party and training session for health department employees. Several other attendees saw Farook leave the function, looking distressed or angry. When Farook returned to the scene just before 11:00 a.m., he and his wife Tashfeen Malik walked into the conference area and began firing; police estimate they fired at least 75 rounds before fleeing in a black, rented SUV. Initially, police believed that the assault was the work of a disgruntled employee. Later, it became clear that the mass shooting was in fact a terrorist attack. Local police, promptly aided by the local FBI, engaged in a massive manhunt for the two shooters. Approximately four hours after the attack, law enforcement personnel located and surrounded the black SUV; a shoot-out ensued that resulted in the deaths of the two attackers and the nonfatal wounding of a police officer. Inside the vehicle were the firearms used in the attack. Not until several days later, however, did the FBI definitively categorize the shootings as a terrorist attack.

By then, investigators had discovered that Farook had made numerous recent trips to Saudi Arabia (where he met his wife) and that Tashfeen Malik had pledged loyalty—online—to the radical extremist Islamic State of Iraq and Syria (ISIS). ISIS quickly praised the California attack but did not claim direct responsibility for it. Farook was a college-educated U.S.-born citizen of Pakistani descent who was a devout Sunni Muslim. His wife, who was born in Pakistan but was raised mainly in Saudi Arabia, was a well-educated pharmacist, although she stopped practicing her profession around 2013, when she met Farook. Farook secured a special U.S. fiancé visa for Tashfeen Malik, and the two were married in 2014. In late May or early June 2015, Malik gave birth to a daughter. At the time of this writing, investigators were still trying to determine how much help the terrorists might have received from outside sources. A search of the couple's apartment turned up tools and materials used to make pipe bombs and a huge cache of ammunition—more than 4,500 rounds. Several days into the investigation, law enforcement apprehended Enrique Marquez, a friend of Farook, who had supplied him with the AR-15 rifles used in the attack. He claimed that Farook had been planning a terrorist attack since at least 2012, and had become increasingly radicalized. Marquez was apparently not involved in the shootings.

Some investigators posited that Farook and Malik's marriage was a sham and was actually intended to provide a cover for their jihadist activities. Not long before the shootings, Farook had secured a $28,500 loan, half of which was given to his mother, who was caring for his daughter at the time. Investigators believed that this was a strong indication that Farook had carefully planned the attack and anticipated the fallout from it. Investigators also discovered that Farook likely had contact with a group of California jihadists operating in Riverside, a town not far from San Bernardino. Occurring on the heels of the November 13, 2015, terrorist attacks in Paris that killed 130 people, the San Bernardino shootings rattled a U.S. public already on edge. On December 6, President Barack Obama delivered a rare Oval Office address in which he attempted to quell public fears of more terrorist attacks, pledged to destroy ISIS, and exhorted Americans not to engage in xenophobia or discriminate against law-abiding Muslims. Nevertheless, this did not prevent Donald Trump, then a leading Republican presidential candidate, from asserting that all Muslims should be prohibited from entering the United States. This prompted an immediate backlash— from both Republicans and Democrats—who argued that such a proposition was un-American and quite likely unconstitutional.

Meanwhile, virtually all Islamic groups in the United States sharply condemned the San Bernardino attack.

Paul G. Pierpaoli Jr.

See also: Baghdadi, Abu Bakr al-; Homegrown Terrorism; Islamic State of Iraq and Syria (ISIS); Jihad

Citations

Goldman, Adam, Mark Bergman, and Missy Ryan. "San Bernardino Shooter's Neighbor Who Bought Rifle Is Cooperating with Authorities," *The Washington Post,* December 10, 2015.

"San Bernardino Shootings Investigated as Terrorism," *BBC News,* December 4, 2015.

Schmidt, Michael S., and Richard Pérez-Peña. "F.B.I. Treating San Bernardino Attack as Terrorism Case," *The New York Times,* December 4, 2015.

Sanchez, Ilich Ramirez (Carlos the Jackal)

Ilich Ramirez Sanchez, better known as Carlos the Jackal, is a Venezuela-born freelance terrorist who mostly worked for the Popular Front for the Liberation of Palestine (PFLP). He was tied to a number of incidents between 1973 and 1975, including:

- The planning of the September 28, 1973, takeover of a train of Soviet Jewish émigrés in Austria by Sa'aqa (Thunderbolt).
- The December 31, 1973, shooting of Joseph E. Sieff, president of the Marks and Spencer store chain, honorary vice president of the Zionist Federation of Great Britain, and president of the Joint Palestinian Appeal in London.
- The January 24, 1974, bombing of the Israeli-owned Hapoalim in London.

- The August 3, 1974, bombings of two small cars and a minibus parked outside the offices of two anti-Arab newspapers, *L'Aurore* and *Minute,* and the United Jewish Social Fund in Paris.
- A September 15, 1974, grenade attack on a drugstore located at the Saint-Germaine shopping complex in Paris.
- The November 18, 1974, assassination of Alan Quartermaine, a British insurance broker, who was hit twice in the neck and killed when his chauffeur-driven Rolls Royce stopped at a King's Road traffic light in London. Authorities believe Carlos may have mistaken Quartermaine for a Jewish member of Parliament who also drove a Rolls Royce and lived nearby (although others suspected some sort of Provisional Irish Republican Army involvement).
- The planning for the January 13, 1975, RPG-7 attack on an El Al 707 in Orly Airport.

On July 27, 1975, three French intelligence officers visited Sanchez's apartment in Paris, acting on a tip-off from a PFLP insider, Michel Moukharbal. After a 30-minute interrogation, they took him to the Direction de la surveillance du territoire (DST, or the Directorate of Territorial Surveillance) headquarters for further questioning. After arriving, he excused himself on the pretext of needing to go to the restroom, only to reemerge with a Czech automatic pistol that he used to kill Moukharbal and officers Raymond Dous and Jean Donatini; Commissaire Principal Jean Herranz was also wounded in the throat.

Sanchez escaped, next surfacing on December 21, 1975, when he led the six-member PFLP team that took over a ministerial meeting of the Organization of Petroleum Exporting Countries (OPEC) in

Vienna and seized 70 hostages, including 11 oil ministers. This was followed by the bombing of the Radio Free Europe building in Munich (February 21, 1981), an attack on West Berlin's Kurfürstendamm shopping mall (August 25, 1983), a threat to kill Bonn interior minister Friedrich Zimmermann if authorities prosecuted Gabriele Kröcher-Tiedemann for her role in the 1975 attack on the OPEC headquarters in Vienna (September 1983), and the bombing of a French TGV high-speed train en route from Marseilles to Paris that killed 3 and injured 10 (December 31, 1983).

On June 21, 1990, an Austrian newspaper reported that Sanchez had operated from East Berlin with the consent of Erich Honecker and former minister of state security Erich Mielke. Following the collapse of the Berlin Wall, he apparently moved to Syria. However, he was reportedly expelled from the country on September 21, 1991, and, having been denied entry to Libya, finally went to Yemen.

Sanchez was eventually arrested in Sudan on August 14, 1994, and extradited to France. He went on trial on December 12, 1997, for the triple homicides of Dous, Donatini, and the Lebanese informant Moukharbal in June 1975. He was found guilty of the charges, and on December 24 was sentenced to life in prison. Sanchez appealed the verdict on the grounds that he was not permitted to confront his accusers, but he was unsuccessful in swaying the court.

On March 12, 2003, Sanchez again went on trial, this time for committing murder, attempting murder, and carrying out explosions that killed six people in five separate attacks across western Europe. He was convicted on all counts. In a book published that same year, Sanchez praised al-Qaeda leader Osama bin Laden as a shining example. He has since converted to Islam and continues to be held in the Clairvaux prison in eastern France.

In 2005, Sanchez submitted a formal complaint to the European Court of Human Rights, alleging that his years in solitary confinement amounted to inhumane treatment; the court rejected the complaint. In May 2007, Sanchez was brought up on new charges stemming from his activities in France in the early 1980s, which included murder and wanton destruction of property. In his ensuing 2011 trial in Paris, Sanchez denied the charges against him, which now included bombings in which 11 people died and more than 100 others were injured. On December 15, 2011, Sanchez was convicted and sentenced to another life term in prison. In June 2013, he lost his appeal of the 2011 conviction, and his second life term in prison was upheld. In October 2015, French officials charged Sanchez with perpetrating an attack on a drugstore in 1974, during which 2 people died and 34 others were injured. On March 28, 2017, Sanchez was convicted and sentenced to a third life term in prison for the 1974 attack.

Peter Chalk

See also: Popular Front for the Liberation of Palestine (PFLP)

Citations

Bellamy, Patrick. "Carlos the Jackal: Trail of Terror, Parts 1 and 2," *Trutv Crime Library,* www.trutv.com/library/crime/terrorists _spies/terrorists/jackal/12.htm.

"Carlos the Jackal Faces New Trial," *BBC News*, May 4, 2007.

"Carlos the Jackal—Three Decades of Crime," *BBC News*, December 24, 1997.

Follain, John. *Jackal: The Complete Story of the Legendary Terrorist, Carlos the Jackal*. New York: Arcade, 1988.

Smith, Colin. *Carlos: Portrait of a Terrorist*. New York: Holt, Rinehart and Winston, 1976.

Sendero Luminoso

Sendero Luminoso (Shining Path), a Peruvian insurgent organization established by Abimael Guzman, took its name from a saying attributed to José Carlos Mariátegui, founder of Peru's first Communist Party: Marxism-Leninism will open the shining path to revolution.

Guzman, a professor of philosophy at the University of San Cristóbal de Huamanga in southeastern Peru from 1962 until 1978, had become interested in the plight of the region's Quechua natives. In the late 1970s he organized his student followers into a clandestine and hierarchical structure in preparation for armed struggle. A strong believer in Chinese Communist leader Mao Tse-tung theory of mobilizing the peasantry as opposed to the traditional Latin American approach of city dwellers, Guzman eschewed evolutionary socialism and sought to bring about a dictatorship of the proletariat that would include cultural revolution and eventually lead to world revolution and the achievement of pure communism.

By 1980, Shining Path was ready to carry out terrorist activities against anyone associated with or supportive of the so-called bourgeois order. Shining Path's early campaigns greatly exacerbated the tensions between landless peasants in the highlands and giant coastal cooperatives supported by the government. The organization encouraged the peasants to invade these cooperatives to occupy or loot them. The Peruvian government launched a counterinsurgency effort in 1982, placing 19 provinces under a state of emergency. Although Shining Path was responsible for many casualties among peasants, government forces were responsible for many more. Guerrilla warfare between the group and the increasingly militarized government raged for the next decade.

Shining Path assassinated highly placed public figures and wounded or killed many members of the security forces. The insurgency also ruined efforts of Peruvian president Alan García to regenerate locally based capitalist development in Peru. To make matters worse, Shining Path revolutionaries had made an arrangement with the coca growers, providing them with protection in exchange for payment from the profits of the illicit trade.

Guzman, or Chairman Gonzalo as he was known within the organization, developed a powerful cult of personality that attracted significant support from the nation's Andean Indians as well as from Spanish-speaking city dwellers. Guzman not only championed a people's war against the government and the right wing, but by the early 1990s he also believed that any group on the left that sought to use nonviolent methods to improve the plight of the poor was his enemy. Thus, in 1991 Shining Path terrorists killed four mothers and their children for their work with a committee that distributed free milk to children. Shining Path also killed the president of a local Catholic charity and two foreign relief workers from an evangelical agency and blew up a sophisticated agricultural experimental station sponsored by the Japanese government. With this kind of destruction, Shining Path made it impossible to get any kind of help to the poor people most affected by the nation's economic crisis. In Puno Province alone, the government estimated in 1991 that the insurgency put an end to more than US$100 million worth of economic and developmental aid.

By 1992, Shining Path's activities had claimed an estimated 23,000 lives and resulted in property damage of some US$22 billion. Most of the victims were peasants. Faced with a deteriorating situation, in April 1992 President Alberto Fujimori carried out what amounted to a coup against his own presidency. He dissolved the congress and the judiciary branch, suspended the constitution, and declared himself the head of the provisional government. These extreme measures did not arouse great opposition within Peru, as most citizens saw them as a necessary response to a desperate situation.

Fujimori's enhanced security efforts led to the capture of Guzman on September 12, 1992. Brought before a military tribunal in October 1992, he was convicted of terrorist activities and sentenced to life imprisonment without parole. (In 2004, his first trial having been declared illegal, Guzman was again tried and convicted, this time by a civilian court, and his previous sentence was upheld.) In 1994 from his cell, Guzman offered peace terms to end the insurgency. This act had the effect of splintering Shining Path, some members of which continue insurgent activities in the countryside in hopes of reaching a peace agreement with the government, while others are now involved in the cocaine trade.

Spencer C. Tucker

See also: Fuerzas Armadas Revolucionárias de Colombia (FARC); Taliban

Citations

Gorriti Ellenbogen, Gustavo. *The Shining Path: A History of the Millenarian War in Peru*. Chapel Hill: University of North Carolina Press, 1999.

Palmer, David Scott, ed. *Shining Path of Peru*. New York: St. Martin's, 1992.

Poole, Deborah, and Gerardo Renique. *Peru: Time of Fear*. New York: Monthly Review Press, 1992.

Taylor, Lewis. *Shining Path: Guerrilla War in Peru's Northern Highlands*. Liverpool: Liverpool University Press, 2006.

September 11 Attacks

On September 11, 2001, the worst act of terrorism in the history of the United States destroyed the twin towers of the World Trade Center in New York City and part of the Pentagon in Virginia. The attacks killed nearly 3,000 people at the World Trade Center and almost 200 at the Pentagon. In an intricate plot, terrorists hijacked four planes and crashed one into each tower of the World Trade Center and one into the Pentagon. The fourth plane crashed into a field in western Pennsylvania, presumably after its passengers attempted to overtake the hijackers. Officials believe that plane was headed for the White House or Camp David.

American Airlines Flight 11 from Boston was the first plane to crash, hitting the north tower of the World Trade Center at 8:45 a.m. At 9:03 a.m., United Airlines Flight 175 from Boston hit the south tower. At 9:40 a.m., the Federal Aviation Administration (FAA) stopped all air traffic nationwide for the first time in history. The FAA also diverted all incoming international flights to Canada. However, the order came too late. At 9:43 a.m., American Airlines Flight 77 from Dulles Airport in Virginia crashed into the Pentagon, and at 10:10 a.m., United Airlines Flight 93 crashed near Shanksville,

Smoke clouds and debris at Ground Zero, site of the World Trade Center towers destroyed in the terrorist attack of September 11, 2001. The 9/11 attacks marked the beginning of the Global War on Terrorism and a seemingly endless conflict between the West and Islamic terrorists motivated by the ideology of Salafi-jihadism. (U.S. Air Force)

Pennsylvania. All were cross-country flights carrying full loads of fuel.

Both towers of the World Trade Center eventually collapsed, the south tower at 10:05 a.m. and the north tower at 10:28 a.m. The collapse killed thousands of people who were attempting to evacuate the buildings (including several hundred New York City firefighters who were dispatched after the first plane hit), as well as other firefighters at the scene, police officers, rescue workers, and onlookers outside the buildings.

The chaotic day included evacuations at the White House, U.S. State Department, and Capitol Building. President George W. Bush was flown from Florida to a bunker at a U.S. Air Force base in Nebraska, the Canadian and Mexican borders were put on the highest state of alert, and all U.S. military personnel around the world were put on high alert. All potential targets around the United States were evacuated (including airports); all nonessential employees at the North Atlantic Treaty Organization (NATO) headquarters in Brussels, Belgium, were sent home; and Israel evacuated all its diplomatic missions.

In the initial days after the attacks, the full extent of the damage was still unclear. Rescue crews continued their search and rescue missions at the World Trade Center and the Pentagon, digging through millions of tons of rubble. The stock market remained closed until September 17, sending the already lagging U.S. economy into further distress. Airlines began announcing layoffs, as consumers expressed fears of flying. To help offset this, the U.S. government quickly established the September 11th Victim Compensation Fund, which provided monetary compensation to the families of victims who agreed not to file any lawsuits related to the attacks. Despite complaints about the strict mathematical approach to determining how

much money each family would receive, only 80 lawsuits were filed, making the fund a success in shielding the airlines. In addition, the world rallied in support, and for the first time in history, NATO invoked Article 5 of the North Atlantic Treaty (1949), which states that an attack on one member of the alliance is an attack on all members and calls for the implementation of collective self-defense. Donations to such charities as the Red Cross and the United Way reached unprecedented heights.

On September 20, Bush became the first president to address an emergency joint session of the U.S. Congress since Franklin D. Roosevelt gave his War Message to Congress on December 8, 1941, after the Japanese attack on Pearl Harbor. During Bush's speech, he pledged that justice would be done to those responsible and announced the creation of the Office of Homeland Security. Bush appointed Pennsylvania governor Tom Ridge as the first director of the Cabinet-level office responsible for unifying a federal plan to combat domestic terrorism (the office later became part of the cabinet as the Department of Homeland Security). Bush also used the speech to condemn domestic hate crimes against Arab Americans, who suffered from scattered violence throughout the United States after the attacks.

In the aftermath of the World Trade Center and Pentagon attacks, the U.S. government called for the implementation of an overall strategy of vigilance to deter terrorism. Bush underlined the particular need for international cooperation in his speech on September 20: "This is not, however, just America's fight. And what is at stake is not just America's freedom. This is the world's fight. This is civilization's fight." Indeed, the tragedy had not happened to only the United States; as New York is one of the most internationally diverse cities in the world, the victims originated from more than 100 different countries. The international response showed that many countries understood the tragedy was theirs as well.

Unlike previous terrorist attacks, there were no credible claims of responsibility. However, Saudi millionaire and known terrorist Osama bin Laden was named the prime suspect; he was also believed to have been behind the World Trade Center bombing in 1993, the U.S. embassy bombings in Africa in 1998, and the USS *Cole* bombing in 2000. Soon after the attacks, all nations cut diplomatic ties with Afghanistan's ruling Taliban government, said to be harboring bin Laden, and many demanded that he be handed over. On October 7, Operation Enduring Freedom was launched against the Taliban. U.S.-led forces quickly toppled the regime, and Afghanistan began a new government with the support of the United States and United Nations. Meanwhile, the U.S. Federal Bureau of Investigation quickly identified 19 alleged hijackers, all Muslims from Middle Eastern countries. Hundreds of people believed to be linked to or have information about the hijackers were detained or arrested in the United States and throughout the world.

In September 2002, Bush heeded political pressure and created the National Commission on Terrorist Attacks Upon the United States, which was charged with investigating the events leading up to the attacks, including any intelligence failures that might have occurred. After more than a year of hearings and inquiries, the commission concluded that though the attacks certainly came as a shock, they should not have come as a surprise. The commission reported that the United States' intelligence community was poorly organized and the country was ill prepared to react to the attacks. However,

according to the executive summary of the commission's report, "we cannot know whether any single step or series of steps would have defeated them" because of al-Qaeda's resourcefulness and flexibility. In light of the failures of the intelligence and defense communities, the commission recommended several sweeping reforms. These included creating a national counterterrorism center and "unifying the intelligence community with a new National Intelligence Director." In addition, the commission recommended enhancing diplomatic relationships in the Middle East, particularly with Islamic groups that may have been alienated by the United States' war on terrorism. Congress has passed legislation incorporating some of the September 11 Commission's recommendations, including reorganization of the intelligence community.

Philip J. MacFarlane

See also: Al-Qaeda; Bin Laden, Osama; Global War on Terror; Taliban; Zawahiri, Ayman al-

Citations

Dudley, William, ed. *The Attack on America, September 11, 2001*. San Diego, CA: Greenhaven Press, 2002.

Halliday, Fred. *Two Hours That Shook the World. September 11, 2001: Causes and Consequences*. London: Saqi Books, 2002.

Jess, Sara, et al. *America Attacked: Terrorists Declare War on America*. San Jose, CA: University Press, 2001.

Suri, Abu Musab al-

One of militant Islam's most prolific strategic theorists in the past 30 years and a member of the al-Qaeda terrorist organization, Abu Musab al-Suri was born in Aleppo, Syria, in 1958; his birth name reportedly was Mustafa Setmariam Nasar. Al-Suri experienced a religious awakening in 1980 after studying engineering at the University of Aleppo for four years. Joining a branch of the Syrian Muslim Brotherhood, he left Syria in 1980, never to return because of the severe repression by the Assad regime of the Islamic opposition. Despite al-Suri's exile, he maintained his Syrian roots and connections—al-Suri means "the Syrian" in Arabic—and was considered the Syrian representative in al-Qaeda's highest leadership circles. Al-Suri traveled widely after leaving Syria. He is known to have resided in Jordan, Saudi Arabia, Iraq, and France (mid-1980s), Afghanistan (1987–1992), Spain (1992–1997), and Afghanistan again (1997–2002). While in Spain he married a Spanish woman. During his first visit to Afghanistan, he met both Abdullah Azzam and Osama bin Laden, the founders of al-Qaeda. Al-Suri may have received sanctuary in Iran after Operation Enduring Freedom began in late 2001, and he reportedly traveled to Iraq to visit Ansar al-Islam's camp in Kurdistan prior to the U.S.-led invasion of Iraq (Operation Iraqi Freedom) in March 2003.

In November 2004 the U.S. government offered a $5 million reward for information leading to his capture. Al-Suri is best known for his prolific theoretical writing and speaking on jihad (holy war) and the appropriate strategies for waging war against the West. His writings are notable for their systematic efforts to learn from past mistakes. His first book, *The Syrian Islamic Jihadist Revolution: Pains and Hopes,* was published around 1990 in Peshawar. In the 1990s, he established a media center called the Islamic

Conflict Studies Bureau LTD and was able to create major media opportunities for bin Laden and al-Qaeda leadership in the 1996–1998 period. During this period, al-Suri wrote a number of studies and analyses of jihadist efforts in the Middle East, Central Asia, and South Asia. His 160-page *Musharraf's Pakistan: The Problem, the Solution, and the Necessary Obligation* was published in late 2004. It called for the overthrow of the Pervez Musharraf regime, a call later echoed by al-Qaeda second in command Ayman al-Zawahiri. At about the same time, al-Suri finally completed the 1,600-page *Call to Global Islamic Resistance,* a work he had begun in the early 1990s that articulates his ideas for a new global guerrilla warfare strategy based on a decentralized model of organization. He also hoped to write a book on jihad guerrilla strategy titled *The Fundamentals for Jihadi Guerrilla Warfare in Light of the Conditions of the Contemporary American Campaign* and based on his lectures and research in Afghanistan, but he was arrested before the manuscript could be completed. Several transcripts of his lectures on this topic have been released on jihadi websites since his arrest.

Suri apparently had strong reservations about the September 11 attacks. On the one hand, he recognized their mobilizing effect on the Islamic community. On the other hand, he also recognized that the attacks provided a justification for U.S. invasion, which shattered the jihadi movement. This recognition led to his publication of *Call to Global Islamic Resistance* in which he argued that the old local and regional covert organizations (*tanzims*) were no longer an effective way of conducting revolution. Their large hierarchical organization, firmly rooted geographically, raised too many risks in an era of dominant U.S. military and political influence and active opposition from many local governments. Al-Suri instead argued that a transnational structure based on small cells held together by common doctrine and ideology could carry out terror operations at lower risk. This also would create a deterritorialized jihadist war in which operations are carried out on a global scale and resistance to occupation is not confined to the theater in question. Al-Suri himself insisted in his writings that he was primarily a theorist and thinker, not an executor of operations. However, he is suspected of having had deep operational involvement in a variety of conflicts and, since 2001, attacks or attempted attacks on Western states. He fought with al-Qaeda and the Taliban in Afghanistan, where his experiences during American air strikes contributed strongly to his reassessment of proper resistance tactics. He was suspected of involvement in the March 2004 Madrid bombing attacks and has been linked in some reports to attacks in London in July 2005. British authorities reportedly suspect that he had some involvement in the 1995 Paris Metro bombings, and he has significant ties with terrorist cells in both Europe and the Maghreb, as well as a record of support for the Algerian terrorist organization Armed Islamic Group (GIA).

Some reports also link him with Abu Musab al-Zarqawi, as both men are associated with a virulent dislike of Shia Islam. However, al-Suri might have acquired this position because of the sectarian situation in Syria. At least one account notes that the intellectually sophisticated and articulate al-Suri must have had a strong ideological impact on the barely educated al-Zarqawi. Al-Suri also ran a major training camp called al-Ghuraba ("The Aliens") in Afghanistan during 2000–2001 that trained foreign fighters for al-Qaeda and the Taliban. Also, he is reported to have assisted in al-Qaeda's experiments with chemical weapons. Al-Suri almost certainly trained al-Qaeda operatives who went back to Europe and created sleeper cells. Interestingly, al-Suri was linked with a group of secessionists inside al-Qaeda who reportedly rejected bin Laden's leadership and pledged loyalty to the Taliban. Al-Suri had to take an oath of obedience to Mullah Mohammed Omar, leader of the Taliban, to run his training camp. Al-Suri himself denied rumors of a split, however, and emphasized his close links with al-Qaeda leadership, including his invitation to bin Laden's wedding in 2000. The nature of the connection to al-Qaeda is, in some respects, irrelevant, as al-Suri's writings provide the basis for a school of jihadi strategic studies that have profoundly affected al-Qaeda and other transnational terrorist networks and have raised significant concern for Western analysts and policy makers. In late 2005, Pakistani security forces reportedly captured al-Suri in Quetta, Pakistan. He was then allegedly transferred to American custody, but his current location is unknown. In more recent years, there has been speculation that al-Suri is being held at a secret Central Intelligence Agency (CIA) prison compound on the island of Diego Garcia in the Indian Ocean. The U.S. government has since confirmed that al-Suri was indeed captured in Quetta in 2005, but it has steadfastly refused to divulge his whereabouts. In April 2014, an al-Qaeda spokesman stated that al-Suri remained imprisoned.

Timothy D. Hoyt

See also: Al-Qaeda; Global War on Terror; Jihad; Madrid Commuter Train Bombings (2004); Zarqawi, Abu Musab al-

Citations

Lacey, Jim, ed. *A Terrorist's Call to Global Jihad: Deciphering Abu Musab al-Suri's Islamic Jihad Manifesto.* Annapolis, MD: Naval Institute Press, 2008.

Lia, Brynjar. *Architect of Global Jihad: The Life of Al-Qaeda Strategist Abu Mus'ab Al-Suri.* New York: Columbia University Press, 2008.

T

Taliban

The word *Taliban* means "students" and is an Arabic word used in many Muslim countries for a political and religious movement begun in Afghanistan in the 1990s. In the mid-1990s, however, Afghan students studying in Pakistani madrassas (schools) adopted the name for a political-religious movement that eventually established an Islamic government in much of Afghanistan. Many in the Taliban also served as mujahideen during the Soviet-Afghan War. When Soviet forces invaded Afghanistan in December 1979, many young Afghan boys and other non-combatants fled the country and were lodged in refugee camps in Iran and Pakistan. During the 10-year Soviet occupation, more than 2 million refugees, mainly Pashtuns, found refuge in Pakistan's North-West Frontier Province, especially the tribal areas. The province was also home to hundreds of madrassas run by the Deobandi sect as well as to Wahhabi-influenced schools established by wealthy Saudi donors. Tens of thousands of Afghan and Pakistani boys thus received an Islamic education in these madrassas.

Soviet forces departed Afghanistan in 1989, and Afghan communist forces met final defeat in 1992, but civil war between rival mujahideen leaders erupted soon afterward. Much of the fighting pitted Pashtuns against ethnic Tajiks, Uzbeks, and Hazaras of northern and central Afghanistan. Pakistan, which hoped to establish lucrative trade routes with Central Asia, sought a strong Pashtun-dominated government to provide stability. By the mid-1990s, many refugee children were old enough to fight, and their strict Islamic education made them ideal recruits for the Taliban. The Taliban emerged in 1994 when Mullah Mohammed Omar led a small group of fighters in liberating several villages from local warlords. In late 1994 Pakistan enlisted the Taliban's support. Omar and approximately 200 fighters overran Spin Boldak and Kandahar and in the process captured many weapons, including tanks, artillery, and aircraft. Their success prompted thousands of Afghan and Pakistani students to join them. By early 1995 the Taliban controlled much of the Pashtun regions of the country. Thereafter, the Taliban confronted better-organized non-Pashtun forces in northern Afghanistan.

Both sides committed numerous atrocities, mainly against rival ethnic groups. Despite several defeats, the Taliban captured Herat in 1995, Kabul in 1996, Mazar-e Sharif in 1998, and Taloqan, a city in northeastern Afghanistan, in 1999. By 2000 fighting had largely stalemated, with the non-Pashtun Northern Alliance bottled up in northeastern Afghanistan and portions of central Afghanistan, although it still controlled Afghanistan's United Nations (UN) seat. Pakistan, Saudi Arabia, and the United Arab Emirates were the only countries to recognize the Taliban government. Pakistan, Saudi Arabia, and various Arab Gulf states also provided weapons to the Taliban, while India, Iran, Russia, and the Central Asian states supported the Northern Alliance. Ironically, the United States initially leaned toward supporting the Taliban, but that changed after the

Taliban ambassador to Pakistan Abdul Salem Zaeef (foreground) during a news conference in Islamabad, Pakistan, on September 21, 2001. Afghanistan's Taliban rulers refused to hand over terrorist leader Osama bin Laden, warning that U.S. attempts to apprehend him by force could plunge the whole region into crisis. The United States entered into a war with the Taliban in October 2001 for its role in harboring Osama bin Laden and al-Qaeda. Sixteen plus years after the initial American invasion of Afghanistan, the U.S. still finds itself at war with the Taliban. Most experts believe that the only way to end the war is through prolonged political negotiations that include members of the Taliban. (Visual News/Getty Images)

Taliban offered sanctuary to the terrorist group al-Qaeda.

Widespread human rights violations by the Taliban provoked international condemnation, but the Taliban consistently ignored outside criticism. Its version of government was perhaps the harshest ever seen in the Muslim world. Women were virtually imprisoned in their homes, medieval-like Islamic punishment became routine for criminal offenses, and international aid organizations were expelled, with no attempt to provide for millions of destitute Afghans. The Taliban even went so far as to destroy priceless historical and cultural treasures such as the Buddhas of Bamiyan, which they claimed were blasphemous to Islam. The Taliban's downfall came following the September 11, 2001, terrorist attacks against the United States, when the Americans and other allies launched major military operations in support of the Northern Alliance in October 2001.

The United States sought to topple the Taliban because it had failed to turn over al-Qaeda leader Osama bin Laden after the attacks and because it continued to give refuge to terrorists. Disenchanted Pashtuns rose up as well and established the Southern Alliance. Within weeks, most of the Taliban and foreign jihadists had fled to the tribal areas, where they found sanctuary. The regions of southern Afghanistan and western Pakistan have historically resisted British, Afghan, and Pakistani control. Fearing internal consequences, the Pakistani government did not conduct sustained counterinsurgency operations there after the September 11 attacks. Consequently, the Taliban used the area to rebuild its forces. Although initially weakened, the Taliban remains a potent threat in the Pashtun regions of Afghanistan, and Pakistan and coalition forces continue to do battle with its fighters in Afghanistan. Since 2007 the number of Taliban-inspired attacks in Afghanistan has risen steadily, so much so that the United States and other coalition nations have had to expend more troops and resources to counter the Taliban resurgence. In the spring of 2009, however, with Pakistani national security threatened by Taliban advances and under heavy pressure from the United States, the Pakistani military commenced major offensive operations against Taliban-controlled areas of northwestern Pakistan.

Chuck Fahrer

See also: Al-Qaeda; Global War on Terror; Haqqani Network; Tehrik-i-Taliban Pakistan (TTP)

Citations

Coll, Steve. *Ghost Wars: The Secret History of the CIA, Afghanistan, and Bin Laden, from the Soviet Invasion to September 10, 2001.* New York: Penguin, 2004.

Goodson, Larry P. *Afghanistan's Endless War: State Failure, Regional Politics, and the Rise of the Taliban.* Seattle: University of Washington Press, 2001.

Tehrik-i-Taliban Pakistan (TTP)

The Tehrik-i-Taliban Pakistan (TTP) emerged as a result of a secret 2007 shura (council) that cemented a deal between 40 commanders from Pakistan's tribal belt as well as the settled districts of Swat, Bannu, Tank, Lakki Marwat, Dera Ismail Khan, Kohistan, Buner, and Malakand. The current leader is Hakimullah Mehsud, who took over the reins of the organization after its founder, Baitullah Mehsud, was killed by a missile from a Central Intelligence Agency (CIA) drone in August 2009. The group includes the Tehrik-e-Nefaz-e-Shariat-e-Mohammadi (Movement for the Enforcement of Islamic Law), which briefly took over the Swat Valley in 2007 and was hitherto described as one of the most dangerous jihadist entities in Pakistan.

As of February 2009, the TTP's strength was estimated to be between 15,000 and 20,000, with armed cadres present in all the tribal agencies of the Federally Administered Tribal Areas (FATA) as well as several districts of the North West Frontier Province (NWFP, now known as Khyber Pakhtunkhwa Province). Islamabad banned the organization on August 25, 2008, in addition to freezing its assets and bank accounts and barring it from making media appearances.

The TTP espouses a highly militant agenda that calls for a defensive jihad against the Pakistani Army, enforcement of sharia law, and a united Islamist onslaught on allied troops in Afghanistan. It is virulently opposed to the central government in Islamabad and has been directly linked to as many as 90 percent of all suicide operations that have taken place in Pakistan since 2007. Some of TTP's more notable attacks have included the assassination of Prime Minister Benazir Bhutto in December 2007; the bombing of the Islamabad Marriott in September 2008 (undertaken in collaboration with Lashkar-e-Jhangvi [LeJ]); an assault on a police academy in Lahore in March 2009; a brazen attack on a police academy in Manawan in April 2009; a suicide bombing of a Shia mosque in the town of Chakwal, just south of the capital, again in April 2009; assaults on three law enforcement agencies in Lahore, the offices of the World Food Program in Islamabad, the army's headquarters in Rawalpindi, and crowded markets in Peshawar and the Shangla District of the Swat Valley—all in October 2009; a January 2010 bombing of a volleyball match in Lakki Marwat, in northwestern Pakistan, that left more than 93 people dead; and a multipronged assault against the U.S. consulate in Peshawar in April 2010.

The TTP is widely acknowledged to have forged a close ideological and operational relationship with Osama bin Laden. After the initiation of the post-9/11 bombing campaign in Afghanistan, Baitullah Mehsud gave sanctuary to fleeing al-Qaeda members in South Waziristan, a move that was reciprocated with the provision of funds, operational planners, and military experts. The TTP subsequently emerged as one of bin Laden's most trusted allies in Pakistan. The group developed an extensive network of training camps in the tribal areas to teach raw recruits guerrilla tactics and transform committed jihadists into suicide bombers. Many of these militants were then dispatched across both sides of the Pakistani-Afghan border, both to attack U.S., North Atlantic Treaty Organization (NATO), and allied troops and also to target prominent sites inside Pakistan itself.

A further indication of the TTP's close alignment with al-Qaeda emerged in early 2009, when the TTP formed the Shura Ittehadul Mujahideen (the Council of United Mujahideen). Primarily a move to reinforce solidarity among the movement's component organizations, the shura issued a one-page statement written in Urdu that both affirmed a joint commitment to combat American troops in Afghanistan and declared an oath of allegiance to Mullah Omar and Osama bin Laden.

After Baitullah Mehsud was killed in a U.S. drone attack in 2009, leadership briefly transferred to his brother, Hakimullah Mehsud. The latter died as a result of injuries sustained in another drone attack in January 2013 as did Qari Hussain (also known as Ustad-e-Fidaeen, "teacher of suicide cadres"), Hakimullah's cousin. A senior lieutenant and head of the group's suicide operation, Hussain is thought to have planned the string of organized attacks that struck Pakistan in October 2009, many of which were allegedly undertaken in conjunction with al-Qaeda in revenge for the army's offensives in the Swat Valley.

At the time of writing, the core of the TTP's remaining strength was concentrated in the Aurakzai tribal region. In an effort to clear the region, the Pakistani military was engaged in an intensive offensive, codenamed Kwakh Ba De Sham (a Pashtun expression roughly translated as "I will teach you a lesson" or "I will fix you"), aimed at destroying the TTP's leadership, crippling its ability to train and launch attacks, and denying it a safe haven in which it might be able to regroup.

Peter Chalk

See also: Al-Qaeda; Haqqani Network; Taliban

Citations

Giustozzi, Antonio. *Koran, Kalashnikov and Laptop: The New-Taliban Insurgency in Afghanistan.* London: Hurst Books, 2007.

Khan, Haji. "Taliban Rename Their Group," *The Nation* (Pakistan), February 23, 2009, http://nation.com.pk/23-Feb-2009/taliban-rename-their-group.

Laub, Zachary. "Pakistan's New Generation of Terrorists," Council on Foreign Relations, Washington, DC, and New York, October 26, 2009, www.cfr.org/backgrounder/pakistans-new-generation-terrorists.

Moreau, Ron, and Sami Yousafzi. "The End of Al Qaeda?" *Newsweek,* August 29, 2009.

"Tribal Tribulations: The Pakistan Taliban in Waziristan," *Jane's Intelligence Review,* February 2009.

Tunisian Beach Resort Attack

On June 26, 2015, in the Mediterranean resort town of Port El Kantaoui, Tunisia, a lone gunman opened fire on beachgoers and guests at a beachfront hotel, an incident that showed the capability of terrorists to murder civilians in such a venue. The resulting massacre killed 38 civilians, including 30 British tourists, and wounded 39 others. The gunman, Seifeddine Rezgui Yacoubi, a radicalized, disaffected Tunisian, was also killed in the attack. The June assault is part of a larger trend that has resulted in increased terrorist activity in Tunisia, which heretofore had been considered a relatively safe country. Just three months earlier, three terrorists attacked a popular museum in Tunis, which resulted in more than 20 deaths. The attack began about noontime on the beach facing the upscale Riu Imperial Marhaba Hotel. After lounging on the beach, and even having spoken to some of the beachgoers, Yacoubi began shooting guests with a Russian automatic assault rifle that he had hidden in a beach umbrella. After shooting a number of people on the beach, he entered the hotel and again began shooting. After several chaotic and terror-filled minutes, the hotel's security guards apprehended and killed him.

The subsequent investigation concluded that Yacoubi was the only gunman, but the Tunisian government strongly suspected that he received assistance from outside sources. Tunisian authorities believe that Yacoubi had connections to the militant Islamist group known as Ansar al-Sharia, a loose network of Islamic terrorists that are thought to operate in seven Middle Eastern and North African countries. Nevertheless, other observers claim that Yacoubi had ties to the Islamic State of Iraq and Syria (ISIS). The government's investigation of the resort killings suggests that the gunman was a chronic cocaine user; high levels of the drug were found in his body at autopsy. Officials believe that Yacoubi had been drawn to Islamic extremism during the Libyan Civil War and may have been angered about the world's seeming unwillingness to intervene in the bloody Syrian Civil War. Concerned about the rise in terrorist activity in Tunisia, Tunisian president Beji Caid Essebsi urged a more cohesive international effort to combat terrorism and took measures to crack down on homegrown religious extremism. Within weeks, scores of mosques led by radical imams were shut down while the government sought to extinguish financial networks that were funding terrorist activity within Tunisia. The Tunisian government also decided to dispatch reserve army troops to secure high-profile areas and landmarks. Because tourism is a major industry in Tunisia, there is now concern that the recent terror attacks will staunch the flow of tourists into the country. The resort massacre was the deadliest terrorist attack in modern Tunisia's history.

Paul G. Pierpaoli Jr.

See also: Islamic State of Iraq and Syria (ISIS); Ivory Coast Beach Resort Attack

Citations

Armstrong, Jeremy, and Dan Warburton. "Tunisia Terror Attack: ISIS Killer High on Drugs When He Carried Out Massacre," *Mirror,* July 2, 1015, www.mirror.co.uk /news/world-news/tunisia-terror-attack-isis -killer-5977381, accessed September 10, 2015.

"Deadly Terrorist Attack on Tunisia Tourist Hotel in Sousse Resort," *The Guardian,* June 26, 2015, www.theguardian.com/world /2015/jun/26/tunisia-tourist-hotel-repor tedly-attacked, accessed September 10, 2015.

"Tunisia to Shut Illegal Mosques as IS Claims Deadly Hotel Attack," AFP and AP, *Times of Israel,* June 27, 2015, www.timesofisrael .com/islamic-state-claims-deadly-hotel -attack-in-tunisia, accessed September 10, 2015.

U

Ulster Volunteer Force (UVF)

The Ulster Volunteer Force (UVF) is the oldest Protestant loyalist paramilitary organization in Northern Ireland. An earlier version of the UVF had been formed in 1912 and was active in fighting before World War I against Irish Home Rule. UVF's opposition to Irish Home Rule led to the creation of a separate Northern Ireland. After this success, the UVF had withered way in the middle 1920s. Catholic agitation for equality in economic and political rights in Northern Ireland in the early 1960s led to the resurrection of the UVF. Ulster's Protestant politicians decided in 1965 to reconstitute the UVF to replace the moderate government of Terence O'Neill and replace it with a more resolute Ulster Protestant government. Gusty Spence and other Protestant leaders plotted the strategy for the UVF in a pub on Shankill Road in Belfast in 1966. The goal of the UVF was to preserve Protestant domination in Northern Ireland and fight against the Provisional Irish Republican Army. In 1966, the Ulster government declared the UVF as an illegal organization after its role in the murders of Catholics became known. Leaders of the UVF were willing to achieve this goal by either violence or by negotiations. A cease-fire in 1973 and unsuccessful negotiations with both the Provisional IRA and the Official IRA proved this intent.

Regardless, the Ulster Volunteer Force developed a reputation for violence. Beginning in 1966, members of the UVF carried out a series of terrorist attacks on Catholics. One such attack on December 4, 1971, when UVF activists bombed McGurk's Bar in Belfast, Northern Ireland, killing 15 Catholics. Its most spectacular and bloody operation, however, was the May 17, 1974, car bombings in Dublin and Monaghan, Republic of Ireland, that claimed the lives of 32 people and wounded more than 200 others. In the late 1970s, a subunit of the UVF earned the reputations as the "Shankill Butchers" for their brutal killings of Catholics. Eight members of the Shankill Butchers were arrested and sentenced to life imprisonment on February 20, 1979. Leadership of the UVF decided that these violent acts were counterproductive because they were alienating even Protestant supporters. These activities had also resulted in most of the veteran UVF leaders serving prison time. This exodus of veteran leaders led to a new generation of UVF leadership. In early 1991, the new leadership concluded an alliance with the Ulster Defence Association and formed a Combined Loyalist Military Command (CLMC) to coordinate operations between the groups.

Leaders of the UVF decided in the mid-1990s to moderate their terrorist image. They implemented a cease-fire in October 1994 and formed the Progressive Unionist Party (PUP) to serve as the political wing of the UVF. Parliamentary leaders of the PUP have been Billy Hutchinson and David Ervine. Both have been elected to the Northern Ireland Assembly. Gusty Spence still retains influence in the PUP, but he has broken most of his ties with the rest of the UVF. Leadership of both the PUP and the UVF has been supportive of the Good Friday Accord. Backing this peace accord, however, has led to open warfare between the UVF and the Ulster Freedom Fighters (UFF). Members of both the UVF and the UFF have been assassinated in an ongoing loyalist feud. This feud has died out since the imprisonment of Johnny "Mad Dog" Adair, the head of the UFF.

Stephen E. Atkins

See also: Loyalist Volunteer Force (LVF); Provisional Irish Republican Army (PIRA)

Citations

Bruce, Steve. *The Red Hand: Protestant Paramilitaries in Northern Ireland.* Oxford, UK: Oxford University Press, 1992.

Dillon, Martin. *God and the Gun: The Church and Irish Terrorism.* New York: Routledge, 1990.

Taylor, Peter. *Loyalists: War and Peace in Northern Ireland.* New York: TV Books, 1999.

UPS/FedEx Bomb Plot

On November 1, 2010, authorities narrowly averted a sophisticated terrorist bombing that was to have involved two explosive-packed printer cartridges that were being shipped to synagogues in Chicago onboard United Parcel Service (UPS) and FedEx cargo planes. The plot was linked to Al-Qaeda in the Arabian Peninsula (AQAP) and was discovered after a tip-off from Saudi intelligence.

The printer cartridges originated in Sana'a, Yemen, and were loaded on two passenger aircraft that flew first to Doha, Qatar, and then to Dubai on October 31, 2010. After arriving in the United Arab Emirates (UAE), the cartridges were to have been shipped to the United States via two different routes, one onboard a UPS cargo plane bound for Chicago via Cologne in Germany and the East Midlands Airport in the United Kingdom, the other direct as a FedEx parcel. The latter was intercepted before it left Dubai following a warning from Saudi officials. However, the former departed as planned. After authorities confirmed that the FedEx package was indeed a bomb, they alerted Britain's Secret Intelligence Service (SIS, or MI6), who quickly quarantined the UPS plane after it arrived at the East Midlands Airport. Officers from the Metropolitan Police's Counter Terrorism Command removed the toner cartridge at 3:30 a.m. and took it to a nearby freight-distribution center for further inspection. At first, no trace of explosives was found, and at 10 a.m. the package was deemed safe. Four hours later, after officers received additional information from Saudi Arabia and Dubai, the cartridge was hastily reexamined and found to contain PETN, a powerful compound that is hard to detect. The cartridge was subsequently removed and made safe.

The sophistication of the intercepted devices led officials to speculate that al-Qaeda or an affiliated organization was behind the plot. The hunch was quickly confirmed. In the November issue of its English-language magazine *Inspire,* AQAP assumed full responsibility, devoting the entire publication to detailing the technology in the attempted attacks. The group scoffed at the notion that the operation, which it called Hemorrhage, had been a failure, claiming that the main aim had been to disrupt global air cargo systems. It further pointed out that the plot had cost only $4,200 to execute but that the resulting panic across the globe would almost certainly force the United States and other Western countries to spend billions of dollars in new security measures.

The chief suspect behind the attempted bombings was later determined to be

Ibrahim Hassan al-Asiri, a 28-year-old engineer and the son of a Saudi career soldier. Also known as Abu Saleh, he was a key figure in AQAP and had previously recruited his younger brother Abdullah in an unsuccessful attempt to assassinate Prince Mohammad bin Naif, Riyadh's deputy interior minister and head of counterterrorism. After that incident al-Asiri was placed at the top of Saudi Arabia's list of 85 most wanted terrorists, causing him to flee the kingdom for Yemen, where he established links with Anwar al-Awlaki, a radical American Islamist cleric who acted as AQAP's principal ideologue. Besides being implicated in the UPS/FedEx plot, al-Asiri was also believed to have made the bomb that Umar Farouk Abdulmutallab used in an attempt to destroy a U.S. passenger plane as it landed at Detroit International Airport on Christmas Day, 2009. That device, like the modified printer cartridges, was composed of PETN.

Peter Chalk

See also: Al-Awlaki, Anwar; Al-Qaeda in the Arabian Peninsula (AQAP); Christmas Day Airline Terror Plot (2009)

Citations

"Bomb Plot Cost Just $4,200, Brags al-Qaeda," *South China Morning Post* (Hong Kong), November 22, 2010.

Fresco, Adam, Richard Ford, and Giles Whittell. "Security Overhaul after al-Qaeda's Bomb Technology Fools the Experts," *The Times* (UK), November 1, 2010.

"Parcels Suspect Sent Brother on Suicide Mission," *The Times* (UK), November 1, 2010.

USA Patriot Act

The Patriot Act is a piece of legislation passed by the United States Congress and signed into law by President George W. Bush on October 26, 2001. It was prompted by the September 11, 2001, terrorist attacks on the United States. The Patriot Act greatly expanded U.S. government intelligence and law enforcement powers, thereby supposedly boosting the government's ability to combat terrorism. The legislation was renewed on March 9, 2006. Critics of the Patriot Act assert that it threatens and violates civil liberties. Supporters of the bill insist that it is vital to protecting America from terrorism and, according to the Department of Justice (DOJ), has led to the conviction of 261 defendants in terrorism cases.

The Patriot Act of 2001 amended federal criminal, banking, money-laundering, and immigration laws. For example, it authorizes "roving" wiretap authorization of a suspect rather than of a particular communication device. Two sections of the law amend immigration laws dealing with "excludable aliens" from entering the United States and allow the government to deport or detain aliens for associating with terrorists. Section 802 of the act created the new category of the crime of domestic terrorism, while Sections 803 and 805, respectively, punish people who either "harbor" or provide "material" support for, or conspire with, terrorists and terrorist organizations. Most of the criticism of the Patriot Act has been directed at Section Two of the law. For example, by authorizing so-called sneak and peek warrants without having to immediately notify the suspect that their home or property has been searched, the act is said to violate the Fourth Amendment to the U.S. Constitution. According to the DOJ, however, such warrants have been used for decades against organized crime and drug dealers, and the U.S. Supreme Court has ruled that in some circumstances, the Fourth Amendment to the Constitution does not require immediate notification that a search warrant has been conducted. Section 215 allows the Federal Bureau of Investigation (FBI) to order any person or entity to turn over "any tangible things" for an authorized investigation to protect against international terrorism or clandestine intelligence activities. Besides allegedly violating the Fourth Amendment, this section is also said to violate freedom of speech, according to the America Civil Liberties Union (ACLU).

Defenders of the Patriot Act note that Section 215 can only be used with the approval of one of three high-ranking FBI officials to obtain foreign intelligence information "not concerning a United States person" or "to protect against international terrorism or clandestine intelligence activities." It prohibits investigations based solely on activities protected by the First Amendment and requires the FBI to notify Congress every year of all investigations it has conducted. In addition, those served with a 215 order can challenge its legality. Critics of the Patriot Act also object to Section 218 because it expands the authority of a secret federal court, the Foreign Intelligence Surveillance Court (FISC), to approve searches and wiretaps if foreign intelligence is a "significant purpose" of the investigation. This is counter to the 1978 Foreign Intelligence Surveillance Act (FISA) standard of "primary purpose." The ACLU argues that Section 218 violates the Fourth Amendment because it extends the FBI's authority to spy on Americans for "intelligence purposes," without having to prove a crime has been or will be committed. Because those targeted for surveillance under Section 218 are never notified that they are under investigation and cannot challenge the warrant because the proceedings of the FISC are secret, the ACLU warns that the potential for abuse of power is immense. Under the FISA, foreign

intelligence had to be the "primary purpose" of wiretaps and searches; the new standard of "significant purpose" is defended to overcome a "wall" that prohibited information sharing and cooperation between intelligence and criminal investigations. Because of this "wall," in August 2001, the FBI refused to allow criminal investigators to assist an intelligence investigation to locate two terrorists—Khalid al-Midhar and Nawaf al-Hazmi—who a month later piloted the plane into the Pentagon on September 11.

For all the claims of alleged abuse and violations to civil liberties by the Patriot Act, *USA Today* reported on March 1, 2006, that according to the Chairman of the House Judiciary Committee (and sponsor of the Patriot Act), Representative James Sensenbrenner Jr. Congress had found no violations of civil liberties. Yet the ACLU pointed out that on January 23, 2004, a U.S. federal judge ruled Section 805 of the Patriot Act—which prohibits providing "expert advice or assistance" to designated international terrorist organizations—unconstitutional because it is vague. And on April 9, 2004, another federal judge ruled that Section 505, which allows the FBI to issue a "national security letter" demanding information about customers and subscribers from email and Internet service providers without any court review or approval, was also unconstitutional. On December 16, 2005, the *New York Times* revealed that following the September 11 attacks, President Bush authorized the National Security Agency (NSA) to eavesdrop on international phone calls without a warrant, sparking a heated legal controversy. Bush maintained that his authority as commander in chief gave him the authority to protect the United States from terrorist threats and that on September 18, 2001, Congress recognized this when it authorized the president to use all necessary means to apprehend terrorists.

By not seeking a warrant from the FISC, however, the ACLU maintained that this program was illegal and violated both the Fourth Amendment and the 1978 FISA. The DOJ, however, noted that the NSA program is "narrowly focused, aimed only at international calls targeted at al-Qaeda and related groups, and only applies to communications where one party is outside the U.S." This argument, however, convinced none of the act's critics. Furthermore, leaders from both parties, along with the leaders of the House and Senate Intelligence Committees, were briefed about the phone-tapping program a dozen or more times since 2001. Director of the Central Intelligence Agency (CIA) Michael Hayden stated on December 19, 2005, that this program "has been successful in detecting and preventing attacks inside the U.S." Nevertheless, the battle continues to rage over the extent and appropriateness of the Patriot Act, with many critics arguing that the law violates basic constitutional rights and has the potential to turn the nation into a secretive police state. Supporters, on the other hand, claim that the Patriot Act has made America safer and is a small price to pay to ensure that there is not another September 11.

On May 26, 2011, President Barack Obama signed into law the Patriot Sunsets Extension Act, which ensured a four-year renewal of three pivotal Patriot Act items: roving wiretaps; searches of business records; and surveillance of so-called "lone wolf" individuals suspected of having the intention and means to carry out acts of terrorism. Many of Obama's supporters and detractors of the Patriot Act sharply criticized the extensions, but the White House insisted that they were necessary for ensuing the national security of the United States. In

2013, revelations (many of which were tied to the leaking of classified information by Edward Snowden, a U.S. defense contractor) about the extent of government surveillance precipitated significant public outrage. Even U.S. Representative Sensenbrenner claimed that the government had overstepped its bounds by collecting telephone and Internet data of tens of millions of innocent Americans who had no ties whatsoever to terrorism. In early 2014, Obama was forced to admit that this mega data collection had probably gone too far and ordered steps to reduce such surveillance. Nevertheless, many critics of the Patriot Act and its provisions were far from appeased.

Stefan Brooks

See also: Global War on Terror; September 11 Attacks

Citations

Bake, Stewart A. *Patriot Debates: Experts Debate the USA Patriot Act.* Chicago: American Bar Association, 2005.

Ball, Howard. *The USA Patriot Act: A Reference Handbook.* Santa Barbara, CA: ABC-CLIO, 2004.

U.S. Embassy (East Africa) Bombings

The 1998 bombings of the U.S. embassies in Nairobi, Kenya, and Dar es Salaam, Tanzania, killed 224 people, including 12 Americans, and injured more than 5,000 people. Two truck bomb explosions orchestrated by suicide bombers affiliated with al-Qaeda detonated within 10 minutes of each other on August 7, 1998. These attacks were simultaneous and symbolic, two characteristics that would go on to become hallmarks of al-Qaeda-style attacks in the continued salvo against that group's war against the West.

Fazul Abdullah Mohammed is recognized as the "mastermind" of the bombings. An East African by birth, he was crucial in recruiting people from the area into al-Qaeda. He would go on to be "al-Qaeda's longest-serving and most senior operative in East Africa" before his death in 2011. Osama bin Laden was placed on the FBI's top 10 most wanted list after his role in organizing the attack. He became the focus of the Clinton administration as the leader of al-Qaeda, and would remain at large until his death in 2011, shortly before Mohammed's death. Abdullah Ahmed Abdullah was known as al-Qaeda's most experienced operational planner, and is still wanted for his role in the 1998 bombings. Adel Abdul Bary, who helped bin Laden issue threats, and several others are currently imprisoned in the United States for their roles in aiding the attacks.

The bombings were done in retaliation for American involvement in the alleged torture of four members of Egyptian Islamic Jihad, a terrorist group linked to al-Qaeda whose goal is to establish an Islamic State in Egypt. This event was most significant because it brought increased American attention to bin Laden and al-Qaeda. Although al-Qaeda was responsible for numerous instances of terrorism in the Middle East during the 1990s, these bombings killed such a large amount of people and did so much damage that direct American attention to it was warranted. The escalation of the conflict between bin Laden's al-Qaeda and the United States would only get worse in the coming years, culminating in the extensive terrorist attacks of September 9, 2001.

Colin P. Clarke

See also: Al-Qaeda; Bin Laden, Osama; September 11 Attacks; USS *Cole* Bombing; World Trade Center (New York) Bombing (1993)

Citations

Bennett, Brian. "Al Qaeda Operative Key to 1998 U.S. Embassy Bombings Killed in Somalia," *Los Angeles Times,* June 12, 2011.

Department of State. International Information Programs. "U.S. Embassy Bombings," International Security (IIP/T/IS), *Usinfo .state.gov,* August 7, 1998.

"The 1998 United States Embassy Bombings," *Crime Scene Database,* October 18, 2016.

Weiser, Benjamin. "Egyptian Gets 25-Year Term in 1998 Embassy Bombings; Judge Calls Plea Deal Generous," *The New York Times,* February 6, 2015.

USS *Cole* Bombing

The attack on USS *Cole* in Yemen marked the first time terrorists successfully targeted a modern U.S. Navy warship. On October 12, 2000, the 8,600-ton displacement (full load), 506-foot-long U.S. Navy destroyer *Cole* (DDG-67) was docked in the Yemeni port of Aden for a refueling stop. At 11:18 a.m. local time, 2 suicide bombers in a small harbor skiff pulled alongside the anchored ship and detonated explosives. The blast killed both bombers and 17 members of the *Cole*'s crew; another 39 were injured. The explosives blew a gaping hole in the ship's hull that measured 35 feet high and 36 feet long. Crewmembers aboard the *Cole* clearly recollect having seen the 2 men as they approached the ship.

The bombers, however, made no untoward moves and indeed appeared friendly. Several aboard the *Cole* believed that the men were workers for the harbor services, collecting trash or performing some other kind of

The U.S. Navy destroyer *Cole* being towed from the port city of Aden, Yemen, by the ocean-going tug USNS *Catawba* following the attack on the destroyer on October 12, 2000, that badly damaged the *Cole* and killed 17 members of its crew. The attack against the *Cole* was one of the opening salvos in the war between al-Qaeda and the United States. (U.S. Department of Defense)

routine task. When the skiff neared the ship, there was no warning of trouble until the explosion. Three days later, the stricken destroyer was taken aboard the Norwegian ship *Blue Marlin* off Yemen and transported to the United States. It reached its home port of Norfolk, Virginia, in December and continued on to Pascagoula, Mississippi, for extensive renovations. Repairs took approximately one year and cost more than $240 million. While still undergoing repair, the ship was towed a short distance to a mooring at Ingalls Shipbuilding in southern Mississippi on September 16, 2001, in a symbolic message of the nation's resolve following the September 11, 2001, World Trade Center and Pentagon attacks. U.S. and Yemeni officials

stated on the day after the bombing that key suspects in the affair had fled to safety in Afghanistan.

There was no immediate credible claim of responsibility, but American officials made al-Qaeda and Osama bin Laden the focus of their investigation. Still, however, some military and national security officials faulted the Bill Clinton and George W. Bush administrations for failing to take appropriate retaliatory measures after the bombing. The *Cole* bombing prompted an investigation into the ease with which the attackers were able to approach the ship. An initial Pentagon inquiry found that the commanding officer had acted reasonably and that the facts did not warrant any punitive action against him or any other member of the *Cole*'s crew. Coordination between U.S. and Yemeni officials investigating the incident was aided by a counterterrorism agreement signed by Yemen and the United States in 1998, and the trial of 12 suspects formally commenced in June 2004. In late September 2004, Abd al-Rahim al-Nashiri and Jamal Mohammad al-Badawi both received the death penalty for their participation in the terrorist act. Four other participants were sentenced 5 to 10 years in jail.

Paul G. Pierpaoli Jr.

See also: Al-Qaeda; Bin Laden, Osama; September 11 Attacks; U.S. Embassy (East Africa) Bombings

Citations

Williams, Paul. *The Al Qaeda Connection: International Terrorism, Organized Crime, and the Coming Apocalypse.* Amherst, NY: Prometheus Books, 2005.

Wright, Lawrence. *The Looming Tower: Al-Qaeda and the Road to 9/11.* New York: Vintage Books, 2007.

W

Weapons of Mass Destruction

Weapons of mass destruction (WMDs) are biological, chemical, and nuclear weapons capable of inflicting mass casualties. Use of these weapons is viewed as not only immoral but contrary to international law and the laws of war because WMDs have the ability to kill indiscriminately, meaning that their destructive nature is not limited to just combatants or military assets. During the Cold War, fears about nuclear weapons and their use was commonplace. Nevertheless, these weapons were under tight control, and neither side dared employ them for fear of the total destruction that a retaliatory strike would bring. With the end of the Cold War, however, nuclear proliferation has become a significant problem, and the likelihood of a rogue state or terrorist group attaining WMDs, including nuclear weapons, has increased substantially.

During the Iran-Iraq War (1980–1988), Iraq employed chemical weapons on Iranian troops, something that Iraqi dictator Saddam Hussein publicly admitted to in December 2006 during his trial for war crimes. It remains in dispute whether Iran employed them as well. The Iran-Iraq War was also the first conflict since World War I in which chemical weapons, apart from tear gas, had been employed. In 1988, as part of an operation to suppress a revolt by Iraqi Kurds, the Hussein government unleashed a chemical attack on the northern Iraqi town of Halabja, killing at least 5,000 people in the first recorded event of such weapons used against civilians. The terrorist bombings in Japan in 1994 and 1995 in which chemical weapons were released in a Tokyo neighborhood and subway reminded the world of the destructive capability of WMDs.

Since the terror attacks of September 11, 2001, the fear of and danger posed by WMDs has increased significantly, owing to the desire of terrorist groups such as al-Qaeda and their affiliates to acquire and employ such weapons against the United States and other countries. The September 11 terrorist attacks on the United States and the 2004 Madrid bombings and 2005 London bombings clearly demonstrated the ability and willingness of al-Qaeda to engage in terrorism to inflict mass casualties, leaving no doubt about their willingness to use WMDs in future terrorist attacks. In March and April 2006 in Iraq, al-Qaeda is believed to have been responsible for a series of terrorist chemical attacks using chlorine gas that killed dozens and sickened hundreds.

Because of the instability and recurrence of war and conflict in the Middle East, the presence of WMDs has only heightened the arms race between Arab states and Israel and also among Arab states themselves. Egypt, Syria, Algeria, and Iran were believed to have significant stockpiles of biological and chemical weapons. In 2003, Libya, seeking to normalize relations with the United States and Europe and to end its international isolation and reputation as a sponsor of terrorism, announced that it was abandoning its WMD programs. Some observers have suggested that President George W. Bush's decision to invade Iraq in 2003 and Libya's failure to end its isolation and convince the UN to lift its sanctions prompted this change of behavior.

Egypt was the first country in the Middle East to develop chemical weapons, which may have been prompted, at least in part, by Israel's construction of a nuclear reactor in 1958. The size of Egypt's chemical weapons arsenal is thought to be perhaps as extensive as Iraq's prior to the 1991 Persian Gulf War, although the end of hostilities between Egypt and Israel since the 1978 Camp David Accords may have obviated the need for maintaining the same quantities of such weapons.

In 1993, as part of the Arab campaign against Israel's nuclear weapons program, Egypt and Syria (along with Iraq) refused to sign the Chemical Weapons Convention (CWC), which bans the acquisition, development, stockpiling, transfer, retention, and use of chemical weapons. These states also refused to sign the Biological Weapons Convention (BWC) of 1975, which prohibits the development, production, acquisition, transfer, retention, stockpiling, and use of biological and toxin weapons. Iraq later signed the BWC. The extent of Egypt's biological weapons program is unknown, but it clearly has the ability to develop such weapons if it already does not have weaponized stockpiles.

With respect to nuclear weapons, Israel is believed to possess as many as 100 nuclear warheads, although the Israeli government has never overtly confirmed possessing such weapons. On December 12, 2006, Israeli prime minister Ehud Olmert admitted in an interview that Israel possessed nuclear weapons, only to be contradicted by a government spokesman the next day denying that Olmert had made such an admission. In the meantime, Israel has refused to sign the Nuclear Non-Proliferation Treaty (NPT) and has not allowed UN International Atomic Energy Agency (IAEA) inspectors to inspect its suspected nuclear sites.

Israel has repeatedly shown its willingness to use force to maintain its suspected nuclear monopoly and deny any Arab state the ability to acquire or develop nuclear weapons. In 1981, the Israeli Air Force destroyed an Iraqi nuclear reactor site under construction at Osirak, Iraq. Iran is currently enriching uranium for what it claims are peaceful purposes, but the United States and much of western Europe have accused Iran of aspiring to build nuclear weapons. That state's refusal to cooperate with the IAEA led the UN in December 2006 and March 2007 to impose sanctions on Iran as punishment for its defiance. In late 2013, however, multilateral talks resulted in a preliminary framework within which Iran would work with the IAEA. In July 2015, negotiators in Geneva achieved a comprehensive agreement regarding Iran's nuclear capabilities. Although Republicans in the United States as well as by Israeli prime minister Benjamin Netanyahu bitterly criticized the deal, it did strictly limit Iran's nuclear activities for a number of years and guaranteed regular IAEA inspections of Iran's nuclear facilities. The agreement was implemented in early 2016, when many economic sanctions against Iran were eased or lifted.

In the fall of 2013, amid the ongoing Syrian Civil War, Syrian president Bashar al-Assad agreed to the complete destruction of his nation's chemical weapons arsenal. He agreed to this as a way to avoid air strikes by the United States and other nations in retaliation for several chemical weapon attacks against his own people. As of mid-2014, most of Syria's chemical weapons had been destroyed or removed from the country.

North Korea, however, has repeatedly disregarded calls for it to abandon its nuclear weapons program. It tested its first weapon in 2006; subsequent tests occurred in 2009, 2013, 2016, and 2017. The tests have usually occurred when tensions with South Korea and its allies were running very high. The North Koreans claimed that the January 2016 test was that of a hydrogen (or thermonuclear) weapon, but that claim could not be independently substantiated, and many experts in the West doubted Pyongyang's ability to construct and successfully test a hydrogen bomb. In the meantime, North Korea continued to develop its ballistic missile program, a development that has many concerned that North Korea could conceivably place a nuclear weapon on a ballistic missile, thereby threatening its neighbors, including Japan, with nuclear destruction.

Stefan Brooks

See also: Al-Qaeda; Al-Qaeda in Iraq (AQI); Global War on Terror

Citations

Hayes, Stephen F. *The Connection: How al Qaeda's Collaboration with Saddam Hussein Has Endangered America*. New York: HarperCollins, 2004.

Hutchinson, Robert. *Weapons of Mass Destruction: The No-Nonsense Guide to Nuclear, Chemical and Biological Weapons Today*. London: George Weidenfeld & Nicholson, 2003.

"Iraq: Timeline of UNSCOM Related Events," MidEastWeb, www.mideastweb.org/iraq timelineunscom.htm, accessed on October 27, 2006.

Langford, R. Everett. *Introduction to Weapons of Mass Destruction: Radiological, Chemical, and Biological*. Hoboken, NJ: Wiley-Interscience, 2004.

Meyer, Adrianne. *Greek Fire, Poison Arrows, and Scorpion Bombs: Biological and Chemical Warfare in the Ancient World*. Woodstock, NY: Overlook-Duckworth, 2003.

Woodward, Bob. *Plan of Attack*. New York: Simon & Schuster, 2004.

Weathermen

The radical faction of the Students for a Democratic Society (SDS), founded in 1969, advocated violent means to alter American society. In January 1960, student activists organized the SDS to promote civil rights and protest the nuclear arms race. By 1965, however, the group had shifted its primary focus to spearheading opposition to the Vietnam War. SDS protest activities included petition drives, draft-resistance training, and campus protests. These efforts were successful in raising opposition to the war but were not successful in changing U.S. government policy. As a result, the SDS began to radicalize. During the SDS national convention at Ann Arbor, Michigan, in December 1968, SDS delegates split into opposing camps. Some delegates wanted to adopt revolutionary violence as a political tactic, first to end the draft and then to end the war. After the convention, the radical factions began to encourage and engage in violent protests against what would become America's longest war.

The Weathermen (sometimes known as the Weatherman Underground) were one of the most violent of these factions. The name was adapted from a Bob Dylan song. The Weathermen specifically grew out of an SDS national war council held in Austin, Texas, in March 1969. This council resolved to promote "armed struggle" as the only way to transform American society. Members of the Weathermen agreed with the council's conclusions, and in October organized some 600 people to engage in violent protests in Chicago. The protests, designed to occur simultaneously with the trial of the Chicago Eight, became known as the "Days of Rage" and earned the Weathermen sufficient notoriety to catch the attention of the FBI, particularly because of the protests' reliance on arson and bombings to assault the federal government.

During the Chicago riots the Weathermen blew up a statue dedicated to police officers who had been killed during the 1886 Haymarket Riot. After the city of Chicago rebuilt the statue, the Weathermen blew it up a second time in October 1970. Rioters also rampaged through tony sections of the city, including the Gold Coast, smashing windows and vandalizing cars. The riot resulted in 28 injured policemen, 6 Weathermen shot and injured, and 68 Weathermen arrested. In 1970 the Weathermen also perpetrated violent acts in New York City. The philosophical foundations of the Weathermen were Marxist in nature: militant struggle was the key to striking out against the state and building a revolutionary consciousness among the young, particularly the white working class. The message was antiracist and anti-imperialist; the goal was a radical counterculture that provoked arguments and incited fights within itself and with its opponents. In the end, the Weathermen sought to impose a classless communist-oriented world order. The group also sought accommodation with the burgeoning black liberation and Black Power movements.

The Weathermen thought that perpetual criticism would force America's youths to continually question the political establishment and reverse the corruption of once democratic American ideals. The radicals believed that most Americans understood their political message and the reasons that they considered violent tactics necessary. In fact, an overwhelming number of Americans regarded the Weathermen's activities as criminal and supported efforts by federal law enforcement agencies to end their activities in the early 1970s. The Weathermen faded rapidly after the 1973 Paris Peace Accords ended the Vietnam War, and by 1977 the organization had dissolved entirely.

Tracy R. Szczepaniak

See also: Homegrown Terrorism

Citations

Gitlin, Todd. *The Sixties: Years of Hope, Days of Rage*. New York: Bantam Books, 1987.

Jacobs, Harold. *The Weathermen*. Berkeley, CA: Ramparts Press, 1971.

Miller, James. *Democracy Is in the Streets: From Port Huron to the Siege of Chicago*. New York: Simon & Schuster, 1987.

O'Neill, William L. *Coming Apart: An Informal History of America in the 1960s*. New York: Times Books, 1971.

Viorst, Milton. *Fire in the Streets: America in the 1960s*. New York: Simon & Schuster, 1979.

Westgate Mall Attack

On September 21, 2013, four terrorists carrying AK-47s and hand grenades launched an attack at the Westgate shopping complex in Nairobi, Kenya. The attack killed 67 people and injured hundreds more. The militants were all members of the al-Qaeda–linked Somali terrorist group al-Shabaab.

Eventually, the Kenyan military killed four of the perpetrators after a lengthy gun battle and hostage situation. It remains somewhat unclear how many perpetrators there actually were, with some sources claiming that the security forces killed all terrorists involved, while others claim that several terrorists may have escaped.

As previously mentioned, the attack was carried out by al-Shabaab, which translates roughly to "the youth," and is a fundamentalist Islamic terrorist group that fights for the creation of an Islamic State in Somalia. It is known to have received funding and arms from al-Qaeda, and shares an ideology, although at various times some of its members have professed allegiance to the Islamic State of Iraq and Syria (ISIS). Al-Shabaab desires to implement sharia law, and seeks to spread its beliefs while punishing nonbelievers or apostates, including Muslims who engage in activities deemed un-Islamic. With roots throughout the Horn of Africa, al-Shabaab ultimately desires to spread its roots farther into Africa, and eventually unite with al-Qaeda in the Middle East.

Shortly after the attack at Westgate, al-Shabaab's now-defunct Twitter account claimed responsibility and attempted to use the social media platform to express its motivations. The group had previously warned Kenya's government that failure to remove its forces from Somalia "would have severe consequences." Accordingly, al-Shabaab claimed that the Westgate attack was in retaliation for Kenya's failure to end involvement in an African Union military effort against al-Shabaab. One particular tweet claimed, "For long we have waged war against the Kenyans in our land, now it's time to shift the battleground and take the war to their land."

The Westgate mall in Nairobi was chosen because it was a popular destination for Westerners and wealthy Kenyans, all viewed as enemies of al-Shabaab. Numerous expatriates, including Brits, Canadians, Americans, and Israelis, were known to frequent Westgate, and although the majority of victims were Kenyan, at least a dozen other nationalities were represented among the dead. Multiple survivors claimed that the gunmen told all Muslims to evacuate the mall, making clear that this was supposed to be an attack on non-Muslims only.

Although several of the perpetrators were suspected to have escaped, the Kenyan government arrested and charged multiple suspects for aiding and abetting the gunmen, but none of the gunmen were ever charged or prosecuted. After the attack, dozens of Western nations, including many that had one or more of their own nationals die, condemned the attack and pledged more support to combating al-Shabaab in Somalia and Kenya. This was the largest terrorist attack in eastern Africa since the U.S. embassy bombings in 1998.

Colin P. Clarke

See also: Al-Shabaab; Garissa University Attack; U.S. Embassy (East Africa) Bombings

Citations

Blair, Edmund, and Richard Lough. "Islamists Claim Gun Attack on Nairobi Mall, at Least 39 Dead," *Reuters*, September 21, 2013.

Daniel, Douglas. "39 People Killed in Kenya Mall Attack Claimed by Somali Militants; Hostages Still Held," *The Washington Post,* September 21, 2013.

Masters, Jonathan. "Al-Shabab," *Council on Foreign Relations*, n.d.

Pearson, Michael, and Nima Elbagir. "Kenyan Police Vow to 'Finish and Punish' Westgate Mall Terrorists," *CNN*, September 23, 2013.

World Trade Center (New York) Bombing (1993)

At 12:18 p.m. on Friday, February 26, 1993, Islamist terrorists exploded a bomb in the underground garage, level B-2, of One World Trade Center (north tower)—the first attempt by Islamist terrorists to destroy the World Trade Center complex, which failed to seriously damage the structure. They employed a yellow Ford Econoline Ryder rental truck filled with 1,500 pounds of explosives. The bomb was built using a mix of fuel oil and fertilizer with a nitroglycerin booster. The conspirators were militant Islamists led by Ramzi Ahmed Yousef, who was of Kuwaiti and Pakistani descent with connections to the al-Qaeda terrorist organization. Yousef confessed to American authorities after his capture that they had selected the World Trade Center complex because it was "an overweening symbol of American arrogance." Other participants were Mohammed Salameh, Nidal Ayyad, Mahmud Abuhalima, and, to a lesser extent, the cleric Sheikh Omar Abdel-Rahman.

Beginning in January 1993, Yousef and his fellow conspirators began to locate and buy the ingredients for the bomb. They required everything, ranging from a safe place to work to storage lockers, tools, chemicals, plastic tubs, fertilizer, and lengths of rubber tubing. It took about $20,000 to build the bomb, although Yousef had wanted more money so that he could build an even bigger bomb. Most of the funds were raised in the United States, but some money came from abroad. Yousef's uncle, Khalid Sheikh Mohammed, had sent him $600 dollars for the bomb. It was Yousef's intention for the explosion to bring down the north tower of the World Trade Center complex; its impact on the south tower, he hoped, would bring it down also. This expectation was too high, however, as the north tower shook in the explosion but withstood its force without major structural damage. Despite the force of the explosion, casualties were relatively low. The bomb produced a crater 22 feet wide and 5 stories deep within the garage structure.

The force of the explosion came close to breaching the so-called bathtub, a structure that prevented water from the Hudson River from pouring into the underground areas of the complex and into the subway system. If

this breach had occurred, the resulting catastrophic loss of life would likely have eclipsed the losses from the subsequent attacks on September 11, 2001. Six people—John DiGiovanni, Bob Kirk-Patrick, Steve Knapp, Bill Backo, Wilfredo Mercado, and Monica Rodriguez-Smith—were killed in the attack, and more than 1,000 were injured. The New York City Fire Department responded with 775 firefighters from 135 companies, but they arrived too late to do anything but tend to the wounded and carry away the dead. It took nearly 10 hours to get everyone out because the elevators shorted out in the explosion and power to the staircases failed. Evacuations took place in the dark and in the midst of heavy smoke. The tower was repaired at a cost of $510 million, and the complex reopened in less than one month. The bombing was significant in revealing how vulnerable the World Trade Center complex was to terrorist attacks.

At first investigators believed that a transformer had blown up, but once they began examining the site, it became obvious that a large bomb had detonated. Within five hours the FBI and the New York City Police Department had confirmed that a bomb had caused the explosion. The next question was determining responsibility for the blast. There had been 20 calls to the police claiming responsibility, but this was not unusual. At first it was believed that the deed was the work of Balkan extremists upset with U.S. policy there, but the investigation was just beginning. Within weeks, the investigating team of 700 FBI agents had identified or arrested all of the World Trade Center bombers. What broke the case was the discovery of a unique vehicle identification number on the frame of the Ryder truck. From that number they learned that Salameh had rented the van because he had reported the van stolen and was trying to recover the $400 deposit.

Salameh was arrested while trying to collect the deposit. Investigators then turned to identify his fellow conspirators, and Yousef was finally determined to be the leader of the plot. By the time authorities had identified Yousef as the leader and maker of the bomb, he was already in Pakistan planning other operations. Ultimately a CIA and FBI team captured him there, but not before he had initiated several other plots. Yousef had always been a freelancer, but there was evidence that he had connections with al-Qaeda operatives before and after the World Trade Center bombing. Following a series of trials, the participants in the bomb plot were found guilty and received life sentences. Yousef was sentenced to 240 years in solitary confinement.

Stephen E. Atkins

See also: Al-Qaeda; Bin Laden, Osama; September 11 Attacks

Citations

Bell, J. Bowyer. *Murders on the Nile: The World Trade Center and Global Terror.* San Francisco: Encounter Books, 2003.

Caram, Peter. *The 1993 World Trade Center Bombing: Foresight and Warning.* London: Janus, 2001.

Davis, Mike. *Duda's Wagon: A Brief History of the Car Bomb.* London: Verso, 2007.

Lance, Peter. *1000 Years for Revenge: International Terrorism and the FBI, the Untold Story.* New York: Regan Books, 2003.

Reeve, Simon. *The New Jackals: Ramzi Yousef, Osama bin Laden, and the Future of Terrorism.* Boston: Northeastern University Press, 1999.

Z

Zarqawi, Abu Musab al-

Abu Musab al-Zarqawi was the founder and leader of Tanzom Qa'idat al-Jihadi Bilad al-Rafidayn (QJBR, or Al-Qaeda of Jihad in the Land of the Two Rivers), otherwise known as Al-Qaeda in Iraq (AQI). As the leader of this group, al-Zarqawi gained notoriety for a number of high-profile terrorist attacks that, together with his declaration of official allegiance to al-Qaeda in 2004, ultimately propelled him to international infamy. To many, he represented the face of the foreign jihadist campaign in Iraq and, by extension, the face of the spectacular violence that plagued the country following the U.S.-led invasion. He was killed in a U.S. air strike on June 7, 2006.

Born Ahmad Fadeel al-Nazal al-Khalayleh in October 1966, al-Zarqawi was raised in the Jordanian industrial city of Zarqa. Situated just northeast of Amman, the city is marked by Palestinian refugee camps dotting its outskirts and high unemployment and crime rates. Unlike many other senior al-Qaeda leaders, who were largely scions of wealthy families or successful professionals before becoming jihadists, al-Zarqawi entered the Salafi-jihadist world from a background as a violent petty thug. A Bedouin of the Bani-Hasan tribe, he was born into a crowded household of 10. His father passed away when al-Zarqawi was 17, and shortly thereafter al-Zarqawi began his descent into a life of heavy drinking and crime. He eventually dropped out of school, possessing scant formal education at that point. Soon after, he was thrown into jail for drug possession and sexual assault.

Al-Zarqawi's first stint in prison likely served as a catalyst that propelled him down a long path of radicalization. Upon his release, he traveled to Afghanistan in 1989, eager to take part in jihad against the Soviets. By the time he arrived, however, the war was winding down. Al-Zarqawi played a minimal role in the tail end of the conflict, primarily writing a jihadist newsletter and later participating in skirmishes between the various factions still fighting after the Soviet withdrawal.

During his stay in Afghanistan, al-Zarqawi based himself in the country's eastern province of Khost. Its close physical proximity to Pakistan facilitated the initial meetings between al-Zarqawi and his first spiritual adviser, Abu Muhammad al-Maqdisi in Peshawar, Pakistan. According to counterterrorism analyst Brian Fishman, al-Maqdisi would play a pivotal role in al-Zarqawi's intellectual evolution by convincing him that attacking the "near enemy"—namely, Arab regimes regarded as too close to the West and apostate—should be prioritized over the "far enemy," the United States and its Western allies.

After studying under al-Maqdisi in Peshawar and positioning himself on the periphery of the waning jihad in Afghanistan, al-Zarqawi returned home to Jordan in the early 1990s. Spurred on by the teachings of al-Maqdisi and the prioritization of the near enemy, al-Zarqawi began plotting against the Jordanian state. Jordanian authorities eventually caught him with explosives in 1994, and he was thrown in jail, where he was reunited with al-Maqdisi. In prison,

Al-Qaeda in Iraq (AQI) leader Abu Musab al-Zarqawi was killed by U.S. forces in early June 2006. Zarqawi waged a highly sectarian war against Iraqi Shiites while also fighting American troops. His death marked a turning point for AQI, but not the end of the group which would ultimately morph into ISIL. (AFP/Getty Images)

al-Zarqawi gained a reputation among fellow prisoners for his discipline in memorizing the Quran and his strict enforcement of prison rules. He evolved into a leader, feared and respected by fellow prisoners. His time in jail also offered al-Zarqawi the chance to further his studies under his spiritual mentor al-Maqdisi, who possessed experience in the operational side of jihad and thus proved crucial in the development of the man who would go on to lead Al-Qaeda in Iraq (AQI).

Following his release from prison as part of an amnesty program in 1999, al-Zarqawi renewed his efforts to attack the Jordanian state and was implicated in the millennium hotel-bombing plot that intended to target the Radisson SAS Hotel in Amman. This attack ultimately failed, and al-Zarqawi was forced to flee back to Pakistan in 1999. His time in

Peshawar was brief, and he eventually traveled to Kandahar, Afghanistan, the birthplace of the Taliban and the home of their leadership. Many believe he first met with Osama bin Laden there, though some allege that the two met during his first stay in the region roughly a decade earlier. Al-Zarqawi and bin Laden's meeting was not without tension. Al-Zarqawi refused to pledge allegiance to al-Qaeda on the basis of their strategic disagreement over the prioritization of the near enemy versus the far enemy. Nonetheless, he was permitted to remain in the country. Allegedly with $5,000 in help from bin Laden, al-Zarqawi set up a terrorist training camp in Herat Province in northwestern Afghanistan, laying the foundations for Jamaat al-Tawhid wa'a Jihad, which he would later transform into QJBR.

Upon the invasion of Afghanistan during Operation Enduring Freedom (OEF), al-Zarqawi briefly resisted U.S. and coalition forces, losing many of his fighters in battle. However, these losses forced him to flee Afghanistan to northern Iraq via Iran. In Iraq he quickly linked up with a Kurdistan-based separatist group, Ansar al-Islam (AaI). Jordanian intelligence officials believe that this stay in Iraq was short-lived and that al-Zarqawi slipped back into Jordan via Syria in late 2002. There, they allege, al-Zarqawi helped plot the assassination of U.S. diplomat Laurence Foley outside his home in Amman in 2002. Al-Zarqawi was ultimately convicted in absentia and sentenced to death in Jordan for the assassination. Regardless of the veracity of the claim that al-Zarqawi was physically present in Jordan at the time of the assassination, most believe his Jordanian associates carried it out under his orders.

Al-Zarqawi maintained his connections to Iraq during this period. In fact, his presence there was cited as a key connection between the Iraqi state and international terrorism in a major speech that then secretary of state Colin Powell gave before the United Nations Security Council on February 5, 2003, in the run-up to the invasion of Iraq. Powell described al-Zarqawi as "an associate and collaborator of Osama bin Laden and his al Qaeda lieutenants." This claim proved to be overstated due to the disagreements between al-Zarqawi and bin Laden and the lack of an al-Qaeda presence in Iraq. Nonetheless, having spent time with members of AaI in Iraqi Kurdistan, al-Zarqawi positioned himself well for the U.S. invasion in 2003. Shortly after the invasion, al-Zarqawi headed farther south to the Sunni Triangle along with the cadres he had built up through his connections to militant networks in Jordan, Afghanistan, and Iraq.

Following the U.S.-led invasion of Iraq, al-Zarqawi played a pivotal role in the Iraqi insurgency that emerged. Al-Zarqawi helped facilitate the inflow of foreign fighters, many of whom entered the country from Syria and some of whom hailed from al-Zarqawi's networks in Jordan. Alongside these fighters, he launched a series of spectacular and violent attacks on high-profile targets throughout Iraq, including the 2003 attacks on the Jordanian embassy and the United Nations headquarters as well as the first sectarian attacks in the country, most prominently the 2003 bombing of the Imam Ali mosque in Najaf. The group eventually gained mainstream international notoriety for the videotaped beheading of Pennsylvania businessman Nicholas Berg on May 7, 2004. Notably, it is widely believed that al-Zarqawi himself personally wielded the knife used in the killing.

In a major development, in October 2004, al-Zarqawi pledged allegiance to bin Laden and al-Qaeda, changing the name of Jamaat al-Tawhid wa'a Jihad to QJBR. Bin Laden, in turn, released a statement in December 2004 that proclaimed al-Zarqawi the emir of AQI. This development came in spite of the aforementioned doctrinal differences over the near enemy and the far enemy and the fact that al-Zarqawi had earlier rejected joining al-Qaeda in Afghanistan in 1999. Moreover, formal al-Qaeda affiliation would not bring the group financial gain. Indeed, an intercepted letter from 2005 revealed that Ayman al-Zawahiri, al-Qaeda's second in command, in fact requested financial assistance from al-Zarqawi's group in Iraq. However, al-Qaeda affiliation offered al-Zarqawi a number of crucial advantages, namely, a larger calling card and a brand name that could propel QJBR to the vanguard of the Sunni jihadist component of the Iraqi insurgency.

This official linkage to al-Qaeda, along with the Berg beheading and the United Nations bombing, vastly inflated al-Zarqawi's reputation in Iraq's insurgency. Already a high-value target for U.S. forces (a $25 million bounty rested on his head), his group's presence in Fallujah and throughout the Sunni Triangle was a key impetus behind the second battle of Fallujah during the late fall of 2004. During this battle, U.S. forces attempted to drive core elements of the Sunni insurgency, not just al-Zarqawi's jihadists but also Iraqi Sunni nationalists, from the region. Most analysts believe that al-Zarqawi fled the city well before the battle, and he lived to fight on.

Despite QJBR's formal affiliation with al-Qaeda, al-Zarqawi and senior al-Qaeda leaders still maintained their ideological differences. First, there was still the issue of the near enemy versus the far enemy. Al-Zarqawi still believed in prioritizing the former, while al-Qaeda's senior leadership believed in focusing on the latter. Second, there was the issue of attacks against Iraq's Shia. Although al-Zarqawi had no qualms about attacking Shiite targets, al-Qaeda believed that the zeal with which he undertook such attacks harmed the overall operation in Iraq. Fellow Muslims found these attacks difficult to comprehend, according to an intercepted letter from al-Zawahiri to al-Zarqawi. Despite condemning the Shia for their "treason" in assisting American forces, al-Zawahiri wondered whether or not such attacks should be deemphasized in favor of operations against U.S. forces and the Iraqi state. Even al-Zarqawi's former mentor, al-Maqdisi, echoed these concerns, publishing a tract publicly questioning al-Zarqawi's killings of Iraqi Shia.

These key disagreements between al-Qaeda's senior leaders and al-Zarqawi ultimately came to a head at the time of the November 9, 2005, Amman hotel bombings in Jordan. Al-Zarqawi was believed to be behind the attacks, which targeted three hotels throughout Amman, killing scores of people and wounding over a hundred others. In addition to their sheer magnitude, the bombings garnered international notoriety because its victims included a number of members of a wedding party. Notably, al-Qaeda distanced itself from the attack.

Despite these disagreements, al-Zarqawi forged ahead with his plan to foment sectarian conflict in Iraq. Arguably the most devastating example of this strategy was the infamous Golden Mosque (also known as the al-Askariya mosque) bombing in Samarra on February 22, 2006. In the attack, al-Zarqawi's cadres placed a series of explosives inside the al-Askariya mosque, a famous Shiite holy site, and detonated them, destroying much of the interior of the mosque but not actually resulting in any casualties. The resulting sectarian violence led to hundreds of deaths and was part of al-Zarqawi's overall strategy to initiate sectarian civil war within the country. Al-Zarqawi's plan involved attacking Shiite targets to trigger reprisal attacks from Shiites, which in turn brought more retaliatory actions from Sunnis. Such a cycle would stifle U.S. aims of creating a functioning Iraqi state and thus allow QJBR to establish an Islamic emirate within the country.

As al-Zarqawi saw continued success in his jihadist campaign, he became an increasing focus of coalition forces. Although at first the United States had relatively scant information on their target (there were three known photos of al-Zarqawi, in each of which his look varied greatly), U.S. efforts to target his network vastly improved over time. In fact, al-Zarqawi narrowly escaped U.S. efforts to kill him in April and November 2005. He ultimately met his end on

June 7, 2006. With the help of both human intelligence and signals intelligence, U.S. and Iraqi forces ultimately tracked an associate of his, Sheik Abd-Al-Rahman, to a safe house just north of Baquba. In the middle of a meeting between Rahman and al-Zarqawi, two U.S. F-16C fighter jets dropped two 500-pound bombs on the safe house, killing al-Zarqawi along with his associate and six others, including one of his wives and their child. Al-Zarqawi's body was seized by U.S. forces and quickly identified. Al-Qaeda's Ayman al-Zawahiri later confirmed his death.

Nate Shestak

See also: Al-Qaeda; Al-Qaeda in Iraq (AQI); Bin Laden, Osama; Zawahiri, Ayman al-

Citations

Cordesman, Anthony H. *The Islamists and the Zarqawi Factor.* Washington, DC, Center for Strategic and International Studies, June 23, 2006.

Fishman, Brian. "After Zarqawi: The Dilemmas and Future of Al Qaeda in Iraq," *Washington Quarterly* 29, no. 4 (Autumn 2006).

Fishman, Brian. "Zarqawi's Jihad: Inside the Mind of Iraq's Most Notorious Man." Working paper, Combating Terrorism Center, West Point, NY, April 26, 2006.

Michael, George. "The Legend and Legacy of Abu Musab al-Zarqawi," *Defence Studies* 7, no. 3 (September 2007).

Zawahiri, Ayman al-

Ayman al-Zawahiri is the leader of al-Qaeda, after the death of Osama bin Laden. Al-Zawahiri merged his group into al-Qaeda in the late 1990s, making his contingent of Egyptians influential in the operations of al-Qaeda. Al-Zawahiri came from a prominent Egyptian family of medical doctors and religious leaders. He was born on June 19, 1951, in al-Sharquiyyah, Egypt. Both sides of his family have roots going back to Saudi Arabia, and his mother's family claims descent from the Prophet Muhammad. His father was a professor at Cairo University's medical school. At an early age, al-Zawahiri joined the Muslim Brotherhood; his first arrest by the Egyptian police was at age 15 in 1966. After studying medicine at the University of Cairo, al-Zawahiri qualified as a physician in 1974, and then received a master's degree in surgical medicine in 1978. Al-Zawahiri left medicine for political agitation against the Egyptian government of President Anwar Sadat.

Inspiring his conversion to Islamic militancy were the writings of Sayyid Qutb, the ideological and spiritual leader of the Muslim Brotherhood. He was shocked by Qutb's execution in 1966 by the Nasser regime enough so that he considered forming a clandestine Islamist group. While still in medical school, al-Zawahiri was instrumental in founding the terrorist group Islamic Jihad in 1973. This group's mission was to direct armed struggle against the Egyptian state. It did not take the Egyptian government long to ban activities of the Islamic Jihad. In the aftermath of the 1981 assassination of President Anwar Sadat, Egyptian authorities arrested al-Zawahiri. He had learned of the plot against Sadat only a few hours before it went into operation and had advised against proceeding because the plot was premature and destined to fail. Al-Zawahiri has claimed that prison authorities treated him brutally. After a trial and acquittal for his role in the assassination plot against Sadat, al-Zawahiri served a three-year prison sentence for illegal possession of arms. His stay in prison only increased his militancy. In prison, al-Zawahiri and Sheikh Omar Abdel-Rahman shared their views. Under torture, al-Zawahiri assisted the police in capturing some of his associates in the Islamic Jihad. After his release from prison, al-Zawahiri resumed his antigovernment activities.

In 1984 he assumed the leadership of Islamic Jihad after the Egyptian police arrested its former head, Lieutenant Colonel Abbud al-Zumar. Al-Zawahiri fled Egypt for Jeddah, Saudi Arabia, in 1985 in the middle of President Hosni Mubarak's purge of Egyptian dissidents. There he worked in a medical dispensary. In Jeddah in 1986, al-Zawahiri first met Osama bin Laden. The ongoing war against the Soviets in Afghanistan attracted al-Zawahiri, and he decided to move to Pakistan. Soon after arriving in Pakistan, al-Zawahiri started coordinating plans between his Islamic Jihad and the Afghan Arabs fighting against Soviet forces in Afghanistan. He served as the chief adviser to bin Laden in the creation of the al-Qaeda network in 1988. Al-Zawahiri also engaged in a campaign to undermine bin Laden's relationship with Abdullah Azzam. Azzam's assassination benefited al-Zawahiri, but there is no concrete evidence that he played any role in it. The Pakistani security service concluded that six associates of al-Zawahiri carried out the assassination.

For several years in the early 1990s, al-Zawahiri played a dual role as a member of al-Qaeda and as a leader of the Islamic Jihad. Al-Zawahiri left Pakistan and moved to Sudan with bin Laden in 1992. His closeness to Egypt allowed him to plot against the Egyptian government of President Mubarak. Al-Zawahiri's goal from the beginning was to overthrow the Egyptian government and replace it with an Islamic State. As head of the Islamic Jihad, he planned the unsuccessful assassination attempt on Egyptian president Mubarak during his visit to Addis Ababa on June 25, 1995. This failure led to the Sudanese government expelling him and

his followers from Sudan. His activities for al-Qaeda kept him traveling around the world. Bin Laden sent al-Zawahiri to Somalia to aid the opposition to American intervention there. Then he was active in building support for the Bosnian Muslims in their separatist war against Yugoslavia. Next he coordinated aid for Albanian Muslims in the Kosovo War. Finally, al-Zawahiri received the assignment to set up terrorist operations in Europe and the United States.

He visited the United States in 1996 to inspect sites for possible terrorist operations there. His conclusion was that major terrorist activities could be undertaken against American targets in the United States. Al-Zawahiri returned to Afghanistan to join bin Laden. He decided to merge his Egyptian Islamic Jihad group into al-Qaeda in 1998 for a combination of political, financial, and operational reasons. In 1997 al-Zawahiri had been implicated in his group's participation in the terrorist massacre of 58 European tourists and 4 Egyptian security guards at Luxor, Egypt. This terrorist act was so brutal that it caused a backlash in both Egyptian public opinion and among the leadership of the Egyptian Islamic Jihad. It led to a schism within its leadership, with a significant number of the leaders concluding a cease-fire with the Egyptian government. Al-Zawahiri opposed the cease-fire with what he considered to be an apostate government. He led a much-weakened Egyptian Islamic Jihad into an alliance with al-Qaeda. Al-Zawahiri's influence over bin Laden had grown over the years. Bin Laden was neither as intellectual nor as militant as al-Zawahiri. Al-Zawahiri's views were expressed in the tract *Knights Under the Prophet's Banner*. In this work al-Zawahiri justified the use of violence as the only way to match the brute military force of the West led by the United States. For this reason it is necessary to target American targets, the tract posits, and the most effective way to do this is by the use of human bombs.

The proposed strategy was to inflict enough damage on the United States that its citizens will demand that their government change policies toward Israel and the Arab world. This treatise was written before the September 11 attacks, but such attacks were obviously in its author's mind. In his position as number two in al-Qaeda, al-Zawahiri served as the chief adviser to bin Laden. Because of his more radical religious views, al-Zawahiri pushed bin Laden toward more radical positions. Al-Zawahiri was aware of the September 11 plot from the beginning, but stayed in the background. The subsequent loss of Afghanistan as a staging area for al-Qaeda forced al-Zawahiri into hiding along with bin Laden. Al-Zawahiri and bin Laden kept in contact, but they stayed in separate areas to avoid the possibility of al-Qaeda's chief leaders being wiped out in a single attack by the Americans and their allies.

On August 1, 2008, CBS News speculated that al-Zawahiri may have been seriously injured or even killed during a July 28 missile strike on a village in South Waziristan. This conjecture was based on an intercepted letter dated July 29 that urgently called for a doctor to treat al-Zawahiri. On August 2, however, senior Taliban commander Maulvi Omar dismissed the report as false. It was assumed that al-Zawahiri became the leader of al-Qaeda following bin Laden's death during a firefight with U.S. Special Forces at a compound in Abbottabad, Pakistan, on May 1, 2011 (May 2 Pakistani local time). This was confirmed on June 16 when it was announced on several al-Qaeda websites that al-Zawahiri had succeeded bin Laden as chief commander of al-Qaeda. In June 2013 al-Zawahiri argued against the merger of the Islamic State of Iraq with the Syrian-based Jabhat al-Nusra into the Islamic State of Iraq and the Levant, as had been declared in April by Abu Bakr al-Baghdadi. The U.S. State Department has offered a $25 million dollar reward for information leading to al-Zawahiri's apprehension. He is under worldwide sanctions by the United Nations Security Council Resolution 1267 Committee as a member or affiliate of al-Qaeda.

Stephen E. Atkins

See also: Al-Qaeda; Bin Laden, Osama; Egyptian Islamic Jihad (EIJ); Qutb, Sayyid; September 11 Attacks; Taliban

Citations

Gunaratna, Rohan. *Inside Al Qaeda: Global Network of Terror.* New York: Berkley Publishing Group, 2003.

Haddad, Yvonne, and Jane Smith. *The Islamic Understanding of Death and Resurrection.* Oxford: Oxford University Press, 2002.

Rabasa, Angel. *Beyond al-Qaeda: Part 1, The Global Jihadist Movement and Beyond al-Qaeda; Part 2, The Outer Rings of the Terrorist Universe.* Santa Monica, CA: RAND Corporation, 2006.

Primary Source Documents

Editor's Note: The Significance and Analysis sections for Documents 1–11 and Document 13 were written by Paul J. Springer.

I. Osama bin Laden's Declaration of War Upon the United States

When: August 23, 1996

Where: Khartoum, Sudan

Significance: This document laid out Osama bin Laden's grievances against the West, and against the United States in particular. He formally declared his intention, that his followers should engage in acts of terrorism and other violence as a means to expel Western influence from the Arabian Peninsula.

DOCUMENT:

It should not be hidden from you that the people of Islam had suffered from aggression, iniquity and injustice imposed on them by the Zionist-Crusaders alliance and their collaborators; to the extent that the Muslims blood became the cheapest and their wealth as loot in the hands of the enemies. Their blood was spilled in Palestine and Iraq. The horrifying pictures of the massacre of Qana, in Lebanon are still fresh in our memory. Massacres in Tajakestan, Burma, Cashmere, Assam, Philippine, Fatani, Ogadin, Somalia, Erithria, Chechnia and in Bosnia-Herzegovina took place, massacres that send shivers in the body and shake the conscience. All of this and the world watch and hear, and not only didn't respond to these atrocities, but also with a clear conspiracy between the USA and its' allies and under the cover of the iniquitous United Nations, the dispossessed people were even prevented from obtaining arms to defend themselves.

The people of Islam awakened and realised that they are the main target for the aggression of the Zionist-Crusaders alliance. All false claims and propaganda about "Human Rights" were hammered down and exposed by the massacres that took place against the Muslims in every part of the world.

The latest and the greatest of these aggressions, incurred by the Muslims since the death of the Prophet (ALLAH'S BLESSING AND SALUTATIONS ON HIM) is the occupation of the land of the two Holy Places -the foundation of the house of Islam, the place of the revelation, the source of the message and the place of the noble Ka'ba, the Qiblah of all Muslims- by the armies of the American Crusaders and their allies. (We bemoan this and can only say: "No power and power acquiring except through Allah").

Under the present circumstances, and under the banner of the blessed awakening which is sweeping the world in general and the Islamic world in particular, I meet with you today. And after a long absence, imposed on the scholars (Ulama) and callers (Da'ees) of Islam by the iniquitous crusaders movement under the leadership of the USA; who fears that they, the scholars and callers of Islam, will instigate the Ummah of Islam against its' enemies as their ancestor scholars-may Allah be pleased with them- like Ibn Taymiyyah and Al'iz Ibn Abdes-Salaam did. And therefore the Zionist-Crusader alliance resorted to killing and arresting the truthful Ulama and the working Da'ees (We are not praising or sanctifying them; Allah sanctify whom He pleased). They killed the Mujahid Sheikh Abdullah Azzaam, and they arrested the Mujahid Sheikh Ahmad Yaseen and the Mujahid Sheikh Omar Abdur Rahman (in America).

Quick efforts were made by each group to contain and to correct the situation. All agreed that the country is heading toward a great catastrophe, the depth of which is not known except by Allah. One big merchant commented: "the king is leading the state into 'sixty-six' folded disaster", (We bemoan this and can only say: "No power and power acquiring except through Allah"). Numerous princes share with the people their feelings, privately expressing their concerns and objecting to the corruption, repression and the intimidation taking place in the country. But the competition between influential princes for personal gains and interest had destroyed the country. Through its course of actions the regime has torn off its legitimacy:

1. Suspension of the Islamic Shari'ah law and exchanging it with man made civil law. The regime entered into a bloody confrontation with the truthful Ulamah and the righteous youths (we sanctify

nobody; Allah sanctify Whom He pleaseth).

2. The inability of the regime to protect the country, and allowing the enemy of the Ummah—the American crusader forces- to occupy the land for the longest of years. The crusader forces became the main cause of our disastrous condition, particularly in the economical aspect of it due to the unjustified heavy spending on these forces. As a result of the policy imposed on the country, especially in the field of oil industry where production is restricted or expanded and prices are fixed to suit the American economy ignoring the economy of the country. Expensive deals were imposed on the country to purchase arms. People asking what is the justification for the very existence of the regime then?

But -to our deepest regret- the regime refused to listen to the people accusing them of being ridiculous and imbecile. The matter got worse as previous wrong doings were followed by mischief's of greater magnitudes. All of this taking place in the land of the two Holy Places! It is no longer possible to be quiet. It is not acceptable to give a blind eye to this matter.

But with the grace of Allah, the majority of the nation, both civilians and military individuals are aware of the wicked plan. They refused to be played against each others and to be used by the regime as a tool to carry out the policy of the American-Israeli alliance through their agent in our country: the Saudi regime.

If there are more than one duty to be carried out, then the most important one should receive priority. Clearly after Belief (Imaan) there is no more important duty than pushing the American enemy out of the holy land. No other priority, except Belief, could be considered before it; the people of knowledge, Ibn Taymiyyah, stated: "to fight in defence of religion and Belief is a collective duty; there is no other duty after Belief than fighting the enemy who is corrupting the life and the religion. There is no preconditions for this duty and the enemy should be fought with one best abilities. (ref: supplement of Fatawa). If it is not possible to push back the enemy except by the collective movement of the Muslim people, then there is a duty on the Muslims to ignore the minor differences among themselves; the ill effect of ignoring these differences, at a given period of time, is much less than the ill effect of the occupation of the Muslims' land by the main Kufr. Ibn Taymiyyah had explained this issue and emphasized the importance of dealing with the major threat on the expense of the minor one. He described the situation of the Muslims and the Mujahideen and stated that even the military personnel who are not practicing Islam are not exempted from the duty of Jihad against the enemy.

Under such circumstances, to push the enemy-the greatest Kufr- out of the country is a prime duty. No other duty after Belief is more important than the duty of had. Utmost effort should be made to prepare and instigate the Ummah against the enemy, the American-Israeli alliance- occupying the country of the two Holy Places and the route of the Apostle (Allah's Blessings and Salutations may be on him) to the Furthest Mosque (Al-Aqsa Mosque). Also to remind the Muslims not to be engaged in an internal war among themselves, as that will have grieve consequences namely:

1. consumption of the Muslims human resources as most casualties and fatalities will be among the Muslims people.
2. Exhaustion of the economic and financial resources.
3. Destruction of the country infrastructures.
4. Dissociation of the society.
5. Destruction of the oil industries. The presence of the USA Crusader military forces on land, sea and air of the states of the Islamic Gulf is the greatest danger threatening the largest oil reserve in the world. The existence of these forces in the area will provoke the people of the country and induces aggression on their religion, feelings and prides and push them to take up armed struggle against the invaders occupying the land; therefore spread of the fighting in the region will expose the oil wealth to the danger of being burned up. The economic interests of the States of the Gulf and the land of the two Holy Places will be damaged and even a greater damage will be caused to the economy of the world. I would like here to alert my brothers, the Mujahideen, the sons of the nation, to protect this (oil) wealth and not to include it in the battle as it is a great Islamic wealth and a large economical power essential for the soon to be established Islamic state, by Allah's Permission and Grace. We also warn the aggressors, the USA, against burning this Islamic wealth (a crime which they may commit in order to prevent it, at the end of the war, from falling in the hands of its legitimate owners and to cause economic damages to the competitors of the USA in Europe or the Far East, particularly Japan which is the major consumer of the oil of the region).
6. Division of the land of the two Holy Places, and annexing of the northerly part of it by Israel. Dividing the land of the two Holy Places is an essential demand of the Zionist-Crusader alliance. The existence of such a large

country with its huge resources under the leadership of the forthcoming Islamic State, by Allah's Grace, represent a serious danger to the very existence of the Zionist state in Palestine. The Nobel Ka'ba, -the Qiblah of all Muslims- makes the land of the two Holy Places a symbol for the unity of the Islamic world. Moreover, the presence of the world largest oil reserve makes the land of the two Holy Places an important economical power in the Islamic world. The sons of the two Holy Places are directly related to the life style (Seerah) of their forefathers, the companions, may Allah be pleased with them. They consider the Seerah of their forefathers as a source and an example for re-establishing the greatness of this Ummah and to raise the word of Allah again. Furthermore the presence of a population of fighters in the south of Yemen, fighting in the cause of Allah, is a strategic threat to the Zionist-Crusader alliance in the area. The Prophet (ALLAH'S BLESSING AND SALUTATIONS ON HIM) said: (around twelve thousands will emerge from Aden/Abian helping - the cause of- Allah and His messenger, they are the best, in the time, between me and them) narrated by Ahmad with a correct trustworthy reference.

7. An internal war is a great mistake, no matter what reasons are there for it. the presence of the occupier-the USA- forces will control the outcome of the battle for the benefit of the international Kufr.

Muslims Brothers of land of the two Holy Places:

It is incredible that our country is the world largest buyer of arms from the USA and the area biggest commercial partners of the Americans who are assisting their Zionist brothers in occupying Palestine and in evicting and killing the Muslims there, by providing arms, men and financial supports.

To deny these occupiers from the enormous revenues of their trading with our country is a very important help for our Jihad against them. To express our anger and hate to them is a very important moral gesture. By doing so we would have taken part in (the process of) cleansing our sanctities from the crusaders and the Zionists and forcing them, by the Permission of Allah, to leave disappointed and defeated.

We expect the woman of the land of the two Holy Places and other countries to carry out their role in boycotting the American goods.

If economical boycotting is intertwined with the military operations of the Mujahideen, then defeating the enemy will be even nearer, by the Permission of Allah. However if Muslims don't co-operate and support their Mujahideen brothers then, in effect, they are supplying the army of the enemy with financial help and extending the war and increasing the suffering of the Muslims.

The security and the intelligence services of the entire world can not force a single citizen to buy the goods of his/her enemy. Economical boycotting of the American goods is a very effective weapon of hitting and weakening the enemy, and it is not under the control of the security forces of the regime.

Few days ago the news agencies had reported that the Defense Secretary of the Crusading Americans had said that "the explosion at Riyadh and Al-Khobar had taught him one lesson: that is not to withdraw when attacked by coward terrorists."

We say to the Defence Secretary that his talk can induce a grieving mother to laughter! and shows the fears that had enshrined you all. Where was this false courage of yours when the explosion in Beirut took place on 1983 AD (1403 A.H). You were turned into scattered pits and pieces at that time; 241 mainly marines soldiers were killed. And where was this courage of yours when two explosions made you to leave Aden in less than twenty four hours!

But your most disgraceful case was in Somalia; where- after vigorous propaganda about the power of the USA and its post cold war leadership of the new world order- you moved tens of thousands of international force, including twenty eight thousands American soldiers into Somalia. However, when tens of your solders were killed in minor battles and one American pilot was dragged in the streets of Mogadishu you left the area carrying disappointment, humiliation, defeat and your dead with you. Clinton appeared in front of the whole world threatening and promising revenge, but these threats were merely a preparation for withdrawal. You have been disgraced by Allah and you withdrew; the extent of your impotence and weaknesses became very clear. It was a pleasure for the "heart" of every Muslim and a remedy to the "chests" of believing nations to see you defeated in the three Islamic cities of Beirut, Aden and Mogadishu.

I say to the Secretary of Defense: The sons of the land of the two Holy Places had come out to fight against the Russian in Afghanistan, the Serb in Bosnia-Herzegovina and today they are fighting in Chechenia and -by the Permission of Allah- they have been made victorious over your partner, the Russians. By the command of Allah, they are also fighting in Tajakistan.

I say: Since the sons of the land of the two Holy Places feel and strongly believe that fighting (Jihad) against the Kuffar in every part of the world, is absolutely essential; then they would be even more enthusiastic, more

powerful and larger in number upon fighting on their own land- the place of their births- defending the greatest of their sanctities, the noble Ka'ba (the Qiblah of all Muslims). They know that the Muslims of the world will assist and help them to victory. To liberate their sanctities is the greatest of issues concerning all Muslims; It is the duty of every Muslims in this world.

I say to you William (Defense Secretary) that: These youths love death as you love life. They inherit dignity, pride, courage, generosity, truthfulness and sacrifice from father to father. They are most delivering and steadfast at war. They inherit these values from their ancestors (even from the time of the Jaheliyyah, before Islam). These values were approved and completed by the arriving Islam as stated by the messenger of Allah (Allah's Blessings and Salutations may be on him): "I have been send to perfecting the good values". (Saheeh Al-Jame' As-Sagheer).

Those youths know that their rewards in fighting you, the USA, is double than their rewards in fighting some one else not from the people of the book. They have no intention except to enter paradise by killing you. An infidel, and enemy of God like you, cannot be in the same hell with his righteous executioner.

Terrorising you, while you are carrying arms on our land, is a legitimate and morally demanded duty. It is a legitimate right well known to all humans and other creatures. Your example and our example is like a snake which entered into a house of a man and got killed by him. The coward is the one who lets you walk, while carrying arms, freely on his land and provides you with peace and security.

The youths hold you responsible for all of the killings and evictions of the Muslims and the violation of the sanctities, carried out by your Zionist brothers in Lebanon; you openly supplied them with arms and finance. More than 600,000 Iraqi children have died due to lack of food and medicine and as a result of the unjustifiable aggression (sanction) imposed on Iraq and its nation. The children of Iraq are our children. You, the USA, together with the Saudi regime are responsible for the shedding of the blood of these innocent children. Due to all of that, whatever treaty you have with our country is now null and void.

Source: This document was originally published in Arabic in the London newspaper, *Al Quds al Arabi*. This translation can be found at https://ctc.usma.edu/posts/declaration-of-jihad-against-the-americans-occupying-the-land-of-the-two-holiest-sites-english-translation-2.

Analysis: With this message, Osama bin Laden declared his intention to engage in terrorism, and any other form of resistance, until all nonbelievers were forced to depart from the Arabian Peninsula. The full document, which is more than 30 pages long when translated into English, contains a list of grievances along with a series of justifications for engaging in violence. Many of his complaints revolved around the Saudi government, which he felt was complicit in allowing an invasion and occupation of the Holy Land of Islam. By attempting to lay the blame for the subsequent violence upon the United States and Saudi Arabia, he sought to absolve his followers for any of their misdeeds. Unfortunately, the document was not taken seriously by many American officials, who believed that al-Qaeda had very limited reach and little chance of striking a major blow against American interests. Even the bombing of two U.S. embassies in sub-Saharan Africa and the attack upon the USS *Cole* did little to move the American government to significant action, and

American domestic security measures were woefully inadequate on September 11, 2001, even in the face of this naked declaration of intent to engage in hostilities.

2. "Jihad Against Jews and Crusaders"

When: February 23, 1998
Where: Jalalabad, Afghanistan
Significance: This is the second *fatwa* issued by Osama bin Laden, in this case on behalf of the World Islamic Front. Like his first declaration, this communiqué called for faithful Muslims around the globe to engage in jihad against the United States until it evacuated the Arabian Peninsula and ceased meddling in the Middle East.

DOCUMENT: Declaration of the World Islamic Front

Praise be to God, who revealed the Book, controls the clouds, defeats factionalism, and says in His Book: "But when the forbidden months are past, then fight and slay the pagans wherever ye find them, seize them, beleaguer them, and lie in wait for them in every stratagem (of war)"; and peace be upon our Prophet, Muhammad Bin-'Abdallah, who said: I have been sent with the sword between my hands to ensure that no one but God is worshipped, God who put my livelihood under the shadow of my spear and who inflicts humiliation and scorn on those who disobey my orders.

The Arabian Peninsula has never—since God made it flat, created its desert, and encircled it with seas—been stormed by any forces like the crusader armies spreading in it like locusts, eating its riches and wiping out its plantations. All this is happening at a time in which nations are attacking Muslims like people fighting over a plate of food. In the light of the grave situation and the lack of support, we and you are obliged to discuss current events, and we should all agree on how to settle the matter.

No one argues today about three facts that are known to everyone; we will list them, in order to remind everyone:

First, for over seven years the United States has been occupying the lands of Islam in the holiest of places, the Arabian Peninsula, plundering its riches, dictating to its rulers, humiliating its people, terrorizing its neighbors, and turning its bases in the Peninsula into a spearhead through which to fight the neighboring Muslim peoples.

If some people have in the past argued about the fact of the occupation, all the people of the Peninsula have now acknowledged it. The best proof of this is the Americans' continuing aggression against the Iraqi people using the Peninsula as a staging post, even though all its rulers are against their territories being used to that end, but they are helpless.

Second, despite the great devastation inflicted on the Iraqi people by the crusader-Zionist alliance, and despite the huge number of those killed, which has exceeded 1 million . . . despite all this, the Americans are once against trying to repeat the horrific massacres, as though they are not content with the protracted blockade imposed after the ferocious war or the fragmentation and devastation.

So here they come to annihilate what is left of this people and to humiliate their Muslim neighbors. Third, if the Americans' aims behind these wars are religious and economic, the aim is also to serve the Jews' petty state and divert attention from its occupation of Jerusalem and murder of Muslims there. The best proof of this is their eagerness to destroy Iraq, the strongest

neighboring Arab state, and their endeavor to fragment all the states of the region such as Iraq, Saudi Arabia, Egypt, and Sudan into paper statelets and through their disunion and weakness to guarantee Israel's survival and the continuation of the brutal crusade occupation of the Peninsula.

All these crimes and sins committed by the Americans are a clear declaration of war on God, his messenger, and Muslims. And ulema have throughout Islamic history unanimously agreed that the jihad is an individual duty if the enemy destroys the Muslim countries. This was revealed by Imam Bin-Qadamah in "Al- Mughni," Imam al-Kisa'i in "Al-Bada'i," al-Qurtubi in his interpretation, and the shaykh of al-Islam in his books, where he said: "As for the fighting to repulse [an enemy], it is aimed at defending sanctity and religion, and it is a duty as agreed [by the ulema]. Nothing is more sacred than belief except repulsing an enemy who is attacking religion and life." On that basis, and in compliance with God's order, we issue the following fatwa to all Muslims:

The ruling to kill the Americans and their allies—civilians and military—is an individual duty for every Muslim who can do it in any country in which it is possible to do it, in order to liberate the al-Aqsa Mosque and the holy mosque [Mecca] from their grip, and in order for their armies to move out of all the lands of Islam, defeated and unable to threaten any Muslim. This is in accordance with the words of Almighty God, "and fight the pagans all together as they fight you all together," and "fight them until there is no more tumult or oppression, and there prevail justice and faith in God."

This is in addition to the words of Almighty God: "And why should ye not fight in the cause of God and of those who, being weak, are ill-treated (and oppressed)?—women and children, whose cry is: 'Our Lord, rescue us from this town, whose people are oppressors; and raise for us from thee one who will help!' "

We—with God's help—call on every Muslim who believes in God and wishes to be rewarded to comply with God's order to kill the Americans and plunder their money wherever and whenever they find it. We also call on Muslim ulema, leaders, youths, and soldiers to launch the raid on Satan's U.S. troops and the devil's supporters allying with them, and to displace those who are behind them so that they may learn a lesson.

Almighty God said: "O ye who believe, give your response to God and His Apostle, when He calleth you to that which will give you life. And know that God cometh between a man and his heart, and that it is He to whom ye shall all be gathered."

Almighty God also says: "O ye who believe, what is the matter with you, that when ye are asked to go forth in the cause of God, ye cling so heavily to the earth! Do ye prefer the life of this world to the hereafter? But little is the comfort of this life, as compared with the hereafter. Unless ye go forth, He will punish you with a grievous penalty, and put others in your place; but Him ye would not harm in the least. For God hath power over all things."

Almighty God also says: "So lose no heart, nor fall into despair. For ye must gain mastery if ye are true in faith."

Source: This document was originally published in Arabic in the London newspaper *Al Quds al Arabi*. Translation by the Federation of American Scientists, www.fas.org/irp/world/para/docs/980223-fatwa.htm.

Analysis: In 1996, international pressure upon the government of Sudan led it to expel Osama bin Laden and his followers.

However, the Saudi government had already revoked his citizenship, leaving him very few locations in which to regroup. An invitation from the Taliban, the theocracy ruling Afghanistan, drew bin Laden and his followers back to the site of his earlier activities as a mujahideen fighting against Soviet occupation. This declaration was issued by bin Laden, but signed by many other prominent radical Islamists, suggesting that a rudimentary alliance was forming between various factions opposed to Western influence in Saudi Arabia. Once again, bin Laden presented his position as a logical and defensible reaction to the American presence in Saudi Arabia. He also suggests that his call for jihad was motivated by the sufferings of other Arab Muslims, specifically the people of Iraq who were subjected to occasional attack as part of the enforcement of a no-fly zone, and who had lived under the effects of a de facto blockade for nearly a decade. By bin Laden's reckoning, more than one million Iraqi children died as a result of American actions, and thus, any casualties inflicted by al-Qaeda's terror attacks would pale in comparison to the scale of lives lost in Iraq.

3. "International Convention for the Suppression of the Financing of Terrorism"

When: December 9, 1999
Where: United Nations, New York City
Significance: Recognizing that the reach and capacity of terrorist organizations is largely dependent upon their ability to acquire resources, particularly financial support, the United Nations General Assembly adopted a convention designed to hinder the ability of terror organizations to obtain and internationally transfer finances.

DOCUMENT: International Convention for the Suppression of the Financing of Terrorism

The States Parties to this Convention,

Deeply concerned about the worldwide escalation of acts of terrorism in all its forms and manifestations,

Noting that the Declaration on Measures to Eliminate International Terrorism also encouraged States to review urgently the scope of the existing international legal provisions on the prevention, repression and elimination of terrorism in all its forms and manifestations, with the aim of ensuring that there is a comprehensive legal framework covering all aspects of the matter,

Considering that the financing of terrorism is a matter of grave concern to the international community as a whole,

Noting that the number and seriousness of acts of international terrorism depend on the financing that terrorists may obtain,

Noting also that existing multilateral legal instruments do not expressly address such financing,

Being convinced of the urgent need to enhance international cooperation among States in devising and adopting effective measures for the prevention of the financing of terrorism, as well as for its suppression through the prosecution and punishment of its perpetrators,

Have agreed as follows:

Article 2

1. Any person commits an offence within the meaning of this Convention if that person by any means, directly or indirectly, unlawfully and willfully, provides or collects funds with the intention that they should be used or in the knowledge that they are to be used, in full or in part, in order to carry out:

A. An act which constitutes an offence within the scope of and as defined in one of the treaties listed in the annex; or

B. Any other act intended to cause death or serious bodily injury to a civilian, or to any other person not taking an active part in the hostilities in a situation of armed conflict, when the purpose of such act, by its nature or context, is to intimidate a population, or to compel a government or an international organization to do or to abstain from doing any act.

Article 4

Each State Party shall adopt such measures as may be necessary:

a. To establish as criminal offences under its domestic law the offences set forth in article 2;

b. To make those offences punishable by appropriate penalties which take into account the grave nature of the offences.

Article 6

Each State Party shall adopt such measures as may be necessary, including, where appropriate, domestic legislation, to ensure that criminal acts within the scope of this Convention are under no circumstances justifiable by considerations of a political, philosophical, ideological, racial, ethnic, religious or other similar nature.

Article 7

1. Each State Party shall take such measures as may be necessary to establish its jurisdiction over the offences set forth in article 2 when:

a. The offence is committed in the territory of that State;

b. The offence is committed on board a vessel flying the flag of that State or an aircraft registered under the laws of that State at the time the offence is committed;

c. The offence is committed by a national of that State.

Article 12

1. States Parties shall afford one another the greatest measure of assistance in connection with criminal investigations or criminal or extradition proceedings in respect of the offences set forth in article 2, including assistance in obtaining evidence in their possession necessary for the proceedings.

2. States Parties may not refuse a request for mutual legal assistance on the ground of bank secrecy.

3. The requesting Party shall not transmit nor use information or evidence furnished by the requested Party for investigations, prosecutions or proceedings other than those stated in the request without the prior consent of the requested Party.

Source: "International Convention for the Suppression of the Financing of Terrorism." A/RES/54/109, Annex, www.un.org/law/cod/finterr.htm. Used by permission of the United Nations.

Analysis: This convention was hailed as a specific, measurable way to take action against terror organizations. Once again, the United Nations General Assembly recognized the danger that terror organizations might represent to civilized society, and attempted to enable member states to cooperate in reducing or eliminating international financing of terrorism. As had been true in virtually every United Nations resolution regarding terrorism, this convention required an international aspect before it could be considered applicable to any given financial transaction. Thus, terror organizations were still free to obtain financing from domestic sources, at least from the UN perspective, although presumably such financing would still be illegal under domestic law. Perhaps most importantly, this convention required states to share banking information with one another, and prohibited adherents from shielding information under banking secrecy laws. However, any information shared under the provisions of this convention could only be used to counteract terror organizations, offering some degree of protection to members of the international banking community who expressed objections to sharing their information.

4. Authorization for the Use of Military Force

When: September 18, 2001
Where: Washington, DC
Significance: This act, passed by the Senate and House of Representatives and signed into law, authorized the president of the United States to utilize military force to end the threat of terror attacks upon the United States. Such force could be applied wherever necessary, and against any nation, organization, or individual who, in the president's determination, was involved in the attacks, harbored anyone who participated or planned them, or represents a future threat of further attacks.

DOCUMENT:

107th Congress
Joint Resolution

To authorize the use of United States Armed Forces against those responsible for the recent attacks launched against the United States.

Whereas, on September 11, 2001, acts of treacherous violence were committed against the United States and its citizens; and

Whereas, such acts render it both necessary and appropriate that the United States
exercise its rights to self-defense and to protect United States citizens both at home
and abroad; and

Whereas, in light of the threat to the
national security and foreign policy of the
United States posed by these grave acts of
violence; and

Whereas, such acts continue to pose an
unusual and extraordinary threat to the
national security and foreign policy of the
United States; and

Whereas, the President has authority under
the Constitution to take action to deter and
prevent acts of international terrorism against
the United States: Now, therefore, be it

*Resolved by the Senate and House of
Representatives of the United States of
America in Congress assembled,*

SECTION 1. SHORT TITLE.

This joint resolution may be cited as the
"Authorization for Use of Military Force."

SEC. 2. AUTHORIZATION FOR USE OF UNITED STATES ARMED FORCES.

(a) IN GENERAL.—That the President is
authorized to use all necessary and appropriate force against those nations, organizations,
or persons he determines planned, authorized, committed, or harbored such organizations or persons, in order to prevent any
future acts of international terrorism against
the United States by such nations, organizations or persons.

(b) WAR POWERS RESOLUTION
REQUIREMENTS.—

(1) SPECIFIC STATUTORY
AUTHORIZATION.—Consistent with section 8(a)(1) of the War Powers Resolution,
the Congress declares that this section is
intended to constitute specific statutory
authorization within the meaning of section 5(b) of the War Powers Resolution.

(2) APPLICABILITY OF OTHER
REQUIREMENTS.—Nothing in this reso-
lution supercedes any requirement of the
War Powers Resolution.

Approved September 18, 2001

Source: Public Law 107-40; 115 Stat. 225

Analysis: The Authorization for Use of
Military Force (AUMF) was the formal
mechanism by which the legislature granted
approval to President George W. Bush, and
his successors in the office, to utilize military
force against the perpetrators of the September 11 attacks and any person, organization,
or nation allied with them or offering them
safe haven. It was initially interpreted by the
public as a license to attack Afghanistan, and
if necessary, to launch a ground invasion with
the purpose of destroying al-Qaeda and capturing or killing its leader, Osama bin Laden.
However, because the AUMF was passed only
a week after the attacks, and the investigation
had not made a final determination regarding
who was definitely responsible for them, it
was a decidedly vague document. Al-Qaeda
had already established "franchises" in the
Arabian Peninsula, and was on the verge of
forming alliances with other terror organizations in Africa and the Middle East. Thus,
the AUMF authorized the deployment of
American troops to a wide variety of locations around the globe, eventually leading to
activities ranging from western Africa to the
Philippine Islands. Because the AUMF did
not specify al-Qaeda as the primary target,
and because it left open the possibility of
attacking nations or organizations allied with
the September 11 attackers, it has been used

to justify the invasion of Iraq in 2003; intervention in Libya in 2011; aerial attacks in Yemen and Somalia against al-Qaeda affiliates; and the deployment of troops to Iraq and Syria to confront the forces of the Islamic State.

5. USA Patriot Act of 2001 (Public Law No. 107-56)

When: October 26, 2001
Where: Washington, DC
Significance: The USA Patriot Act, passed in the immediate aftermath of the September 11 attacks, provided significant information-gathering powers to U.S. government agencies, but was perceived by many to substantially impede upon American privacy rights guaranteed to all citizens.

DOCUMENT:

SUMMARY AS OF:
10/24/2001—Passed House without amendment.

Uniting and Strengthening America by Providing Appropriate Tools Required to Intercept and Obstruct Terrorism (USA PATRIOT ACT) Act of 2001

Title I: Enhancing Domestic Security Against Terrorism—Establishes in the Treasury the Counterterrorism Fund.

(Sec. 102) Expresses the sense of Congress that: (1) the civil rights and liberties of all Americans, including Arab Americans, must be protected, and that every effort must be taken to preserve their safety; (2) any acts of violence or discrimination against any Americans be condemned; and (3) the Nation is called upon to recognize the patriotism of fellow citizens from all ethnic, racial, and religious backgrounds.

(Sec. 103) Authorizes appropriations for the Federal Bureau of Investigation's (FBI) Technical Support Center.

(Sec. 104) Authorizes the Attorney General to request the Secretary of Defense to provide assistance in support of Department of Justice (DOJ) activities relating to the enforcement of Federal criminal code (code) provisions regarding the use of weapons of mass destruction during an emergency situation involving a weapon (currently, chemical weapon) of mass destruction.

(Sec. 105) Requires the Director of the U.S. Secret Service to take actions to develop a national network of electronic crime task forces throughout the United States to prevent, detect, and investigate various forms of electronic crimes, including potential terrorist attacks against critical infrastructure and financial payment systems.

(Sec. 106) Modifies provisions relating to presidential authority under the International Emergency Powers Act to: (1) authorize the President, when the United States is engaged in armed hostilities or has been attacked by a foreign country or foreign nationals, to confiscate any property subject to U.S. jurisdiction of a foreign person, organization, or country that he determines has planned, authorized, aided, or engaged in such hostilities or attacks (the rights to which shall vest in such agency or person as the President may designate); and (2) provide that, in any judicial review of a determination made under such provisions, if the determination was based on classified information such information may be submitted to the reviewing court ex parte and in camera.

Title II: Enhanced Surveillance Procedures—Amends the Federal criminal code to authorize the interception of wire, oral, and electronic communications for the production of evidence of: (1) specified chemical weapons or terrorism offenses; and (2) computer fraud and abuse.

(Sec. 203) Amends rule 6 of the Federal Rules of Criminal Procedure (FRCrP) to permit the sharing of grand jury information that involves foreign intelligence or counterintelligence with Federal law enforcement, intelligence, protective, immigration, national defense, or national security officials (such officials), subject to specified requirements.

Authorizes an investigative or law enforcement officer, or an attorney for the Government, who, by authorized means, has obtained knowledge of the contents of any wire, oral, or electronic communication or evidence derived therefrom to disclose such contents to such officials to the extent that such contents include foreign intelligence or counterintelligence.

Directs the Attorney General to establish procedures for the disclosure of information (pursuant to the code and the FRCrP) that identifies a United States person, as defined in the Foreign Intelligence Surveillance Act of 1978 (FISA).

Authorizes the disclosure of foreign intelligence or counterintelligence obtained as part of a criminal investigation to such officials.

(Sec. 204) Clarifies that nothing in code provisions regarding pen registers shall be deemed to affect the acquisition by the Government of specified foreign intelligence information, and that procedures under FISA shall be the exclusive means by which electronic surveillance and the interception of domestic wire and oral (current law) and electronic communications may be conducted.

(Sec. 205) Authorizes the Director of the FBI to expedite the employment of personnel as translators to support counterterrorism investigations and operations without regard to applicable Federal personnel requirements. Requires: (1) the Director to establish such security requirements as necessary for such personnel; and (2) the Attorney General to report to the House and Senate Judiciary Committees regarding translators.

(Sec. 206) Grants roving surveillance authority under FISA after requiring a court order approving an electronic surveillance to direct any person to furnish necessary information, facilities, or technical assistance in circumstances where the Court finds that the actions of the surveillance target may have the effect of thwarting the identification of a specified person.

(Sec. 207) Increases the duration of FISA surveillance permitted for non-U.S. persons who are agents of a foreign power.

(Sec. 208) Increases (from seven to 11) the number of district court judges designated to hear applications for and grant orders approving electronic surveillance. Requires that no fewer than three reside within 20 miles of the District of Columbia.

(Sec. 209) Permits the seizure of voice-mail messages under a warrant.

(Sec. 210) Expands the scope of subpoenas for records of electronic communications to include the length and types of service utilized, temporarily assigned network addresses, and the means and source of payment (including any credit card or bank account number).

(Sec. 211) Amends the Communications Act of 1934 to permit specified disclosures to Government entities, except for records revealing cable subscriber selection of video programming from a cable operator.

(Sec. 212) Permits electronic communication and remote computing service providers to make emergency disclosures to a governmental entity of customer electronic communications to protect life and limb.

(Sec. 213) Authorizes Federal district courts to allow a delay of required notices of the execution of a warrant if immediate notice may have an adverse result and under other specified circumstances.

(Sec. 214) Prohibits use of a pen register or trap and trace devices in any investigation to protect against international terrorism or clandestine intelligence activities that is conducted solely on the basis of activities protected by the first amendment to the U.S. Constitution.

(Sec. 215) Authorizes the Director of the FBI (or designee) to apply for a court order requiring production of certain business records for foreign intelligence and international terrorism investigations. Requires the Attorney General to report to the House and Senate Intelligence and Judiciary Committees semi-annually.

(Sec. 216) Amends the code to: (1) require a trap and trace device to restrict recoding or decoding so as not to include the contents of a wire or electronic communication; (2) apply a court order for a pen register or trap and trace devices to any person or entity providing wire or electronic communication service in the United States whose assistance may facilitate execution of the order; (3) require specified records kept on any pen register or trap and trace device on a packet-switched data network of a provider of electronic communication service to the public; and (4) allow a trap and trace device to identify the source (but not the contents) of a wire or electronic communication.

(Sec. 217) Makes it lawful to intercept the wire or electronic communication of a computer trespasser in certain circumstances.

(Sec. 218) Amends FISA to require an application for an electronic surveillance order or search warrant to certify that a significant purpose (currently, the sole or main purpose) of the surveillance is to obtain foreign intelligence information.

(Sec. 219) Amends rule 41 of the FRCrP to permit Federal magistrate judges in any district in which terrorism-related activities may have occurred to issue search warrants for searches within or outside the district.

(Sec. 220) Provides for nationwide service of search warrants for electronic evidence.

(Sec. 221) Amends the Trade Sanctions Reform and Export Enhancement Act of 2000 to extend trade sanctions to the territory of Afghanistan controlled by the Taliban.

Title IV: Protecting the Border

Subtitle B: Enhanced Immigration Provisions—Amends the Immigration and Nationality Act to broaden the scope of aliens ineligible for admission or deportable due to terrorist activities to include an alien who: (1) is a representative of a political, social, or similar group whose political endorsement of terrorist acts undermines U.S. antiterrorist efforts; (2) has used a position of prominence to endorse terrorist activity, or to persuade others to support such activity in a way that undermines U.S. antiterrorist efforts (or the child or spouse of such an alien under specified circumstances); or (3) has been associated with a terrorist organization and intends to engage in threatening activities while in the United States.

(Sec. 411) Includes within the definition of "terrorist activity" the use of any weapon or dangerous device.

Redefines "engage in terrorist activity" to mean, in an individual capacity or as a member of an organization, to: (1) commit or to incite to commit, under circumstances indicating an intention to cause death or serious bodily injury, a terrorist activity; (2) prepare or plan a terrorist activity; (3) gather information on potential targets for terrorist activity; (4) solicit funds or other things of value for a terrorist activity or a terrorist organization (with an exception for lack of knowledge); (5) solicit any individual to engage in prohibited conduct or for terrorist organization membership (with an exception for lack of knowledge); or (6) commit an act that the actor knows, or reasonably should know, affords material support, including a safe house, transportation, communications, funds, transfer of funds or other material financial benefit, false documentation or identification, weapons (including chemical, biological, or radiological weapons), explosives, or training for the commission of a terrorist activity; to any individual who the actor knows or reasonably should know has committed or plans to commit a terrorist activity; or to a terrorist organization (with an exception for lack of knowledge).

Defines "terrorist organization" as a group: (1) designated under the Immigration and Nationality Act or by the Secretary of State; or (2) a group of two or more individuals, whether related or not, which engages in terrorist-related activities.

Provides for the retroactive application of amendments under this Act. Stipulates that an alien shall not be considered inadmissible or deportable because of a relationship to an organization that was not designated as a terrorist organization prior to enactment of this Act. States that the amendments under this section shall apply to all aliens in exclusion or deportation proceedings on or after the date of enactment of this Act.

Directs the Secretary of State to notify specified congressional leaders seven days prior to designating an organization as a terrorist organization. Provides for organization redesignation or revocation.

(Sec. 412) Provides for mandatory detention until removal from the United States (regardless of any relief from removal) of an alien certified by the Attorney General as a suspected terrorist or threat to national security. Requires release of such alien after seven days if removal proceedings have not commenced, or the alien has not been charged with a criminal offense. Authorizes detention for additional periods of up to six months of an alien not likely to be deported in the reasonably foreseeable future only if release will threaten U.S. national security or the safety of the community or any person. Limits judicial review to habeas corpus proceedings in the U.S. Supreme Court, the U.S. Court of Appeals for the District of Columbia, or any district court with jurisdiction to entertain a habeas corpus petition. Restricts to the U.S. Court of Appeals for the District of Columbia the right of appeal of any final order by a circuit or district judge.

(Sec. 413) Authorizes the Secretary of State, on a reciprocal basis, to share criminal- and terrorist-related visa lookout information with foreign governments.

(Sec. 414) Declares the sense of Congress that the Attorney General should: (1) fully implement the integrated entry and exit data system for airports, seaports, and land border ports of entry with all deliberate speed; and (2) begin immediately establishing the Integrated Entry and Exit Data System Task Force. Authorizes appropriations.

Requires the Attorney General and the Secretary of State, in developing the integrated entry and exit data system, to focus on the use of biometric technology and the development of tamper-resistant documents readable at ports of entry.

(Sec. 415) Amends the Immigration and Naturalization Service Data Management Improvement Act of 2000 to include the Office of Homeland Security in the Integrated Entry and Exit Data System Task Force.

(Sec. 416) Directs the Attorney General to implement fully and expand the foreign student monitoring program to include other approved educational institutions like air flight, language training, or vocational schools.

(Sec. 417) Requires audits and reports on implementation of the mandate for machine readable passports.

(Sec. 418) Directs the Secretary of State to: (1) review how consular officers issue visas to determine if consular shopping is a problem; and (2) if it is a problem, take steps to address it, and report on them to Congress.

Title V: Removing Obstacles to Investigating Terrorism—Authorizes the Attorney General to pay rewards from available funds pursuant to public advertisements for assistance to DOJ to combat terrorism and defend the Nation against terrorist acts, in accordance with procedures and regulations established or issued by the Attorney General, subject to specified conditions, including a prohibition against any such reward of $250,000 or more from being made or offered without the personal approval of either the Attorney General or the President.

(Sec. 502) Amends the State Department Basic Authorities Act of 1956 to modify the Department of State rewards program to authorize rewards for information leading to: (1) the dismantling of a terrorist organization in whole or significant part; and (2) the identification or location of an individual who holds a key leadership position in a terrorist organization. Raises the limit on rewards if the Secretary State determines that a larger sum is necessary to combat terrorism or defend the Nation against terrorist acts.

(Sec. 503) Amends the DNA Analysis Backlog Elimination Act of 2000 to qualify a Federal terrorism offense for collection of DNA for identification.

(Sec. 504) Amends FISA to authorize consultation among Federal law enforcement officers regarding information acquired from an electronic surveillance or physical search in terrorism and related investigations or protective measures.

(Sec. 505) Allows the FBI to request telephone toll and transactional records, financial records, and consumer reports in any investigation to protect against international terrorism or clandestine intelligence activities only if the investigation is not conducted solely on the basis of activities protected by the first amendment to the U.S. Constitution.

(Sec. 506) Revises U.S. Secret Service jurisdiction with respect to fraud and related activity in connection with computers. Grants the FBI primary authority to investigate specified fraud and computer related activity for cases involving espionage, foreign counter-intelligence, information protected against unauthorized disclosure for reasons of national defense or foreign relations, or restricted data, except for offenses affecting Secret Service duties.

(Sec. 507) Amends the General Education Provisions Act and the National Education Statistics Act of 1994 to provide for disclosure of educational records to the Attorney General in a terrorism investigation or prosecution.

Title VIII: Strengthening the Criminal Laws Against Terrorism—Amends the Federal criminal code to prohibit specific terrorist acts or otherwise destructive, disruptive, or violent acts against mass transportation vehicles, ferries, providers, employees, passengers, or operating systems.

(Sec. 802) Amends the Federal criminal code to: (1) revise the definition of "international terrorism" to include activities that appear to be intended to affect the conduct of government by mass destruction; and (2) define "domestic terrorism" as activities that occur primarily within U.S. jurisdiction, that involve criminal acts dangerous to human life, and that appear to be intended to intimidate or coerce a civilian population, to influence government policy by intimidation or coercion, or to affect government conduct by mass destruction, assassination, or kidnapping.

(Sec. 803) Prohibits harboring any person knowing or having reasonable grounds to believe that such person has committed or to be about to commit a terrorism offense.

(Sec. 804) Establishes Federal jurisdiction over crimes committed at U.S. facilities abroad.

(Sec. 805) Applies the prohibitions against providing material support for terrorism to offenses outside of the United States.

(Sec. 806) Subjects to civil forfeiture all assets, foreign or domestic, of terrorist organizations.

(Sec. 808) Expands: (1) the offenses over which the Attorney General shall have primary investigative jurisdiction under provisions governing acts of terrorism transcending national boundaries; and (2) the offenses included within the definition of the Federal crime of terrorism.

(Sec. 809) Provides that there shall be no statute of limitations for certain terrorism offenses if the commission of such an offense resulted in, or created a foreseeable risk of, death or serious bodily injury to another person.

(Sec. 810) Provides for alternative maximum penalties for specified terrorism crimes.

(Sec. 811) Makes: (1) the penalties for attempts and conspiracies the same as those for terrorism offenses; (2) the supervised release terms for offenses with terrorism predicates any term of years or life; and (3) specified terrorism crimes Racketeer Influenced and Corrupt Organizations statute predicates.

(Sec. 814) Revises prohibitions and penalties regarding fraud and related activity in connection with computers to include specified cyber-terrorism offenses.

(Sec. 816) Directs the Attorney General to establish regional computer forensic laboratories, and to support existing laboratories, to develop specified cyber-security capabilities.

(Sec. 817) Prescribes penalties for knowing possession in certain circumstances of biological agents, toxins, or delivery systems, especially by certain restricted persons.

Title IX: Improved Intelligence—Amends the National Security Act of 1947 to require the Director of Central Intelligence (DCI) to establish requirements and priorities for foreign intelligence collected under the Foreign Intelligence Surveillance Act of 1978 and to provide assistance to the Attorney General (AG) to ensure that information derived from electronic surveillance or physical searches is disseminated for efficient and effective foreign intelligence purposes. Requires the inclusion of international terrorist activities within the scope of foreign intelligence under such Act.

(Sec. 903) Expresses the sense of Congress that officers and employees of the intelligence community should establish and maintain intelligence relationships to acquire information on terrorists and terrorist organizations.

(Sec. 904) Authorizes deferral of the submission to Congress of certain reports on intelligence and intelligence-related matters until: (1) February 1, 2002; or (2) a date after February 1, 2002, if the official involved certifies that preparation and submission on February 1, 2002, will impede the work of officers or employees engaged in counterterrorism activities. Requires congressional notification of any such deferral.

(Sec. 905) Requires the AG or the head of any other Federal department or agency with law enforcement responsibilities to expeditiously disclose to the DCI any foreign intelligence acquired in the course of a criminal investigation.

(Sec. 906) Requires the AG, DCI, and Secretary of the Treasury to jointly report to Congress on the feasibility and desirability of reconfiguring the Foreign Asset Tracking Center and the Office of Foreign Assets Control to provide for the analysis and dissemination of foreign intelligence relating to the financial capabilities and resources of international terrorist organizations.

(Sec. 907) Requires the DCI to report to the appropriate congressional committees on the establishment and maintenance of the National Virtual Translation Center for timely and accurate translation of foreign intelligence for elements of the intelligence community.

(Sec. 908) Requires the AG to provide a program of training to Government officials regarding the identification and use of foreign intelligence.

Source: The preceding summary of the USA Patriot Act of 2001 can be found at the Library of Congress website, www.justice.gov/archive/ll/highlights.htm, and is courtesy of the Congressional Research Service. The full text of the USA PATRIOT Act of 2001 is found at www.gpo.gov/fdsys/pkg/PLAW-107publ56/pdf/PLAW-107publ56.pdf.

Analysis: More than anything, the USA Patriot Act was designed to remove barriers to counterterrorism activities that had arisen through bureaucratic inefficiencies, poor cooperation between intelligence and law enforcement agencies, and time-consuming or expensive methods of intercepting communications of terrorist suspects. However, some critics claimed that the act gave the federal government unprecedented powers for surveillance without sufficient judicial oversight. One of the most effective aspects of the act was that it significantly tightened controls upon the international transfer of cash and financial instruments, and it had a major effect upon money-laundering practices. In the years following its passage, a number of civil rights groups brought lawsuits against provisions of the act, although the majority of it remained intact. In March 2006, Congress made most of the intelligence collection aspects of the USA PATRIOT Act permanent, eliminating the sunset provision that accompanied the original legislation. This renewal made clear that congressional leaders believed the act had proven effective in the war on terror, and also that the war was likely to continue for the foreseeable future.

6. Final Report of the National Commission on Terrorist Attacks Upon the United States

When: July 22, 2004
Where: Washington, DC
Significance: The *Final Report of the National Commission on Terrorist Attacks Upon the United States* represents the official government account regarding the September 11 attacks. Not only did the commission seek to identify the failures in security measures that allowed the attack to succeed, it was also charged with making broad and specific recommendations for the federal government to counter future attacks and more effectively prosecute the war on terror.

DOCUMENT: Excerpts from the Executive Summary, *Final Report of the National Commission on Terrorist Attacks Upon the United States*

A Shock, Not a Surprise

The 9/11 attacks were a shock, but they should not have come as a surprise. Islamist extremists had given plenty of warning that they meant to kill Americans indiscriminately and in large numbers. Although Usama Bin Ladin himself would not emerge as a signal threat until the 1990s, the threat of Islamist terrorism grew over the decade.

In February 1993, a group led by Ramzi Yousef tried to bring down the World Trade Center with a truck bomb. They killed six and wounded a thousand. Plans by Omar Abdel Rahman and others to blow up the Holland and Lincoln tunnels and other New York City landmarks were frustrated when the plotters were arrested. In October 1993, Somali tribesmen shot down U.S. helicopters, killing 18 and wounding 73 that came to be known as "Black Hawk down." Years later it would be learned that those Somali tribesmen had received help from al Qaeda.

In early 1995, police in Manila uncovered a plot by Ramzi Yousef to blow up a dozen U.S. airliners while they were flying over the Pacific. In November 1995, a car bomb exploded outside the office of the U.S. program manager for the Saudi National Guard in Riyadh, killing five Americans and two others. In June 1996, a truck bomb demolished the Khobar Towers apartment complex in Dharan, Saudi Arabia, killing 19 U.S. servicemen and wounding hundreds. The Attack was carried out primarily by Saudi Hezbollah, an organization that had received help from the government of Iran.

Until 1997, the U.S. intelligence community viewed Bin Ladin as a financier of terrorism, not as a terrorist leader. In February 1998, Usama Bin Ladin and four others issued a self-styled fatwa, publicly declaring that it was God's decree that every Muslim should try his utmost to kill any American, military or civilian, anywhere in the world, because of American "occupation" of Islam's holy places and aggression against Muslims.

In August 1998, Bin Ladin's group, al Qaeda, carried out near-simultaneous truck bomb attacks on the U.S. embassies in Nairobi, Kenya, and Dar es Salaam, Tanzania. The attacks killed 224 people, including 12 Americans, and wounded thousands more.

In December 1999, Jordanian police foiled a plot to bomb hotels and other sites frequented by American tourists, and a U.S. Customs agent arrested Ahmed Ressam at the U.S. Canadian border as he was smuggling in explosives intended for an attack on Los Angeles International Airport.

In October 2000, an al Qaeda team in Aden, Yemen, used a motorboat filled with explosives to blow a hole in the side of a destroyer, the USS *Cole*, almost sinking the vessel and killing 17 American sailors.

The 9/11 attacks on the World Trade Center and the Pentagon were far more elaborate, precise, and destructive than any of these earlier assaults. But by September 2001, the executive branch of the U.S. government, the Congress, the news media, and the American public had received clear warning that Islamic terrorists meant to kill Americans in high numbers.

September 11, 2001

The day began with the 19 hijackers getting through a security checkpoint system that they had evidently analyzed and knew how to defeat. Their success rate in penetrating the system was 19 for 19. They took over the four flights, taking advantage of air crews and cockpits that were not prepared for the contingency of a suicide hijacking.

On 9/11, the defense of U.S. air space depended on close interaction between two federal agencies: the Federal Aviation Administration (FAA) and North American Aerospace Defense Command (NORAD). Existing protocols on 9/11 were unsuited in every respect for an attack in which hijacked planes were used as weapons.

What ensued was a hurried attempt to improvise a defense by civilians who had never handled a hijacked aircraft that attempted to disappear, and by a military unprepared for the transformation of commercial aircraft into weapons of mass destruction.

A shootdown authorization was not communicated to the NORAD air defense sector until 28 minutes after United 93 had crashed in Pennsylvania. Planes were scrambled, but ineffectively, as they did not know where to go or what targets they were to intercept. And once the shootdown order was given, it was not communicated to the pilots. In short, while leaders in Washington believed that the fighters circling above them had been instructed to "take out" hostile aircraft, the only orders actually conveyed to the pilots were to "ID type and tail."

Like the national defense, the emergency response on 9/11 was necessarily improvised.

In New York City, the Fire Department of New York, the New York Police Department, the Port Authority of New York and New Jersey, the building employees, and the occupants of the buildings did their best to cope with the effects of almost unimaginable events—unfolding furiously over 102 minutes. Casualties were nearly 100 percent at and above the impact zones and were very high among first responders who stayed in danger as they tried to save lives. Despite weaknesses in preparations for disaster, failure to achieve unified incident command, and inadequate communications among responding agencies, all but approximately one hundred of the thousands of civilians who worked below the impact zone escaped, often with help from the emergency responders.

At the Pentagon, while there were also problems of command and control, the emergency response was generally effective. The Incident Command System, a formalized management structure for emergency response in place in the National Capital Region, overcame the inherent complications of a response across local, state, and federal jurisdictions.

Operational Opportunities

We write with the benefit and handicap of hindsight. We are mindful of the danger of being unjust to men and women who made choices in conditions of uncertainty and in circumstances over which they often had little control.

Nonetheless, there were specific points of vulnerability in the plot and opportunities to disrupt it. Operational failures—opportunities that were not or could not be exploited by the organizations and systems of that time—included

- not watchlisting future hijackers Hazmi and Mihdhar, not trailing them after they traveled to Bangkok, and not informing the FBI about one future hijacker's U.S. visa or his companion's travel to the United States;
- not sharing information linking individuals in the *Cole* attack to Mihdhar;
- not taking adequate steps in time to find Mihdhar or Hazmi in the United States;
- not linking the arrest of Zacarias Moussaoui, described as interested in flight training for the purpose of using an airplane in a terrorist act, to the heightened indications of attack;
- not discovering false statements on visa applications;
- not recognizing passports manipulated in a fraudulent manner;
- not expanding no-fly lists to include names from terrorist watchlists;
- not searching airline passengers identified by the computer-based CAPPS screening system; and
- not hardening aircraft cockpit doors or taking other measures to prepare for the possibility of suicide hijackings.

GENERAL FINDINGS

Since the plotters were flexible and resourceful, we cannot know whether any single step or series of steps would have defeated them. What we can say with confidence is that none of the measures adopted by the U.S. government from 1998 to 2001 disturbed or even delayed the progress of the al Qaeda plot. Across the government, there were failures of imagination, policy, capabilities, and management.

Imagination

The most important failure was one of imagination. We do not believe leaders understood the gravity of the threat. The terrorist danger from Bin Ladin and al Qaeda was not a major topic for policy debate among the public, the media, or in the Congress. Indeed, it barely came up during the 2000 presidential campaign.

Al Qaeda's new brand of terrorism presented challenges to U.S. governmental institutions that they were not well-designed to meet. Though top officials all told us that they understood the danger, we believe there was uncertainty among them as to whether this was just a new and especially venomous version of the ordinary terrorist threat the United States had lived with for decades, or it was indeed radically new, posing a threat beyond any yet experienced.

As late as September 4, 2001, Richard Clarke, the White House staffer long responsible for counterterrorism policy coordination, asserted that the government had not yet made up its mind how to answer the question: "Is al Qida a big deal?"

A week later came the answer.

Policy

Terrorism was not the overriding national security concern for the U.S. government under either the Clinton or the pre-9/11 Bush administration.

The policy challenges were linked to this failure of imagination. Officials in both the

Clinton and Bush administrations regarded a full U.S. invasion of Afghanistan as practically inconceivable before 9/11.

Capabilities

Before 9/11, the United States tried to solve the al Qaeda problem with the capabilities it had used in the last stages of the Cold War and its immediate aftermath. These capabilities were insufficient. Little was done to expand or reform them.

The CIA had minimal capacity to conduct paramilitary operations with its own personnel, and it did not seek a large-scale expansion of these capabilities before 9/11. The CIA also needed to improve its capability to conduct intelligence from human agents.

At no point before 9/11 was the Department of Defense fully engaged in the mission of countering al Qaeda, even though this was perhaps the most dangerous foreign enemy threatening the United States.

America's homeland defenders faced outward. NORAD itself was barely able to retain any alert bases at all. Its planning scenarios occasionally considered the danger of hijacked aircraft being guided to American targets, but only aircraft that were coming from overseas.

The most serious weaknesses in agency capabilities were in the domestic arena. The FBI did not have the capability to link the collective knowledge of agents in the field to national priorities. Other domestic agencies deferred to the FBI.

FAA capabilities were weak. Any serious examination of the possibility of a suicide hijacking could have suggested changes to fix glaring vulnerabilities—expanding no-fly lists, searching passengers identified by the CAPPS screening system, deploying federal air marshals domestically, hardening cockpit doors, alerting air crews to a different kind of hijacking possibility than they had been trained to expect. Yet the FAA did not adjust either its own training or training with NORAD to take account of threats other than those experienced in the past.

Management

The missed opportunities to thwart the 9/11 plot were also symptoms of a broader inability to adapt the way government manages problems to the new challenges of the twenty-first century. Action officers should have been able to draw on all available knowledge about al Qaeda in the government. Management should have ensured that information was shared and duties were clearly assigned across agencies, and across the foreign-domestic divide.

There were also broader management issues with respect to how top leaders set priorities and allocated resources. For instance, on December 4, 1998, DCI Tenet issued a directive to several CIA officials and the DDCI for Community Management, stating: "We are at war. I want no resources or people spared in this effort, either inside CIA or the Community." The memorandum had little overall effect on mobilizing the CIA or the intelligence community. This episode indicates the limitations of the DCI's authority over the direction of the intelligence community, including agencies within the Department of Defense.

The U.S. government did not find a way of pooling intelligence and using it to guide the planning and assignment of responsibilities for joint operations involving entities as disparate as the CIA, the FBI, the State Department, the military, and the agencies involved in homeland security.

WHAT TO DO? A GLOBAL STRATEGY

The enemy is not just "terrorism." It is the threat posed specifically by Islamist terrorism, by Bin Ladin and others who draw on a long tradition of extreme intolerance within a minority strain of Islam that does not distinguish politics from religion, and distorts both.

The enemy is not Islam, the great world faith, but a perversion of Islam. The enemy goes beyond al Qaeda to include the radical ideological movement, inspired in part by al Qaeda, that has spawned other terrorist groups and violence. Thus our strategy must match our means to two ends: dismantling the al Qaeda network and, in the long term, prevailing over the ideology that contributes to Islamist terrorism.

The first phase of our post-9/11 efforts rightly included military action to topple the Taliban and pursue al Qaeda. This work continues. But long-term success demands the use of all elements of national power: diplomacy, intelligence, covert action, law enforcement, economic policy, foreign aid, public diplomacy, and homeland defense. If we favor one tool while neglecting others, we leave ourselves vulnerable and weaken our national effort.

What should Americans expect from their government? The goal seems unlimited: Defeat terrorism anywhere in the world. But Americans have also been told to expect the worst: An attack is probably coming; it may be more devastating still.

Vague goals match an amorphous picture of the enemy. Al Qaeda and other groups are popularly described as being all over the world, adaptable, resilient, needling little higher-level organization, and capable of anything. It is an image of an omnipotent hydra of destruction. That image lowers expectations of government effectiveness.

It lowers them too far. Our report shows a determined and capable group of plotters. Yet the group was fragile and occasionally left vulnerable by the marginal, unstable

people often attracted to such causes. The enemy made mistakes. The U.S. government was not able to capitalize on them.

No president can promise that a catastrophic attack like that of 9/11 will not happen again. But the American people are entitled to expect that officials will have realistic objectives, clear guidance, and effective organization. They are entitled to see standards for performance so they can judge, with the help of their elected representatives, whether the objectives are being met.

We propose a strategy with three dimensions: (1) attack terrorists and their organizations, (2) prevent the continued growth of Islamic terrorism, and (3) protect against and prepare for terrorist attacks.

HOW TO DO IT? A DIFFERENT WAY OF ORGANIZING GOVERNMENT

The strategy we have recommended is elaborate, even as presented here very briefly. To implement it will require a government better organized than the one that exists today, with its national security institutions designed half a century ago to win the Cold War. Americans should not settle for incremental, ad hoc adjustments to a system created a generation ago for a world that no longer exists.

Our detailed recommendations are designed to fit together. Their purpose is clear: to build unity of effort across the U.S. government. As one official now serving on the front lines overseas put it to us: "One fight, one team."

We call for unity of effort in five areas, beginning with unity of effort on the challenge of counterterrorism itself:

- unifying strategic intelligence and operational planning against Islamist terrorists across the foreign-domestic divide with a National Counterterrorism Center;

- unifying the intelligence community with a new National Intelligence Director;
- unifying the many participants in the counterterrorism effort and their knowledge in a network-based information sharing system that transcends traditional governmental boundaries
- unifying and strengthening congressional oversight to improve quality and accountability; and
- strengthening the FBI and homeland defenders.

* * *

We call on the American people to remember how we all felt on 9/11, to remember not only the unspeakable horror but how we came together as a nation—one nation. Unity of purpose and unity of effort are the way we will defeat this enemy and make America safer for our children and grandchildren.

We look forward to a national debate on the merits of what we have recommended, and we will participate vigorously in that debate.

Source: National Commission on Terrorist Attacks Upon the United States, *Executive Summary of the Final Report of the National Commission on Terrorist Attacks Upon the United States.* The Executive Summary, and the full report plus all supporting documents, is available at http://govinfo.library.unt.edu/911/report/index.htm.

Analysis: The 9/11 Commission brought together dozens of elective officials, government experts, respected scholars, and other community leaders to investigate the September 11 attacks and make policy and structural recommendations for future efforts to defend against terrorist attacks. It was created at the behest of both houses of Congress and President George W. Bush. Formed in late 2002, the commission held 12 public hearings sessions, beginning on

March 31, 2003, and ending on June 17, 2004. In those hearings, hundreds of individuals offered testimony, evidence, and counsel to the commission, which ultimately consolidated its findings in the final report. The commission found ample opportunities for the U.S. government to disrupt the September 11 attacks, but that failures to understand the nature of the threat, the inability of agencies to efficiently cooperate with one another, and a certain degree of overconfidence about the effectiveness of existing security measures all conspired to render the U.S. civilian air traffic system vulnerable to attack and exploitation. Once the attack commenced, although individuals and organizations did their best to respond quickly and properly, there was simply no mechanism for a coordinated response, and hence, the only factor that served to spoil the ambitions of the hijackers was the initiative of the passengers aboard one of the attacked aircraft.

The final report of the commission proved very evenhanded in determining blame for the failures on September 11, but its primary objective was to offer recommendations for future initiatives that might prevent further catastrophic attacks upon the homeland. The commission went so far as to recommend a radical reorganization of the nation's military, intelligence, and law enforcement agencies, recognizing that the existing structure had been created more than a generation earlier, and no longer fit the needs of the nation in the modern security environment. Although not all of the commission's recommendations were put into action, the final report served as a catalyst for a renewed discussion of the proper security apparatus of the United States, and allowed for a reasoned solution rather than a knee-jerk reaction in the immediate aftermath of the September 11 attacks.

7. Al Qaeda Training Manual

When: October 2002
Where: Manchester, England
Significance: This manual was discovered during a raid on a home used by al-Qaeda militants. It was translated into English and introduced into evidence in a New York court during the trial of suspects associated with the 1998 embassy bombings in Dar es Salaam and Nairobi.

DOCUMENT:

First lesson

General Introduction
Principles of Military Organization:

Military Organization has three main principles without which it cannot be established:

1. Military Organization commander and advisory council
2. The soldiers (individual members)
3. A clearly defined strategy

Military Organization Requirements:

The Military Organization dictates a number of requirements to assist it in confrontation and endurance. These are:

1. Forged documents and counterfeit currency
2. Apartments and hiding places
3. Communication means
4. Transportation means
5. Information
6. Arms and ammunition
7. Transport

Missions Required of the Military Organization:

The main mission for which the Military Organization is responsible is:

The overthrow of the godless regimes and their replacement with an Islamic regime. Other missions consist of the following:

1. Gathering information about the enemy, the land, the installations, and the neighbors.
2. Kidnapping enemy personnel, documents, secrets, and arms.
3. Assassinating enemy personnel as well as foreign tourists.
4. Freeing the brothers who are captured by the enemy.
5. Spreading rumors and writing statements that instigate people against the enemy..
6. Blasting and destroying the places of amusement, immorality, and sin; not a vital target.
7. Blasting and destroying the embassies and attacking vital economic centers..
8. Blasting and destroying bridges leading into and out of the cities.

Importance of the Military Organization:

1. Removal of those personalities that block the call's path. All types of military and civilian intellectuals and thinkers for the state.
2. Proper utilization of the individuals' unused capabilities.
3. Precision in performing tasks, and using collective views on completing a job from all aspects, not just one.
4. Controlling the work and not fragmenting it or .deviating from it.
5. Achieving long-term goals such as the establishment of an Islamic state and short-term goals such as operations against enemy individuals and sectors.
6. Establishing the conditions for possible confrontation with the regressive regimes and their persistence.

7. Achieving discipline in secrecy and through tasks.

Second Lesson

Necessary qualifications and characteristics for the organization's members

1. Islam:
The member of the Organization must be Moslem. How can an unbeliever, someone from a revealed religion [Christian, Jew], a secular person, a communist, etc. protect Islam and Moslems and defend their goals and secrets when he does not believe in that religion [Islam]? The Israeli Army requires that a fighter be of the Jewish religion. Likewise, the command leadership in the Afghan and Russian armies requires anyone with an officer's position to be a member of the communist party.

2. Commitment to the Organization's Ideology:
This commitment frees the Organization's members from conceptual problems.

3. Maturity:
The requirements of military work are numerous, and a minor cannot perform them. The nature of hard and continuous work in dangerous conditions requires a great deal of psychological, mental, and intellectual fitness, which are not usually found in a minor.

4. Sacrifice:
He [the member] has to be willing to do the work and undergo martyrdom for the purpose of achieving the goal and establishing the religion of majestic Allah on earth.

5. Listening and Obedience:
In the military, this is known today as discipline. It is expressed by how the member obeys the orders given to him. That is what our religion urges.

6. Keeping Secrets and Concealing Information
[This secrecy should be used] even with the closest people, for deceiving the enemies is not easy.

7. Free of Illness
The Military Organization's member must fulfill this important requirement.

8. Patience
[The member] should have plenty of patience for [enduring] afflictions if he is overcome by the enemies. He should not abandon this great path and sell himself and his religion to the enemies for his freedom. He should be patient in performing the work, even if it lasts a long time.

9. Tranquility and "Unflappability"
[The member] should have a calm personality that, allows him to endure psychological traumas such as those involving bloodshed, murder, arrest, imprisonment, and reverse psychological traumas such as killing one or all of his Organization's comrades. [He should be able] to carry out the work.

10. Intelligence and Insight
When the prophet—Allah bless and keep him—sent Hazifa Ben Al-Yaman to spy on the polytheist and [Hafiza] sat among them, Abou Soufian said, "Let each one of you look at his companion." Hazifa said to his companion, "Who are you?" The companion replied, "So-and-so son of so-and-so."

11. Caution and Prudence
In his battle against the king of Tomedia, the Roman general Speer sent an emissary to discuss with that king the matter of truce between the two armies. In reality, he had sent him to learn about the Tomedians' ability to fight. The general picked Lilius, one of

his top commanders, for that task and sent with him some of his officers, disguised as slaves. During that mission, one of the king's officers, Sifax, pointed to one of the [disguised] slaves and yelled, "That slave is a Roman officer I had met in a neighboring city. He was wearing a Roman uniform." At that point, Lilius used a clever trick and managed to divert the attention of the Tomedians from that by turning to the disguised officer and quickly slapping him on the face a number of times. He reprimanded him for wearing a Roman officer's uniform when he was a slave and for claiming a status that he did not deserve. The officer accepted the slaps quietly. He bowed his head in humility and shame, as slaves do. Thus, Sifax men thought that officer was really a slave because they could not imagine that a Roman officer would accept these hits without defending himself.

12. Truthfulness and Counsel
The Commander of the faithful Omar Ibn Al-Khattab—may Allah be pleased with him—asserted that this characteristic was vital in those who gather information and work as spies against the Moslems' enemies. He [Omar] sent a letter to Saad Ibn Abou Wakkas—may Allah be pleased with him—saying, "If you step foot on your enemies' land, get spies on them. Choose those whom you count on for their truthfulness and advice, whether Arabs or inhabitants of that land. Liars' accounts would not benefit you, even if some of them were true; the deceiver is a spy against you and not for you.

13. Ability to Observe and Analyze
The Israeli Mossad received news that some Palestinians were going to attack an Israeli El Al airplane. That plane was going to Rome with Golda Meir—Allah's curse upon her—the Prime Minister at the time, on board. The Palestinians had managed to use a clever trick that allowed them to wait for the arrival of the plane without being questioned by anyone. They had beaten a man who sold potatoes, kidnaped him, and hidden him. They made two holes in the top of that peddler's cart and placed two tubes next to the chimney through which two Russian-made "Strella" missiles could be launched. The Mossad officers traveled the airport back and forth looking for [anything] that [could] lead them to the Palestinians. One officer passed the potato cart twice without noticing anything. On his third time, he noticed three chimneys, but only one of them was working with smoke coming out of it. He quickly steered toward the cart and hit it hard. The cart overturned, and the Palestinians were captured.

14. Ability to Act, Change Positions, and Conceal Oneself

Third Lesson

Counterfeit Currency and Forged Documents

Financial Security Precautions:

1. Dividing operational funds into two parts: One part is to be invested in projects that offer financial return, and the other is to be saved and not spent except during operations.
2. Not placing operational funds [all] in one place.
3. Not telling the Organization members about the location of the funds.
4. Having proper protection while carrying large amounts of money.
5. Leaving the money with non-members and spending it as needed.

Forged Documents (Identity Cards, Records Books, Passports) The following security precautions should be taken:

1. Keeping the passport in a safe place so it would not be seized by the security apparatus, and the brother it belongs to would have to negotiate its return. (I'll give you your passport if you give me information)

2. All documents of the undercover brother, such as identity cards and passport, should be falsified.

3. When the undercover brother is traveling with a certain identity card or passport, he should know all pertinent [information] such as the name, profession, and place of residence.

4. The brother who has special work status (commander, communication link) should have more than one identity card and passport. He should learn the contents of each, the nature of the [indicated] profession, and the dialect of the residence area listed in the document . . .

5. The photograph of the brother in these documents should be without a beard. It is preferable that the brother's public photograph [on these documents] be also without a beard. If he already has one [document] showing a photograph with a beard, he should replace it.

6. When using an identity document in different names, no more than one such document should be carried at one time.

7. The validity of the falsified travel documents should always be confirmed.

8. All falsification matters should be carried out through .the command and not haphazardly.

9. Married brothers should not add their wives to their passports.

10. When a brother is carrying the forged passport of a certain country, he should not travel to that country. It is easy to detect forgery at the airport, and the dialect of the brother is different from that of the people from that country.

Security Precautions Related to the Organizations' Given Names:

1. The name given by the Organization [to the brother] should not be odd in comparison with other names used around him.

2. A brother should not have more than one name in the area where he lives.

Fourth Lesson

Organization

Military Bases "Apartments and Hiding Places"

Definition of Bases:

These are apartments, hiding places, command centers, etc., in which secret operations are executed against the enemy.

These bases may be in cities, and are [then] called homes or apartments. They may be in mountainous, harsh terrain far from the enemy, and are [then] called hiding places or bases.

During the initial stages, the Military Organization usually uses apartments in cities as places for launching assigned missions, such as collecting information, observing members of the ruling regime, etc.

Hiding places and bases in mountains and harsh terrain are used at later stages, from which Jihad [holy war] groups are dispatched to execute assassination operations of enemy individuals, bomb their centers, and capture their weapons. In some Arab countries such as Egypt, where there are no mountains or harsh terrain, all stages of Jihad work would take place in cities. The opposite was true in Afghanistan, where initially Jihad work was in the cities, then the warriors shifted to mountains and harsh terrain. There, they started battling the Communists.

Security Precautions Related to Apartments:

1. Choosing the apartment carefully as far as the location, the size for the work necessary (meetings, storage, arms, fugitives, work preparation).
2. It is preferable to rent apartments on the ground floor to facilitate escape and digging of trenches.
3. Preparing secret locations in the apartment for securing documents, records, arms, and other important items.
4. Preparing ways of vacating the apartment in case of a surprise attack (stands, wooden ladders).
5. Under no circumstances should anyone know about the apartment except those who use it.
6. Providing the necessary cover for the people who frequent the apartment (students, workers, employees, etc.
7. Avoiding seclusion and isolation from the population and refraining from going to the apartment at suspicious times.
8. It is preferable to rent these apartments using false names, appropriate cover, and non-Moslem appearance.
9. A single brother should not rent more than one apartment in the same area, from the same agent, or using the same rental office.
10. Care should be exercised not to rent apartments that are known to the security apparatus [such as] those used for immoral or prior Jihad activities.
11. Avoiding police stations and government buildings. Apartments should not be rented near those places.
12. When renting these apartments, one should avoid isolated or deserted locations so the enemy would not be able to catch those living there easily.
13. It is preferable to rent apartments in newly developed areas where people do not know one another. Usually, in older quarters people know one another and strangers are easily identified, especially since these quarters have many informers.
14. Ensuring that there is has been no surveillance prior to the members entering the apartment.
15. Agreement among those living in the apartment on special ways of knocking on the door and special signs prior to entry into the building's main gate to indicate to those who wish to enter that the place is safe and not being monitored. Such signs include hanging out a towel, opening a curtain, placing a cushion in a special way, etc.
16. If there is a telephone in the apartment, calls should be answered in an agreed-upon manner among those who use the apartment. That would prevent mistakes that would, otherwise, lead to revealing the names and nature of the occupants.
17. For apartments, replacing the locks and keys with new ones. As for the other entities (camps, shops, mosques), appropriate security precautions should be taken depending on the entity's importance and role in the work.
18. Apartments used for undercover work should not be visible from higher apartments in order not to expose the nature of the work.

19. In a newer apartment, avoid talking loud because prefabricated ceilings and walls [used in the apartments] do not have the same thickness as those in old ones.
20. It is necessary to have at hand documents supporting the undercover [member]. In the case of a physician, there should be an actual medical diploma, membership in the [medical] union, the government permit, and the rest of the routine procedures known in that country.
21. The cover should blend well [with the environment]. For example, selecting a doctor's clinic in an area where there are clinics, or in a location suitable for it.
22. The cover of those who frequent the location should match the cover of that location. For example, a common laborer should not enter a fancy hotel because that would be suspicious and draw attention.

Source: Department of Justice, https://www.justice.gov/sites/default/files/ag/legacy/2002/10/08/manualpart1_1.pdf.

Analysis: This training manual covers the basics of undercover tradecraft. It incorporates elements of Carlos Marighella's *Minimanual of the Urban Guerrilla,* as well as Mao Tse-tung's theory of insurrections. Although it is not the only such training manual discovered in materials held by al-Qaeda operatives, this manual offered very practical advice regarding the most common Western detection methods for potential terrorist attacks. Its discovery was a chilling reminder that al-Qaeda and other terror organizations continually seek to refine their methods of infiltration and attack, and disseminate the best practices to their members. The original manual had a substantial number of religious references to inspire readers and justify their activities, in addition to the operational guidance.

8. Abu Musab al-Zarqawi's Letter to al-Qaeda Leadership

When: 2004
Where: Iraq
Significance: Al-Zarqawi quickly became the most feared man in Iraq due to his leadership of the al-Qaeda offshoot operating in the aftermath of the American-led invasion. At his direction, al-Qaeda attacks were launched against coalition forces and Iraqi citizens, particularly members of the Shia majority. Even Osama bin Laden expressed some reservations at the ferocity of al-Zarqawi's attacks, particularly those targeting Muslim civilians, but he was incapable of corralling al-Zarqawi's activities.

DOCUMENT:

Even if our bodies are far apart, the distance between our hearts is close.

Our solace is in the saying of the Imam Malik. I hope that both of us are well. I ask God the Most High, the Generous, [to have] this letter reach you clothed in the garments of health and savoring the winds of victory and triumph. Amen.

I send you an account that is appropriate to [your] position and that removes the veil and lifts the curtain from the good and bad [that are] hidden in the arena of Iraq.

As you know, God favored the [Islamic] nation with jihad on His behalf in the land of Mesopotamia. It is known to you that the arena here is not like the rest. It has positive elements not found in others, and it also has negative elements not found in others. Among the greatest positive elements of this arena is that it is jihad in the Arab heartland. It is a stone's throw from the lands of the two Holy Precincts and the al-Aqsa [Mosque]. We know from God's religion that the true, decisive battle between infidelity and Islam is in this land, i.e., in [Greater] Syria and its surroundings. Therefore, we must spare no effort and strive urgently to establish a foothold in this land. Perhaps God may cause something to happen thereafter. The current situation, o courageous shaykhs, makes it necessary for us to examine this matter deeply, starting from our true Law and the reality in which we live.

Here is the current situation as I, with my limited vision, see it. I ask God to forgive my prattle and lapses. I say, having sought help from God, that the Americans, as you know well, entered Iraq on a contractual basis and to create the State of Greater Israel from the Nile to the Euphrates and that this Zionized American Administration believes that accelerating the creation of the State of [Greater] Israel will accelerate the emergence of the Messiah. It came to Iraq with all its people, pride, and haughtiness toward God and his Prophet. It thought that the matter would be somewhat easy. Even if there were to be difficulties, it would be easy. But it collided with a completely different reality. The operations of the brother mujahidin began from the first moment, which mixed things up somewhat. Then, the pace of operations quickened. This was in the Sunni Triangle, if this is the right name for it. This forced the Americans to conclude a deal with the Shi'a, the most evil of mankind. The deal was concluded on [the basis that] the Shi'a would get two-thirds of the booty for having stood in the ranks of the Crusaders against the mujahidin.

First: The Makeup [of Iraq]

In general, Iraq is a political mosaic, an ethnic mixture, and scattered confessional and sectarian disparities that only a strong central authority and a overpowering ruler have been able to lead, beginning with Ziyad Ibn Abihi (tr. note: 7th century A.D.) and ending with Saddam. The future faces difficult choices. It is a land of great hardships and difficulties for everyone, whether he is serious or not.

As for the details:

1. The Kurds

In their two Barazani and Talabani halves, these have given the bargain of their hands and the fruit of their hearts to the Americans. They have opened their land to the Jews and become their rear base and a Trojan horse for their plans. They (the Jews) infiltrate through their lands, drape themselves in their banners, and take them as a bridge over which to cross for financial control and economic hegemony, as well as for the espionage base for which they have built a large structure the length and breadth of that land. In general, Islam's voice has died out among them—the Kurds—and the glimmer of religion has weakened in their homes. The Iraqi Da'wa has intoxicated them, and the good people among them, few as they are, are oppressed and fear that birds will carry them away.

3 [sic]. The Shi'a

[They are] the insurmountable obstacle, the lurking snake, the crafty and malicious scorpion, the spying enemy, and the penetrating venom. We here are entering a battle on two levels. One, evident and open, is with an attacking enemy and patent infidelity. [Another is] a difficult, fierce battle with a crafty enemy who wears the garb of a friend, manifests agreement, and calls for comradeship, but harbors ill will and twists up peaks and crests.

Their greatest [act of] worship is to curse the Muslim friends of God from first to last. These are the people most anxious to divide the Muslims. Among their greatest principles are leveling charges of infidelity and damning and cursing the elite of those who have ruled matters, like the orthodox caliphs and the 'ulama' of the Muslims, because of their belief that anyone who does not believe in the infallible imam, who is not present, does not believe in God and his Prophet, may God bless him and grant him salvation.

Second: The Current Situation and the Future

There is no doubt that the Americans' losses are very heavy because they are deployed across a wide area and among the people and because it is easy to procure weapons, all of which makes them easy and mouth-watering targets for the believers. But America did not come to leave, and it will not leave no matter how numerous its wounds become and how much of its blood is spilled. It is looking to the near future, when it hopes to disappear into its bases secure and at ease and put the battlefields of Iraq into the hands of the foundling government with an army and police that will bring the behavior of Saddam and his myrmidons back to the people. There is no doubt that the space in which we can move has begun to shrink and that the grip around the throats of the mujahidin has begun to tighten. With the deployment of soldiers and police, the future has become frightening.

Third: So Where are We?

Despite the paucity of supporters, the desertion of friends, and the toughness of the times, God the Exalted has honored us with good harm to the enemy. Praise be to God, in terms of surveillance, preparation, and planning, we have been the keys to all of the martyrdom operations that have taken place except those in the north. Praise be to God, I have completed 25 [operations] up to now, including among the Shi'a and their

symbolic figures, the Americans and their soldiers, the police and soldiers, and the coalition forces. God willing, more are to come. What has prevented us from going public is that we have been waiting until we have weight on the ground and finish preparing integrated structures capable of bearing the consequences of going public so that we appear in strength and do not suffer a reversal. We seek refuge in God. Praise be to God, we have made good strides and completed important stages. As the decisive moment approaches, we feel that [our] body has begun to spread in the security vacuum, gaining locations on the ground that will be the nucleus from which to launch and move out in a serious way, God willing.

Fourth: The Work Plan

After study and examination, we can narrow our enemy down to four groups.

1. The Americans

These, as you know, are the most cowardly of God's creatures. They are an easy quarry, praise be to God. We ask God to enable us to kill and capture them to sow panic among those behind them and to trade them for our detained shaykhs and brothers.

2. The Kurds

These are a lump [in the throat] and a thorn whose time to be clipped has yet to come. They are last on the list, even though we are making efforts to harm some of their symbolic figures, God willing.

3. Soldiers, Police, and Agents

These are the eyes, ears, and hands of the occupier, through which he sees, hears, and delivers violent blows. God willing, we are determined to target them strongly in the coming period before the situation is consolidated and they control arrest[s].

4. The Shi'a

These in our opinion are the key to change. I mean that targeting and hitting them in [their] religious, political, and military depth will provoke them to show the Sunnis their rabies and bare the teeth of the hidden rancor working in their breasts.

5. The Work Mechanism

Our current situation, as I have previously told you, obliges us to deal with the matter with courage and clarity and to move quickly to do so because we consider that [unless we do so] there will be no result in which religion will appear. The solution that we see, and God the Exalted knows better, is for us to drag the Shi'a into the battle because this is the only way to prolong the fighting between us and the infidels. We say that we must drag them into battle for several reasons, which are:

1. They, i.e., the Shi'a, have declared a secret war against the people of Islam. They are the proximate, dangerous enemy of the Sunnis, even if the Americans are also an archenemy. The danger from the Shi'a, however, is greater and their damage is worse and more destructive to the [Islamic] nation than the Americans, on whom you find a quasi-consensus about killing them as an assailing enemy.
2. They have befriended and supported the Americans and stood in their ranks against the mujahidin. They have spared and are still sparing no effort to put an end to the jihad and the mujahidin.
3. Our fighting against the Shi'a is the way to drag the [Islamic] nation into the battle. We speak here in some detail. We have said before that the Shi'a have put on the uniforms of the Iraqi army, police,

and security [forces] and have raised the banner of preserving the homeland and the citizen. Under this banner, they have begun to liquidate the Sunnis under the pretext that they are saboteurs, remnants of the Ba'th, and terrorists spreading evil in the land. With strong media guidance from the Governing Council and the Americans, they have been able to come between the Sunni masses and the mujahidin. I give an example that brings the matter close to home in the area called the Sunni Triangle—if this is the right name for it. The army and police have begun to deploy in those areas and are growing stronger day by day. They have put chiefs [drawn] from among Sunni agents and the people of the land in charge. In other words, this army and police may be linked to the inhabitants of this area by kinship, blood, and honor. In truth, this area is the base from which we set out and to which we return. When the Americans disappear from these areas—and they have begun to do so—and these agents, who are linked by destiny to the people of the land, take their place, what will our situation be?

5 (sic)—The Timing for Implementation

It is our hope to accelerate the pace of work and that companies and battalions with expertise, experience, and endurance will be formed to await the zero hour when we will begin to appear in the open, gain control the land at night, and extend it into daylight, the One and Conquering God willing. We hope that this matter, I mean the zero hour, will [come] four months or so before the promised government is formed. As you can see, we are racing against time. If we are able, as we hope, to turn the tables on them and thwart their plan, this will be good. If the other [scenario] [happens]—and we seek refuge in God—and the government extends its control over the country, we will have to pack our bags and break camp for another land in which we can resume carrying the banner or in which God will choose us as martyrs for his sake.

6. What About You?

You, gracious brothers, are the leaders, guides, and symbolic figures of jihad and battle. We do not see ourselves as fit to challenge you, and we have never striven to achieve glory for ourselves. All that we hope is that we will be the spearhead, the enabling vanguard, and the bridge on which the [Islamic] nation crosses over to the victory that is promised and the tomorrow to which we aspire. This is our vision, and we have explained it. This is our path, and we have made it clear. If you agree with us on it, if you adopt it as a program and road, and if you are convinced of the idea of fighting the sects of apostasy, we will be your readied soldiers, working under your banner, complying with your orders, and indeed swearing fealty to you publicly and in the news media, vexing the infidels and gladdening those who preach the one-ness of God. On that day, the believers will rejoice in God's victory. If things appear otherwise to you, we are brothers, and the disagreement will not spoil [our] friendship. [This is} a cause [in which] we are cooperating for the good and support-ing jihad. Awaiting your response, may God preserve you as keys to good and reserves for Islam and its people. Amen, amen.

Peace and the mercy and blessings of God be upon you.

Source: U.S. State Department. Translation by the Coalition Provisional Authority, February 2004, http://2001-2009.state.gov/p/nea/rls/31694.htm.

Analysis: Al-Zarqawi's letter makes it extremely clear that he perceived the Shia of Iraq to be the foremost enemy to be con-fronted, with the American-led coalition occupying Iraq as the secondary enemy. In this communication, he gives lip service to following the dictates of bin Laden and the high command of al-Qaeda, but also makes it clear that he intended to continue his extremely bloody attacks upon soft targets. Al-Zarqawi's ultimate goal was to provoke an Islamic civil war of extermina-tion, in the expectation that superior Sunni numbers and resources would allow the annihilation of the Shia, whom he consid-ered the most evil of humans due to their heresy. Had al-Zarqawi's plan been carried to fruition, the insurgency in Iraq would likely have devolved even further into sectarian violence, and might very well have grown to engulf the entire Middle East in conflict.

9. Osama bin Laden's Letter to the American People

When: November 1, 2004
Where: Afghanistan
Significance: With this letter, bin Laden attempted to reach the American people directly with his claims regarding the Sep-tember 11 attacks and the U.S. responses. He made the case that the attacks were the direct result of American policies, and would be repeated in the future if the United States did not cease meddling in the internal affairs of Middle Eastern nations.

DOCUMENT:

Praise be to Allah who created the creation for his worship and commanded them to be just and permitted the wronged one to retaliate against the oppressor in kind. To proceed:

Peace be upon he who follows the guidance: People of America this talk of mine is for you and concerns the ideal way to prevent another Manhattan, and deals with the war and its causes and results.

Before I begin, I say to you that security is an indispensable pillar of human life and that free men do not forfeit their security, contrary to Bush's claim that we hate freedom.

If so, then let him explain to us why we don't strike for example—Sweden? And we know that freedom-haters don't possess defiant spirits like those of the 19 - may Allah have mercy on them.

No, we fight because we are free men who don't sleep under oppression. We want to restore freedom to our nation, just as you lay waste to our nation. So shall we lay waste to yours.

No one except a dumb thief plays with the security of others and then makes himself believe he will be secure. Whereas thinking people, when disaster strikes, make it their priority to look for its causes, in order to prevent it happening again.

But I am amazed at you. Even though we are in the fourth year after the events of September 11th, Bush is still engaged in distortion, deception and hiding from you the real causes. And thus, the reasons are still there for a repeat of what occurred.

So I shall talk to you about the story behind those events and shall tell you truthfully about the moments in which the decision was taken, for you to consider.

I say to you, Allah knows that it had never occurred to us to strike the towers. But after it became unbearable and we witnessed the oppression and tyranny of the American/Israeli coalition against our people in Palestine and Lebanon, it came to my mind.

The events that affected my soul in a direct way started in 1982 when America permitted the Israelis to invade Lebanon and the American Sixth Fleet helped them in that. This bombardment began and many were killed and injured and others were terrorized and displaced.

I couldn't forget those moving scenes, blood and severed limbs, women and children sprawled everywhere. Houses destroyed along with their occupants and high rises demolished over their residents, rockets raining down on our home without mercy.

The situation was like a crocodile meeting a helpless child, powerless except for his screams. Does the crocodile understand a conversation that doesn't include a weapon? And the whole world saw and heard but it didn't respond.

In those difficult moments many hard-to-describe ideas bubbled in my soul, but in the end they produced an intense feeling of rejection of tyranny, and gave birth to a strong resolve to punish the oppressors.

And as I looked at those demolished towers in Lebanon, it entered my mind that we should punish the oppressor in kind and that we should destroy towers in America in order that they taste some of what we tasted and so that they be deterred from killing our women and children.

And that day, it was confirmed to me that oppression and the intentional killing of innocent women and children is a deliberate American policy. Destruction is freedom and democracy, while resistance is terrorism and intolerance.

This means the oppressing and embargoing to death of millions as Bush Sr. did in Iraq in the greatest mass slaughter of children mankind has ever known, and it means the throwing of millions of pounds of bombs and explosives at millions of children—also in

Iraq—as Bush Jr did, in order to remove an old agent and replace him with a new puppet to assist in the pilfering of Iraq's oil and other outrages.

So with these images and their like as their background, the events of September 11th came as a reply to those great wrongs, should a man be blamed for defending his sanctuary?

Is defending oneself and punishing the aggressor in kind, objectionable terrorism? If it is such, then it is unavoidable for us.

This is the message which I sought to communicate to you in word and deed, repeatedly, for years before September 11th.

And you can read this, if you wish, in my interview with Scott in Time Magazine in 1996, or with Peter Arnett on CNN in 1997, or my meeting with John Weiner in 1998.

You can observe it practically, if you wish, in Kenya and Tanzania and in Aden. And you can read it in my interview with Abdul Bari Atwan, as well as my interviews with Robert Fisk.

The latter is one of your compatriots and co-religionists and I consider him to be neutral. So are the pretenders of freedom at the White House and the channels controlled by them able to run an interview with him? So that he may relay to the American people what he has understood from us to be the reasons for our fight against you?

If you were to avoid these reasons, you will have taken the correct path that will lead America to the security that it was in before September 11th. This concerned the causes of the war.

As for its results, they have been, by the grace of Allah, positive and enormous, and have, by all standards, exceeded all expectations. This is due to many factors, chief among them, that we have found it difficult to deal with the Bush administration in light of the resemblance it bears to the regimes in our countries, half of which are ruled by the military and the other half which are ruled by the sons of kings and presidents.

Our experience with them is lengthy, and both types are replete with those who are characterized by pride, arrogance, greed and misappropriation of wealth. This resemblance began after the visits of Bush Sr. to the region.

At a time when some of our compatriots were dazzled by America and hoping that these visits would have an effect on our countries, all of a sudden he was affected by those monarchies and military regimes, and became envious of their remaining decades in their positions, to embezzle the public wealth of the nation without supervision or accounting.

So he took dictatorship and suppression of freedoms to his son and they named it the Patriot Act, under the pretense of fighting terrorism. In addition, Bush sanctioned the installing of sons as state governors, and didn't forget to import expertise in election fraud from the region's presidents to Florida to be made use of in moments of difficulty.

All that we have mentioned has made it easy for us to provoke and bait this administration. All that we have to do is to send two mujahidin to the furthest point east to raise a piece of cloth on which is written al-Qaida, in order to make the generals race there to cause America to suffer human, economic, and political losses without their achieving for it anything of note other than some benefits for their private companies.

This is in addition to our having experience in using guerrilla warfare and the war of attrition to fight tyrannical superpowers, as we, alongside the mujahidin, bled Russia for 10 years, until it went bankrupt and was forced to withdraw in defeat.

All Praise is due to Allah.

So we are continuing this policy in bleeding America to the point of bankruptcy. Allah willing, and nothing is too great for Allah.

That being said, those who say that al-Qaida has won against the administration in the White House or that the administration has lost in this war have not been precise, because when one scrutinizes the results, one cannot say that al-Qaida is the sole factor in achieving those spectacular gains.

Rather, the policy of the White House that demands the opening of war fronts to keep busy their various corporations—whether they be working in the field of arms or oil or reconstruction—has helped al-Qaida to achieve these enormous results.

And so it has appeared to some analysts and diplomats that the White House and us are playing as one team towards the economic goals of the United States, even if the intentions differ.

And it was to these sorts of notions and their like that the British diplomat and others were referring in their lectures at the Royal Institute of International Affairs. [When they pointed out that] for example, al-Qaida spent $500,000 on the event, while America, in the incident and its aftermath, lost—according to the lowest estimate—more than $500 billion.

Meaning that every dollar of al-Qaida defeated a million dollars by the permission of Allah, besides the loss of a huge number of jobs.

As for the size of the economic deficit, it has reached record astronomical numbers estimated to total more than a trillion dollars.

And even more dangerous and bitter for America is that the mujahidin recently forced Bush to resort to emergency funds to continue the fight in Afghanistan and Iraq, which is evidence of the success of

the bleed-until-bankruptcy plan—with Allah's permission.

It is true that this shows that al-Qaida has gained, but on the other hand, it shows that the Bush administration has also gained, something of which anyone who looks at the size of the contracts acquired by the shady Bush administration-linked megacorporations, like Halliburton and its kind, will be convinced. And it all shows that the real loser is . . . you.

It is the American people and their economy. And for the record, we had agreed with the Commander-General Muhammad Ataa, Allah have mercy on him, that all the operations should be carried out within 20 minutes, before Bush and his administration noticed.

It never occurred to us that the commander-in-chief of the American armed forces would abandon 50,000 of his citizens in the twin towers to face those great horrors alone, the time when they most needed him.

But because it seemed to him that occupying himself by talking to the little girl about the goat and its butting was more important than occupying himself with the planes and their butting of the skyscrapers, we were given three times the period required to execute the operations—all praise is due to Allah.

And it's no secret to you that the thinkers and perceptive ones from among the Americans warned Bush before the war and told him: "All that you want for securing America and removing the weapons of mass destruction—assuming they exist—is available to you, and the nations of the world are with you in the inspections, and it is in the interest of America that it not be thrust into an unjustified war with an unknown outcome."

But the darkness of the black gold blurred his vision and insight, and he gave priority to private interests over the public interests of America.

So the war went ahead, the death toll rose, the American economy bled, and Bush became embroiled in the swamps of Iraq that threaten his future. He fits the saying "like the naughty she-goat who used her hoof to dig up a knife from under the earth".

So I say to you, over 15,000 of our people have been killed and tens of thousands injured, while more than a thousand of you have been killed and more than 10,000 injured. And Bush's hands are stained with the blood of all those killed from both sides, all for the sake of oil and keeping their private companies in business.

Be aware that it is the nation who punishes the weak man when he causes the killing of one of its citizens for money, while letting the powerful one get off, when he causes the killing of more than 1000 of its sons, also for money.

And the same goes for your allies in Palestine. They terrorize the women and children, and kill and capture the men as they lie sleeping with their families on the mattresses, that you may recall that for every action, there is a reaction.

Finally, it behooves you to reflect on the last wills and testaments of the thousands who left you on the 11th as they gestured in despair. They are important testaments, which should be studied and researched.

Among the most important of what I read in them was some prose in their gestures before the collapse, where they say: "How mistaken we were to have allowed the White House to implement its aggressive foreign policies against the weak without supervision."

It is as if they were telling you, the people of America: "Hold to account those who have caused us to be killed, and happy is he who learns from others' mistakes."

And among that which I read in their gestures is a verse of poetry. "Injustice chases its people, and how unhealthy the bed of tyranny."

As has been said: "An ounce of prevention is better than a pound of cure."

And know that: "It is better to return to the truth than persist in error." And that the wise man doesn't squander his security, wealth and children for the sake of the liar in the White House.

In conclusion, I tell you in truth, that your security is not in the hands of Kerry, nor Bush, nor al-Qaida. No.

Your security is in your own hands. And every state that doesn't play with our security has automatically guaranteed its own security.

And Allah is our Guardian and Helper, while you have no Guardian or Helper. All peace be upon he who follows the Guidance.

Source: English translation of a speech delivered by videotape on Al Jazeera Television, www .aljazeera.com/archive/2004/11/2008491633364 57223.html.

Analysis: Although there are elements of ideology and religion contained within this letter, bin Laden definitely changed his approach to communications with the American public, particularly when compared to his earlier messages to the West, referenced in his statement. Rather than attempting to convince Americans to renounce their religions and embrace Islam, he instead chose to appeal on the grounds of economics and justice. He accused the Bush administration of placing private financial interests ahead of the lives of American citizens. At the same time, he threatened that terror attacks against American interests would continue as long as the American public did not repudiate the government's activities. Placing them in the context of historical attacks upon Muslim citizens and drawing the connection between Israel and the United States, bin Laden sought to provoke a public outcry for isolationism as a means of saving the lives of military personnel and avoiding further budgetary deficits.

10. Brian Michael Jenkins, Testimony before the House Committee on Homeland Security

When: May 26, 2010
Where: Washington, DC
Significance: Jenkins is a RAND analyst who studies the danger presented by homegrown terrorists within the United States. In this testimony, he offered a broad overview of the threat from radicalized U.S. citizens.

DOCUMENT:

A Determined, Resilient, Opportunistic and Adaptable Foe

Nearly nine years after 9/11, the principal terrorist threat still comes from a galaxy of jihadist groups that subscribe to or have been influenced by al Qaeda's ideology of a global armed struggle against the West. The complexity of the movement defies easy assessment. The ability of al Qaeda's central leadership to directly project its power through centrally planned and managed terrorist attacks has been reduced. Terrorist organizations now confront a more hostile operating environment: Al Qaeda has not been able to carry out a major terrorist attack in the West since the London bombings of 2005. For the time being, it has concentrated its resources and efforts on the conflicts in Afghanistan and Pakistan.

This should not imply that we are at a tipping point in the struggle against terrorism. Al Qaeda, its affiliates, and its allies, remain determined to continue to attack, and they have proved to be resilient, opportunistic, and adaptable, capable of morphing to meet new circumstances. Complacency on our part would be dangerous.

A More Decentralized Terrorist Campaign

To carry on its international terrorist campaign, al Qaeda now relies on its affiliates, principally in North Africa, Iraq, and the Arabian Peninsula, and on its continuous exhortation to followers to do whatever they can, wherever they are. Other terrorist groups, while concentrating on local contests, have adopted al Qaeda's vision of a global struggle and may launch their own attacks or assist volunteers seeking support.

Emphasis on Do-It-Yourself Terrorism

The United States remains al Qaeda's primary target. Some analysts believe that al Qaeda is under growing pressure to prove that it can carry out another attack on U.S. soil in order to retain its credentials as the vanguard of the jihadist movement. Such an attack could take the form of an operation planned from abroad, like the Christmas Day airline bombing attempt, or it could be do-it-yourself attempts by homegrown terrorists responding to al Qaeda's call to action. Inevitably, one or more of these attacks may succeed.

Terrorist attempts are not evidence of our failure to protect the nation from terrorism, nor should they be cause for feigned outrage and divisive finger-pointing. They provide opportunities to learn lessons and improve defenses. The attempts reflect that we are at war—although the term has been largely discarded—and as in any war, the other side attacks.

America's Homegrown Terrorists

According to a recent RAND paper, there were 46 reported cases of radicalization and recruitment to jihadist terrorism in the United States between 9/11 and the end of 2009. This number does not include attacks from abroad. In all, 125 persons were involved in the 46 cases. Two more cases and several more arrests in 2010 bring the total to 131 persons. Half of the cases involve single individuals; the remainder are tiny conspiracies. The number of cases and the number of persons involved both increased sharply in 2009. Whether this presages a trend we cannot yet say. But these cases tell us that radicalization and recruitment to jihadist terrorism do happen here. They are clear indications of terrorist intent. The threat is real.

No Deep Reservoirs of Potential Recruits

Fortunately, the number of homegrown terrorists, most of whom are Muslims, is a tiny turnout in a Muslim American community of perhaps 3 million. (By contrast, several thousand Muslim Americans serve in the U.S. armed forces.) Al Qaeda's exhortations to violence are not resonating among the vast majority of Muslim Americans. There are veins of extremism, handfuls of hotheads, but no deep reservoirs from which al Qaeda can recruit. America's would-be jihadists are not Mao's fish swimming in a friendly sea.

The cases do not indicate an immigration or border-control problem. Almost all of those arrested for terrorist-related crimes are native-born or naturalized U.S. citizens or legal permanent residents. Most of them have lived in the United States for many years. There is no evidence that they were radicalized before coming to the United States. No armies of "sleepers" have infiltrated the country.

The Criminal Justice System Works

The cases also tell us that the U.S. criminal justice system works. With the exception of Jose Padilla, who was initially held as an enemy combatant, the individuals arrested in these cases (except for those who left to join jihad fronts abroad) were brought before U.S. courts and convicted or now await trial.

About a quarter of those identified have links with jihadist groups—al Qaeda, Lashkar-e-Taiba, or the Taliban—but there is no underground network of foreign terrorist operatives, and there are no terrorist gangs in the United States like those active in the 1970s, when the level of terrorist violence was much higher than it is today.

Amateurs are Still Dangerous

Twenty-five of the 131 terrorists identified in the United States since 9/11 received some kind of terrorist indoctrination or training. Judging by the results, it was not very good. Al Qaeda clearly has quality-control problems. The plots have been amateurish. Only two attempts succeeded in causing casualties—significantly, both were carried out by lone gunmen, a problem in the United States that transcends terrorism. But amateurs are still dangerous. There is no long mile between the terrorist wannabe and the lethal zealot.

America's jihadists may suffer from substandard zeal. Only one became a suicide bomber, although Major Nidal Hasan may not have expected to survive his murderous rampage at Fort Hood. The rest planned to escape.

Most American jihadists appear to have radicalized themselves rather than having been recruited in the traditional sense.

However, itinerant proselytizing recruiters appear in some of the cases, and active recruiting does occur in prisons. Many homegrown terrorists begin their journey to violent jihad on the Internet.

Diverse Personal Motives

The process of radicalization and recruitment to jihadist terrorist violence is complex and reflects a combination of individual circumstances and ideological motivations. Personal crisis and political cause are often paired in the process.

What does the jihadist acolyte seek in terrorism? Although recruitment may involve the rhetoric of religious belief, turning to violent jihad does not seem to result from profound religious discernment. Few jihadists appear to have more than a superficial knowledge of Islam. On the other hand, radicalization and recruitment do appear to be opportunities for an ostentatious display of piety, conviction, and commitment to their beliefs, ultimately expressed in violence.

Jihadists often use the need to avenge perceived assaults on Islam—insults to the religion, atrocities inflicted upon its believers, aggression by infidels against its people and territory, anger at specific U.S. policies—to justify their actions. These certainly are jihadist recruiting themes, but volunteer terrorists also view jihad as an opportunity for adventure, a chance to gain status in a subculture that exalts violence, to overcome perceived personal humiliation and prove manliness, to demonstrate prowess, to be perceived as a warrior in an epic struggle.

For lonely hearts, joining jihad offers a camaraderie that can sweep the more malleable along to schemes they would otherwise not have contemplated. For those who feel powerless, violent action offers the secret pleasures of clandestinity and power that come with the decision to kill.

Al Qaeda's ideology also has become a vehicle for resolving personal discontents, an opportunity to start life over, to transcend personal travail and turmoil through bloody violence, to soothe a restless soul with the spiritual comfort of an absolute ideology that dismisses the *now* as a brief passage between a glorious mythical past and eternal paradise. The jihadist may see terrorism as a path to glory in every sense of that word.

The Message to Would-Be Terrorists: No Path to Glory

Dealing with domestic radicalization does not mean countering jihadist propaganda. It means applying the law. What one believes is a matter of conscience. What one does to impose his or her beliefs on others concerns everyone. When a course of action involves the threat or use of violence, it becomes a matter of law. America's response to homegrown terrorism must, above all, be based upon the law.

The individualistic quality of radicalization and recruitment to jihadist terrorism in the United States suggests a counter-recruitment strategy that focuses on dissuading individuals from joining al Qaeda's version of jihad. This can be accomplished not through ideological or theological debate with al Qaeda's online communicators, but by deterrence through arrests, by treating terrorists and would-be terrorists as ordinary criminals, by stripping them of political pretensions.

The message to would-be terrorists should be that they can trust no one. They will fail. They will be detected and apprehended. They will be treated as ordinary criminals and will spend a long time in a prison cell. They will receive no applause. They will disgrace their families and their communities. They will be labeled fools. Their lives will be wasted. There will be no glory.

Authorities could go further and consider something like Italy's so-called "repentant program," in which convicted terrorists were offered reduced sentences in return for their cooperation. This kind of program differs from routine plea-bargaining and from efforts abroad to rehabilitate terrorists. A "repentant" program would reward those who not only provide authorities with operational intelligence, but also contribute to understanding the recruitment process itself, and who actively participate in efforts to discourage others from following the same destructive path. It would let the denunciations of al Qaeda motivator al-Awlaki come from his own acolytes.

Local Authorities are Best Placed to Counter Recruiting

Preventing future terrorist attacks will require the active cooperation of the American Muslim community, which is the target of jihadist recruiting. It will require effective domestic intelligence collection. Both are best accomplished by local authorities.

The first line of defense against radicalization and recruitment to jihadist terrorism in the Muslim-American community *is* the Muslim-American community. America's invasion of Iraq, its support for Ethiopia's invasion of Somalia, and its current military efforts in Afghanistan and Pakistan have created some pockets of resentment, but polls indicate little support for al Qaeda's jihadist fantasies among American Muslims. Cooperation against terrorism means more than the public denunciations of al Qaeda that many non-Muslim Americans demand as proof of Muslims' patriotism, nor should tips to police be the sole metric.

Much of the defense against jihadist radicalization will be invisible—quiet discouragement, interventions by family members and friends, and when necessary, discreet assistance to the authorities. Reports indicate that this is already taking place.

Community policing can maintain the cooperation that is needed. This does not involve police in religious or political debates, which are matters for the community. It requires building and maintaining trust between the community and local authorities and understanding local communities and diasporas, their problems, and their concerns.

Community cooperation will not prevent all terrorist attempts. Respected community leaders may have limited influence over more radical elements or may have no clue about tiny conspiracies or individuals who are on an interior journey to terrorism.

Members of the community must realize that while they play an important role in discouraging terrorism, they cannot be intermediaries in criminal investigations or intelligence operations aimed at preventing terrorist attacks. American Muslims should not regard themselves or be perceived by others as targets because they are Muslims. But being Muslim brings no privileged or separate status.

Disruption of Terrorist Plots: An Undeniable Intelligence Success

Twenty-five of the reported cases of homegrown terrorism involved plots to carry out attacks in the United States. Only three— including the failed Times Square bombing attempt—got as far as implementation, an undeniable intelligence success. And no doubt, other terrorist plots have been disrupted without arrests, while the publicized success of authorities has had a deterrent effect on still other plotters.

Intelligence has improved since 9/11. Federal government agencies share more information with each other and with local police departments and fusion centers, although there are still some problems. But connecting dots is not enough, and the emphasis on information-sharing should not distract us from the difficult and delicate task of domestic intelligence collection.

Domestic Intelligence Collection Remains Haphazard

The diffuse nature of today's terrorist threat and the emphasis on do-it-yourself terrorism challenge the presumption that knowledge of terrorist plots will come first to federal authorities, who will then share this information with state and local authorities. It is just as likely—perhaps more likely—that local law enforcement could be the first to pick up the clues of future conspiracies.

Local police departments are best placed to collect domestic intelligence. Their ethnic composition reflects the local community. They know the territory. They don't rotate to a new city every three or four years. They report to local authorities. But they often lack an understanding of intelligence and require resources and training.

Despite the clear need for improved domestic intelligence, collection remains haphazard. The Joint Terrorism Task Forces are extremely effective, but they are case-oriented, and investigation differs from intelligence. The fusion centers are venues for sharing information and have diverse responsibilities, but few collect intelligence.

An Army of On-Line Jihadists but Few Terrorists

The Internet plays an important role in contemporary terrorism, as jihadists have effectively demonstrated. It allows global communications, critical to a movement determined to build an army of believers. It facilitates recruiting. It is accessible to seekers, reinforcing and channeling their anger.

It creates online communities of like-minded extremists, engaging them in constant activity. It is a source of instruction. It facilitates clandestine communication.

The Internet, however, has not enabled al Qaeda, despite its high volume of sophisticated communications, to provoke a global intifada. Its websites and chat rooms outnumber its Western recruits. Its on-line exhortations to Americans have produced a very meager return—an army of on-line jihadists, but only a tiny cohort of terrorists in the real world. And while the Internet offers would-be terrorists a continuing tutorial on tactics and improvised weapons, again thus far, this has not yet significantly improved terrorist skills.

Moreover, the Internet provides insights into jihadist thinking and strategy and has proved to be a source of intelligence leading to arrests. This must be kept in perspective when considering countermeasures. These might include ways to address the issue of anonymity and facilitate investigations—and here, terrorist use of the Internet represents only one facet of a much larger problem of cyber-crime.

I have no doubt that jihadists will attempt further terrorist attacks. Some will succeed. That is war. But I also have no doubt that these attacks will not defeat this republic or destroy its values without our active complicity, as long as we do not yield to terror.

Source: "Internet Terror Recruiting and Tradecraft: How Can We Address an Evolving Tool While Protecting Free Speech." Hearing before the Subcommittee on Intelligence, Information Sharing, and Terrorism Risk Assessment, May 26, 2010. Serial No. 111–67. Washington, DC: Government Printing Office, 2010.

Analysis: It is illustrative that Jenkins notes a significant rise in radicalization efforts and homegrown jihadism beginning in 2009.

This shift was a deliberate effort on the part of al-Qaeda to conduct some form of attacks within the United States, and suggests that U.S. efforts at national security and counterterrorism had inhibited the chances of al-Qaeda operatives infiltrating and attacking. Instead, al-Qaeda recruiters began to focus upon the use of the Internet for communication with potential radicals within the United States, focusing upon the young and marginalized elements of Muslim communities in America. Although this approach yielded some successes, the net effect has not been close to what al-Qaeda leadership hoped to achieve. Jenkins argues that the key to preventing homegrown terrorism is to control the narrative that surrounds such activities, and prevent the potential actors from being seen as anything but pathetic criminals bent upon destruction, far from the heroic image that many have been presented as the ideal.

II. National Strategy for Counterterrorism

When: July 2011
Where: Washington, DC
Significance: Although the 2010 National Security Strategy placed much less emphasis upon the threat of terrorism than previous editions, President Obama's administration released a stand-alone document to discuss the overarching strategy governing the U.S. counterterrorism efforts under his regime.

DOCUMENT:

Overview of the National Strategy for Counterterrorism
This National Strategy for Counterterrorism articulates our government's approach to countering terrorism and identifies the range of tools critical to this Strategy's success. This Strategy builds on groundwork laid by previous strategies and many aspects of the United States Government's enduring approach to countering terrorism. At the same time, it outlines an approach that is more focused and specific than were previous strategies.

The United States deliberately uses the word "war" to describe our relentless campaign against al-Qa'ida. However, this Administration has made it clear that we are not at war with the tactic of terrorism or the religion of Islam. We are at war with a specific organization—al-Qa'ida.

U.S. efforts require a multidepartmental and multinational effort that goes beyond traditional intelligence, military, and law enforcement functions. We are engaged in a broad, sustained, and integrated campaign that harnesses every tool of American power—military, civilian, and the power of our values—together with the concerted efforts of allies, partners, and multilateral institutions. These efforts must also be complemented by broader capabilities, such as diplomacy, development, strategic communications, and the power of the private sector. In addition, there will continue to be many opportunities for the Executive Branch to work with Congress, consistent with our laws and our values, to further empower our counterterrorism professionals with the tools and resources necessary to maximize the effectiveness of our efforts.

Structure of the Strategy. This Strategy sets out our overarching goals and the steps necessary to achieve them. It also includes specific areas of focus tailored to the regions, domains, and groups that are most important to achieving the President's goal of disrupting, dismantling, and defeating al-Qa'ida and its affiliates and adherents while protecting the American people.

The *Overarching Goals* articulate the desired end states that we aim to create, understanding that success requires integrated, enduring, and adaptive efforts. Success also requires strategic patience: Although some of these end states may not be realized for many years, they will remain the focus of what the United States aims to achieve.

The *Areas of Focus* are the specific regions and al-Qa'ida-affiliated groups that the Strategy prioritizes.

The Threat We Face

The preeminent security threat to the United States continues to be from *al-Qa'ida and its affiliates and adherents.*

A decade after the September 11, 2001 terrorist attacks, the United States remains at war with al-Qa'ida. Although the United States did not seek this conflict, we remain committed, in conjunction with our partners worldwide, to disrupt, dismantle, and eventually defeat al-Qa'ida and its affiliates and adherents to ensure the security of our citizens and interests.

The death of Usama bin Laden marked the most important strategic milestone in our effort to defeat al-Qa'ida. It removed al-Qa'ida's founder and leader and most influential advocate for attacking the United States and its interests abroad. But, as the President has made clear, Usama bin Laden's demise does not mark the end of our effort. Nor does it mark the end of al-Qa'ida, which will remain focused on striking the United States and our interests abroad.

Since 2001 the United States has worked with its partners around the globe to put relentless pressure on al-Qa'ida—disrupting terrorist plots, measurably reducing the financial support available to the group, and

inflicting significant leadership losses. Despite our many successes, al-Qa'ida continues to pose a direct and significant threat to the United States.

In addition to plotting and carrying out specific attacks, al-Qa'ida seeks to inspire a broader conflict against the United States and many of our allies and partners. To rally individuals and groups to its cause, al-Qa'ida preys on local grievances and propagates a self-serving historical and political account. It draws on a distorted interpretation of Islam to justify the murder of Muslim and non-Muslim innocents. Countering this ideology—which has been rejected repeatedly and unequivocally by people of all faiths around the world—is an essential element of our strategy.

Although its brutal tactics and mass murder of Muslims have undermined its appeal, al-Qa'ida has had some success in rallying individuals and other militant groups to its cause. Where its ideology does resonate, the United States faces an evolving threat from groups and individuals that accept al-Qa'ida's agenda, whether through formal alliance, loose affiliation, or mere inspiration. Affiliated movements have taken root far beyond al-Qa'ida's core leadership in Afghanistan and Pakistan, including in the Middle East, East Africa, the Maghreb and Sahel regions of northwest Africa, Central Asia, and Southeast Asia. Although each group is unique, all aspire to advance al-Qa'ida's regional and global agenda—by destabilizing the countries in which they train and operate, attacking U.S. and other Western interests in the region, and in some cases plotting to strike the U.S. Homeland.

Adherence to al-Qa'ida's ideology may not require allegiance to al-Qa'ida, the organization. Individuals who sympathize with or actively support al-Qa'ida may be inspired to violence and can pose an ongoing threat, even if they have little or no formal contact with al-Qa'ida. Global communications and connectivity place al-Qa'ida's calls for violence and instructions for carrying it out within easy reach of millions. Precisely because its leadership is under such pressure in Afghanistan and Pakistan, al-Qa'ida has increasingly sought to inspire others to commit attacks in its name. Those who in the past have attempted attacks in the United States have come from a wide range of backgrounds and origins, including U.S. citizens and individuals with varying degrees of overseas connections and affinities.

Beyond al-Qa'ida, other foreign terrorist organizations threaten U.S. national security interests. These groups seek to undermine the security and stability of allied and partner governments, foment regional conflicts, traffic in narcotics, or otherwise pursue agendas that are inimical to U.S. interests. Whether these are groups that operate globally, as Hizballah or Hamas do, or are terrorist organizations located and focused domestically, we are committed to working vigorously and aggressively to counter their efforts and activities even as we avoid conflating them and al-Qa'ida into a single enemy.

Principles That Guide our Counterterrorism Efforts

Although the terrorist organizations that threaten us are far from monolithic, our CT efforts are guided by core principles: Adhering to U.S. Core Values; Building Security Partnerships; Applying CT Tools and Capabilities Appropriately; and Building a Culture of Resilience

We are committed to upholding our most cherished values as a nation not just because doing so is right but also because doing so enhances our security. Adherence to those core values—respecting human rights, fostering good governance, respecting privacy and civil liberties, committing to security and transparency, and upholding the rule of law—enables us to build broad international coalitions to act against the common threat posed by our adversaries while further delegitimizing, isolating, and weakening their efforts.

The United States is dedicated to upholding the rule of law by maintaining an effective, durable legal framework for CT operations and bringing terrorists to justice. U.S. efforts with partners are central to achieving our CT goals, and we are committed to building security partnerships even as we recognize and work to improve shortfalls in our cooperation with partner nations.

Our CT efforts must also address both near and long-term considerations—taking timely action to protect the American people while ensuring that our efforts are in the long-term security interests of our country. Our approach to political change in the Middle East and North Africa illustrates that promoting representative and accountable governance is a core tenet of U.S. foreign policy and directly contributes to our CT goals.

At the same time, we recognize that no nation, no matter how powerful, can prevent every threat from coming to fruition. That is why we are focused on building a culture of resilience able to prevent, respond to, or recover fully from any potential act of terror directed at the United States.

Adhering to U.S. Core Values

The United States was founded upon a belief in a core set of values that is written into our founding documents and woven into the very fabric of our society. Where terrorists offer injustice, disorder, and destruction the United States must stand for freedom, fairness, equality, dignity, hope, and opportunity. The power and appeal of our values enables the United States to build a broad coalition to act collectively against the common threat posed by terrorists, further delegitimizing, isolating, and weakening our adversaries.

- Respect for Human Rights. Our respect for universal rights stands in stark contrast with the actions of al-Qa'ida, its affiliates and adherents, and other terrorist organizations. Contrasting a positive U.S. agenda that supports the rights of free speech, assembly, and democracy with the death and destruction offered by our terrorist adversaries helps undermine and undercut their appeal, isolating them from the very population they rely on for support. Our respect for universal rights must include living them through our own actions. Cruel and inhumane interrogation methods are not only inconsistent with U.S. values, they undermine the rule of law and are ineffective means of gaining the intelligence required to counter the threats we face. We will maximize our ability to collect intelligence from individuals in detention by relying on our most effective tool—the skill, expertise, and professionalism of our personnel.
- Encouraging Responsive Governance. Promoting representative, responsive governance is a core tenet of U.S. foreign policy and directly contributes to our CT goals. Governments that place the will of their people first and encourage peaceful change directly contradict the al-Qa'ida ideology. Governments that are responsive to the needs of their citizens diminish the discontent of their people and the associated drivers and grievances that al-Qa'ida actively attempts to exploit. Effective governance reduces the traction and space for al-Qa'ida, reducing

its resonance and contributing to what it fears most—irrelevance.
- Respect for Privacy Rights, Civil Liberties, and Civil Rights. Respect for privacy rights, civil liberties, and civil rights is a critical component of our Strategy. Indeed, preservation of those rights and liberties is essential to maintain the support of the American people for our CT efforts. By ensuring that CT policies and tools are narrowly tailored and applied to achieve specific, concrete security gains, the United States will optimize its security and protect the liberties of its citizens.
- Balancing Security and Transparency. Democratic institutions function best in an environment of transparency and open discussion of national issues. Wherever and whenever possible, the United States will make information available to the American people about the threats we face and the steps being taken to mitigate those threats. A well-informed American public is a source of our strength. Information enables the public to make informed judgments about its own security, act responsibly and with resilience in the face of adversity or attack, and contribute its vigilance to the country's collective security. Yet at times, some information must be protected from disclosure—to protect personnel and our sources and methods of gathering information and to preserve our ability to counter the attack plans of terrorists.

Upholding the Rule of Law. Our commitment to the rule of law is fundamental to supporting the development of an international, regional, and local order that is capable of identifying and disrupting terrorist attacks, bringing terrorists to justice for their acts, and creating an environment in every country around the world that is inhospitable to terrorists and terrorist organizations.

Maintaining an Effective, Durable Legal Framework for CT Operations. In the immediate aftermath of the September 11, 2001 attacks, the United States Government was confronted with countering the terrorist threat in an environment of legal uncertainty in which long-established legal rules were applied to circumstances not seen before in this country. Since then we have refined and applied a legal framework that ensures all CT activities and operations are placed on a solid legal footing. Moving forward, we must ensure that this legal framework remains both effective and durable. To remain effective, this framework must provide the necessary tools to defeat U.S. adversaries and maintain the safety of the American people. To remain durable this framework must withstand legal challenge, survive scrutiny, and earn the support of Congress and the American people as well as our partners and allies. It must also maintain sufficient flexibility to adjust to the changing threat and environment.

Bringing Terrorists to Justice. The successful prosecution of terrorists will continue to play a critical role in U.S. CT efforts, enabling the United States to disrupt and deter terrorist activity; gather intelligence from those lawfully held in U.S. custody; dismantle organizations by incarcerating key members and operatives; and gain a measure of justice by prosecuting those who have plotted or participated in attacks. We will work with our foreign partners to build their willingness and capacity to bring to justice suspected terrorists who operate within their borders. When other countries are unwilling or unable to take action against terrorists within their borders who threaten the United States, they should be taken into U.S. custody

and tried in U.S. civilian courts or by military commission.

Building Security Partnerships

The United States alone cannot eliminate every terrorist or terrorist organization that threatens our safety, security, or interests. Therefore, we must join with key partners and allies to share the burdens of common security.

- *Accepting Varying Degrees of Partnership.* The United States and its partners are engaged in the full range of cooperative CT activities—from intelligence sharing to joint training and operations and from countering radicalization to pursuing community resilience programs. The United States partners best with nations that share our common values, have similar democratic institutions, and bring a long history of collaboration in pursuit of our shared security. With these partners the habits of cooperation established in other security-related settings have transferred themselves relatively smoothly and efficiently to CT.

In some cases partnerships are in place with countries with whom the United States has very little in common except for the desire to defeat al-Qa'ida and its affiliates and adherents. These partners may not share U.S. values or even our broader vision of regional and global security. Yet it is in our interest to build habits and patterns of CT cooperation with such partners, working to push them in a direction that advances CT objectives while demonstrating through our example the value of upholding human rights and responsible governance. Furthermore, these partners will ultimately be more stable and successful if they move toward these principles.

- *Leveraging Multilateral Institutions.* To counter violent extremists who work in scores of countries around the globe, the United States is drawing on the resources and strengthening the activities of multilateral institutions at the international, regional, and subregional levels. Working with and through these institutions can have multiple benefits: It increases the engagement of our partners, reduces the financial burden on the United States, and enhances the legitimacy of our CT efforts by advancing our objectives without a unilateral, U.S. label. The United States is committed to strengthening the global CT architecture in a manner that complements and reinforces the CT work of existing multilateral bodies. In doing so, we seek to avoid duplicating and diluting our own or our partners' efforts, recognizing that many of our partners have capacity limitations and cannot participate adequately across too broad a range of multilateral fora.

Source: White House. National Strategy for Counterterrorism, June 2011, https://obamawhitehouse .archives.gov/blog/2011/06/29/national-strategy -counterterrorism.

Analysis: As a public document, the National Strategy for Counterterrorism obviously cannot reveal the tactical plans for the United States regarding military, law enforcement, and intelligence agency activities regarding terrorist organizations. Rather, the document is intended to explain the broad foundations of the U.S. approach to winning the war on terror. In particular, the refusal to forego fundamental rights guaranteed by the Constitution, even in the face of a terrorist threat, is key to understanding the federal approach to counterterrorism. Furthermore, the United States offers a competing vision for the means by which different cultures and nations should interact with one another, on the grounds of mutual respect and acceptance of diversity. It is important to note the strong international partnership approach preferred by the Obama administration, which is in stark contrast to the Bush administration's position that in the war on terror, there can be no neutral ground, and thus nations were either with or against the United States. The hard line adopted by Bush alienated many world leaders, while the Obama administration attempted to bring as many nations into the coalition against terrorism as possible.

12. Executive Order 13584 of September 9, 2011

When: Thursday, September 15, 2011
Where: Washington, DC
Significance: This order was intended to put the United States on more firm footing with winning the "battle of the narrative" against terrorist and insurgent groups. Despite having one of the world's strongest militaries, the United States has consistently fallen short in its ability to counter terrorists' use of the Internet to both recruit new followers and terrorize their adversaries. Although this document was signed in 2011, proof of America's inability to counter terrorists' use of social media has been evident in the long-running conflict with the Islamic State of Iraq and Syria (ISIS), which has relied to a great extent on the Internet to spread its messages to followers around the globe.

Document: Executive Order 13584 of September 9, 2011

Developing an Integrated Strategic Counterterrorism Communications Initiative

and Establishing a Temporary Organization to Support Certain Government-Wide Communications Activities Directed Abroad

By the authority vested in me as President by the Constitution and the laws of the United States of America, including section 2656 of title 22, United States Code, and section 3161 of title 5, United States Code, it is hereby ordered as follows:

Section 1. *Policy.* The United States is committed to actively countering the actions and ideologies of al-Qa'ida, its affiliates and adherents, other terrorist organizations, and violent extremists overseas that threaten the interests and national security of the United States. These efforts take many forms, but all contain a communications element and some use of communications strategies directed to audiences outside the United States to counter the ideology and activities of such organizations. These communications strategies focus not only on the violent actions and human costs of terrorism, but also on narratives that can positively influence those who may be susceptible to radicalization and recruitment by terrorist organizations.

The purpose of this Executive Order is to reinforce, integrate, and complement public communications efforts across the executive branch that are (1) focused on countering the actions and ideology of al-Qa'ida, its affiliates and adherents, and other international terrorist organizations and violent extremists overseas, and (2) directed to audiences outside the United States. This collaborative work among executive departments and agencies (agencies) brings together expertise, capabilities, and resources to realize efficiencies and better coordination of U.S. Government communications investments to combat terrorism and extremism.

Sec. 2. *Assigned Responsibilities to the Center for Strategic Counterterrorism Communications.*

(a) Under the direction of the Secretary of State (Secretary), the Center for Strategic Counterterrorism Communications (Center) that has been established in the Department of State by the Secretary shall coordinate, orient, and inform Government-wide public communications activities directed at audiences abroad and targeted against violent extremists and terrorist organizations, especially al-Qa'ida and its affiliates and adherents, with the goal of using communication tools to reduce radicalization by terrorists and extremist violence and terrorism that threaten the interests and national security of the United States. Consistent with section 404o of title 50, United States Code, the Center shall coordinate its analysis, evaluation, and planning functions with the National Counterterrorism Center. The Center shall also coordinate these functions with other agencies, as appropriate.

Executive branch efforts undertaken through the Center shall draw on all agencies with relevant information or capabilities, to prepare, plan for, and conduct these communications efforts.

(b) To achieve these objectives, the Center's functions shall include:

(i) monitoring and evaluating narratives (overarching communication themes that reflect a community's identity, experiences, aspirations, and concerns) and events abroad that are relevant to the development of a U.S. strategic counterterrorism narrative designed to counter violent extremism and terrorism that threaten the interests and national security of the United States;

(ii) developing and promulgating for use throughout the executive branch the U.S. strategic counterterrorism narratives and public communications strategies to counter the messaging of violent extremists and terrorist organizations, especially al-Qa'ida and its affiliates and adherents;

(iii) identifying current and emerging trends in extremist communications and communications by al-Qa'ida and its affiliates and adherents in order to coordinate and provide thematic guidance to U.S. Government communicators on how best to proactively promote the U.S. strategic counterterrorism narrative and policies and to respond to and rebut extremist messaging and narratives when communicating to audiences outside the United States, as informed by a wide variety of Government and non-government sources, including non-governmental organizations, academic sources, and finished intelligence created by the intelligence community;

(iv) facilitating the use of a wide range of communications technologies, including digital tools, by sharing expertise among agencies, seeking expertise from external sources, and extending best practices; (v) identifying and requesting relevant information from agencies, including intelligence reporting, data, and analysis; and (vi) identifying shortfalls in U.S. capabilities in any areas relevant to the Center's mission and recommending necessary enhancements or changes.

(c) The Secretary shall establish a Steering Committee composed of senior representatives of agencies relevant to the Center's mission to provide advice to the Secretary on the operations and strategic orientation of the Center and to ensure adequate support for the Center. The Steering Committee shall meet not less than every 6 months. The Steering Committee shall be chaired by the Under Secretary of State for Public Diplomacy. The Coordinator for Counterterrorism of the Department of State shall serve as Vice Chair. The Coordinator of the Center shall serve as Executive Secretary. The Steering Committee shall include one senior representative designated by the head of each of the following agencies: the Department of Defense, the Department of Justice, the Department of Homeland Security, the Department of the Treasury, the National Counterterrorism Center, the Joint Chiefs of Staff, the Counterterrorism Center of the Central Intelligence Agency, the Broadcast Board of Governors, and the Agency for International Development. Other agencies may be invited to participate in the Steering Committee at the discretion of the Chair.

Sec. 3. *Establishment of a Temporary Organization.*

(a) There is established within the Department of State, in accordance with section 3161 of title 5, United States Code, a temporary organization to be known as the Counterterrorism Communications Support Office (CCSO).

(b) The purpose of the CCSO shall be to perform the specific project of supporting agencies in Government-wide public communications activities targeted against violent extremism and terrorist organizations, especially al-Qa'ida and its affiliates and adherents, to audiences abroad by using communication tools designed to counter violent extremism and terrorism that threaten the interests and national security of the United States.

(c) In carrying out its purpose set forth in subsection (b) of this section, the CCSO shall:

(i) support agencies in their implementation of whole-of-government public communications activities directed at audiences abroad, including by providing baseline research on characteristics of these audiences, by developing expertise and studies on aspirations, narratives, information strategies and tactics of violent extremists and terrorist organizations overseas, by designing and developing sustained campaigns on specific areas of interest to audiences abroad, and by developing expertise on implementing highly focused social media campaigns; and

(ii) perform such other functions related to the specific project set forth in subsection (b) of this section as the Secretary may assign.

(d) The CCSO shall be headed by a Director selected by the Secretary, with the advice of the Steering Committee. Its staff may include, as determined by the Secretary: (1) personnel with relevant expertise detailed on a non-reimbursable basis from other agencies; (2) senior and other technical advisers; and (3) such other personnel as the Secretary may direct to support the CCSO. To accomplish this mission, the heads of agencies participating on the Steering Committee shall provide to the CCSO, on a non-reimbursable basis, assistance, services, and other support including but not limited to logistical and administrative support and details of personnel. Non-reimbursable details shall be based on reasonable requests from the Secretary in light of the need for specific expertise, and after consultation with the relevant agency, to the extent permitted by law.

(e) The CCSO shall terminate at the end of the maximum period permitted by section 3161(a)(1) of title 5, United States Code, unless sooner terminated by the Secretary consistent with section 3161(a)(2) of such title.

Sec. 4. *General Provisions.*

(a) Nothing in this order shall be construed to impair or otherwise affect:

(i) authority granted by law to an agency, or the head thereof; or

(ii) functions of the Director of the Office of Management and Budget relating to budgetary, administrative, or legislative proposals.

(b) This order shall be implemented consistent with applicable law and subject to the availability of appropriations.

(c) This order is not intended to, and does not, create any right or benefit, substantive or procedural, enforceable at law or in equity by any party against the United States, its departments, agencies, or entities, its officers, employees, or agents, or any other person.

THE WHITE HOUSE,

September 9, 2011.

Source: The White House Office of the Press Secretary, https://obamawhitehouse.archives.gov/the-press-office/2011/09/09/executive-order-13584-developing-integrated-strategic-counterterrorism-c.

Analysis: This document is essentially a recognition that the United States needs to improve its abilities—across the entire spectrum of government—to counter the actions, activities, and ideology of al-Qaeda and other violent extremist groups whose messages retain broad resonance with large segments of varying populations. By passing an executive order, the Obama administration sought to provide legislation that would back the requirements necessary to become more effective in communicating strategically to both U.S. adversaries and allies. As noted in the document, these communications strategies laid out focus on both the human costs of terrorism as well as the narratives that often influence populations and individuals susceptible to radicalization and recruitment by terrorist organizations. In some ways, this document can be considered a precursor to other initiatives that would follow and continue today, including programs to counter violent extremism (CVE), radicalization, and homegrown terrorism within the United States.

13. President Obama's Address to the Nation on U.S. Counterterrorism Strategy

When: December 6, 2015
Where: Washington, DC
Significance: Four days before these remarks, two radicalized individuals entered a community center in San Bernardino, California, and opened fire upon a meeting with semi-automatic weapons. They killed 14 civilians and wounded more than a dozen. Hours later, the suspects were killed in a firefight with local law enforcement. As the investigation unfolded, the president chose to offer remarks on the incident in a national address.

DOCUMENT:

Good evening. On Wednesday, 14 Americans were killed as they came together to celebrate the holidays. They were taken from family and friends who loved them deeply. They were White and Black, Latino and Asian, immigrants and American-born, moms and dads, daughters and sons. Each of them served their fellow citizens, and all of them were part of our American family.

Tonight I want to talk with you about this tragedy, the broader threat of terrorism, and how we can keep our country safe.

The FBI is still gathering the facts about what happened in San Bernardino, but here is what we know. The victims were brutally murdered and injured by one of their coworkers and his wife. So far, we have no evidence that the killers were directed by a terrorist organization overseas or that they were part of a broader conspiracy here at home. But it is clear that the two of them have—had gone down the dark path of radicalization, embracing a perverted interpretation of Islam that calls for war against America and the West. They had stockpiled assault weapons, ammunition, and pipe bombs. So this was an act of terrorism, designed to kill innocent people.

Our Nation has been at war with terrorists since Al Qaida killed nearly 3,000 Americans on 9/11. In the process, we've hardened our defenses, from airports to financial centers to other critical infrastructure. Intelligence and law enforcement agencies have disrupted countless plots here and overseas and worked around the clock to keep us safe. Our military and counterterrorism professionals have relentlessly pursued terrorist networks overseas, disrupting safe havens in several different countries, killing Usama bin Laden, and decimating Al Qaida's leadership.

Over the last few years, however, the terrorist threat has evolved into a new phase. As we've become better at preventing complex, multifaceted attacks like 9/11, terrorists turned to less complicated acts of violence like the mass shootings that are all too common in our society. It is this type of attack that we saw at Fort Hood in 2009, in Chattanooga earlier this year, and now in San Bernardino. And as groups like ISIL grew stronger amidst the chaos of war in Iraq and then Syria, and as the Internet erases the distance between countries, we see growing efforts by terrorists to poison the minds of people like the Boston Marathon bombers and the San Bernardino killers.

For 7 years, I have confronted this evolving threat each morning in my intelligence briefing. And since the day I took this office, I've authorized U.S. forces to take out terrorists abroad precisely because I know how real the danger is. As Commander in Chief, I have no greater responsibility than the security of the American people. As a father to two young daughters who are the most precious part of my life, I know that we see ourselves with friends and coworkers at a holiday party like the one in San Bernardino. I know we see our kids in the faces of the young people killed in Paris. And I know that after so much war, many Americans are asking whether we are confronted by a cancer that has no immediate cure.

Well, here's what I want you to know: The threat from terrorism is real, but we will overcome it. We will destroy ISIL and any other organization that tries to harm us. Our success won't depend on tough talk or abandoning our values or giving into fear. That's what groups like ISIL are hoping for. Instead, we will prevail by being strong and smart, resilient and relentless, and by drawing upon every aspect of American power.

Here's how. First, our military will continue to hunt down terrorist plotters in any country where it is necessary. In Iraq and Syria, airstrikes are taking out ISIL leaders, heavy weapons, oil tankers, infrastructure. And since the attacks in Paris, our closest allies—including France, Germany, and the United Kingdom—have ramped up their contributions to our military campaign, which will help us accelerate our effort to destroy ISIL.

Second, we will continue to provide training and equipment to tens of thousands of Iraqi and Syrian forces fighting ISIL on the ground so that we take away their safe havens. In both countries, we're deploying special operations forces who can accelerate that offensive. We've stepped up this effort since the attacks in Paris, and we'll continue to invest more in approaches that are working on the ground.

Third, we're working with friends and allies to stop ISIL's operations: to disrupt plots, cut off their financing, and prevent them from recruiting more fighters. Since the attacks in Paris, we've surged intelligence sharing with our European allies. We're working with Turkey to seal its border with Syria. And we are cooperating with Muslim-majority countries—and with our Muslim communities here at home—to counter the vicious ideology that ISIL promotes online.

Fourth, with American leadership, the international community has begin—begun to establish a process—and timeline—to pursue ceasefires and a political resolution to the Syrian war. Doing so will allow the Syrian people and every country, including our allies, but also countries like Russia, to focus on the common goal of destroying ISIL, a group that threatens us all.

This is our strategy to destroy ISIL. It is designed and supported by our military commanders and counterterrorism experts, together with 65 countries that have joined an American-led coalition. And we constantly examine our strategy to determine when additional steps are needed to get the job done. That's why I've ordered the Departments of State and Homeland Security to review the visa waiver program [visa program; White House correction.] under which the female terrorist in San Bernardino originally came to this country. And that's why I will urge high-tech and law enforcement leaders to make it harder for terrorists to use technology to escape from justice.

Finally, if Congress believes, as I do, that we are at war with ISIL, it should go ahead and vote to authorize the continued use of military force against these terrorists. For over a year, I have ordered our military to take thousands of airstrikes against ISIL targets. I think it's time for Congress to vote to demonstrate that the American people are united and committed to this fight.

My fellow Americans, these are the steps that we can take together to defeat the terrorist threat. Let me now say a word about what we should not do. We should not be drawn once more into a long and costly ground war in Iraq or Syria. That's what groups like ISIL want. They know they can't defeat us on the battlefield. ISIL fighters were part of the insurgency that we faced in Iraq. But they also know that if we occupy foreign lands, they can maintain insurgencies for years, killing thousands of our troops, draining our resources, and using our presence to draw new recruits.

The strategy that we are using now—airstrikes, special forces, and working with local forces who are fighting to regain control of their own country—that is how we'll achieve a more sustainable victory. And it won't require us sending a new generation of Americans overseas to fight and die for another decade on foreign soil.

Here's what else we cannot do. We cannot turn against one another by letting this fight

be defined as a war between America and Islam. That too is what groups like ISIL want. ISIL does not speak for Islam. They are thugs and killers, part of a cult of death, and they account for a tiny fraction of more than a billion Muslims around the world, including millions of patriotic Muslim Americans who reject their hateful ideology. Moreover, the vast majority of terrorist victims around the world are Muslim. If we're to succeed in defeating terrorism, we must enlist Muslim communities as some of our strongest allies, rather than push them away through suspicion and hate.

That does not mean denying the fact that an extremist ideology has spread within some Muslim communities. This is a real problem that Muslims must confront, without excuse. Muslim leaders here and around the globe have to continue working with us: to decisively and unequivocally reject the hateful ideology that groups like ISIL and Al Qaida promote; to speak out against not just acts of violence, but also those interpretations of Islam that are incompatible with the values of religious tolerance, mutual respect, and human dignity.

But just as it is the responsibility of Muslims around the world to root out misguided ideas that lead to radicalization, it is the responsibility of all Americans, of every faith, to reject discrimination. It is our responsibility to reject religious tests on who we admit into this country. It's our responsibility to reject proposals that Muslim Americans should somehow be treated differently. Because when we travel down that road, we lose. That kind of divisiveness, that betrayal of our values, plays into the hands of groups like ISIL. Muslim Americans are our friends and our neighbors, our coworkers, our sports heroes. And yes, they are our men and women in uniform who are willing to die in defense of our country. We have to remember that.

My fellow Americans, I am confident we will succeed in this mission because we are on the right side of history. We were founded upon a belief in human dignity, that no matter who you are or where you come from or what you look like or what religion you practice, you are equal in the eyes of God and equal in the eyes of the law. Even in this political season, even as we properly debate what steps I and future Presidents must take to keep our country safe, let's make sure we never forget what makes us exceptional. Let's not forget that freedom is more powerful than fear; that we have always met challenges—whether war or depression, natural disasters or terrorist attacks—by coming together around our common ideals as one Nation and one people. So long as we stay true to that tradition, I have no doubt America will prevail.

Thank you. God bless you, and may God bless the United States of America.

Source: Weekly Compilation of Presidential Documents, 2015, no. 0874, https://www.gpo.gov/fdsys/browse/collection.action?collectionCode=CPD

Analysis: The San Bernardino attacks resulted in one of the deadliest terror attacks in U.S. history. The perpetrators, Syed Rizwan Farook and Tashfeen Malik, were soon proven to be radical Islamists who had pledged their support to the Islamic State. Malik, who had entered the United States on a fiancé visa, appeared to be the first of the pair to be radicalized, marking one of the rare known occurrences of a wife radicalizing her husband. The couple left behind a two-year old child, an action that also does not fit the normal profile of lone-wolf attackers.

President Obama took pains to remind the nation that the vast majority of Muslims do not agree with the aims of the Islamic State, but in a nod to the political realities, he did acknowledge the dangers associated with radicalization efforts being conducted by violent extremists. Building off of the ramifications of a single attack, the President called for Congress to renew and expand the authorization to use military force to explicitly allow military attacks against the Islamic State.

14. Executive Order 13780 of March 6, 2017

When: March 9, 2017
Where: Washington, DC, Federal Register Vol. 82, No. 45
Significance: This order was essentially labeled a "Muslim ban" by the popular media and was extremely unpopular with large swaths of the American public, leading to a major backlash against the Trump administration. Thousands of Americans across the country protested the ban, with many arguing that several countries *not* listed on the order—Saudi Arabia and Pakistan, to name a few—posed an even more dire threat to the United States but were not listed due to politics. As of late 2017, the ban had been revised and was still undergoing scrutiny in various federal courts.

Executive Order 13780 of March 6, 2017

Protecting the Nation From Foreign Terrorist Entry Into the United States
By the authority vested in me as President by the Constitution and the laws of the United States of America, including the Immigration and Nationality Act (INA), 8 U.S.C. 1101 et seq., and section 301 of title 3, United States Code, and to protect the

Nation from terrorist activities by foreign nationals admitted to the United States, it is hereby ordered as follows:

Section 1. *Policy and Purpose.* (a) It is the policy of the United States to protect its citizens from terrorist attacks, including those committed by foreign nationals. The screening and vetting protocols and procedures associated with the visa-issuance process and the United States Refugee Admissions Program (USRAP) play a crucial role in detecting foreign nationals who may commit, aid, or support acts of terrorism and in preventing those individuals from entering the United States. It is therefore the policy of the United States to improve the screening and vetting protocols and procedures associated with the visa-issuance process and the USRAP.

(b) On January 27, 2017, to implement this policy, I issued Executive Order 13769 (Protecting the Nation from Foreign Terrorist Entry into the United States).

(i) Among other actions, Executive Order 13769 suspended for 90 days the entry of certain aliens from seven countries: Iran, Iraq, Libya, Somalia, Sudan, Syria, and Yemen. These are countries that had already been identified as presenting heightened concerns about terrorism and travel to the United States. Specifically, the suspension applied to countries referred to in, or designated under, section 217(a)(12) of the INA, 8 U.S.C. 1187(a)(12), in which Congress restricted use of the Visa Waiver Program for nationals of, and aliens recently present in, (A) Iraq or Syria, (B) any country designated by the Secretary of State as a state sponsor of terrorism (currently Iran, Syria, and Sudan), and (C) any other country designated as a country of concern by the Secretary of Homeland Security, in consultation with the Secretary of State and the Director of National Intelligence. In 2016, the Secretary of Homeland Security designated Libya, Somalia, and Yemen as additional countries of concern for travel purposes, based on consideration of three statutory factors related to terrorism and national security: "(I) whether the presence of an alien in the country or area increases the likelihood that the alien is a credible threat to the national security of the United States; (II) whether a foreign terrorist organization has a significant presence in the country or area; and (III) whether the country or area is a safe haven for terrorists." 8 U.S.C. 1187(a)(12)(D)(ii). Additionally, Members of Congress have expressed concerns about screening and vetting procedures following recent terrorist attacks in this country and in Europe.

(ii) In ordering the temporary suspension of entry described in subsection (b)(i) of this section, I exercised my authority under Article II of the Constitution and under section 212(f) of the INA, which provides in relevant part: "Whenever the President finds that the entry of any aliens or of any class of aliens into the United States would be detrimental to the interests of the United States, he may by proclamation, and for such period as he shall deem necessary, suspend the entry of all aliens or any class of aliens as immigrants or nonimmigrants, or impose on the entry of aliens any restrictions he may deem to be appropriate." 8 U.S.C. 1182(f). Under these authorities, I determined that, for a brief period of 90 days, while existing screening and vetting procedures were under review, the entry into the United States of certain aliens from the seven identified countries—each afflicted by terrorism in a manner that compromised the ability of the United States to rely on normal decision-making procedures about travel to the United States—would be detrimental to the interests of the United States. Nonetheless, I permitted the Secretary of State and the Secretary of Homeland Security to grant case-by-case waivers when they determined that it was in the national interest to do so.

(iii) Executive Order 13769 also suspended the USRAP for 120 days. Terrorist groups have sought to infiltrate several nations through refugee programs. Accordingly, I temporarily suspended the USRAP pending a review of our procedures for screening and vetting refugees. Nonetheless, I permitted the Secretary of State and the Secretary of Homeland Security to jointly grant case-by-case waivers when they determined that it was in the national interest to do so.

(iv) Executive Order 13769 did not provide a basis for discriminating for or against members of any particular religion. While that order allowed for prioritization of refugee claims from members of persecuted religious minority groups, that priority applied to refugees from every nation, including those in which Islam is a minority religion, and it applied to minority sects within a religion. That order was not motivated by animus toward any religion, but was instead intended to protect the ability of religious minorities—whoever they are and wherever they reside—to avail themselves of the USRAP in light of their particular challenges and circumstances.

(c) The implementation of Executive Order 13769 has been delayed by litigation. Most

significantly, enforcement of critical provisions of that order has been temporarily halted by court orders that apply nationwide and extend even to foreign nationals with no prior or substantial connection to the United States. On February 9, 2017, the United States Court of Appeals for the Ninth Circuit declined to stay or narrow one such order pending the outcome of further judicial proceedings, while noting that the "political branches are far better equipped to make appropriate distinctions" about who should be covered by a suspension of entry or of refugee admissions.

(d) Nationals from the countries previously identified under section 217(a)(12) of the INA warrant additional scrutiny in connection with our immigration policies because the conditions in these countries present heightened threats. Each of these countries is a state sponsor of terrorism, has been significantly compromised by terrorist organizations, or contains active conflict zones. Any of these circumstances diminishes the foreign government's willingness or ability to share or validate important information about individuals seeking to travel to the United States. Moreover, the significant presence in each of these countries of terrorist organizations, their members, and others exposed to those organizations increases the chance that conditions will be exploited to enable terrorist operatives or sympathizers to travel to the United States. Finally, once foreign nationals from these countries are admitted to the United States, it is often difficult to remove them, because many of these countries typically delay issuing, or refuse to issue, travel documents.

(e) The following are brief descriptions, taken in part from the Department of State's Country Reports on Terrorism 2015 (June 2016), of some of the conditions in six of the previously designated countries that demonstrate why their nationals continue to present heightened risks to the security of the United States:

(i) *Iran*. Iran has been designated as a state sponsor of terrorism since 1984 and continues to support various terrorist groups, including Hizballah, Hamas, and terrorist groups in Iraq. Iran has also been linked to support for al-Qa'ida and has permitted al-Qa'ida to transport funds and fighters through Iran to Syria and South Asia. Iran does not cooperate with the United States in counterterrorism efforts.

(ii) *Libya*. Libya is an active combat zone, with hostilities between the internationally recognized government and its rivals. In many parts of the country, security and law enforcement functions are provided by armed militias rather than state institutions. Violent extremist groups, including the Islamic State of Iraq and Syria (ISIS), have exploited these conditions to expand their presence in the country. The Libyan government provides some cooperation with the United States' counterterrorism efforts, but it is unable to secure thousands of miles of its land and maritime borders, enabling the illicit flow of weapons, migrants, and foreign terrorist fighters. The United States Embassy in Libya suspended its operations in 2014.

(iii) *Somalia*. Portions of Somalia have been terrorist safe havens. Al-Shabaab, an al-Qa'ida-affiliated terrorist group, has operated in the country for years and continues to plan and mount operations within Somalia and in neighboring countries. Somalia has porous borders, and most countries do not recognize Somali identity documents. The Somali government cooperates with the United States in

some counterterrorism operations but does not have the capacity to sustain military pressure on or to investigate suspected terrorists.

(iv) *Sudan*. Sudan has been designated as a state sponsor of terrorism since 1993 because of its support for international terrorist groups, including Hizballah and Hamas. Historically, Sudan provided safe havens for al-Qa'ida and other terrorist groups to meet and train. Although Sudan's support to al-Qa'ida has ceased and it provides some cooperation with the United States' counterterrorism efforts, elements of core al-Qa'ida and ISIS-linked terrorist groups remain active in the country.

(v) *Syria*. Syria has been designated as a state sponsor of terrorism since 1979. The Syrian government is engaged in an ongoing military conflict against ISIS and others for control of portions of the country. At the same time, Syria continues to support other terrorist groups. It has allowed or encouraged extremists to pass through its territory to enter Iraq. ISIS continues to attract foreign fighters to Syria and to use its base in Syria to plot or encourage attacks around the globe, including in the United States. The United States Embassy in Syria suspended its operations in 2012. Syria does not cooperate with the United States' counterterrorism efforts.

(vi) *Yemen*. Yemen is the site of an ongoing conflict between the incumbent government and the Houthi-led opposition. Both ISIS and a second group, al-Qa'ida in the Arabian Peninsula (AQAP), have exploited this conflict to expand their presence in Yemen and to carry out hundreds of attacks. Weapons and other materials smuggled across Yemen's porous borders are used to finance AQAP and other terrorist activities. In 2015, the United States Embassy in Yemen suspended its operations, and embassy staff were relocated out of the country. Yemen has been supportive of, but has not been able to cooperate fully with, the United States in counterterrorism efforts.

(f) In light of the conditions in these six countries, until the assessment of current screening and vetting procedures required by section 2 of this order is completed, the risk of erroneously permitting entry of a national of one of these countries who intends to commit terrorist acts or otherwise harm the national security of the United States is unacceptably high. Accordingly, while that assessment is ongoing, I am imposing a temporary pause on the entry of nationals from Iran, Libya, Somalia, Sudan, Syria, and Yemen, subject to categorical exceptions and case-by-case waivers, as described in section 3 of this order.

(g) Iraq presents a special case. Portions of Iraq remain active combat zones. Since 2014, ISIS has had dominant influence over significant territory in northern and central Iraq. Although that influence has been significantly reduced due to the efforts and sacrifices of the Iraqi government and armed forces, working along with a United States-led coalition, the ongoing conflict has impacted the Iraqi government's capacity to secure its borders and to identify fraudulent travel documents. Nevertheless, the close cooperative relationship between the United States and the democratically elected Iraqi government, the strong United States diplomatic presence in Iraq, the significant presence of United States forces in Iraq, and Iraq's commitment to combat ISIS justify different treatment for Iraq. In particular, those Iraqi government forces that have fought to regain more than half of the territory previously dominated by ISIS have shown steadfast determination and earned enduring respect as they battle an armed group that is the common enemy of Iraq and the United States. In addition, since Executive Order 13769 was issued, the Iraqi government has expressly undertaken steps to enhance travel documentation, information sharing, and the return of Iraqi nationals subject to final orders of removal. Decisions about issuance of visas or granting admission to Iraqi nationals should be subjected to additional scrutiny to determine if applicants have connections with ISIS or other terrorist organizations, or otherwise pose a risk to either national security or public safety.

(h) Recent history shows that some of those who have entered the United States through our immigration system have proved to be threats to our national security. Since 2001, hundreds of persons born abroad have been convicted of terrorism-related crimes in the United States. They have included not just persons who came here legally on visas but also individuals who first entered the country as refugees. For example, in January 2013, two Iraqi nationals admitted to the United States as refugees in 2009 were sentenced to 40 years and to life in prison, respectively, for multiple terrorism-related offenses. And in October 2014, a native of Somalia who had been brought to the United States as a child refugee and later became a naturalized United States citizen was sentenced to 30 years in prison for attempting to use a weapon of mass destruction as part of a plot to detonate a bomb at a crowded Christmas-tree-lighting ceremony in Portland, Oregon. The Attorney General has reported to me that more than 300 persons who entered the United States as refugees are currently the subjects of counterterrorism investigations by the Federal Bureau of Investigation.

(i) Given the foregoing, the entry into the United States of foreign nationals who may commit, aid, or support acts of terrorism remains a matter of grave concern. In light of the Ninth Circuit's observation that the political branches are better suited to determine the appropriate scope of any suspensions than are the courts, and in order to avoid spending additional time pursuing litigation, I am revoking Executive Order 13769 and replacing it with this order, which expressly excludes from the suspensions categories of aliens that have prompted judicial concerns and which clarifies or refines the approach to certain other issues or categories of affected aliens.

Sec. 2. *Temporary Suspension of Entry for Nationals of Countries of Particular Concern During Review Period.* (a) The Secretary of Homeland Security, in consultation with the Secretary of State and the Director of National Intelligence, shall conduct a worldwide review to identify whether, and if so what, additional information will be needed from each foreign country to adjudicate an application by a national of that country for a visa, admission, or other benefit under the INA (adjudications) in order to determine that the individual is not a security or public-safety threat. The Secretary of Homeland Security may conclude that certain information is needed from particular countries even if it is not needed from every country.

(b) The Secretary of Homeland Security, in consultation with the Secretary of State and the Director of National Intelligence,

shall submit to the President a report on the results of the worldwide review described in subsection (a) of this section, including the Secretary of Homeland Security's determination of the information needed from each country for adjudications and a list of countries that do not provide adequate information, within 20 days of the effective date of this order. The Secretary of Homeland Security shall provide a copy of the report to the Secretary of State, the Attorney General, and the Director of National Intelligence.

(c) To temporarily reduce investigative burdens on relevant agencies during the review period described in subsection (a) of this section, to ensure the proper review and maximum utilization of available resources for the screening and vetting of foreign nationals, to ensure that adequate standards are established to prevent infiltration by foreign terrorists, and in light of the national security concerns referenced in section 1 of this order, I hereby proclaim, pursuant to sections 212(f) and 215(a) of the INA, 8 U.S.C. 1182(f) and 1185(a), that the unrestricted entry into the United States of nationals of Iran, Libya, Somalia, Sudan, Syria, and Yemen would be detrimental to the interests of the United States. I therefore direct that the entry into the United States of nationals of those six countries be suspended for 90 days from the effective date of this order, subject to the limitations, waivers, and exceptions set forth in sections 3 and 12 of this order.

(d) Upon submission of the report described in subsection (b) of this section regarding the information needed from each country for adjudications, the Secretary of State shall request that all foreign governments that do not supply such information regarding their nationals begin providing it within 50 days of notification.

(e) After the period described in subsection (d) of this section expires, the Secretary of Homeland Security, in consultation with the Secretary of State and the Attorney General, shall submit to the President a list of countries recommended for inclusion in a Presidential proclamation that would prohibit the entry of appropriate categories of foreign nationals of countries that have not provided the information requested until they do so or until the Secretary of Homeland Security certifies that the country has an adequate plan to do so, or has adequately shared information through other means. The Secretary of State, the Attorney General, or the Secretary of Homeland Security may also submit to the President the names of additional countries for which any of them recommends other lawful restrictions or limitations deemed necessary for the security or welfare of the United States.

(f) At any point after the submission of the list described in subsection (e) of this section, the Secretary of Homeland Security, in consultation with the Secretary of State and the Attorney General, may submit to the President the names of any additional countries recommended for similar treatment, as well as the names of any countries that they recommend should be removed from the scope of a proclamation described in subsection (e) of this section.

(g) The Secretary of State and the Secretary of Homeland Security shall submit to the President a joint report on the progress in implementing this order within 60 days of the effective date of this order, a second report within 90 days of the effective date of this order, a third report within 120 days of the effective date of this order, and a fourth report within 150 days of the effective date of this order.

Sec. 3. *Scope and Implementation of Suspension.*

(a) *Scope.* Subject to the exceptions set forth in subsection (b) of this section and any waiver under subsection (c) of this section, the suspension of entry pursuant to section 2 of this order shall apply only to foreign nationals of the designated countries who:

(i) are outside the United States on the effective date of this order;

(ii) did not have a valid visa at 5:00 p.m., eastern standard time on January 27, 2017; and

(iii) do not have a valid visa on the effective date of this order.

(b) Exceptions. The suspension of entry pursuant to section 2 of this order shall not apply to:

(i) any lawful permanent resident of the United States;

(ii) any foreign national who is admitted to or paroled into the United States on or after the effective date of this order;

(iii) any foreign national who has a document other than a visa, valid on the effective date of this order or issued on any date thereafter, that permits him or her to travel to the United States and seek entry or admission, such as an advance parole document;

(iv) any dual national of a country designated under section 2 of this order when the individual is traveling on a passport issued by a nondesignated country;

(v) any foreign national traveling on a diplomatic or diplomatic-type visa, North Atlantic Treaty Organization visa, C–2 visa for travel to the United Nations, or G–1, G–2, G–3, or G–4 visa; or

(vi) any foreign national who has been granted asylum; any refugee who has already been admitted to the United States; or any individual who has been granted withholding of removal, advance parole, or protection under the Convention Against Torture.

(c) *Waivers*. Notwithstanding the suspension of entry pursuant to section 2 of this order, a consular officer, or, as appropriate, the Commissioner, U.S. Customs and Border Protection (CBP), or the Commissioner's delegee, may, in the consular officer's or the CBP official's discretion, decide on a case-by-case basis to authorize the issuance of a visa to, or to permit the entry of, a foreign national for whom entry is otherwise suspended if the foreign national has demonstrated to the officer's satisfaction that denying entry during the suspension period would cause undue hardship, and that his or her entry would not pose a threat to national security and would be in the national interest. Unless otherwise specified by the Secretary of Homeland Security, any waiver issued by a consular officer as part of the visa issuance process will be effective both for the issuance of a visa and any subsequent entry on that visa, but will leave all other requirements for admission or entry unchanged. Case-by-case waivers could be appropriate in circumstances such as the following:

(i) the foreign national has previously been admitted to the United States for a continuous period of work, study, or other long-term activity, is outside the United States on the effective date of this order, seeks to reenter the United States to resume that activity, and the denial of reentry during the suspension period would impair that activity;

(ii) the foreign national has previously established significant contacts with the United States but is outside the United States on the effective date of this order for work, study, or other lawful activity;

(iii) the foreign national seeks to enter the United States for significant business or professional obligations and the denial of entry during the suspension period would impair those obligations;

(iv) the foreign national seeks to enter the United States to visit or reside with a close family member (e.g., a spouse, child, or parent) who is a United States citizen, lawful permanent resident, or alien lawfully admitted on a valid nonimmigrant visa, and the denial of entry during the suspension period would cause undue hardship;

(v) the foreign national is an infant, a young child or adoptee, an individual needing urgent medical care, or someone whose entry is otherwise justified by the special circumstances of the case;

(vi) the foreign national has been employed by, or on behalf of, the United States Government (or is an eligible dependent of such an employee) and the employee can document that he or she has provided faithful and valuable service to the United States Government;

(vii) the foreign national is traveling for purposes related to an international organization designated under the International Organizations Immunities Act (IOIA), 22 U.S.C. 288 et seq., traveling for purposes of conducting meetings or business with the United States Government, or traveling to conduct business on behalf of an international organization not designated under the IOIA;

(viii) the foreign national is a landed Canadian immigrant who applies for a visa at a location within Canada; or

(ix) the foreign national is traveling as a United States Government-sponsored exchange visitor.

Sec. 4. *Additional Inquiries Related to Nationals of Iraq.* An application by any Iraqi national for a visa, admission, or other immigration benefit should be subjected to thorough review, including, as appropriate, consultation with a designee of the Secretary of Defense and use of the additional information that has been obtained in the context of the close U.S.-Iraqi security partnership, since Executive Order 13769 was issued, concerning individuals suspected of ties to ISIS or other terrorist organizations and individuals coming from territories controlled or formerly controlled by ISIS. Such review shall include consideration of whether the applicant has connections with ISIS or other terrorist organizations or with territory that is or has been under the dominant influence of ISIS, as well as any other information bearing on whether the applicant may be a threat to commit acts of terrorism or otherwise threaten the national security or public safety of the United States.

Sec. 5. *Implementing Uniform Screening and Vetting Standards for All Immigration Programs.* (a) The Secretary of State, the Attorney General, the Secretary of Homeland Security, and the Director of National Intelligence shall implement a program, as part of the process for adjudications, to identify individuals who seek to enter the United States on a fraudulent basis, who support terrorism, violent extremism, acts of violence toward any group or class of people within the United States, or who present a risk of causing harm subsequent to their entry. This program shall include the development of a uniform baseline for screening and vetting standards and procedures, such as in-person interviews; a database of identity documents proffered by applicants to ensure that duplicate documents are not used by multiple applicants; amended application forms that include questions aimed at identifying fraudulent answers and malicious intent; a mechanism to ensure that applicants are who they claim to be; a mechanism to assess whether applicants may commit, aid, or support any kind of violent, criminal, or terrorist acts after entering the United States; and any other appropriate means for ensuring the proper collection of all information necessary for a rigorous evaluation of all grounds of inadmissibility or grounds for the denial of other immigration benefits.

(b) The Secretary of Homeland Security, in conjunction with the Secretary of State, the Attorney General, and the Director of National Intelligence, shall submit to the President an initial report on the progress of the program described in subsection (a) of this section within 60 days of the effective date of this order, a second report within 100 days of the effective date of this order, and a third report within 200 days of the effective date of this order.

Sec. 6. *Realignment of the U.S. Refugee Admissions Program for Fiscal Year 2017.* (a) The Secretary of State shall suspend travel of refugees into the United States under the USRAP, and the Secretary of Homeland Security shall suspend decisions on applications for refugee status, for 120 days after the effective date of this order, subject to waivers pursuant to subsection (c) of this section. During the 120-day period, the Secretary of State, in conjunction with the Secretary of Homeland Security and in consultation with the Director of National Intelligence, shall review the USRAP application and adjudication processes to determine what additional procedures should be used to ensure that individuals seeking admission as refugees do not pose a threat to the security and welfare of the United States, and shall implement such additional procedures. The suspension described in this subsection shall not apply to refugee applicants who, before the effective date of this order, have been formally scheduled for transit by the Department of State. The Secretary of State shall resume travel of refugees into the United States under the USRAP 120 days after the effective date of this order, and the Secretary of Homeland Security shall resume making decisions on applications for refugee status only for stateless persons and nationals of countries for which the Secretary of State, the Secretary of Homeland Security, and the Director of National Intelligence have jointly determined that the additional procedures implemented pursuant to this subsection are adequate to ensure the security and welfare of the United States.

(b) Pursuant to section 212(f) of the INA, I hereby proclaim that the entry of more than 50,000 refugees in fiscal year 2017 would be detrimental to the interests of the United States, and thus suspend any entries in excess of that number until such time as I determine that additional entries would be in the national interest.

(c) Notwithstanding the temporary suspension imposed pursuant to subsection (a) of this section, the Secretary of State and the Secretary of Homeland Security may jointly determine to admit individuals to the United States as refugees on a case-by-case basis, in their discretion, but only so long as they determine that the entry of such individuals as refugees is in the national interest and does not pose a threat to the security or welfare of the United States, including in circumstances such as the following: the individual's entry would enable the United States to conform its conduct to a preexisting international agreement or arrangement, or the denial of entry would cause undue hardship.

(d) It is the policy of the executive branch that, to the extent permitted by law and as practicable, State and local jurisdictions be granted a role in the process of determining the placement or settlement in their jurisdictions of aliens eligible to be admitted to the United States as refugees. To that end, the Secretary of State shall examine existing law to determine the extent to which, consistent with applicable law, State and local jurisdictions may have greater involvement in the process of determining the placement or resettlement of refugees in their jurisdictions, and shall devise a proposal to lawfully promote such involvement.

Sec. 7. *Rescission of Exercise of Authority Relating to the Terrorism Grounds of Inadmissibility.* The Secretary of State and the Secretary of Homeland Security shall, in consultation with the Attorney General, consider rescinding the exercises of authority permitted by section 212(d)(3)(B) of the INA, 8 U.S.C. 1182(d)(3)(B), relating to the terrorism grounds of inadmissibility, as well as any related implementing directives or guidance.

Sec. 8. *Expedited Completion of the Biometric Entry-Exit Tracking System.* (a) The Secretary of Homeland Security shall expedite the completion and implementation of a biometric entry-exit tracking system for in-scope travelers to the United States, as recommended by the National Commission on Terrorist Attacks Upon the United States.

(b) The Secretary of Homeland Security shall submit to the President periodic reports on the progress of the directive set forth in subsection (a) of this section. The initial report shall be submitted within 100 days of the effective date of this order, a second report shall be submitted within 200 days of the effective date of this order, and a third report shall be submitted within 365 days of the effective date of this order. The Secretary of Homeland Security shall submit further reports every 180 days thereafter until the system is fully deployed and operational.

Sec. 9. *Visa Interview Security.* (a) The Secretary of State shall immediately suspend the Visa Interview Waiver Program and ensure compliance with section 222 of the INA, 8 U.S.C. 1202, which requires that all individuals seeking a nonimmigrant visa undergo an in-person interview, subject to specific statutory exceptions. This suspension shall not apply to any foreign national traveling on a diplomatic or diplomatic-type visa, North Atlantic Treaty Organization visa, C–2 visa for travel to the United Nations, or G–1, G–2, G–3, or G–4 visa; traveling for purposes related to an international organization designated under the IOIA; or traveling for purposes of conducting meetings or business with the United States Government.

(b) To the extent permitted by law and subject to the availability of appropriations, the Secretary of State shall immediately expand the Consular Fellows Program, including by substantially increasing the number of Fellows, lengthening or making permanent the period of service, and making language training at the Foreign Service Institute available to Fellows for assignment to posts outside of their area of core linguistic ability, to ensure that nonimmigrant visa-interview wait times are not unduly affected.

Sec. 10. *Visa Validity Reciprocity.* The Secretary of State shall review all nonimmigrant visa reciprocity agreements and arrangements to ensure that they are, with respect to each visa classification, truly reciprocal insofar as practicable with respect to validity period and fees, as required by sections 221(c) and 281 of the INA, 8 U.S.C. 1201(c) and 1351, and other treatment. If another country does not treat United States nationals seeking nonimmigrant visas in a truly reciprocal manner, the Secretary of State shall adjust the visa validity period, fee schedule, or other treatment to match the treatment of United States nationals by that foreign country, to the extent practicable.

Sec. 11. *Transparency and Data Collection.* (a) To be more transparent with the American people and to implement more effectively policies and practices that serve the national interest, the Secretary of Homeland Security, in consultation with the Attorney General, shall, consistent with applicable law and national security, collect and make publicly available the following information:

(i) information regarding the number of foreign nationals in the United States who have been charged with terrorism-related offenses while in the United States; convicted of terrorism-related offenses while in the United States; or removed from the United States based on terrorismrelated activity, affiliation with or provision of material support to a terrorism-related organization, or any other nationalsecurity-related reasons;

(ii) information regarding the number of foreign nationals in the United States who have been radicalized after entry into the

United States and who have engaged in terrorism-related acts, or who have provided material support to terrorism-related organizations in countries that pose a threat to the United States;

(iii) information regarding the number and types of acts of gender-based violence against women, including so-called "honor killings," in the United States by foreign nationals; and

(iv) any other information relevant to public safety and security as determined by the Secretary of Homeland Security or the Attorney General, including information on the immigration status of foreign nationals charged with major offenses.

(b) The Secretary of Homeland Security shall release the initial report under subsection (a) of this section within 180 days of the effective date of this order and shall include information for the period from September 11, 2001, until the date of the initial report. Subsequent reports shall be issued every 180 days thereafter and reflect the period since the previous report.

Sec. 12. *Enforcement.* (a) The Secretary of State and the Secretary of Homeland Security shall consult with appropriate domestic and international partners, including countries and organizations, to ensure efficient, effective, and appropriate implementation of the actions directed in this order.

(b) In implementing this order, the Secretary of State and the Secretary of Homeland Security shall comply with all applicable laws and regulations, including, as appropriate, those providing an opportunity for individuals to claim a fear of persecution or torture, such as the credible fear determination for aliens covered by section 235(b)(1)(A) of the INA, 8 U.S.C. 1225(b)(1)(A).

(c) No immigrant or nonimmigrant visa issued before the effective date of this order shall be revoked pursuant to this order.

(d) Any individual whose visa was marked revoked or marked canceled as a result of Executive Order 13769 shall be entitled to a travel document confirming that the individual is permitted to travel to the United States and seek entry. Any prior cancellation or revocation of a visa that was solely pursuant to Executive Order 13769 shall not be the basis of inadmissibility for any future determination about entry or admissibility.

(e) This order shall not apply to an individual who has been granted asylum, to a refugee who has already been admitted to the United States, or to an individual granted withholding of removal or protection under the Convention Against Torture. Nothing in this order shall be construed to limit the ability of an individual to seek asylum, withholding of removal, or protection under the Convention Against Torture, consistent with the laws of the United States.

Sec. 13. *Revocation.* Executive Order 13769 of January 27, 2017, is revoked as of the effective date of this order.

Sec. 14. *Effective Date.* This order is effective at 12:01 a.m., eastern daylight time on March 16, 2017.

Sec. 15. *Severability.* (a) If any provision of this order, or the application of any provision to any person or circumstance, is held to be invalid, the remainder of this order and the application of its other provisions to any other persons or circumstances shall not be affected thereby.

(b) If any provision of this order, or the application of any provision to any person or circumstance, is held to be invalid because of the lack of certain procedural requirements, the relevant executive branch officials shall implement those procedural requirements.

Sec. 16. *General Provisions.* (a) Nothing in this order shall be construed to impair or otherwise affect:

(i) the authority granted by law to an executive department or agency, or the head thereof; or

(ii) the functions of the Director of the Office of Management and Budget relating to budgetary, administrative, or legislative proposals.

(b) This order shall be implemented consistent with applicable law and subject to the availability of appropriations.

(c) This order is not intended to, and does not, create any right or benefit, substantive or procedural, enforceable at law or in equity by any party against the United States, its departments, agencies, or entities, its officers, employees, or agents, or any other person.

THE WHITE HOUSE,

March 6, 2017.

Source: From the White House Office of the Press Secretary, www.whitehouse.gov/the-press-office /2017/03/06/executive-order-protecting-nation -foreign-terrorist-entry-united-states.

Analysis: This piece of legislation remains one of the most controversial laws enacted by the Trump administration during its first year in office. The order is an attempt to prevent travel to the United States by foreign nationals from a list of countries designated to be associated with a high risk of terrorism. Most of these nations are in the Middle East and North Africa and as such, are predominantly Muslim countries. The order has come under criticism from many domestic civilian and political opponents who argue that most acts of terrorism committed against the United States on its home soil comes from American citizens. Therefore, this travel ban would likely not make the country or its citizens much safer, while serving to inflame tensions around the world in many of the countries where the United States needs and will continue to need the most assistance from law enforcement, intelligence, and security services of these nations.

Chronology of Modern Terrorism

May 1, 1961
Antulio Ramirez Ortiz hijacks a National Airlines plane and demands transportation to Cuba. It is the first U.S. aircraft hijacking.

October 25, 1978
President Jimmy Carter signs the Foreign Intelligence Surveillance Act, designed to facilitate investigations of foreign citizens suspected of espionage or terrorism.

December 26, 1979
Soviet forces enter Afghanistan in support of a puppet regime, triggering a decade-long war against the mujahideen.

October 23, 1983
Hezbollah operatives detonate truck bombs at American and French compounds in Beirut, killing 242 U.S. troops and 58 French troops.

August 11, 1988
Osama bin Laden and Abdullah Azzam found al-Qaeda.

December 21, 1988
Pan Am Flight 103 is destroyed over Lockerbie, Scotland, when a bomb detonates aboard the airplane. A total of 270 people are killed, including 11 hit by falling wreckage.

Libyan intelligence agents are later blamed for the attack.

February 15, 1989
Soviet forces complete their withdrawal from Afghanistan.

August 2, 1990
Iraqi forces invade Kuwait and threaten attacks upon Saudi Arabia.

February 26, 1993
A truck bomb detonates in the World Trade Center, killing 6 and wounding more than 1,000. Ramzi Ahmed Yousef is later proven to be the organizer of the attack.

March 20, 1995
Aum Shinrikyo members release sarin nerve gas on the Tokyo subway system during rush hour. Twelve commuters are killed, and more than 5,000 are incapacitated.

April 19, 1995
Timothy McVeigh detonates a truck bomb outside the Alfred P. Murrah Building in Oklahoma City, killing 169.

June 25, 1996
A truck bomb detonates outside of Khobar Towers, a U.S. military housing facility in

Dhahran, Saudi Arabia, killing 19 U.S. personnel and wounding more than 500.

August 23, 1996
Osama bin Laden formally declares war upon the United States and demands the evacuation of all Western troops from Saudi Arabia.

August 7, 1998
Bombs explode outside the U.S. embassies in Nairobi, Kenya, and Dar es Salaam, Tanzania. Twelve U.S. citizens and nearly 300 foreign citizens are killed, and more than 5,000 are wounded.

August 20, 1998
In retaliation for the bombings of U.S. embassies in Kenya and Tanzania, Tomahawk cruise missiles strike al-Qaeda camps in Afghanistan and Sudan.

June 7, 1999
The Federal Bureau of Investigation places al-Qaeda leader Osama bin Laden on the "Ten Most Wanted" list.

October 12, 2000
The USS *Cole* is attacked by an explosives-laden boat, killing 17 sailors and injuring 39.

January 25, 2001
President William Clinton's outbound counterterrorism adviser, Richard Clarke, warns incoming National Security Adviser Condoleezza Rice about the dangers presented by al-Qaeda.

May 30, 2001
Federal Aviation Administration security manager Michael Canavan implores airlines to pay greater attention to security measures.

August 6, 2001
Central Intelligence Agency analysts deliver a briefing to President George W. Bush, warning of an imminent al-Qaeda attack upon the United States.

September 11, 2001
Nineteen al-Qaeda operatives simultaneously hijack four aircraft. Two are deliberately flown into the World Trade Center in New York City, one is flown into the Pentagon in Washington, DC, and one crashes in a field in Pennsylvania. A total of 2,996 are killed in the attacks; thousands more are wounded.

September 18, 2001
The U.S. Congress formally passes the Authorization for the Use of Military Force, allowing President Bush to use the military and intelligence assets of the nation to hunt down the perpetrators of the September 11 attacks.

September 20, 2001
President George W. Bush addresses a joint session of Congress and vows revenge upon al-Qaeda for the September 11 attacks.

September 28, 2001
Hezbollah commander Sayyed Hassan Nasrallah blames the September 11 attacks upon a joint U.S.-Israeli plot to justify an invasion of the Middle East.

September 28, 2001
The UN General Assembly passes a resolution calling upon all member states to freeze the assets of al-Qaeda and affiliated groups.

September–October 2001
An unknown perpetrator mails envelopes laced with anthrax spores to five media

outlets and two U.S. senators, prompting several building closures and causing five deaths.

October 7, 2001
The United States commences air strikes against Taliban and al-Qaeda targets in Afghanistan.

October 26, 2001
President George W. Bush signs the USA Patriot Act into law.

November 10, 2001
President George W. Bush addresses the UN General Assembly and calls upon member nations for support in the war against al-Qaeda.

December 22, 2001
Richard Reid attempts to detonate explosives hidden in his shoes while aboard American Airlines Flight 63.

January 9, 2002
John Yoo provides the Bush administration rationale for detaining captured enemies at Guantanamo Bay but not providing them with prisoner-of-war status under the Geneva Convention.

March 21, 2002
Secretary of Defense Donald Rumsfeld institutes a military tribunal system to put al-Qaeda members on trial for terrorism activities.

October 12, 2002
Suicide bombers outside a nightclub in Bali, Indonesia, kill more than 200, including 7 Americans.

November 15, 2002
The National Commission on Terrorist Attacks upon the United States, also called the 9/11 Commission, is chartered and tasked with investigating the 9/11 attacks.

November 2002
Osama bin Laden releases a letter to the American people explaining al-Qaeda's grievances and explaining how to end terror attacks against the U.S. homeland.

March 20, 2003
A U.S.-led coalition commences an invasion of Iraq, ostensibly to disarm the Iraqi government of weapons of mass destruction and eliminate its support of terror organizations.

April 16, 2003
Secretary of Defense Donald Rumsfeld authorizes specific "enhanced interrogation techniques."

March 11, 2004
Ten bombs detonate aboard Madrid commuter trains, killing nearly 200. The attacks occur 30 months after 9/11.

March 24, 2004
Former presidential counterterrorism adviser Richard Clarke testifies before the 9/11 Commission and apologizes to the nation for failing to detect and prevent the September 11 attacks.

June 28, 2004
The U.S. Supreme Court issues decisions in *Rasul v. Bush* and *Hamdan v. Rumsfeld*.

July 22, 2004
The 9/11 Commission releases its final report.

July 7, 2005
Four suicide bombers attack subway trains in London, killing more than 50.

June 7, 2006
An air strike kills Abu Musab al-Zarqawi, commander of Al-Qaeda in Iraq.

February 10, 2007
General David Petraeus is named commander of Multi-National Force–Iraq, and begins implementing a major troop surge in the hope of providing stability.

March 10, 2007
Khalid Sheikh Mohammed formally confesses to planning the 9/11 attacks, in addition to a host of other al-Qaeda operations, during a Combatant Status Review tribunal hearing at Guantanamo Bay, Cuba.

November 5, 2009
Major Nidal Malik Hasan, an army psychiatrist, opens fire at a military facility in Fort Hood, Texas, killing 13 and wounding 30.

December 25, 2009
Umar Farouk Abdulmutallab attempts to detonate a bomb on an international flight. He had smuggled the explosives onto the airplane by concealing them in his underwear.

April 28, 2010
Anthony Romero, president of the American Civil Liberties Union, writes an open letter to President Barack Obama calling for an end to extrajudicial targeted killings.

May 1, 2010
Faisal Shahzad attempts to detonate a car bomb in Times Square.

September 23, 2010
Iranian president Mahmoud Ahmadinejad delivers a speech before the UN General Assembly in which he blames the 9/11 attacks upon a U.S. government plot. A general walkout ensues.

May 2, 2011
U.S. Navy SEALs attack a compound in Abbottabad, Pakistan, and kill Osama bin Laden.

June 16, 2011
Al-Qaeda's website formally announces the succession of Ayman al-Zawahiri to command the organization.

September 30, 2011
American-born al-Qaeda spokesperson Anwar al-Awlaki is killed by a missile fired by an unmanned aircraft in Yemen.

February 9, 2012
Somalian terror organizational al-Shabaab formally announces its allegiance to al-Qaeda.

September 11, 2012
Militants attack the U.S. consulate in Benghazi, Tripoli, and assassinate Ambassador J. Christopher Stevens.

April 15, 2013
Two bombs explode near the finish line of the Boston Marathon. Chechen brothers Dzhokhar and Tamerlan Tsarnaev are later found to have placed the bombs.

June 13, 2014
The United States commences air strikes targeting the Islamic State of Iraq and the Levant.

December 28, 2014
The North Atlantic Treaty Organization formally ends combat operations in Afghanistan.

January 3–7, 2015
Boko Haram militants attack several northern Nigerian villages, killing more than 2,000 civilians.

January 7, 2015
Gunmen linked to Al-Qaeda in the Arabian Peninsula attack the offices of *Charlie Hebdo,* a satire magazine based in Paris, France, killing 12 and wounding 10.

March 18, 2015
Three Islamic State gunmen attack the Bardo Museum in Tunis, killing 22 victims, including 20 foreign tourists. One of the attackers remains at large.

March 26–27, 2015
Al-Shabaab operatives attack the Makka al-Mukarama hotel in Mogadishu, Somalia, killing 24 and wounding 28.

June 26, 2015
Seifeddine Rezgui Yacoubi, an Islamic State operative, opens fire at a tourist resort near Sousse, Tunisia, killing 38 tourists and wounding 39 more.

October 10, 2015
Members of the Islamic State detonate two suicide bombs in Ankara, Turkey, killing 102 and wounding 508.

October 31, 2015
Metrojet Flight 9268 is destroyed after a bomb exploded during the flight, killing 224 mostly Russian passengers and crew. The Islamic State took credit for the attack, and claimed it was retaliation for Russian air strikes in Syria.

November 12, 2015
Two suicide bombers attack a Beirut suburb, killing 43 mostly Shia victims. The Islamic State later claims responsibility.

November 13, 2015
Eight attackers launch three coordinated attacks at six locations in Paris, France,

killing 130 and wounding nearly 400. The attackers are members of the Islamic State.

December 2, 2015
Syed Rizwan Farook and Tashfeen Malik attack a community center in San Bernardino, California, killing 14 and wounding 21. They are later shown to have pledged allegiance to the Islamic State.

January 15–16, 2016
Al-Qaeda in the Islamic Maghreb operatives attack a restaurant and hotel in Ouagadougou, Burkina Faso, killing 30 and wounding 60.

January 20, 2016
Tehrik-i-Taliban Pakistan gunmen attack Bacha Khan University in Charsadda, Pakistan, killing 20 and wounding 60.

March 22, 2016
Suicide bombers linked to the Islamic State attacked a metro station and an airport in Brussels, killing 32 and injuring 340.

June 12, 2016
Omar Mateen opens fire in an Orlando nightclub, killing 49 and wounding 53. He pledges allegiance to the Islamic State in a telephone call to 911 during the attack.

July 1, 2016
Five men attacked a café in Dhaka, Bangladesh, and took hostages. Twenty-four were killed and 50 injured. The attackers were linked to the Islamic State.

July 14, 2016
Mohamed Lahouaiej-Bouhlel drives a cargo truck into crowds celebrating Bastille Day in Nice, France, killing 85 and wounding 307. Two days later the Islamic State claimed responsibility for the attack.

August 20, 2016
Suicide bomber targets a Kurdish wedding in Gaziantep, Turkey. Fifty-seven people were killed and 66 injured. The Islamic State is thought to be responsible for the attack.

September 25, 2016
A video showed the Islamic State slaughtering at least 100 Iraqi civilians in Iraq.

October 24, 2016
Both the Islamic State and Lashkar-e-Jhangvi claimed credit for an attack in Quetta on a police training college where 60 were killed and another 120 injured.

December 19, 2016
Anis Amri, a 24 year old Tunisian asylum seeker, hijacked a truck and drove it into a Christmas market in Breitscheidplatz, Berlin, killing 12 and injuring 56. ISIS claimed responsibility and released a video of Amri pledging allegiance to Abu Bakr al-Baghdadi.

January 1, 2017
A gunman killed 39 people in a shooting on New Year's Eve at the Reina nightclub in Istanbul, Turkey. The gunman was linked to the Islamic State.

January 2, 2017
A series of car bombings perpetrated by the Islamic State killed 56 and injured another 122 in Baghdad.

March 8, 2017
Multiple gunmen affiliated with the Islamic State launched an attack on a military hospital in Kabul. Reports on the death toll ranged from the mid-40s to over 100 people killed.

March 22, 2017
Khalid Masood drove a vehicle into pedestrians on Westminster Bridge in London, killing four and injuring many others before crashing the vehicle and subsequently stabbing a police officer to death before being shot dead himself.

April 9, 2017
Suicide bombings by the Islamic State killed 30 people and injured at least 70 during Palm Sunday mass services at a Coptic Church in Tanta, Egypt.

May 22, 2017
A British citizen of Libyan decent named Salman Abedi blew himself up at an Ariana Grande concert in Manchester killing at least 22 concertgoers and injuring 116 others. The Islamic State claimed responsibility.

June 3, 2017
Several men inspired by the Islamic State deliberately mowed down multiple pedestrians using a van on the London Bridge. Immediately after, the men drove to Borough Market and stabbed several civilians before being shot by police. Eight people were killed and 48 were injured.

June 7, 2017
The Iranian parliament and the Mausoleum of Ruhollah Khomeini were attacked by seven armed men with pistols and Kalashnikov rifles and claiming to be associated with the Islamic State.

August 12, 2017
A car driven by white supremacist James Alex Fields plowed into a group of people marching peacefully during protests in

Charlottesville, Virginia. A person was killed and 19 were injured.

August 17, 2017

Fifteen civilians were killed and more than 130 others were injured when a van ran over pedestrians in La Rambla of Barcelona, Spain. The attack was claimed by the Islamic State.

September 15, 2017

A crude homemade bomb partially exploded on a District line tube train at Parsons Green tube station, London, injuring 30 people. The attack was claimed by the Islamic State.

October 31, 2017

Sayfullo Saipov, an Uzbek immigrant living in the United States, plowed a rented van into a crowd of pedestrians in New York City, killing 8 people and injuring more than a dozen. Saipov declared his allegiance to the Islamic State.

December 11, 2017

Akeyed Ullah, a Bangladeshi immigrant living in Brooklyn, NY, detonated a pipe bomb in a subway station near Times Square, in Manhattan, NY. Nobody was killed in the incident. Ullah indicated that he was motivated by the Islamic State.

Bibliography

Abu-Amr, Ziad. *Islamic Fundamentalism in the West Bank and Gaza: Muslim Brotherhood and Islamic Jihad.* Bloomington: Indiana University Press, 1994.

Aburish, Said K. *Arafat: From Defender to Dictator.* New York and London: Bloomsbury, 1998.

Abuza, Zachary. *Militant Islam in Southeast Asia.* Boulder: Lynne Rienner, 2003.

Acharya, Arabinda, Syed Adnan Ali Shah Bukhari, and Sadia Sulaiman. "Making Money in the Mayhem: Funding Taliban Insurrection in the Tribal Areas of Pakistan," *Studies in Conflict & Terrorism* 32, no. 2 (2009): 95–108.

Bajoria, Jayshree. *Pakistan's New Generation of Terrorists.* Council on Foreign Relations, Washington, DC, and New York, October 26, 2009.

Bake, Stewart A. *Patriot Debates: Experts Debate the USA Patriot Act.* Chicago: American Bar Association, 2005.

Basile, Mark. "Going to the Source: Why Al-Qaeda's Financial Network Is Likely to Withstand the Current War on Terrorist Financing," *Studies in Conflict & Terrorism* 27, no. 3 (2004): 169–185.

Bergen, Peter L. *The Longest War: The Enduring Conflict between America and Al-Qaeda.* New York: Free Press, 2011.

Bergen, Peter L. *The Osama bin Laden I Know: An Oral History of Al Qaeda's Leader.* New York: Free Press, 2006.

Bever, Lindsey. "'I'm Just a Sociopath,' Dylann Roof Declared after Deadly Church Shooting Rampage, Court Records Say," *Washington Post,* May 17, 2017.

Bloom, Mia. "Ethnic Conflict, State Terror, and Suicide Bombing in Sri Lanka," *Civil Wars* 6, no. 1 (2003): 58–84.

Bloom, Mia. *Dying to Kill: The Allure of Suicide Terror.* New York: Columbia University Press, 2005.

Boot, Max. *The Savage Wars of Peace: Small Wars and the Rise of American Power.* New York: Basic, 2002.

Burke, Jason. *Al-Qaeda: The True Story of Radical Islam.* London: I. B. Tauris, 2003.

Brown, Vahid, and Don Rassler. *Fountainhead of Jihad: The Haqqani Nexus, 1973–2012.* New York: Oxford University Press, 2013.

Byman, Daniel L. "Can Lone Wolves Be Stopped?" *Brookings Institution,* March 15, 2017.

Byman, Daniel. *Deadly Connections: States that Sponsor Terrorism.* Cambridge: Cambridge University Press, 2005.

Byman, Daniel. "Should Hezbollah Be Next?" *Foreign Affairs* (November–December 2003): 54–66.

Byman, Daniel, Peter Chalk, Bruce Hoffman, William Rosenau, and David Brannan. *Trends in Outside Support for Insurgent Movements.* Santa Monica, CA: RAND Corporation, 2001.

Callimachi, Rukmini. "Not 'Lone Wolves' After All: How ISIS Guides World's Terror Plots from Afar," *New York Times,* February 4, 2017.

Callimachi, Rukmini. "Protest of U.S. Terror Listing Offers a Glimpse at Qaeda

Strategy," *New York Times,* November 17, 2016.

Chad, Sheldon, Christina Boyle, and Corina Knoll. "Hunt Is on for Brussels Bombing Suspect: Islamic State Warns of More, Worse Attacks," *Los Angeles Times,* March 23, 2016.

Chalk, Peter. *The Latin American Drug Trade: Scope, Dimensions, Impact, and Response.* Santa Monica, CA: RAND, 2011.

Chalk, Peter, Angel Rabasa, William Rosenau, and Leanne Piggott. *The Evolving Terrorist Threat to Southeast Asia: A Net Assessment.* Santa Monica, CA: RAND, 2009.

Chivers, C. J. " 'All People Are the Same to God': An Insider's Portrait of Joseph Kony." *The New York Times,* December 31, 2010.

Chivers, C. J. "Afghanistan's Hidden Taliban Government," *New York Times,* February 6, 2011.

Clarke, Colin. "Hamas's Strategic Rebranding," *Foreign Affairs,* May 17, 2017.

Clark, Wesley. *Waging Modern War: Bosnia, Kosovo, and the Future of Combat.* New York: PublicAffairs, 2001.

Cochrane, Marisa. "The Fragmentation of the Sadrist Movement." *Iraq Report 12,* Institute for the Study of War, Washington DC, January 2009.

Coll, Steve. "Looking for Mullah Omar," *The New Yorker* 87, no. 45 (January 23, 2012).

Coll, Steve. *Ghost Wars: The Secret History of the CIA, Afghanistan, and Bin Laden, from the Soviet Invasion to September 10, 2001.* New York: Penguin, 2004.

Coogan, Tim Pat. *The IRA: A History.* Greenwood Village, CO: Roberts, 1994.

Cragin, Kim, and Sara Daly. *The Dynamic Terrorist Threat: An Assessment of Group Motivations and Capabilities in a Changing World.* Santa Monica, CA: RAND Corp., 2004.

Crenshaw, Martha. "How Terrorism Declines," *Terrorism Research and Public Policy* 3, no. 1 (Spring 1991): 69–87.

Crenshaw, Martha. "How Terrorism Ends," *United States Institute of Peace,* Special Report, Number 48, Washington, DC: USIP, May 25, 1999.

Cronin, Audrey Kurth. "How al-Qaida Ends: The Decline and Demise of Terrorist Groups," *International Security* 31, no. 1 (Summer 2006): 7–48.

Cruickshank, Paul, and Mohannad Hage Ali. "Abu Musab al-Suri: Architect of the New Al Qaeda," *Studies in Conflict & Terrorism* 30, no. 1 (2007): 1–14.

Davis, Mike. *Duda's Wagon: A Brief History of the Car Bomb.* London: Verso, 2007.

Eggen, Dan. "9/11 Report Says Plotter Saw Self as Superterrorist," *Washington Post,* July 27, 2004, A1.

English, Richard. *Armed Struggle: The History of the IRA.* Oxford: Oxford University Press, 2003.

Esposito, John L. *Unholy War: Terror in the Name of Islam.* New York: Oxford University Press, 2002.

Farrell, William. *Blood and Rage: The Story of the Japanese Red Army.* Lexington, MA: Lexington Books, 1990.

Filkins, Dexter. "Taliban Elite, Aided by NATO, Join Talks for Afghan Peace," *New York Times,* October 19, 2010.

Fishman, Brian. "After Zarqawi: The Dilemmas and Future of Al Qaeda in Iraq," *Washington Quarterly* 29, no. 4 (Autumn 2006).

Follain, John. *Jackal: The Complete Story of the Legendary Terrorist, Carlos the Jackal.* New York: Arcade, 1988.

Fresco, Adam, Richard Ford, and Giles Whittell. "Security Overhaul after al-Qaeda's Bomb Technology Fools the Experts," *The Times* (UK), November 1, 2010.

Giustozzi, Antonio. *Koran, Kalashnikov and Laptop: The New-Taliban Insurgency in Afghanistan.* London: Hurst Books, 2007.

Goldman, Adam, Mark Bergman, and Missy Ryan. "San Bernardino Shooter's Neighbor Who Bought Rifle is Cooperating with Authorities," *Washington Post,* December 10, 2015.

Gunaratna, Rohan. *Inside Al Qaeda: Global Network of Terror.* New York: Berkley Publishing Group, 2003.

Hammes, Thomas X. *The Sling and the Stone: On War in the 21st Century.* St. Paul, MN: Zenith, 2004.

Hashim, Ahmed S. *When Counterinsurgency Wins: Sri Lanka's Defeat of the Tamil Tigers.* Philadelphia: University of Pennsylvania Press, 2012.

Heiberg, Marianne, et al., eds., *Terror, Insurgency, and the State: Ending Protracted Conflicts.* Philadelphia, PA: University of Pennsylvania Press, 2007.

Hoffman, Bruce, and Gordon H. McCormick. "Terrorism, Signaling, and Suicide Attack," *Studies in Conflict & Terrorism* 27, no. 4 (2004): 243–281.

Horgan, John. *The Psychology of Terrorism.* London: Routledge, 2005.

Horgan, John. *Walking Away from Terrorism.* New York: Routledge, 2009.

Jackson, Brian A. "Organizational Decision-Making by Terrorist Groups," in *Social Science for Counterterrorism: Putting the Pieces Together,* edited by Paul K. Davis and Kim Cragin. Santa Monica, CA: RAND Corp., 2009.

Jackson, Brian A., and Bryce Loidolt. "Considering Al-Qa'ida's Innovation Doctrine: From Strategic Texts to "Innovation in Practice," *Terrorism and Political Violence* 25, no. 2 (2013): 284–310.

Jackson, Brian, et al. *Aptitude for Destruction, Volume 2: Case Studies of Organizational Learning in Five Terrorist Groups.* Santa Monica, CA: RAND Corp., 2005.

Jenkins, Brian Michael. *Stray Dogs and Virtual Armies: Radicalization and Recruitment to Jihadist Terrorism in the United States Since 9/11.* Santa Monica, CA: RAND Corp., 2011, OP-343-RC.

Jenkins, Brian. *Will Terrorists Go Nuclear?* Amherst: Prometheus Books, 2008.

Jess, Sara, et al. *America Attacked: Terrorists Declare War on America.* San Jose, CA: University Press, 2001.

Jones, Seth, et al. *Counterterrorism and Counterinsurgency in Somalia: Assessing the Campaign Against al-Shabaab.* Santa Monica, CA: RAND Corp., 2016.

Jones, Seth G. "Al Qaeda in Iran: Why Tehran Is Accommodating the Terrorist Group," *Foreign Affairs,* January 29, 2012.

Jones, Seth G., and Martin C. Libicki. *How Terrorist Groups End: Lessons for Countering Al Qa'ida.* Santa Monica, CA: RAND Corp., 2008.

Kenney, Michael. " 'Dumb' Yet Deadly: Local Knowledge and Poor Tradecraft among Islamist Militants in Britain and Spain," *Studies in Conflict & Terrorism* 33, no. 10 (2010): 911–932.

Kenney, Michael. *From Pablo to Osama: Trafficking and Terrorist Networks, Government Bureaucracies, and Competitive Adaptation.* University Park: Penn State University Press, 2007.

Kepel, Gilles. *Jihad: The Trail of Political Islam.* Cambridge, MA: Belknap, 2003.

Mulaj, Klejda, ed. *Violent Non-State Actors in World Politics.* New York: Columbia University Press, 2010.

Langford, R. Everett. *Introduction to Weapons of Mass Destruction: Radiological, Chemical, and Biological.* Hoboken, NJ: Wiley-Interscience, 2004.

Lia, Brynjar. *Architect of Global Jihad: The Life of Al-Qaeda Strategist Abu Mus'ab Al-Suri.* New York: Columbia University Press, 2008.

Lister, Charles. *The Syrian Jihad.* Oxford: Oxford University Press, 2016.

Livingstone, Neil C., and David Haley. *Inside the PLO.* New York: William Morrow, 1990.

Lou, Michael, and Dan Herbeck. *American Terrorist: Timothy McVeigh and the Oklahoma City Bombing.* New York: Harper Collins, 2001.

Makarenko, Tamara. "Earth Liberation Front Increases Actions across the United States," *Jane's Intelligence Review,* September 2003.

Marcus, Aliza. *Blood and Belief: The PKK and Kurdish Fight for Independence.* New York: NYU Press, 2007.

Masters, Jonathan. "Al-Shabab," *Council on Foreign Relations.* Council on Foreign Relations, n.d.

McCants, William. "The Believer," Brookings Institution, September 1, 2015.

Mitchell, Richard P. *The Society of Muslim Brothers.* Oxford: Oxford University Press, 1993.

Moloney, Ed. *A Secret History of the IRA.* New York: W. W. Norton, 2002.

Moreau, Ron, and Sami Yousafzi. "The End of Al Qaeda?" *Newsweek,* August 29, 2009.

Qutb, Sayyid. *Milestones.* Chicago: Kazi, 1964.

Rabasa, Angel, Peter Chalk, Kim Cragin, Sara A. Daly, Heather S. Gregg, Theodore W. Karasik, Kevin A. O'Brien, and William Rosenau. *Beyond al-Qaeda. Part 1: The Global Jihadist Movement.* Santa Monica, CA: RAND, 2006.

Rabasa, Angel, Robert Blackwill, Peter Chalk, Kim Cragin, Christine C. Fair, Brain Jackson, Brian Jenkins, Seth Jones, Nate Shestak, and Ashley Tellis. *The Lessons of Mumbai.* Santa Monica, CA: RAND, 2009.

Reeve, Simon. *The New Jackals: Ramzi Yousef, Osama bin Laden, and the Future of Terrorism.* Boston: Northeastern University Press, 1999.

Rubin, Alissa J., and Aurelien Breeden. "France Remembers the Nice Attack: 'We Will Never Find the Words,'" *The New York Times,* July 14, 2017.

Savage, Charlie. "Nigerian Indicted in Terrorist Plot," *New York Times,* January 6, 2010.

Schanzer, Jonathan. *Hamas vs. Fatah: The Struggle for Palestine.* New York: St. Martin's Press, 2008.

Schmitt, Eric. "Leader of Qaeda Cell in Syria, Mushin al-Fadhli, Is Killed in Airstrike, U.S. Says," *New York Times,* July 21, 2015.

Seale, Patrick. *Abu Nidal: A Gun for Hire.* New York: Random House, 1992.

Seierstad, Asne. *One of Us: The Story of a Massacre in Norway—and Its Aftermath.*

New York: Farrar, Straus, and Giroux, 2015.

Shane, Scott. "The Lessons of Anwar Al-Awlaki," *New York Times Magazine,* August 27, 2015.

Tankel, Stephen. "Lashkar-e-Taiba: From 9/11 to Mumbai." International Center for the Study of Radicalisation and Political Violence, London, April/May 2009.

Taylor, Bron. "Religion, Violence and Radical Environmentalism: From Earth First! to the Unabomber to the Earth Liberation Front," *Terrorism and Political Violence* 10, no. 4 (Winter 1998).

Taylor, Lewis. *Shining Path: Guerrilla War in Peru's Northern Highlands.* Liverpool: Liverpool University Press, 2006.

Taylor, Peter. *Loyalists.* London: Bloomsbury, 1999.

Turkewitz, Julie, and Frances Robles. "Was the Orlando Gunman Gay? The Answer Continues to Elude the F.B.I.," *The New York Times,* June 25, 2016.

Viorst, Milton. *Fire in the Streets: America in the 1960s.* New York: Simon & Schuster, 1979.

Von Hippel, Karin. *Europe Confronts Terrorism.* New York: Palgrave Macmillan, 2005.

Warrick, Joby. "ISIS's Second-in-Command Hid in Syria for Months. The Day He Stepped Out, the U.S. Was Waiting," *Washington Post,* November 28, 2016.

Wedeman, Ben. "Israel-Palestinian Violence: What You Need to Know," *CNN,* October 15, 2015.

Williams, Paul. *The Al Qaeda Connection: International Terrorism, Organized Crime, and the Coming of the Apocalypse.* Amherst, NY: Prometheus Books, 2005.

Wright, Lawrence. "ISIS's Savage Strategy in Iraq," *The New Yorker,* May 24, 2017.

Wright, Lawrence. *The Looming Tower: Al-Qaeda and the Road to 9/11.* New York: Knopf, 2006.

Editor and Contributors List

VOLUME EDITOR

Colin P. Clarke
Political Scientist
RAND Corporation

CONTRIBUTORS

Christopher Anzalone
Research Fellow
Harvard Kennedy School

Stephen E. Atkins
Adjunct Professor of History
Texas A&M University

Donna Bassett
Senior Manager
The Information Project

Drew Bazil
Graduate student
Georgetown University, Washington, DC

Amy Hackney Blackwell
Independent Scholar

Ben Brandt
Director
Lime Consultancy, UAE

Dr. Stefan Brooks
Assistant Professor of Political Science
Lindsey Wilson College

Stephanie Caravias
Graduate Student
Georgetown University, Washington, DC

Peter Chalk
Senior Analyst
RAND Corporation

Elliot P. Chodoff
University of Haifa
Israel

Julie Dunbar
Editorial Manager
World Geography & Culture/Issues
ABC-CLIO

Dr. Richard M. Edwards
Senior Lecturer
University of Wisconsin Colleges

Dr. Chuck Fahrer
Associate Professor of Geography
Georgia College and State University

Katherine Gould
Independent Scholar

Greg Hannah
Senior Political Scientist
RAND Corporation, Cambridge, UK

Dr. Timothy D. Hoyt
Professor of Strategy and Policy
U.S. Naval War College

Dr. Harry Raymond Hueston II
Independent Scholar

Daniel Katz
Independent Scholar

Philip J. MacFarlane
Independent Scholar

Lisa McCallum
Independent Scholar

Dr. Edward F. Mickolus
Former International Terrorism Analyst
Central Intelligence Agency

Terri Nichols
Independent Scholar

Benjamin P. Nickels
Associate Professor of Counterterrorism
and Counterinsurgency
Africa Center for Strategic Studies

Michael E. Orzetti
Graduate Student
Georgetown University, Washington, DC

Dr. Paul G. Pierpaoli Jr.
Fellow
Military History, ABC-CLIO, Inc.

Dr. Priscilla Roberts
Associate Professor of History
School of Humanities

Honorary Director
Centre of American Studies
University of Hong Kong

Nate Shestak
Graduate Student
Georgetown University,
Washington, DC

Alex Stephenson
Future Plans Office
Asymmetric Warfare Group,
Fort George G. Meade, Maryland

First Lieutenant Tracy R. Szczepaniak
Department of History
U.S. Air Force Academy

Dr. Spencer C. Tucker
Senior Fellow
Military History, ABC-CLIO, Inc.

Lauren Twenhafel
Graduate Student
Georgetown University, Washington, DC

Jose M. Valente
Independent Scholar

Richard Warnes
Senior Political Scientist
RAND Corporation,
Cambridge, UK

Dr. Sherifa Zuhur
Visiting Professor of National
Security Affairs
Regional Strategy and
Planning Department
Strategic Studies Institute
U.S. Army War College

Index

Page numbers in **bold** indicate the location of main entries; (doc.) indicates the entry is a document.

About the Editor

Colin P. Clarke is a political scientist at the RAND Corporation, where his research focuses on terrorism and insurgency. At RAND, Clarke has helped direct studies on ISIS financing and lessons learned from the history of all insurgencies since the end of World War II. He is a lecturer at Carnegie Mellon University and an associate fellow at the International Centre for Counter-Terrorism (ICCT) in The Hague, Netherlands. Clarke is the author of *Terrorism, Inc.: The Financing of Terrorism, Insurgency, and Irregular Warfare.*